FORTRESS
DIVINELY PROTECTED

By R.E. Crofton

R.E. Crofton

Fortress: Divinely Protected

All scriptures given are in the King James Version

Printed in the United States of America

First Edition: June 2017

ISBN: 0692864970
ISBN-13: 978-0692864975

DEDICATION

This book is dedicated to God the Father, God the Son, and God the Holy Spirit, for these three are one. Since the foundation of the world the Holy Trinity knew that I would write this book. God alone is omniscient, omnipotent and omnipresent and His written Word the Bible is truth. As a blood-bought born-again child of God, I was inspired as I wrote this book and created characters, plots, divine intervention, and a type of Church and Christians that have to be birthed in these last days to spiritually stand against the attacks of the devil in the darkest days of humanity in the near future.

May a copy of this book that is destined to be held and read by every appointed son and daughter of God on all seven continents come to pass. May the true church of Jesus Christ arise like a sleeping giant awakened in Holy anger with an unsurpassed zeal for God in these end times and cause every demon and Lucifer himself to tremble in fear. May this fear and trembling be a result of continual prayer forged with faith by an Army of God marching on their knees. May the power of God, His anointing that can break every yoke and His Shekinah glory be manifested to a dying world one last time.

Vengeance is reserved for God to be executed on His enemies. The scriptures declare in Romans 12:19b, "Vengeance is mine; I will repay, saith the Lord." In the end God will have the last say on all those who oppose Him.

If you are born again, may you and I accomplish all that the Spirit of God wants us to achieve in our years remaining on this sin-stained earth.

If you are not saved, may you seek Him while He still may be found!

WITH GOD ALL THINGS ARE POSSIBLE - MATTHEW 19:6

CONTENTS

ACKNOWLEDGMENTS

Special recognition to J. L. Wesley for your invaluable knowledge, insights and contribution in the editing of this book. Your willingness to help me will never be forgotten. Figuratively you put air in my sails in the voyage of this book when I needed it the most. Another round of thanks goes to Sister Pam T. for your willingness to do a final proof read. Your faithfulness in the undertaking was truly a blessing. Your help was at a crucial juncture in time was ordained of God. Jon Michael thanks for your technical help in the formation of the cover of the book and my website. I appreciated your encouragement in the process of completing the book.. I want to recognize Sister Donna for your visionary insights into publishing, assistance and technical knowledge in the making of this book a reality. Finally, a very special thanks to my loving wife Gail who has stood by and aided me in my pursuit of writing through the years. Your labor, encouragement, and faith make the publication of this first book possible.

Chapter 1

THE CHOSEN FEW

4:23:23 AM, Mountain Standard Time, Wednesday, 05/08/20_ _ , Boulder, Colorado, USA

"Starlight, Starlight! Baby, please, wake up. Please, wake up, Baby."

"Ah, ah... what's up, Riv?" River Jenkins is sitting by his pretty 19-year-old bride, Starlight, on their small makeshift wooden bed in the back of their 1967 hippie Volkswagen van trying to wake her up. She yawns and snuggles with her pillow trying to go back to sleep and says, "I'm so tired and sleepy."

"I know it's early, Star. Really, I'm sorry, but I've got to talk to you."

By the tone of River's voice, she instantly knows something is up even in her half-asleep state. As she begins to rub her eyes, she asks, "Well, what's wrong?" Then it hits her. "Oh no! Oh no! You had another one of those dreams from the Lord, didn't you? I knew it!"

"Yes, I think it was a dream, or I mean, I don't know if it was a dream or some kind of a vision from God."

"I just knew it! Okay, now I'm wide awake, River, and you have my undivided attention."

Starlight starts pulling herself up from the old three-inch orange foam mattress covered with a clean but old hand-sewn quilted blanket made from big patches of soft, faded, and torn old blue denim Levi jeans. The mattress is resting on top of a one-half inch sheet of plywood on 1"x 6" pine slats and a wooden bed frame made from 2"x4"s. Underneath the half-inch plywood that supports the relatively thin mattress they sleep on is a large

1

portion of their earthly possessions. Up above their heads are their Grizzly model Bear recurve bows that they love to shoot for target practice. The bows are unstrung and are resting on gray plastic gun racks screwed into the metal upright window frames of the van. Behind the driver's seat is River's black hard plastic guitar case that contains his expensive Fender acoustic guitar that he worked hard to save money for in the summer of his 15th birthday. River's grandfather had taken out all of the bench seats after the van was purchased, so he could live a nomadic, hippie lifestyle in the late 1960's. He had built the small bed in the back of the van to sleep on. River's guitar is held in place by two bungee cords tied to the VW van wall. It rests upon a small RV refrigerator at the foot of the bed that they use to keep their food and drinks cool on extended stays at campgrounds. Almost all of their other belongings are in small cardboard boxes and plastic crates. They are trying to live a minimalist's lifestyle, but the van has gotten increasingly smaller as the months have gone by since their marriage began.

Starlight is now sitting straight up and has pushed back the navy blue flannel sheet and the old Pendleton western style wool blanket away from her body. It is needed for the cool Colorado nights in Boulder. After about 45 years of use, it is becoming frayed and has three small moth eaten holes near the middle of it. Night temperatures have been dipping down into the mid 50's lately. Starlight knows that major change is going to happen with this new revelation River has gotten from God and she is bracing herself for it. Now her legs are crisscrossed Indian style with her back next to the left padded back door of their vintage original 1967 VW van. Her mouth is a little dry, and she reaches backwards with her hand to grab her water bottle that she nightly wedges in between the corner of the bed frame and van. She takes a drink. The van has been their home on the road for about 18 months since they left Redwood, California where they grew up. They have spent a total of nine nights in cheap motels since they got married, mostly when the temperature has gotten really cold. On their one-year anniversary, River splurged and got them a room in a Hampton Inn in Colorado Springs. Starlight thought she had died and gone to heaven.

The paint on the lower half of the outside of the vehicle is light blue and the upper part is white from the factory, or what little of it that is left untouched, because the van is mostly covered with multi-colored hand-painted flowers. River had inherited it from his grandfather, Jack Miller, who had raised him. He had died about a year before River and Starlight decided to leave the Utopian Experimental Community outside of Redwood, California, where they grew up and lived their entire lives. They left the day Starlight turned 18 and got married by a justice of the peace in a nearby town..

River took the death of his grandfather really hard. Two days before he died, his grandfather was very sick in bed, and he told River that he had made a lot of mistakes in his life. Jack admitted to River if he had to do it all over again he would have done a lot of things differently. But River had told his grandfather that he loved him anyway and hugged him tightly. He told him that he was glad he was his grandfather and that he didn't want to lose him. A local preacher by the name of Larry Dunkin felt led by the Lord to visit his old teammate from high school, Jack Miller. He didn't know he had stage four cancer in a very advanced state. Jack had only been recently diagnosed with it about two weeks before. He had been sick for the last couple of months but had never gone to the doctor. He kept fooling himself it was just due to the fact that he was getting older. Larry and Jack had played baseball together at Redwood High School for four years and had been good friends.

Pastor Dunkin knocked on the front door and River answered it. Dunkin explained why he wanted to see his old friend. River was only vaguely familiar with Pastor Dunkin. He explained that his grandfather had not been feeling well but he would check with him. River asked his grandfather if he wanted to see a pastor by the name of Larry Dunkin. His grandfather's tired eyes perked up and he said, "I feel okay enough to see him. I haven't seen Dunk in a good while. Send him in." Jack Miller had resisted the simple message of salvation for years from his friend Larry. But, tonight his heart was soft and the fear of death loomed over him like a dark cloud. An hour later, after a lot of memories were exchanged and a lot of laughter and tears were shed, Pastor Dunkin led Jack Andrew Miller to the Lord. Until his grandfather died two days later, River had never seen his grandfather with so much peace and joy on his face. It was something that played with his mind over and over and he couldn't shake it.

Here his grandfather was dying and yet he seemed happy about it. River asked him about it and his grandfather reassured him that he loved him with all his heart. His grandfather told him he hated leaving him and wished he had more time to spend with him. The reason for his joy and peace was that Jesus Christ had forgiven him from a lifetime of sin and was so real to him. Fear of death and the unknown it brings had totally quit plaguing his mind. Jack Miller had begged River to meet with his friend Dunkin and hear him out about the Lord. But, River was angry at God because his grandfather was so close to death and also because of his dad's accidental death. It would take months and a miracle for River to let go of his anger and resentment toward God.

Jack Miller had raised River since his dad, Canyon, was killed by a drunk driver when he was changing a tire alongside a road near Redwood when River was just nine years old. River and his dad had had a great relationship. Because of the impact of his father's death, River swore to Starlight and his grandfather that he would never drink or get high. It was a promise he had always kept. He didn't make it his mission in life to condemn others that did drink or do drugs. It just wasn't for him. Jack Miller also put away his use of alcohol and recreational pot habit as a result of his son's death and River's commitment.

River's mom split the scene from the Utopian Experimental Community with a charismatic small time drug dealer from Seattle soon after River was born. She supposedly died from a drug overdose of prescription pills two months after leaving the community. Lisa Jenkins had been an army brat and had lived all over the world with her family. She had never liked the idea of being pinned down in one place too long because she got bored and liked change and adventure. She had met Canyon Moore at a local flea market in Redwood and had fallen instantly head over heels in love with him and he with her. But, within less than a year she had fallen out of love with Canyon and would be gone forever.

Jack Miller was the leader of the original hippie members who helped form the commune in 1969 where River and Starlight had been raised. Most of the hippies of the 1960's were the catalysts for the radical cultural revolution of their era; but, in time, these individuals had returned to a more moderate version of their parents' traditional lifestyle long before the turn of the 21st century. The novelty and excitement of their rebellious, free lifestyle had eventually worn off. But, Jack Miller had held on to his 1967 flower covered hippie VW van regardless of the changes. His van was like a monument on wheels to a former way of life of almost complete freedom and carefree rebellion. It had helped him to ride the crest of the wave in his day. When he was younger, he had often referred to it as his chick magnet. On the back of River's inherited genuine hippie van from California was a large painted white peace sign and below it in two inch letters read, "Give peace a chance". But, lately Starlight had told River she wanted to change it to a cross in the middle and paint in white letters, "Give Jesus a chance."

After drinking the water from her bottle and twisting the cap back on, Starlight's voice is a little bit shaky from a combination of frustration and fear clawing their way into her mind. She says, "Oh, oh, River, I don't understand. I don't really understand why this stuff is happening to us." Tears are forming and falling from the corners of her deep blue eyes as she says, "I thought things were going so good for us in here in Boulder. I thought for sure we were in the center of God's will. We finally got some decent money coming in with my cashier job at the New Mane Salon and from your private guitar and harmonica lessons. With our gigs singing in the coffee houses and clubs, we are finally getting our heads above water financially. I thought maybe we could finally settle down and get an apartment and quit living out of this tin can of a van or sleeping in a tent sometimes. But, now I'm scared silly, because the last two times this happened God spared our lives."

"Yea, I know. It's freakin' me out too," says an anxious 20 year old River Jenkins. The angelic vision has shaken him to his core and he repeatedly runs both his hands over his long brown hair pulled back into a ponytail and held in place by a red rubber band.

"River, what exactly did God tell you in your dream-like state, or whatever you want to call it?" asks an inquisitive Starlight.

"Star, this time a huge angel came to me and said his name was Michael and that he was an archangel. Here is the bulk of what he said. The stench of sin of an evil people has reached the nostrils of God and He is repulsed by it - that destruction is coming, but we are in the shadow of the Almighty. Michael told me that just as it rains on the just and the unjust, so will destruction fall on the just and the unjust. He said you and I and our new friend Patrick have been ordained to be set apart for a special purpose.

Michael said all those who make up the generation alive today and those still to come that know God's son, Jesus, intimately were born for such a time as this. God has marked some for martyrdom and others will be preserved for different roles and purposes. He said not to fear death for it is but an exit door to your ultimate eternal reward. The angel made it clear that the power of God will fall on all the true followers and truth seekers of Christ who love Him and His Holy Word the Bible in these end times. They will be part of the Remnant Church Movement that will sweep across this country and to the ends of the earth. He said we will see and need the miraculous in order to sustain ourselves and survive the flood of wickedness that will be released on our country soon because the time is short."

Starlight listens intently as River continues. "Michael also said there are two shepherds, anointed vessels who walk in holiness on the grounds of a Fortress not built with wood, steel, stone, nor mortar. They stand guard over a special flock there and abroad that will be divinely protected in the times to come. Soon these two shepherds will walk in a greater anointing from God, his favor and in experiencing the miraculous. Michael said God wants us to follow them as they follow Him, because God will display His mighty power through them as a witness to all who oppose Him. Michael also said the devil's heart will burn with anger toward them, but they are clothed and protected with strong prayer continually. He said we have been called to music evangelism to reach the last generation that knows not God nor the things of God. A great anointing will be released to us for the work to which we have been called. And last of all, Michael said he and his angel hosts that he commands would continually watch over us and all those who have been selected from the foundation of the world to walk through the fires of the Tribulation to be purified chosen vessels."

"Wow, that is a lot. How in the world did you remember all that?" inquires a surprised Starlight.

"It's like the Holy Spirit downloaded it into my long term memory," replies River confidently. "I can't explain it other than it is embedded into my brain cells."

"With all this taking place, we must be near the start of the tribulation according to all that Michael told you, River. Maybe it's going to start any day, huh?" replies Starlight, who is now full of anticipation and whose faith is beginning to rise.

"Michael never narrowed it down or pinpointed exactly when it would start, but it must be really soon," says River.

"What did Michael the archangel look like, River?"

"Michael is like nine or maybe ten feet tall and wears a long white robe. He has blonde hair down to his shoulders and wears a bright pure golden breast plate. He looks very powerful and intimidating physically. Believe me, he could snap the biggest, baddest, and strongest NFL player in half like a dried up twig if he wanted to, but I wasn't afraid of him."

"River, you're not scared of him?" asks a curious Starlight.

"No, not at all. He is friendly and has what I would call a peaceful looking smile on his face. He said that he had been sent from God Almighty to tells us things that must quickly come to pass. Did he have a sword in his hand, like those angels in the book of Genesis guarding the Garden of Eden from Adam and Eve?" asks Starlight.

"No, and believe me he looks like he doesn't need one either," replies River.

Starlight starts thinking out loud to herself saying, "I wonder if it is the same archangel Michael mentioned in the book of Daniel."

"Yeah, I bet he is the same one, Star. It hadn't occurred to me until now that he probably is the same angel. I have to call Patrick now," declares River.

Surprised, Starlight replies, "Did the angel tell you to?"

"No, I just know that I know that I need to," says River with total confidence. "Again, I can't explain it."

"But is he going to believe you?" asks Starlight as she surveys the surreal circumstances.

"Without a doubt in my mind, I know he will," replies River.

But Starlight begins to reason in her own mind that maybe Patrick won't believe River. After all, she and River have just met that guy. She knows he is a senior and a pre-med student at Colorado A&M University. He is from Philadelphia, Pennsylvania. She doesn't know Patrick O'Malley very well and they are from two entirely different worlds.

Nothing could be closer to the truth than what she has just spoken to River. All she knows about Patrick is that he has a northern accent, seems nice and friendly and came from a rich and affluent family in Philadelphia. She also knows his dad is a well-known, prominent doctor on the east coast. She and River came from another time and place on the west coast, although they cannot escape the fact that they were raised on a genuine California hippie commune known as the Utopian Experimental Community - or UEC, like the members liked to call it. But River and Starlight have coined an identity for themselves. They like to think of themselves as "country fried millennials" in the 21st century.

At UEC there was an abundance of different farm animals on the 525 acres there, hay that had to be hauled from the fields in the summer and stacked in two very large barns, dairy cattle to milk and thousands of chickens to raise for eggs. There were days on the farm in which the winds didn't blow in the people's favor and certain conditions prevailed so that they couldn't escape the smell of fresh animal manure. Also there were two natural small ponds and a small man-made lake Jack had carved out with a bulldozer in the summer of 1971.. The ponds were well stocked with fish that Starlight and River loved to catch and usually released. Indeed the 21st century had brought changes to the commune, but old ways of the hippie culture still had some root. By the grace of God, neither River nor Starlight had embraced all the negative entanglements of that lifestyle. Both had known each other since they were babies, having grown up on the large communal farm. They had been best friends since they were kids. Everyone on the farm knew them and liked them, but they had just always marched to the beat of a different drum than the other young people on the farm.

God had always put a special love in their hearts for each other. River had given Starlight a promise ring when she was 14 and he was 15. Even though both had not been raised in a traditional family or even a somewhat functional family, they both knew they wanted to have a traditional family life one day. Since the day River gave her the promise ring, Starlight had dreamed of one day walking down the aisle in a church. She had always imagined herself in an elegant white wedding dress holding a beautiful bouquet of flowers and marrying River, her knight in shining armor, but dressed in a black tuxedo. However, the complete dream had not come true as of yet. They had moved around a lot until they came to Boulder.

But even in Boulder they had not gotten involved in a Bible believing church, let alone had enough money for a real traditional marriage ceremony. Of the seven churches they visited, they just couldn't find the right church to call home for one reason or another. The churches they visited were either way too liberal or too legalistic. Some services they attended at one big church reminded them of a little Las Vegas with all their entertainment productions to draw more people in. Others were cold and the members were impersonal or shallow. Some believed in the gifts of the spirit, but were walking in the flesh trying to manifest them. Some pastors emphasized the giving of money to the church and prosperity of the believers. Those ministers were always taking numerous offerings in the service. Most of the churches didn't emphasis the teaching of the word, prayer or discipleship, but had social programs as an outreach to the community. A lot of churches had two or three of these characteristics.

Both River and Starlight were born on Utopian Experimental Community property. Experienced midwives were used to help bring them into the world. UEC was a large farm situated ten miles outside the city limits of Redwood. UEC members tried to be as independent as possible from outside interferences impacting their lifestyle, Most locals referred to the farm as the commune or hippie commune outside of town. UEC had been formed by a small number of people who had met at the historic Woodstock Music Festival in White Lake, New York on a dairy farm in August of 1969. Jack Miller had been a good looking guy with a very charismatic personality and was a dreamer. He single handedly had influenced a group of about twenty people to return with him to Redwood and start building a utopian society on his family farm.

Most of the baby boomer generation who founded UEC eventually outgrew their constant diet of free love, drugs, and rock and roll and turned their energies to that of a more compromised capitalistic nature. Half of the original members had left. Still old ways had persisted among some old and

9

newer wanna-be hippie members since UEC was founded in 1969. The community was known for its high quality organic fruits, vegetables, eggs, and milk products. They also purchased and processed other small organic farms vegetables, fruits, grains, eggs and milk in the area that were of equally high quality and sold them under their Utopian Experimental Community label. All of the members of UEC and the other farms in their network were opposed to pesticides, herbicides, steroid usage in their farm animals and genetically modified seeds of any kind. Some UEC members were also known for another type of farming. Several members had been busted over the years by law enforcement officials for clandestine marijuana crops grown on state land that bordered their property. There were always small crops for the needs of certain members of UEC. Pot was never grown as a cash crop to be sold to dealers or people outside the commune.

Starlight was an energetic and spunky young woman with long, shiny blonde hair that was parted in the middle, hung down past her waist and was cut in a v pattern in the back. Her hair was the first thing people noticed about her. Her complexion was always slightly tanned because she loved being outdoors. She and River loved outdoors sports like hiking, rock climbing, bouldering, canoeing, kayaking, horseback riding and archery. She had always enjoyed helping her grandmother Jane and others on the farm do chores. She loved faded comfortable t-shirts and blue jeans and going barefooted as much as possible. A little dirt or manure between her toes never bothered her.

Growing up on the UEC farm had provided her with many fond memories and others she would like to have forgotten. Starlight was down to earth, and even though she had a zest for life, she possessed a gentle spirit about her. People were just naturally drawn to her for different reasons. But a big reason they were attracted to her was because she possessed a rare special gift from God. It was her voice - and when she sang, people were mesmerized by it. She had an amazing natural operatic sounding voice and had never taken any voice lessons in her life. Her voice had a tremendous range and could hit notes that seemed impossible and that she could hold for an extended period of time. River was also a gifted guitar and harmonica player and he had a great voice, too, but it was Starlight who always took center stage. When River and she sang and played their rock folk music at coffee houses, clubs, music festivals and other venues, they usually brought the house down. Since they had both gotten saved about six months before in Colorado Springs, they found themselves gravitating more and more to Christian music. River and Starlight were continually reading and studying the Bible. She had also started writing Christian songs. They had recently in the last few months started finishing their show with the song *Amazing Grace*. Most of their audiences were familiar with folk legend Maggie Blackwood and her classic version of *Amazing Grace*. Starlight would mention that Maggie's style of music and singing had had a tremendous influence on her style of singing and songwriting. Usually she and River would close with their own rendition of *Amazing Grace*. River played the guitar while Starlight sang. Often the unsaved people in the places where they performed were reduced to tears by the conviction of the Holy Spirit touching their hearts when Starlight and River did their version of the song. When they were done performing at the close of the show, they would tell everyone that they were Christians and if anyone needed prayer that they would be glad to pray for them. River would say they were not there to judge or beat anyone over the head with a Bible. Sometimes at least one or two or more would come forward and ask for prayer. Occasionally, Starlight and River would lead someone to Christ, which brought them great joy. Some people who were not interested in God would wait until they were finished ministering to people and tell them how much they enjoyed the show, buy a CD, get an autograph, or find out more about their hippie upbringing, their van and/or their music.

Starlight's maiden name was Weaver. People had often teased her about her name being Starlight Weaver. But, it didn't bother her. Her mom's name was Moonbeam Weaver and she had been born on the same commune just like her. Moonbeam Weaver was in charge of the sales and marketing end of the organic products they produced. She had to travel a lot and was gone much of the time. She tended to be a workaholic. Starlight cried herself to sleep many a night saying to herself that only River really cared about her and loved her. Starlight's grandmother, Jane Weaver, was a radical young woman originally from Chicago, Illinois and had decided to plunge herself deep into the countercultural movement of the 1960's. It was at Woodstock where she met Jack Miller and was captivated with his grand vision of building a utopian hippie farm community in Redwood, California. As one of eight original female founding members of the Utopian Experimental Community, she had risen to taken on a matriarchal role in the community.

Jane Weaver had been a radical wild woman in the 60's and a heavy drug user. But, she had kicked a bad drug habit after she had gotten pregnant with Moonbeam. Since her daughter was born, she had always been a recreational user. Jane Weaver raised Moonbeam to call her by her first name and insisted that Starlight do the same. Jane was a total nonconformist and revolted against old school traditions and social norms on all levels. She could have gotten an illegal abortion in her day, but the fact that she was pregnant and unmarried was still taboo in 1970 when Moonbeam was born. Jane Weaver relished the fact that she was breaking a social norm that had been around before the time of Christ, whom she hated. Organic farming had become her passion and she loved being involved in the day to day operations of the farm as a supervisor over the dairy herd and the quality of dairy products UEC produced. Starlight's grandmother was still a very active and attractive woman in her early 70's and lived a very immoral lifestyle. As a young girl Starlight noticed that Jane would often grow tired or her current boyfriend and quickly find a new one usually from outside of UEC.

****

As they continue their discussion in the van, Starlight says, "River, from everything you said, I would imagine that Patrick is on the same page as we are according to what the angel Michael told you. We've been through something similar to this twice before. But, it is still is hard to believe in these revelations from God. Is Patrick even saved? I mean, I just met him briefly around a week ago at Megan's Roasted Bean Coffeehouse and I don't know him that well."

"Yes, I believe that Michael must have revealed himself to Patrick. And yes, Patrick is definitely saved, Star," replies River. "Pat is a real cool Christian and he can play the bass guitar".

Thank God he is saved. How good is he on the bass, River?, asks Starlight.

"Pat is really good," River replies, "but he says he is just okay".

"When did you hear him play?"

"A couple of days after first meeting him at the coffeehouse, I ran into him at the rock gym. We got to talking about music and he let me listen to

12

some recordings of him playing bass on his smart phone. He and I really hit it off. Not only is he into rock climbing, bouldering and other outdoor activities like us, but best of all he really loves Jesus."

"Oh, well that's cool," responds Starlight. "You didn't tell me all that before."

"Starlight, I just found out four days ago when I ran into him at the rock gym and I forgot to tell you. We exchanged phone numbers at that time."

"Okay, what I want to know now is exactly what does God want us to do according to what the archangel Michael told you? What Michael told you sounds like a riddle about two shepherds who live on the grounds of a fortress not built with stone and mortar. What does that mean?"

"First let me say I didn't tell you this part yet, because you were already having a hard time."

"I know, I know! I'm dealing with it better now," says Starlight, "But what did he tell you that you didn't tell me yet?"

"He said we had to leave Boulder and go southwest of here as soon as possible."

"I already knew we were going to leave, River. It was a given. I have a lot of questions before we just pack up and move. The first question is where to the southwest of here? That's the big question."

"I don't know, Star".

A little frustration can be heard in Starlight's voice as she asks the question. "Well, now I am beginning to regress and understand how Sarah in the book of Genesis must have felt being married to Abraham, wandering around in the desert. "

"That does seem like us. All I know is that Michael said that in the process of leaving it would be made clear to us."

"In that case, we'll just have to wait and find out," replies Starlight. "River, let me ask you another question."

"Shoot, says River."

"Why, why would God not want us to tell more people about leaving Boulder if something is going to happen?" says a distraught Starlight.

"I don't know, Star. I'm not God. Maybe he knows that people just would not believe us if we told them. I don't know what is exactly going to happen, Starlight."

"But, River, my friend Jenny Garcia down at the salon is so close to getting saved."

"Haven't you shared the gospel with her a couple of times and she rejected it?"

"Yes I have," says Star, "More than a couple of times. But, I know in my heart she is so close to getting saved. I left her a tract inside her purse yesterday when I left work. I like her a lot as a friend. Jenny said she and her boyfriend Mark were leaving for Fort Collins last night to visit his brother because his wife just had a baby."

"Hopefully they did, Star. All we can do is pray at this point."

"Okay, well you pray because I'm having a hard time right now."

"Sure. Give me a moment while I move my foot. It seems to be falling asleep. There, okay, that's better, I'll pray now. Dear Lord, you know the beginning from the end. Your son is the alpha and omega. If you have sent the angel Michael to warn us to leave Boulder along with our friend Patrick, we have to submit to your will. There are people we like and care about in this city and we wish everyone would get saved. But, you are God and we have asked your Son Jesus to be our Lord and Savior, both Starlight and myself, as well as Patrick. So please help Starlight, Patrick, and me to bow our knees to your will being done in our lives. Please be with Starlight's friend Jenny and her boyfriend and convict them of their of sins and to say the sinner's prayer in the tract. Please Lord. Amen."

"I am feeling better now, River. I have some peace at least. Please forgive me because I have been acting selfish and like a real cry baby. I really do want Jesus to be my Lord in every area, so I submit to his will. I sincerely want to mature as a disciple of Christ."

"Thanks, Star," says a somewhat relieved River.

"Go ahead and call Patrick, because this is going to be a very interesting conversation."

"Alright, I'm going to place my phone on speaker so you can hear the conversation."

"Great! Go ahead."

River speed dials Patrick's number. When there is a connection, River says, "Patri..."

Patrick blurts out, "River, my body is shaking. I think I'm still dreaming. I'm not sure what just happened. I just experienced something supernatural. An archangel just appeared to me in a dream, or at least I think it was a dream. He said his name was Michael and that God had chosen me and others that I would join with for a special purpose. The angel said that you and Starlight have also been chosen along with a fourth individual who will join us in our first leg of the journey. Michael said we were to walk in faith and be bold and strong in the Lord. He said that in the coming days we will walk through the fires of the Tribulation, but will not be burned but purified. The last thing Michael said was that you were going to call me at the appointed time. I was literally waiting for you to call me, River," says Patrick with a shaky voice.

"Oh my God, River! I've got goose bumps all over me," says Starlight.

"Is that Starlight in the background?" asks a confused and nervous Patrick.

"Yes, that's my wife, and she is also weirded out by all of this supernatural stuff from God. This same thing has happened twice before to us, and had we not obeyed the Lord we would have been killed both times."

"I believe you, River! I believe you. I'm all ears! I was really thinking I was losing my mind. What are you supposed to tell me, River?"

"Pat, I guess I'm supposed to tell you to pack your bags. We're going on a road trip. We have to leave Boulder as soon as possible."

"I started packing my stuff last night after this dream vision thing. I mean, I felt like something was going to happen. I didn't know what. It didn't make any sense. I thought I was going nuts. I just pulled in here eight days ago from Philly and I had basically just unpacked all the things from my SUV into my one bedroom apartment. I was excited that the start of the new fall semester at Colorado A&M is just a few days away. But, last night I was compelled to pack my stuff. All my junk is by the front door of my apartment. If nothing happens and I'm not back in school real soon after it starts and I tell my parents about this, they are going to have me placed in a psychiatric hospital back in Philly. It was hard enough to talk them into letting me attend A&M to study pre-med here instead of the University of William Penn in Philadelphia, where my dad graduated. I have a lot at stake here. River, where did the angel tell you we need to go?"

"He, ah... he ah, it hasn't been revealed yet to me."

"What the heck? You mean you don't know? Oh great! I thought you would have the answer. I feel this sense of doom if I stay and I feel like I'm crazy if I go."

"Look, Patrick, don't freak out! Just chill for a second! Remember what the angel Michael said."

"Okay! Okay! I'm getting a grip in the name of Jesus."

"Super! Throw all your stuff in your SUV and meet us here at the Happy Camper Campground, lot 121. We are in an old 1967 VW van with flowers all over it. You can't miss us," says River.

"Yeah, I know exactly where the campground is. It's right down the road less than a half a mile from Ci Mada Union Laboratories, that huge five story gray mirrored building that's mostly hidden right at the lower tree line of the mountain with huge natural boulders around it."

River's mind is dazed for a second and he says, "Hey, repeat that. Tell me again what the name of the laboratories you mentioned is, Patrick?"

Starlight's eyes light up in complete surprise and rage. Patrick repeats himself. "It's Ci Mada Union Laboratories."

Starlight starts saying, "Oh my God, Oh my God, Oh my God, I don't believe it," as she instantly places her hands over her face and slowly drags them down in disbelief.

Patrick, a bit confused about Starlight's vocal reaction, says, "I... guess you guys have heard of them before."

"Yeah, we have. Especially the last four years before we left home. We just forgot that it was here in Boulder and it's hard to believe it's almost just a stone's throw away from where we are now."

"Well, River, Ci Mada Union Laboratories is one of those buildings that's tucked away and surrounded by tall pine trees, and if you are not looking for it, you can easily overlook it. Guys, I'm sensing that maybe you know something about Ci Mada that I don't know. Is it something regarding genetic research of seeds, plants, and animals?"

"Oh definitely! Yes we do - especially me, Patrick," declares Starlight in an angry tone. "No wonder God is getting us out of here." With a voice of righteous anger, she then goes on to say, "Patrick, listen. Ci Mada has been messing around with mother nature and making gmo seeds and frankenstein foods and animals for years with nothing more than a slap on the wrist. Crooked politicians, departments of governments, and university research centers who are supposed to be looking out for the health of the American people have become rich, fat cats from catering to Ci Mada's demands. So now I'm guessing there's probably an unknown major fault line below our very feet and God is going to drop judgment on that wicked company. He possibly might cause a rift in the earth's crust that is going to appear and hell is going to open its gates and swallow that company. Either that might happen or, who knows, one of those meteorites that have been hitting south of us and elsewhere is going to slam into it and blow it up. I don't know, but that is my spiritual gut feeling. This is probably why the Lord wants us out of here, Patrick.."

River speaks up with emphasis, "Starlight knows all about that evil company and I'm kinda thinking she might be right, Pat, about what is coming."

"That could be the case. I don't know for sure, guys, but I believe we'll find out shortly. In that case, it seems that God wants us to quickly 'get out of

Dodge,'" says Patrick who is sensing the serious nature of the angelic visitation.

Starlight is stunned with the realization that Ci Mada is just down the road from their lot in the campground. "I just didn't know that Ci Mada was basically in my backyard. The fact is, River and I have been so busy, Patrick, just trying to make ends meet financially that I completely forgot that Ci Mada had relocated here three years ago from just north of San Francisco."

Patrick, sensing that Ci Mada might be due for judgment, asks, "So you guys think Ci Mada Union Laboratories is what this supernatural visitation from the archangel Michael is all about?"

"Yeah, in my mind and spirit I believe it's got to be part of the reason," responds River, as he sees Starlight nodding her head in agreement.

"Patrick, my mother, Moonbeam, can't stand that company. I've heard her call them every name in the book a bunch of times, especially during the last two years I was at home."

"Patrick, it is so ironic that we are right down the road from a company opposed to everything Starlight and I have believed in and have been taught about nature, food, and animals. We weren't familiar with this area of Boulder and, after all, this is only our third night in the campground," rationalizes River. From what I could make out from the road when I passed by a few days ago, there's no name on the building."

"Yeah, I know. It's probably for security reasons. Did you guys notice the street address?"

"I did. It's 666 in big letters, and so now the plot thickens. Could somebody be leaving a clue, guys?" replies Starlight in a serious, sarcastic tone, with her right index finger touching the corner of the right side of her mouth and her head tilted towards her right shoulder as the pupils of her eyes pointed upward in the opposite direction. "River, if we had more time, my mom and grandmother and the people back at UEC would be so proud of us if we protested against Ci Mada Union Laboratories."

"Yeah, they would roll out the red carpet and give us a hero's welcome back on the farm, Star," says River with a grin. "But that's not what the angel told us to do."

"I know, Riv. I just thought it would be so cool to do that. Maybe we can come back another time and do that if the Lord wills and Ci Mada hasn't been cast into Hell."

"Yeah, but not this time, Star."

"Hey, guys I heard a lot of rumors over the short time I've been in Boulder. But, I just thought people were blowing things out of proportion. At this moment I'm beginning to remember some things people said about Ci Mada being kind of evil in a lot of ways".

"Oh, definitely, Patrick," says Starlight. "I distinctly remember on more than one occasion Moonbeam said Ci Mada Union had deep ties with the establishment. Their evil foreign-born director who runs that place, whose name I can't remember, was a real creep and she had heard rumors that his dad did genetic research for Hitler. She said Ci Mada was intentionally destroying mother nature and the health of the American people."

"Starlight, all I basically knew about Ci Mada before was that they did genetic research and that they paid good money to pre-med students from the university. Two former friends of mine who were unsaved and who were pre-med students like myself got jobs there making big bucks. They made eighteen dollars an hour at Ci Mada working part-time before school was out doing research. They were also told by their supervisors they could work the whole summer making tons of overtime if they wanted to and possibly get pay raises and bonuses. They had to sign confidential agreements and go through extensive background checks to get the jobs. They told me it was a done deal for me to get a job with the company with me being an upperclassman in pre-med and my GPA being a lot higher than theirs. So I had an interview with a guy named Nash and when he saw I was a born again Christian on my application the interview was basically over at that point. He made up some bogus excuse that he had an important meeting with some VIP's in the company, that he had forgotten about it, and that he would call me in about an hour and a half to continue the interview at another time. He never called me back, so I went on home to Philly this past summer and worked in my dad's medical office shuffling papers around and doing 'gofer' jobs at ten dollars an hour."

"Patrick, that sounds about right knowing what we know about Ci Mada. That company is continually tampering with our fragile food chain, God's creatures, nature in general, and is apparently opposed to the Bible and Christianity. Our families and friends have been committed to high standards in the organic food industry for 50 years and Ci Mada is totally opposed to that industry," says a livid Starlight.

Patrick, with a sense of urgency, now says, "You guys seem to have valid points. In the end, the people who are behind Ci Mada Union will have to answer to God. I understand your passion about not messing around with nature. Anyway, guys, right now I'm taking a deep breath and I'll load everything up. Then I'm going to stop and get some cash at my bank's ATM machine and fill up my gas tank. I'll be there in about 45 minutes. Okay, I will believe with you guys that God will show us the answer as to where to go."

"That's right," River and Starlight agree.

"Bye," says Patrick. "See you soon!"

"Bye," say Starlight and River together.

"Okay, Starlight, before I get sidetracked with all that has happened and what we have discussed just now I want to know how our financial status is right now.

"We've got about $1,650.00 in cash and our special reserve, for when everything goes south."

"Well, remember, Star, those three old U. S. twenty dollar gold pieces dated 1861 that belonged to my grandfather are what we touch last when there is nothing left - period."

"Yeah, I know. "

"You still have our savings and gold tucked away in your old right winter boot under the bed?"

"Yes, River."

"Then I guess we're all good for now."

"We had $2,300.00 two days ago until I had to dip deep into our cash reserve money to put on some new tires and get a front wheel alignment for this old van. The salesman said that tread was not only low but the tires were also very dry rotted. River, with the condition of our tires, the salesman said we could have had a blow out at any time."

"I guess the Lord had it all planned out, Starlight. We probably wouldn't have gotten down the road a hundred miles today with those old tires. Let's get a very quick shower and get ready for Patrick. Our gas tank is filled to the top already and we are ready to roll."

After a quick shower, they both are dressed and Starlight pulls out a jar of organic peanut butter and a pint-sized jar of raw honey to make sandwiches on some 100% stone ground organic wheat bread from a cardboard box in the van. They drink spring water from a local source in stainless steel hiking bottles with their breakfast. When they are finished eating, Starlight is inside the van cleaning things up and packing things away. River is checking the van's oil, as Patrick pulls up in his Toyota FJ Cruiser that is loaded to the max with most of his belongings. The van's oil is just slightly low, so River puts the dipstick back into place. He waves to Patrick in his Toyota SUV, but Patrick looks a little pale. As he gets out of the SUV, his body is shaking a little bit, and he tells River he can't believe he is actually doing this. River is also having a hard time dealing with it, but he smiles, shrugs his shoulders, and says, "Tell me about it."

The air is a little cool and crisp this morning so Patrick unlocks the back-seat door behind the driver's seat to reach for his light jacket when a book falls out of the vehicle and is flat on the ground with the inside cover opened. River reaches down to pick it up and to give it to Patrick when he recognizes the book is opened to highlighted pages 78 and 79. In almost total unbelief he says, "Patrick, where did you get this book?"

"I ordered it online and just finished reading it last night at ten o'clock. I couldn't put it down. It arrived in my school mailbox two days ago."

"Wow! I've been reading that very same book!"

"No! Really? Where did you get your copy?"

"I found it on my van two days ago after coming out of a gas station. It was under my windshield wiper with a note that said, "Read it.'"

"Wow! I wonder if the angel Michael put it there, River?"

"I don't know," responds River in amazement.

Starlight steps out of the van, without knowing what just happened or hearing the conversation of the young men. She is reading the same book Patrick has and is opened to where River had placed a bookmark. She is fixated on two pages River had folded over the corners and wanted to share it with Patrick after he got out of his SUV. Starlight had tuned everything else out of her mind. Just five minutes ago, before she ran across the book, she had been straightening things up in the van and trying to get to her phone between the van's inside wall and the bed frame that she could not budge. River is holding Patrick's copy of the book in his hands, but his back is toward Starlight. Starlight has two pages from the book with her right index finger sandwiched in between them to hold the spot River had folded. As she walks to Patrick's vehicle, she says, "Hi. Patrick. I know it is weird about the vision, but these two guys in this book wrote on pages 78 and 79 that strange things were going to happen to Christians in the end times. They will occur in order for God's prophetic scriptures to be fulfilled to the letter in the end times. They believe God will use divine appointments, coincidences, dreams, visions, signs, angels and miracles in the lives of Christians to combat the god of this world and his demonic forces. They go on and state that these things must happen in order to ensure the church of Jesus Christ complete victory over the Kingdom of Satan in the Tribulation period."

River's voice is quivering as he says, "Of all the things written in that book, what Starlight just said was what stood out the most to me."

River slowly turns around as Patrick's eyes almost bug out of their sockets when he sees the only place he has highlighted in the whole book is what Starlight just read. Patrick knows that a miracle is taking place before his eyes.

River says, "You mean this book, Starlight, *Walking in the Supernatural in the End Times* by Ricky Crawford and Gary Kirkman?"

Starlight finally looks up to see that Patrick has a copy of the same book, that River is holding it in his hands opened to that the same section that is highlighted. She instantly falls to her knees with her arms and hands stretched out upward and cries out with her eyes closed, "Jesus is Lord! Jesus is Lord!. Jesus Christ is Lord! I surrender all to Him and Him alone! I believe God has given us a definite sign and confirmation from heaven!"

Patrick quickly remembers something and, grabbing his book from River, says, "Look here!" as he points to the back of the book. "These two ministers live in Golden Valley, Colorado. Golden Valley is a little cow town in Clark county southwest of here. Listen, guys, this is where we are supposed to go!"

River enthusiastically responds by saying, "Starlight, I'm in total agreement with Patrick. I think what has just happened is a divine sign as to where we are to go. Listen, Star, you don't know it, but when Patrick got out and opened the back door on the driver side, this book fell out to pages 78 and 79 pointing up to the sky."

Starlight, now with her eyes wide open, still on her knees with her arms raised high and waving them gently, says "Hallelujah, God is alive! Romans 8:14 says, 'For as many as are led by the Spirit of God, they are the sons of God'. It sure is exciting to belong to the family of God!"

"Amen, sister!" says a spiritually pumped River.

"This is unbelievable! God is blowing my mind!" says Patrick. "I used to work out with a guy named Forrest at the rock climbing gym in Boulder when I was a sophomore, and he was finishing up his master's degree at the university. He was quite interesting and super nice. Forrest used to witness to me while we climbed, and I just really kind of blew him off concerning Christianity. But he planted some spiritual seeds in my heart. It just took some time for them to sprout. If I remember correctly, at the start of last year I got a letter from him about him being involved with a ministry located in Golden Valley after he graduated. I had completely forgotten about that until just now."

"Okay, guys!" announces Star ecstatically. "There is no doubt in my mind that God sovereignly had you to read the same book that River was reading, and that I was reading River's copy when you pulled up, Patrick. God ordained that without me knowing it. But who are these ministers, Patrick?" she asks, wanting desperately to know.

"They are two ministers that all the big names in Bible prophecy 20 years ago labeled as false prophets and false teachers. Now some of those same famous prophecy teachers on TV and radio are second guessing what they wrote in their own books that sold millions of copies and are saying that Ricky Crawford's and Gary Kirkham's prophetic scriptural interpretations may have some validity."

"In other words," Starlight says in a righteous angry tone, "those ministers are doing some back peddling from what I've picked up in the middle of the book. Isn't that right, Patrick?"

"Yes, absolutely!" responds Patrick. "What they taught in certain areas of prophecy went totally against the flow of what Christians got a steady diet of on Christian TV, radio, and books."

"But I don't understand much Bible prophecy, Patrick. What originally got these two ministers branded as false teachers and such?" asks a puzzled Starlight.

"Well, they are post-tribulationists for one thing," says Patrick.

"Oh, I know what that means," responds a confident Starlight. "It means Christians will go through the Tribulation and not get raptured out before or at the start of it, like that is supposed to scare me or something. If and when God wants me to be a martyr, all I have to say is 'bring it on,' because if I'm absent from the body, then I'm present with the Lord. Hallelujah! I never believed in that fairy tale of a quick escape from the earth called the rapture."

"Maybe you haven't, Starlight, but a lot of Christians believe that doctrine as if it was the gospel," says Patrick with strong conviction.

"Well, all I have to say is a fan of our music felt led to give me an old copy of a book by a guy named James McKeever. After a gig at the Showtime Club in Colorado Springs, he came up and gave us a copy of McKeever's book entitled *Christians Will go through the Tribulation*. I read it as a brand new babe in Christ and it made a lot of sense to me," snaps Starlight.

24

"Me too," says River. "Patrick, Starlight and I have spent most of our time just reading the Bible. When we read and study the Bible, we always pray for the Holy Spirit to reveal nothing but the truth of God's Word to us."

"Absolutely! I'm not interested in the doctrines of men," adds Starlight in a resolute voice.

"I just want to say this one thing, Pat and Star, that is so key for us to remember."

"What, River?" asks a curious Starlight.

"It's this, that if God has gone to this much trouble to use an angel and these divine coincidences to clearly show us to go and see Gary Kirkman and Ricky Crawford, the authors of this book here, then I think we need to sit at their feet and listen to what they have to say," replies River.

"Amen! That's a very true statement. And I want to add that I don't know exactly all the reasons why the Lord has hooked me up with you guys, but I know he has. There is no doubt now in my mind. I have regrets about leaving Boulder, but this whole ordeal is so much bigger than us here."

"Absolutely," agrees Starlight as Patrick nods his head.

"I wish we could somehow reach all these people in Boulder with the Gospel before we leave this city," says Patrick with humility and sadness in his voice.

"I know, but apparently God has work for us to do in Golden Valley in music evangelism with the ministry there," says Starlight, who now has a stream of tears flowing from her eyes.

"The strange thing is that Golden Valley is a two stoplight town and Clark County I think is the smallest county and the poorest in the state," replies a puzzled Patrick.

"Yeah, well, apparently God wants us there and is going to use us somehow," replies River confidently. "Patrick, I think we need to get going."

"Yes, but before we go, I want to loan you guys a really good set of walkie talkies. I think we need them for the trip to Golden Valley. Our cell phones won't work when we have to travel through some of the mountainous areas. I have a GPS screen in my SUV and I'll program it for Golden Valley. We'll be able to use it for some of the trip. I also have a current road atlas for a back up. Are you familiar with this kind of walkie talkie, River?" asks Patrick.

"Oh, yes. We used them on the commune sometimes and this is basically the same kind that Star and I used."

"One last thing before we leave… I have to tell you guys this before we go that this whole thing since last night has seemed surreal. I mean really, I have replayed last night over and over again in my mind at least 100 times. And now I can't believe I'm actually going on a road trip at this time with school soon to start and I might not be coming back here." Somewhere between a thin line of faith and fear he says, "I'm going for it. So I guess let's get on the road," announces a seemingly inspired Patrick.

"We know exactly how you feel, Pat," empathizes River.

"Great! You guys ready to leave?"

"Yes, we are!" River and Starlight loudly reply.

As Starlight and River climb into their van, she tells River, "If we hadn't gone through this before, I would say we are nuts. Just plain fruity and nutty."

"I agree, if it wasn't for the fact that we have gone through two similar circumstances before. Starlight, you know what?"

"What, River?"

"I love you, and we are going to trust God by faith to go before us so we can accomplish His will for our lives."

"Amen, River, I love you too. We are walking by faith in these last days. Hey, River, look! Patrick is taking off."

"Don't worry, Star, I'm going to stay right on his tail."

"It's Golden Valley or Bust!" proclaims Starlight, full of faith and ready for their new spiritual journey to begin.

Chapter 2

THE ROCKY ROAD

8:05:17 AM, Mountain Standard Time, Wednesday, 05/08/20_ _ , near Mountain View, Colorado, USA

"Hey Pat, do you read me?"

"Yeah, loud and clear."

"Hey, man, I'm so sorry, but we need to make another pit stop the next chance we get. My beautiful young bride, Starlight, must be in the Guinness Book of World Records for the smallest bladder."

"You're kidding me. She's incredible," rants Patrick in actual subdued frustration with a good dose of teasing.

 No sooner had the three gotten out of Boulder when Starlight had to go to the restroom at a gas station for the first time. Then Patrick's SUV had a flat tire that took an hour to fix. Starlight had to go again and this time went out in the forest. The guys had to unload all of Patrick's stuff outside of the back of his vehicle to get to the jack and tire lug wrench. Then it took thirty minutes just to get one stubborn lug nut off the wheel in order to remove the flat tire and change it. Frustration was building up in their minds as a result of the setbacks. They then had to put back all of the luggage. Then his one year old SUV started over heating, barely making it to a scenic rest area where she went again. They knew the archangel was looking out for them because River had just purchased an extra gallon of coolant the night before and had it in his van, just the fix to solve the problem.

"Yeah, tell me about it. Now she has to pee a fourth time. We might want to give her a medal for this." River is using humor to try to diffuse the anxiety they are all experiencing from the angelic visitations and whole ordeal of leaving Boulder, which may soon receive some kind of physical judgment of God.

"River, I'm beginning to think that your young bride's bladder is under demonic attack like my vehicle." He then starts laughing so loudly over the walkie-talkie that it makes him start coughing.

When he stops and finally releases his button, River sheepishly says, "It does seem that way, Pat." Now it's his turn. He can't stop laughing.

Starlight snickers for a moment herself, then snatches the walkie-talkie out of River's hand and pushes the button so both of them can hear her and says, "Hey, will you guys stop? Give me a break! Oh, wait a minute, that didn't come out just right."

River swipes the walkie-talkie back from her unexpectedly and quickly pushes the talk button. Trying not to laugh, he looks at Starlight and says, "No, you have made it perfectly clear now." In an effort to sound like a medieval knight, he tells her, "My fair damsel, I can't help but notice that you are in distress. I vow to you we will stop at the next chance, so that your tiny bladder may know rest and so that everything comes out all right."

Starlight is rolling her eyes and tightening the muscles in her cheeks and neck so that her lips are compressing against one another. Having known her his whole life, He recognizes her body language and knows it's time to back off her now. He tells his new friend that they need to stop with the bathroom humor because, otherwise, he might become another fatal driving statistic in the state of Colorado.

"Who's going to be a fatal statistic?" inquires Patrick, who is pretending he can't hear.

"Me!" says River.

"Well, this laughing has been great therapy for me, buddy, because I needed a little comic relief. The intensity of the situation has had me uptight since last night."

"I'm with you."

Starlight motions to River to push the button. "Yeah, humor is a great stress reliever. Unfortunately, it has all been at my expense." She looks at her bearded husband and makes mean faces, pretending she is really mad. He knows she is clowning around now and cracks up at her funny faces. She unbuckles her seat belt and leans way over the armrest of her passenger chair in the VW van jabbing River with her left elbow in his side kind of hard.

He plays it up like a drama king. "Ouch! That hurts! My side will never be the same again. I think you've damaged some of my internal organs."

Quickly refastening her seatbelt, Starlight smiles really big and arrogantly proclaims, "Serves you right for messing with this girl."

Travel time to Golden Valley has been increased with all the bathroom breaks and vehicle problems. The three travelers are in awe of the beautiful scenery in the remote areas of Colorado. They couldn't have asked for a lovelier day with the sun beaming down, a slight mountain breeze whistling between the peaks, and a cool 62 degrees this time of morning. The majestic Rocky Mountains, with sprinkled sections of golden colored aspen trees under a blue sky canopy and fluffy white clouds, has made the trip visually spectacular. At that moment, River is a safe distance behind Patrick, traveling the speed limit in broad daylight, when he notices a huge momma grizzly bear up ahead with two large cubs seemingly coming out from behind two boulders a short distance in front of his friend's SUV. The bears had been completely hidden from their sight by a huge boulder and a smaller one alongside the two lane highway. All three bears quickly charge out to the middle of the highway, then remain motionless as they look at Patrick's SUV coming straight at them.

River yells, "Hold on, Star!"

At that same instance Patrick slams on his brakes fast and hard. The SUV begins swerving back and forth with tires smoking. It looks as if it is going to tip over. In one sense, time seems frozen for each of the three because the grizzlies don't budge an inch. But time is distorted in their minds on the other hand because everything also seems to be happening in a flash. Patrick's vehicle is about ten feet from all three grizzlies before it comes to a sudden, complete stop. River's reaction is to push his brake pedal to the floor board in order to keep the van from crashing into the back of the SUV. The old hippie van's new tires are squealing, and the smell of burning rubber and smoke begin to fill the air in a small black cloud behind the almost out of control '67 van.

Starlight braces herself for crashing into the back of their new friend's vehicle by firmly clinching onto her chair's cracked vinyl armrests with all ten of her fingernails embedded in them. She is screaming at the top of her lungs, "Jesus, Jesus, please helps us!"

In order to avoid hitting Patrick's SUV and to stop from going over the shoulder of the opposite lane, River is able to gain control of his van by the grace of God and steer it to the left of the SUV at the last possible moment. No sooner do both vehicles come to an abrupt halt than a barrage of jagged rocks twice the size of volleyballs and some three feet in diameter come rolling down the middle of the two lane highway. Then in a blur, Starlight sees three more boulders about three feet in diameter go across the road along with smaller boulders coming down the mountainside. After all the noise and commotion, the bear and her cubs casually walk across the road down the mountain and disappear into the tree line fifty yards below the road like nothing had ever happened. In this poor section of Colorado, guardrails alongside the road do not exist. Had River lost control of the van, it could have easily plunged them, and possibly Patrick, over the edge of the road and down the mountainside into the trees and rocks below. Certain death would have resulted.

Not hurt, Patrick notices the bears have disappeared below and he quickly jumps out of his SUV. His body is shaking violently almost to the point of making him look like he is going into shock. For a split second he thinks he is surely going to die. Somehow he manages to overcome the vibration and fear and scouts out the area before possibly encountering any more bears or falling rocks. It seems that he is talking to himself, but he is actually rapidly praying under his breath, thanking God he is still alive. Starlight and River take a jolt because their old van doesn't have shoulder harnesses, only safety belts across their laps. River is a little woozy because he has a small knot on his head from hitting his head on the top of the steering wheel. He had been so busy trying not to hit Patrick's vehicle or some of the rocks that he didn't think to brace himself with both of his arms on the steering wheel as the van came to a whiplash kind of stop. He is conscious, but he has a fair-sized bump on his head that seems to be growing, with a small cut on top and a trace of blood oozing out.

Although Starlight tightened and braced her body just before he slammed on the brakes, she seems fine. She yells, "Riv, Riv, you okay?"

"Yeah, thanks to God. My head hurts a little, but it could have been a lot worse. Those boulders would have killed us if it had it not been for those bears. I never saw the rocks coming down the mountain."

"Oh...Oh, I know, Honey. It just happened... so fast," replies Starlight, who is still trying to keep herself from hyperventilating but quickly remembers to turn on the hazard lights. After only seconds, she is doing a lot better breathing.

"Let's get out and see how Patrick is doing," instructs River with his hand on his head.

"Okay, but you stay put for now." Starlight jumps out of the van. She sprints around the van, with her long blonde hair flopping up and down in the air and bouncing off her back as she comes to his aid. She grabs River's arm as he gets out of the van to make sure he doesn't fall.

Patrick appears to be normal at first glance now as he runs over to the VW van and says, "You guys alright?"

"Yeah, we're still alive, thanks to God. It was only by His grace that we were able to stop," replies a shaken River.

"Yeah, you got that right," says Starlight.

"It all happened so quickly," says a still nervous Patrick. "The bears and rocks came out of nowhere. It's a miracle I was able to stop. If it had not been for those bears staying put in the middle of the road, I know I would have been dead meat."

"The bears didn't act normal," replies River, while touching the knot on his head. "God was truly watching over all of us. All of those smaller rocks were bouncing around, and if one would have come through my windshield, it would've killed us."

"No doubt. How are you feeling, Pat?" asks Starlight, whose breathing has returned to normal.

"Physically I'm fine, but I've been on a mental and emotional roller coaster since last night and I feel drained at this point. Gee, River, your forehead has a good size lump on it."

"Ah, it's nothing. I'll be alright."

Within seconds, drivers in both lanes are quickly stopping and getting out to check on the young travelers. People are saying they can't call 911 from here because it's a dead zone. Locals tell them rock slides happen every once and a while, but it is always because of a lot of rain or melting snow and ice, never on a beautiful day like today. Several people tell them that at exit 19 down the mountain in the town of Mountain View is the Mountain View Diner. They have a land line there they can use if they need to call for an ambulance. The young travelers reassure them all that they are fine, although Patrick and Starlight are concerned about River's head. A few moments pass and they drive their still functioning vehicles backwards to test them. They are hoping and praying that while they are there no more rock slides happen. Starlight then looks up and points her finger at two white goats moving away from their position on the highway. The two mountain goats, high above them, are walking on loose shale rock that is sliding. River and Patrick look up and see them. Patrick says, "I bet they started this rock avalanche."

River agrees, "Yeah, I believe you are right."

Within ten minutes, about twenty drivers and passengers clear off the small rocks and boulders on the highway and get back on their journey. The three young Christians from Boulder are the last to leave. River says that he wants to stop at the diner up ahead and get some coffee. Patrick wants to get ice for his bump too.

Patrick agrees that that sounds like a great idea. "After that whole ordeal, I just want to chill out for a while and get a little bite to eat. But first let me check you out a little bit, River."

"No, no, I'm good - really. I just hit my head a little bit and got my bell rung on the steering wheel. I've had worse falling off while riding horses and rock climbing without a helmet," insists River.

"Well, it doesn't look too bad to be honest with you. But sometimes looks can be deceiving."

"Seriously, Pat, once I get some coffee, I think I'll be fine. I usually have some coffee by this time in the morning, so my headache might also be from lack of caffeine."

"Well, that is a possibility, but I thought I would ask anyway. After all, I'm a pre-med student and my dad is a doctor, so it's second nature to inquire into people's health."

"That's understandable."

"River, once we get to the diner, we need to talk about what's going on. I was joking earlier about us being under demonic attack, but after what just happened, I think I believe it."

"Yeah, it seems that way. God definitely wanted us to leave Boulder, but now it seems the devil doesn't want us to get to Golden Valley."

River and Starlight both express that they believe Michael and other angels are probably working behind the scenes protecting them.

Patrick replies, "Yes, I believe that an angel used those bears to get me to stop. I never saw those rocks and huge boulders coming down the mountain."

"Thank God for his mighty angels," says River who notices his vision has gotten a little blurry.

"Amen! I'll follow you, Pat, to the diner. Okay, River?" He hesitates momentarily about driving. "Oh, no! How about I drive, buddy boy?" says an assertive Starlight in a loving tone because she knows River has a high threshold of pain.

"Alright, you win. You drive to the diner while I take it easy. That sounds good to me. I'll work with you, babe, but will you do me a favor, Star?"

"What's that?"

"Make sure you stop for bears if you see any."

"Oh, yeah, you bet I will!"

Just as they are getting ready to get into their vehicles, River glances up one more time and sees two large white mountain goats high up on the rocky ridge slopes above. One goat is chasing another on loose shale rock. In a low voice, he says, "Look up there where the goats are running on loose rocks with boulders of different sizes right below." Patrick and Starlight look up and see some loose rock sliding downward.

Starlight nervously says, "Let's get out of here before we get entombed by another rock avalanche."

"Absolutely! We're out of here," yells Patrick.

Five minutes have passed since they left the scene where the rock slide occurred when arrive at the shabby Mountain View Diner. River slips his folded red bandana over his forehead to hide his bump just before he walks in the building. As they walk into the restaurant, they notice that its décor looks like it's right out of the early 1970's. No retro look here, just the real deal with a thin layer of dust here and there and yellowing of the walls and ceiling - something that comes with time from years of cooking and smoke from earlier decades when patrons were allowed to smoke freely in public.

Starlight flashes a smile, cocks her head to the right, and says, "Excuse me, gentlemen. I have an appointment with the ladies' restroom."

"Make sure you're not late, Star," replies River jokingly.

Patrick laughs a little and says, "Let's get a booth by the middle of that window over there, River. It really is an awesome few of the mountains. But, seriously, we need to have a talk about all that has happened."

"Sure," responds River.

As they walk over to the booth and sit down, their eyes scan the old diner. They notice the old red vinyl booths with cracked bench seats and padded backs and red and white checkered plastic table cloths. The booths are lined perpendicular to two of the interior walls of the dining area and butt up right next to them. Mushroom-style bar stools with varying degrees of ripped red vinyl from years of wear and tear are next to the front counter. Yellow and red cylinder plastic dispensers with screw on tops and long spouts that contains mustard and ketchup for squirting the condiments on food are on every booth and table and at the counter. Old dusty mounted heads of elk, deer, grizzly bear, wolf, coyote, stuffed bodies of small game and large fish are mounted on the walls and in various poses on shelves and counters. A faded calendar from 1971, held in place by an old rusted thumb tack with an old one dollar bill above it held in place with yellowed scotch tape, hung on the outdated medium dark brown four-by-eight feet sheets of wood paneling from a bygone era. The bill probably represented the first dollar the owner made and the calendar the year the diner opened. Patrick and River feel they have stepped back in time.

A cute and very friendly young waitress with light brown shoulder length layered hair parted in the middle comes over to where they are sitting. She had graduated from Mountain View High School the previous school year in June.

She politely says, "Hi. My name is Emily. Can I get you guys something to drink before you order?"

River responds, "I want a cup of straight black coffee. And my wife said all she wants is some fruit, if you have that. Oh, and one more thing if you don't mind. See if can get me a bag with some ice in it because I hit my head. "

"Are you alright?"

"Yeah, I'm going to be fine once I get some caffeine in me."

"Well, that's good. We only have bananas right now. I can get that for you. Will a bananas be alright?"

"Yes, that's fine."

"It's none of my business," says the waitress apologetically, "but I'm curious. Are you and that young girl I saw going to the bathroom really married?" asks Emily.

"Yes, we are."

"It's just kinda strange you're married."

"Well, we hear this all the time."

Emily, who is in an upbeat mood, says, "The reason I asked is that most people our age wouldn't even bother to get married at this stage of our lives."

"Yes, I know."

"She's going to have your baby, right?"

"No," replies River.

"You got married and something went wrong and she just had an abortion."

"Nope. We just got married early because we love each other."

"Well that's the best answer you can give. How old are you guys anyway?"

"I'm 20, and my name is River. My wife's name is Starlight. She is 19. Our friend Patrick here is 21."

"Emily, my friend here looks older with that thick beard he has, doesn't he?" asks Patrick.

Emily, who also likes to joke around, says, 'Yeah, he really does, but his wife doesn't have a beard and she looks my age."

"Now, that is really funny," snickers Patrick.

"Now I know you aren't from around here with your accent."

"No, you're kidding me, Emily."

"You're from back east somewhere, aren't you?"

"You guessed it. I'm from Philadelphia, Pennsylvania. How old are you?" asks Patrick with equal curiosity.

"I'm also 19 like River's wife, Scarlett."

"It's Starlight," smiles Patrick.

"Oh, sorry," replies an embarrassed Emily as she covers her mouth with her right hand. "I bet you guys must be Colorado A&M students and getting ready for the start of the fall semester."

"No, not exactly," says Patrick.

"Uh, oh. Listen. I would love to talk to you guys some more if you don't mind, but my boss, Ivan over there, is looking at me. Ivan is not only the cook here, but he is also the owner. He says my job is to take care of the customers' orders and to service them when they come in. He doesn't want me to talk too much to them, so I can be free to service our other customers. Emily looks at Patrick and asks, "How about you? You just want something to drink or do you need a menu?"

"No, I don't need a menu, just a large glass of milk and a large pastry. What kind do you have?"

"Well, we have large cinnamon rolls, and they are really delicious. Ivan over there is a good cook, but a better pastry chef."

"Okay, that will work for me. Cinnamon roll it is."

"I'll get your order, guys. I would love to sit and talk with you more, if you don't mind. I'm leaving in a while with my friend Stephanie. We're heading out of Mountain View for a few days on our way to Boulder."

"Sure, we don't mind, do we, River?" responds Patrick in a surprised friendly tone with eyebrows raised.

"Yeah, we can talk," agrees River who's headache is getting worse.

Starlight is walking toward the booth with a smile beaming from ear to ear because she is thankful that everyone is safe and unharmed from the incident on the highway and her bladder is empty. Emily sees her and says, "I got your order, and I love your long, shiny hair. I'll be right back with your food and drinks."

"Thank you very much." Starlight then slides into the booth and nestles up to River. "That girl seems nice."

"Her name is Emily, and she's also pretty funny," replies a smiling Patrick.

"Yeah, she is, ain't she?" adds River as he rolls his eyes at him.

"Yeah, she cracks me up with her inquisitive and lively personality. She wants to sit down and talk with us for a few minutes when she comes back with our order."

"That's fine with me, guys. Maybe we can share the Gospel with her," says Starlight in an upbeat manner.

"Yeah, let's definitely witness to her. River, I know you heard her say that she's leaving with a friend named Stephanie, and they are going to Boulder? For heaven's sake, we can't let her go to Boulder," says an anxious Patrick.

"It also seems like you kind of like her, Pat."

"Now, man, don't start jumping to conclusions," he remarks, slightly embarrassed.

"Remember River what I told you guys. Michael said that a fourth individual would accompany us on this leg of our journey," River recalls aloud. "It's been a short, but crazy, trip so far and I completely forgot about that."

"So let's see what she says about not going to Boulder with her friend and coming with us to Golden Valley. Starlight, will you find out some more about her?" requests Patrick in a curious manner. She is your same age, so she can easily relate to you. Besides, everybody likes you."

"Sure, Patrick. Let's see if she is the one to come with us to Golden Valley. Besides, we can't let her go to Boulder, knowing what we know, without warning her. Okay, I'll do this on one condition."

"What's that?"

"No more busting on me about going to the bathroom."

"Okay, I won't make a pee-p!" chuckles Pat.

"Patrick!" says Starlight in a girlish giggle while staring at him with a mean look in her eyes.

"No, seriously, I promise. I will keep my mouth shut, scout's honor."

"Great! And just so you know, Patrick, I was going to do it anyway. Gotcha!"

He grins as he drops his head down in mock defeat.

"Listen, guys. When Emily comes back, let me do most of the talking to her. River, you and Pat just add a little commentary. In the meantime, River, I need to take care of that cut on your forehead." Starlight grabs a paper napkin from the table, gently removes his bandana and starts lightly dabbing his cut, which is slightly oozing.

"Watch it, Star! You're killing me! Ouch, that hurts."

"Wow, I thought you were tough," teases Starlight. "Since you quit working on the UEC farm, I think you've gotten soft."

"I'm still tough, Star. It's not the cut that hurts. It's the big bump under it when you press hard on it."

Starlight replies teasingly, "Oh, my poor baby, I'll be more delicate with you."

Then Emily returns with a tray of their drinks, a banana, a bag of ice, and a big cinnamon roll.

Patrick is softly laughing. "You guys are sounding like you've been married for years."

"Starlight, I'm beginning to think that Pat is wise beyond his years," jokes River just as he jerks away from her doctoring. Starlight is giggling and trying to gently swab River's forehead some more while he makes an effort to defending himself by blocking her hands from touching him.

"You guys are hilarious," giggles Emily as she hands everyone their drinks and food. She hands River the bag of ice and he quickly, yet gently, places it on the bump.

"Hey, Emily, I think you can talk now because that middle-aged woman just went behind the counter," informs Starlight.

"Yeah, my shift is over. My replacement, Lauren over there, just came in with four customers behind her and now she is on duty." Emily then yells out, "Ivan, I'm off the clock now. Lauren is here."

"Alright, kid. Enjoy your two days off," yells Ivan from the kitchen.

"You want to sit down here, Emily?" inquires Patrick, pointing to the empty section of the booth next to him.

"Sure. Thanks, Patrick," as she slides in beside him.

"Emily, the guys said you wanted to talk to us and that you are about to go to Boulder with a friend?"

"Yeah, that's right, Starlight. But first I've got to say you guys are so different than the people here around my age. I can't put my finger on it. You guys just seem to enjoy life and laugh a lot. The teenagers I grew up with in Mountain View are depressed, really negative, and stay drunk or high on drugs."

Pleased to hear Emily's assessment of them, Starlight explains, "Well, the reason is that we're born again Christians and followers of Jesus Christ, our Lord and Savior. I'd like to talk to you more about God in a minute if you're interested."

"Yes. I would like that. That is so ironic. I've been reading my grandmother's Bible a little and asking God to reveal Himself to me," informs Emily.

"That's great Emily. But first, Emily, I'm curious about why you are going to Boulder," inquires Starlight.

Emily moves her head around and shifts her eyes from right to left, looking to see where Lauren is and if Ivan is still back in the kitchen out of sight before quietly whispering, "I'm waiting on someone I knew from high school. Her name is Stephanie, and she's talked me into going to Boulder to apply for a new job working on an assembly line at a medical laboratory. The place pays $12.50 an hour with good benefits. Stephanie's aunt told her it was a done deal for us to get hired, since she does the hiring. She is the new manager in the human resources department of the company. All we have to do is show up tomorrow and fill out the application to get hired."

"What's the name of the laboratory?" asks Patrick as he discreetly glances at River's and Starlight's eyes with everyone fully anticipating to hear the name Ci Mada Union Laboratories.

Emily sees Ivan stepped out of the kitchen to make a phone call on the land line. He's focused on the call but is closer to where they are sitting, so she quietly whispers the name of the company. "It's Pinkerton Laboratories, and they make placebo pills, tablets, and capsules of different sizes, shapes, and colors. Different pharmaceutical companies use these placebos on people in control groups and then compare the results with those of the actual medicine being tested on people. Some doctors also give these pills to patients that are hypochondriacs. I haven't told Ivan about the new job because he would have a fit. He trusts me and depends upon me a lot with his restaurant. I can also cook just as well as he can because he taught me his trade secrets. So when he leaves on vacation, I'm the cook. This is the third year I've worked for him, this last year full time. Before that I worked only summers and vacations while I was in high school."

The three travelers listen intently as Emily continues. "I left home after graduating from high school. For the last year I have lived in what Ivan calls his mother-in-law's quarters behind his house. His deceased mother-in-law lived in it for eight years before she died a year and a half ago. His wife Mildred and he have been very good to me. I don't want to hurt their feelings. But this diner is run down, as you can see, and Ivan is barely scraping by financially. I don't make much here as a waitress, and we don't get a lot of customers. What I make from tips is usually very small. The overall economy is pretty much flat here in this area of Colorado and I'm going nowhere fast. A lot of people have left here and moved away to find jobs in Boulder and the other big cities and resort areas."

After some thought and a quick prayer in her mind about how to address the situation, Starlight finally plunges in. "Emily, I know you just met us, but I want you to come with us to Golden Valley. It's a really long and unbelievable story about why we are going there, but if you come with us I would be glad to tell you the whole story."

"You guys are really nice and cool, but I can't! I just can't! I need a better job because I have nothing here, nothing at all and no future. I have a little money saved up and I'll need all of that money to move and get set up in Boulder. My mom is in her own little world, and I can't live with her. She is one of few in the area with a really good paying job because she gets a commission on all that she sells as the manager of the Colorado Cannabis Smokehouse Plaza here in town. She's turned into a serious pothead."

"Really?" inquires Patrick.

"Yes," replies Emily. "Rich people stop and smoke pot there from out of state as they travel from Boulder to the ski resorts and other vacation spots. Many of the customers at the store that my mom manages drop some serious cash on pot and the paraphernalia related to it. The Colorado Cannabis Smokehouse includes a huge Las Vegas-style pot parlor, gift shop, a huge gas station, a convenience store, and a fancy spread in their mega buffet restaurant. Their snacks, drinks, and buffet are pretty inexpensive. Their customers will get the munchies after they smoke weed and that is why their food is so cheap. Selling weed and paraphernalia is where they make most of their money."

"So that place is really cutting into Ivan's business here even though the food in the buffet is not as good?" asks River.

"Yeah. Ivan had some money saved up. He was going to totally remodel and upgrade this place until the recession happened in 2008. He then decided to keep on holding on to that money because he didn't know what the future held. Then when they legalized pot in Colorado in 2013, the smokehouse plaza was quickly built. Since then it has hurt his business a lot. He doesn't know what he's going to do now."

"How does his restaurant stay afloat?" asks Patrick.

Emily quickly responds, "Take a bite of the cinnamon roll, Patrick."

He then takes a bite and says, "Man this is great! It's the best I've ever tasted! It's really good." He gives it a thumbs up. Patrick, River and Emily snack on their food and sip their drinks as they listen to their new friend.

Emily goes on and says, "Yeah, Ivan's restaurant is really run down, but the food is really great here. That's what keeps this restaurant's lights on. The smokehouse offsets the money they are losing on food by the huge profits they are making off the pot and drug paraphernalia they sell. The food is not as good there, but it's cheaper. They also sell gas cheaper than anyone else around here and that's another reason people end up eating there."

"So you want to go to Boulder and start a new life it seems," surmises a compassionate Starlight.

"Definitely. My mom is always half stoned at work and then gets really wasted at night. I can't stand being around the smell of pot. It stinks so bad and it makes me to want to throw up. Even the smell of pot on people's clothes makes me nauseated. I had to leave home because of my mom's job and lifestyle. It's hard making it on my own here in Mountain View." Emily has tears welling up in the corners of her eyes.

"Where's your dad, Emily?" inquires a sympathetic Patrick.

"My dad is not even in the picture because he left years ago with the young secretary of the Mormon church we used to attend for a little while when I was a little girl. He married that woman and now lives in Utah with her and their four young children."

"Do you have any other family in the surrounding areas?" asks Starlight.

"No, not anymore. My older brother, Mark, whom I was really close to and loved dearly, joined the Army out of high school and died four years ago in Afghanistan by stepping on a land mine. That whole episode really took my mom over the edge and got her deeper into drugs." Emily breaks down crying. "I've got no one, nothing."

Starlight is getting misty eyed as compassion fills her heart for Emily. She pauses for a moment before she says, "Look at me, Emily. You've got me, River, and Patrick. Your story, Emily, is similar to my story and River's. Listen. As true followers of Christ, we are trying to follow the teachings of the Bible. We know God is real. If you have His Holy Spirit in your heart,

He is all you really need. God can heal your broken heart and give you hope for tomorrow. He can lead you and guide you through life. Nobody knows that any better than Patrick, River and myself."

"What you are saying seems too simple," responds Emily. "God seems dead to me, Starlight, like He doesn't care about me at all."

"He's alive, Emily, and He cares about you tremendously," Starlight assures her the best she can. "It really is very simple. Let me give you a personal example. About 15 minutes before we stepped foot in this place, we were all almost killed by a rock avalanche right up the road. God spared our lives miraculously."

"Are you for real?" asks a sniffling Emily.

"Yes. We saw two white mountain goats. We believe they started the rock slide. A momma grizzly and her two large cubs stepped out from behind two boulders and stopped right in the middle of the road preventing us from getting killed by the huge boulders coming down the mountainside."

"Wait! Sorry, Starlight. That doesn't sound right! What you just told me is a complete lie," says Emily. Starlight, along with River and Patrick, share shocked looks.

"I don't know what you guys are up to. Maybe you three belong to some kind of twisted cult or something far worse," retorts Emily in an angry tone. "What kind of sick mind games are you trying to play with me to lure me away from here to go to Golden Valley? Or who knows where? At first I thought you guys were sincere, but now I'm beginning to feel very uncomfortable around you guys," adds Emily, with suspicion in her voice, and her body fidgeting.

"Emily, everything Starlight said is true. We're not trying to kidnap you or anything. I'd put my hand on the Bible and take an oath," replies Patrick, who almost can't believe what he is hearing. Patrick goes on to say, "God could strike me down dead if Starlight isn't telling you the truth."

"Let me tell you guys one thing," replies Emily in a quiet, angry tone. "I might have grown up in this little hick town, but I've got a brain. Ivan over there is an avid hunter. He's killed every kind of wild game in these forests and mountains around here. I've heard him tell me and at least 20 other people in this very restaurant that there are no white mountain goats around here to be found. He says they aren't within 100 miles of here. No one has ever seen them. Plus huge rock slides almost always happen when it's raining like crazy or when there is snow or ice thawing, not when it's a nice June day like today."

"We have no reason to lie to you," says a concerned River.

"Sure, River. Then I'll ask a local expert on wild game around here, especially since it happened just a few miles up the road from here." Emily raises her voice and says, "Ivan, you have lived in Mountain View your whole life. Are white mountain goats found in this area of Colorado?"

Ivan walks over to the group and adamantly replies, "No, they are not. No one has ever seen them around here, let alone killed one. Believe me, I would have hunted down one years ago if they'd lived in this area, and I'd have had it mounted on one of these walls in here."

"Thanks, Ivan. There, you have the truth."

Just then a Colorado State Trooper by the name of Sgt. Doug Reynolds comes into the diner and hikes up his right leg over one of the bar stools as he sits down on the only red one free of cracks. He leans his massive upper body forward as he places his elbows on the counter. Lauren has gone outside to take the trash to the metal dumpster in the back. Emily automatically slides down in the booth because she doesn't want to get called back into service. Trooper Reynolds, in a loud deep voice, says, "Hey, Ivan. How you doing, ol' buddy?"

Ivan turns around in the doorway of the kitchen and replies in an excited voice, "Trooper Doug, how are you doing?"

"Well, I'll being doing better once I get a cup of your good ol' hot, black coffee in me. You'll never guess it in a hundred years, Ivan. You'll never guess it."

"What are you talking about, Doug?" asks a curious Ivan.

"Well, here's the scoop. Around 20 minutes ago there was a huge rock slide right up the road from you. A motorist and his wife were right behind an SUV and an old hippie van. The old man was all shaken up about it, because he was right there when it happened and almost slammed into a car behind the van. The van almost slid into an SUV in front of it."

Emily's ears perk up as she walks over to the trooper, along with Starlight. "That was our van, Sir, and our friend Patrick was in the first vehicle in front of the rock slide right in front of us," says Starlight.

"I don't know how I missed your van outside. The big box truck Ivan uses for advertising his restaurant must have been hiding it from my sight." Trooper Doug spins around in his bar stool and asks, "Are you kids alright?"

"We're all okay, officer, except my friend here," replies Patrick.

Trooper Doug sees River's forehead and says, "Son, did you hit your head on the steering wheel or windshield?"

"Yes, sir, officer. My head hit the steering wheel, but I'm okay."

"You positive you don't need medical attention?"

"My head is just sore," assures River.

Starlight speaks up. "We're not going to let him drive the van today, just to be on the safe side."

"That's a wise decision, Miss," replies the trooper.

Emily is starting to believe that maybe Starlight, River and Patrick have been telling the truth. "Officer Doug, you were going to tell Ivan something. You said something about Ivan not being able to guess it in a hundred years. What did you mean by that?"

"Emily, that motorist that told me what happened was a local guy. He was so shaken up from the three grizzlies standing in the middle of the highway and the massive rock slide, that I had to pull him over at Exit 16 down the road. I almost gave him a ticket for speeding, but he said it was the worst rock slide he had ever seen in fifty years of living in the area. The episode scared the dickens out of him, so I let him off. I asked him what caused the slide. He said he and his wife had spotted two white mountain goats running across some loose rocks high up on a slope above the highway. He thinks they started the rock slide."

"Well, I'll be a monkey's uncle," says Ivan. "This is a first. I stand to be corrected on there being no white mountain goats in this area." Ivan breaks into a little dance, shuffling his feet to celebrate.

"I thought you would love hearing that, Ivan. Are these guys friends of yours, Emily?" inquires State Trooper Reynolds.

"Yes, they are. I haven't known them very long, but they are really good friends of mine," says Emily with a smile gracing her lips, since she now knows they were telling her the truth. "We are leaving for Golden Valley in a few minutes. Right, guys?"

"Yes, we are," respond River, Starlight, and Patrick in unison with big grins on their faces. Starlight leans over and gives Emily a hug.

"Let me get my stuff after I text Stephanie that I'm not going to Boulder," says Emily, "And we'll go when you guys are done." Ten minutes later, after laughing and talking, they finish their drinks and food. Then Emily says, "Bye, Ivan!. Put my friends' bill on my tab."

Patrick speaks up, "No, I've got it, Emily."

"No way. It's the least I can do for the way I acted and not trusting you guys. I knew in my heart I could, but my mind was telling me different."

"Well, if you insist, Emily," smiles Starlight.

"Okay, kid." Ivan knows she is going somewhere, but doesn't know where. He yells, "See ya! Be careful!"

They walk outside and River head is throbbing now. But he fights through the pain and tells Starlight, "Why don't you let Emily ride with you, and I'll ride with Patrick."

Emily shares, "I don't usually ride with people I don't know, and I can't believe I'm going to Golden Valley. I mean, I don't know why I'm doing this, other than I just feel I can trust you guys and that I'm supposed to go."

As Patrick and River are walking away to get into Patrick's SUV, Emily says, "Stop, guys! Hey, wait. I really want to apologize to you guys about what happened in there. I mean, I don't know what to say."

"It's fine, Emily. You're cool," replies River.

"No problem," adds Patrick. "Life's been hitting you hard, but God is good."

"Hey, listen. It's alright," assures Starlight. The main thing is that you know we are sincere Christians and you can trust us. Now I was wondering is there a place where we can have some privacy to talk with having to whisper, like a park or something?"

"There's a modern rest area about twelve miles down the road. We can stop there and talk."

"That's sounds great," says River who is fighting inwardly to sound positive, but is on the verge of what seems like a migraine.

"Okay, great! Let's hit the road," adds Starlight.

Time flies by, and Starlight and Emily are both in a happy mood as they pull up beside Patrick's SUV at the rest area. Patrick and River got there a minute before and just sat down at a picnic table. River is massaging the temples of his head. The girls are smiling as they approach them.

Patrick chuckles, "Well, I'm wondering what you two girls have been up to."

"Starlight says, "Thank you, Jesus! Praise God! Guys, guess what just happened?"

"What?" inquire River and Patrick.

"Emily just got saved on the way here!"

"Emily, you got saved? Praise God!" replies an exuberant Patrick.

"Yeah, that's what Starlight is calling it. I just asked Jesus into my heart to be my Lord and Savior and to help me to repent and turn from my sinful

49

ways."

"Wow, that is so cool," says an excited Patrick.

"Praise God, Emily!" replies River in a more subdued tone caused by the increasing uneasiness growing in his stomach.

"Thanks, guys. I feel... I mean... I can't really describe it, but I feel different. I don't know how to explain it, but I feel like I've been cleansed of my sins. It's like a burden that has been lifted off my shoulders."

"You've been born again. Welcome to the family of God. Did you talk to her about this morning, Starlight?" asks River.

"Yeah, we lightly touched upon it and then we pulled in here," replies a joyful Starlight.

"This girl here was so ready to get saved. I just can't believe it. She says she has always been interested in God, His supernatural power, and angels. She knows we are in the end times, and she believes us. And she just blurted out that she wanted what we have. I said, "We've got Jesus in our hearts.""

"After what happened back at the diner and talking to Starlight, I felt I could really trust you guys. So I went for it," replies Emily.

"That's great, because we are experiencing some supernatural stuff on this trip," affirms River.

Patrick holds up the back of his book *Walking in the Supernatural in the End Times* with the picture of Gary Kirkman and Ricky Crawford on the back. Emily enthusiastically says, "Hey, I've served those two men before in the diner, and they talked to me about God. They were trying to get me saved, as you call it. I was a Mormon growing up but had gotten disillusioned with the Mormon church, so I heard them out. They were very nice to me and seemed to really care about me. Even Ivan listened to them because that Ricky guy had been a Vietnam vet like Ivan. Also both of those ministers were big hunters, which really tickled Ivan's ears. They left me a $30 tip for a meal that cost around $19. I was blown away. It really came in handy at the time because business was so slow and I was flat broke."

"What else do you know about them, Emily? asks Starlight.

"Well, they have a church called Fortress a short distance from here in Golden Valley, and other churches are linked somehow to them."

"That's exactly what the angel Michael said," exclaims an excited River. Michael said two shepherds live on the grounds of a Fortress not built with stone and mortar and that they are divinely protected. Now, that's a good place to be during the Tribulation period, a Fortress divinely protected by God and His mighty angels."

"Amen to that, brother. I'm curious, Emily. Did they seem weird or odd?" asks Patrick.

"Yes, they did," says Emily.

"How's that?" asks Starlight.

"They were weird and odd in a good sense. I have never met two individuals that seemed more humble, genuinely friendly and trustworthy than those two. In fact, you guys remind me of them."

"Thanks, Emily. That's sweet," says Starlight as she grabs Emily's right shoulder and leans in so their heads are touching.

"But I heard a few rumors that I just don't believe about them," replies Emily.

"What's that?" inquires Patrick.

"Well, I know for a fact they have a community of Christians that live on a big spread of land where their church is located. They told me that themselves," responds Emily.

"We've kinda been there and done that before, right, Starlight?" says River who seems to be doing a little better now with his head and stomach.

"Yeah, just this time two godly ministers run it and a number of sincere born again Christians live in this community," Starlight answers.

"What kind of rumors have you heard about their ministry?" asks Patrick who is very curious.

"Well now, I remember hearing something about them not too long ago. It seemed really off the wall. Just give me a second." Emily pauses and thinks. "Oh, yeah! An older couple from Golden Valley stopped by about two weeks ago at the diner. I overheard them mention those guys in a bizarre conversation. I heard the elderly husband tell his wife that those guys were building an underground bunker headquarters in the mountain on their land for a new kind of Third Reich, for when the big one goes off. He said they were storing up illegal military firearms, high-tech weapons, air-to-ground heat seeking missiles, radiation suits, and I think masks and potassium iodine pills to lead a religious army and rebuild a better America from a heap of ashes."

"The wife said, 'No, no, that is not the correct story.' She said that a close friend of hers said that she had some inside information that it was a religious cult like what happened in Waco, Texas in 1993, and that the two male leaders manipulated their flock with mind control techniques and mind altering prescription drugs purchased in large quantities from Mexico. The two leaders, Crawford and Kirkman, used the drugs on a mass scale in their drinking water on their followers and it turned them into mind controlled zombies, especially the women. The males at the compound were brainwashed into doing all the work and selling these drugs to dealers in the big cities of Colorado to fund their cult. The woman said her friend believed that each leader had a harem of at least 15 women starting at age 18 and up. Also, the leaders were scaring these women with Bible prophecy and teaching them that they could become immortals if they chose to worship them and were obedient to their every whim or desire."

"I'm not buying that garbage," laughs Patrick. "God would not send the archangel Michael to River and me to hook us up with two nut cases in these last days."

"I think the only nut cases were that older couple," agrees Starlight, which causes everybody to laugh. River's head begins to throb because he laughed so hard, but he decides to just ignore it. He hasn't discerned the seriousness of his situation.

"Patrick declares, "These ministers, Crawford and Kirkman, must have something going on that has the devil all worried enough to work overtime and hinder us from trying to get there." Everybody nods in agreement. Then he announces, "Hey, I just remembered! Hasn't Clark County had some meteorites hitting it? It seems like we are heading into the eye of the storm instead away from it."

Starlight quips up. "No, actually no meteorites have hit there."

"Really, Star?" replies River. "Where did you hear this?"

"It was on the radio the other day at the salon. They specifically mentioned Clark County had not been hit, but the surrounding counties have all been hit."

'Wow, guys! Here we go again with Golden Valley popping up. It's located in Clark County," declares River.

"This is so strange. I can't believe I'm actually on my way to Golden Valley instead of Boulder," says Emily with a bit of nervousness in her voice.

Patrick, sensing her nervousness, says, "Emily, God is in control, and this is a divine adventure we have all embarked upon. The angel said that a fourth person would join us, and you have been ordained of God to be that one."

"Yeah, it definitely seems that way," Emily eyes light up and she responds in a little more confident tone now.

"The major reason we wanted to stop and talk here at the rest area was to share Christ with you and give you a little bit more information on why we are going to Golden Valley," informs Patrick. "But Starlight has already taken care of the first part. And it seems you already know the ministers we are going to see in Golden Valley. Also, you have given us some helpful information about their character.

"Yeah, so let's get back on the road. But before we leave, I was wondering if you can get my phone, River," Starlight requests.

River's condition is even worse now than before. He replies, "Sorry... we'll have to get it later, Star? That bed frame is so hard to move, especially with all that junk inside the van and underneath the mattress. Maybe I'll feel better once the coffee kicks in and I'll get it when we get to Golden Valley. It's only about 35 miles away."

"Okay, that's fine, River. Are you really alright? How about some aspirin?"

"Yeah, give me three and I'll be fine." She goes to the van and comes back with the pills and a water bottle. River quickly takes them. Then he says, "Now let's get back on our road trip."

"Are you sure, River?"

"Yeah, let's go."

"Okay, I'm taking you at your word," agrees a somewhat hesitant Patrick.

"Take the lead again, Patrick," instructs Starlight and she kisses River on the side of his head. She tells River when he gets in the SUV to take it easy.

Patrick, who is concerned, tells Starlight, "I'll radio you if he is getting worse."

"Thanks."

"Hey, guys, I'll be okay, once those aspirin kick in," says River. "There's no more swelling of that bump as far as I can tell, so that's a good sign, Star."

"Well, let me know if it changes."

"I promise I will, Starlight,"

"Okay. Then let's go," responds Starlight.

No sooner do they get down the road about three miles than River starts throwing up. He also starts having seizures, and his eyes are rolled back into his eye sockets. Patrick quickly pulls over on the shoulder of the road and radios Starlight. He asks her to ask Emily where the nearest hospital is located. She indicates that the small town of Rock Top has one about two more exits down the highway. Within ten minutes River is the emergency room of the Rock Top Memorial Hospital. He is awake but going in and out of consciousness and is mumbling. He vomited several times right outside the entrance of the emergency room. Patrick and a tall male nurse

54

got him in a wheelchair and got him inside the hospital. After a brief but through examination and x-rays of River's skull, the physician asks Starlight and Patrick a bunch of question as to what happened. Dr. Gibson then tells Starlight and her friends that the young man's condition is really touch and go.

The doctor keeps asking Starlight what her husband hit when he slammed on the breaks. Starlight tells the doctor he hit the steering wheel. The doctor then asked if there is anything else on the steering wheel. Starlight pauses and replies that there is an old rusty metal knob that they sometimes hold unto when they drive.

Dr. Gibson says, "I can't prove it, but I think he hit that when you guys slammed on the brakes."

"Oh, no!" exclaims Starlight.

"But his condition didn't seem that bad, doctor," says Patrick.

"Well, what probably happened was his body was running off the adrenalin rush from the entire crisis. I must assume that his body was able to overcome the initial blow and pain he received, but it quickly caught up with him," the doctor surmises.

Dr. Gibson goes on to say, "River's injury is far more serious than his cut and bump appear to be. The x-rays show that he has a hairline skull fracture and some swelling in his forehead, and he might have internal bleeding. That is what concerns me. The prognosis may not be good and could be even life threatening if the brain starts hemorrhaging."

Upon hearing those words, Starlight seems unmoved and initially even relaxed by the news. However, in reality she is mustering up all the faith in her heart to spiritually fight for River's life.

Dr. Gibson is totally surprised by her reaction, knowing that she and River are married. He starts thinking that maybe she is going into some kind of denial or mild shock from the news. He says, "Young lady, maybe you didn't hear me, but your husband's life hangs in the balance."

Emily covers her face in horror from hearing the bad news about River.

Patrick is rubbing his right cheek with his fingertips thinking about the prophetic words spoken by the angel and how this news about River is going to play out.

Starlight, in emotional turmoil, slowly drops to her knees in front of Dr. Gibson. With her eyes closed and with her hands lifted up to heaven, she starts to sincerely pray from the depths of her heart. Her total focus at this point is crying out to God for the life of her young husband and soul mate. Like a child mesmerized by her favorite TV show and never hearing her mother calling her from the next room, she tunes out everything around her.

The doctor, startled and taken back by her outrageous conduct and religious zeal, orders her to stop praying in public. He indignantly demands, "Mrs. Jenkins, what you are doing is not politically correct in a professional medical environment that services the public of different faiths. What you are doing should be done privately and quietly in the Interreligious Meditation Center down the hall. Please stop and listen to me. I have firm convictions of religious tolerance, but not religious fanaticism."

Everyone in the entire ER area is shocked to see a beautiful young woman crying out to God in prayer with tears rolling down her suntanned skin. However, they are appalled at hearing a medical doctor going into a rant of his absurd political correctness on prayer in public. Although what Starlight is doing seems strange and different to the non-churched people standing in the ER area, Dr. Gibson's behavior seems rather rude, crude and ridiculous at the moment.

Emily and Patrick stand there looking at the doctor with their mouths wide open. Both are thinking, "You've got to be kidding me." Patrick taps Emily on her shoulder. As he grabs her hand, he says, "I'm going to pray." He prays quietly for God to intervene in this ordeal with Dr. Gibson and for River's life. Dr. Gibson now sees two people praying out loud and heads to the counter to call a security guard. Starlight, oblivious to him or anyone else around her, continues to cry out loud to God unashamedly for divine intervention in River's life.

She prays, "Dear Almighty God, Maker of heaven and earth, Creator of the human body and the greatest of all physicians, I ask You to perform an operation with Your hand that can heal. I ask you to please touch River's skull. You died at Golgotha, the place of the skull, for not only his sins and my sins, but also the sins of the whole world. You are the God of miracles, and there is no sickness, no disease, no organ, bone or cell that You cannot heal. Your messenger, Michael, delivered River a message this morning, and I don't believe permanent sickness or death is an option for River now. Please, dear Lord, bring about a miraculous healing in the life of your servant River. But let your will be done on earth as it is heaven in my life and his. Amen!"

As soon as Dr. Gibson starts dialing the number of a security guard to come to the ER area, he instantly starts suffering an anxiety attack and panics. He shouts out loudly, "My eyes are getting blurry. I, I, I, can't see! I can't see anything! I can't see!"

A backslidden 28-year old Christian ER nurse, Amy Choate, is surprised by young Starlight's faith, sincerity, and boldness. Amy had a close and special relationship with God as a child, and as a teenager she had gone on several mission trips to Central America. On these trips she had seen some small miracles and witnessed firsthand divine appointments taking place in her life and others to whom she had witnessed. God was very real to her at that point in her life. But her four years at a liberal college and wild partying had led her down a path away from God. But now she is shocked about Dr. Gibson's anti-Christian stance. She witnessed the whole event and couldn't believe Dr. Gibson's antics and unprofessional behavior. She comes over to Dr. Gibson and grabs his right arm to try to settle him down.

Then she says, "Mrs. Jenkins, that was a beautiful and stirring prayer, and I believe God is going to honor that."

Dr. Gibson calls out, "Nurse!"

"Yes, Dr. Gibson. It's Amy."

"I believe I'm having a reaction to a new anti-anxiety pill I starting taking three days ago. I believe I accidently took two pills this morning instead of one and the loss of my eyesight is one of the side effects. Will you check the pill bottle in the right front pocket of my jacket, because I can't read it. At this moment I'm unable to see anything. I should have exactly seven pills left in my trial size bottle."

She finds it in his pocket, takes a few seconds to count the pills, and says, "Yep, you only have six pills left in the bottle." Though she does not say it aloud, inside she knows the doubling up of the pills is not the reason for the doctor's loss of eyesight. "Doctor, please come with me and I'll take you to Dr. Elkins, the eye specialist on the third floor. Sometimes we need to seek help from a doctor on a higher level."

"I know," replies Dr. Gibson. "Just take me to him immediately." Dr. Gibson then turns around blindly and screams, "Mrs. Jenkins I will deal with you and your male friend later, for this public display of politically incorrect Christian fanaticism in this ER.

Chapter 3

OPERATION SUPER PREDATORS

1:38:46 PM, Mountain Standard Time, Tuesday, 05/07/20_ _, Ci Mada Union Laboratories, World Headquarters, Genetic and Behavioral Modifications Division, Director's Office, Dr. Fritz Von Gunten, Boulder, Colorado, USA

"No, No, No! I refuse to, Wolfgang!" rants an extremely irritated Dr. Von Gunten in his authoritative thick German accent. Thirty years of living in the U.S. had not diminished his accent. The redeeming part of understanding his speech was the fact that he always pronounced the syllables in his words very slowly and distinctly.

"Under no circumstances can I rush Operation Super Predators. I'm willing to abide by the original percentage guidelines the Adamic Society has arrived at concerning the number of my super predators to be released in two weeks across the North American Continent. The sheet is before me, and I have no problem releasing 12 to 15 percent of our specimens, with 15 percent being the absolute maximum number. My work is like the finest of French wines. It can't be rushed, because I'm not running a puppy mill. I'm satisfied that we currently have 697 giant pitwolves that meet my physical qualifications here in Colorado and our remote facilities around the country to be released in rural areas and near large cities over the next year. I'm also satisfied that we have another 322 in Mexico and 464 in Canada. From a purely physical standpoint, the size, strength, speed, jumping ability, and agility of these fine specimens are mind boggling. I'm content with that aspect of their development. Wait just a minute, Wolfgang. I know that is what they want, but there is still some testing that needs to be conducted concerning the final outcome of the shaping and modification of their behavior. Once these issues are resolved, I have no problem releasing much higher percentages of them as time goes on."

"Okay, I'm not going to argue with you, Doctor," replies Wolfgang. "Now please listen, Dr. Von Gunten. Your family and my family go back centuries in Geneva, Switzerland. Everyone respects your work in the Adamic Society, but up until now, you have operated with free reign and have been treated with kid gloves. You must be more flexible, because the agenda has changed. The society always makes adjustments. You have been a member since I was a teenager, and you know what I'm telling you is true."

"Yes, yes, I know."

Dr. Von Gunten has almost always been able to get his way with the society. They know he is eccentric and that stubbornness runs deep in his family. As he is sitting and talking on the phone with his boss, Wolfgang Martin, he is thumping the eraser end of a pencil on his beautiful mahogany desk. The longer he talks with Wolfgang, the harder and faster he thumps, as he subconsciously is releasing the tension that is mounting in his mind.

Wolfgang is getting a little bit peeved and says, "I understand your position and can sympathize with you, Dr. Von Gunten. However, with that being said, Marla told me that the percentage needs to be bumped up to 33 percent of all the current specimens to be released in two weeks.

Upon hearing the dreaded name Marla being involved and the new percentage of 33 percent, Fritz Von Gunten instantly snaps off the top part of his pencil with his thumb and produces a low level growl. Fritz Von Gunten does this in total frustration. He fears Marla and secretly loathes her because of her meddling in his life's work.

Wolfgang picks up on Fritz's growl, but still proceeds in explaining the reason for the new procedures. He states, "The reason the percentage has increased is because the society wants to play off the fear the public is already experiencing with the meteorites that are hitting now mostly in Colorado. Controlled shock and awe, and also the element of surprise are the principles that the Adamic Society operates by in controlling the masses. They use these tactics to herd the people into a certain direction or thought. When opportunities arise, the society is quick to take advantage of them. "So with the meteorites hitting in Colorado the time is now to release the specimens even if they aren't at your 100 percent personal level of satisfaction."

"Wolfgang, you may own the company that I'm a director of but I must be true to myself. I will finish the work that my father and mother started. At this stage, I can't tolerate being pushed to do something that rushes all my years of research. Compromising quantity for quality runs against my very nature. My life's work has been to create the perfect killing machine that strikes fear in the hearts of the masses. May the Adamic Society and my Lord Lucifer be exalted and their goals achieved by the works of my brilliant mind and hands."

Now Wolfgang's frustration level is rising, and he says, "I know you are a perfectionist and I don't doubt your sincerity, but believe me, Fritz, when I say I do not want to get Marla involved in this situation. She tends to be on the ruthless and sadistic side."

"Yes, I know how Marla is. No one has to tell me, Wolfgang. However, I'm sorry. I just can't do it. The society asked me to do a job, and I agreed to the original terms. I'm just trying to accomplish the goal they set before me in a realistic and logical fashion. I've got to go now and analyze the data that has already come in today."

Suddenly he reconsiders what Wolfgang Martin has just said. His own self-preservation now rushes to the forefront of his mind. He knows Marla plays hardball and will not tolerate insubordination. With hesitation in his voice, Dr. Von Gunten says, "I... I might be able to bump up the percentage a few points, possibly to 20 percent. I'm sorry, Wolfgang. I now really have to say goodbye."

"Do not hang up, Fritz!"

Click.....

Dr. Fritz Von Gunten is a Swiss citizen who moved to the United States over three decades ago. He has an impressive resume, having graduated first in his graduate class with a PhD in Human Genetics from the prestigious Heidendorf University in Berlin. He followed up with a PhD in psychology two years later from Harver University, again at the top of his class. Von Gunten had been a triple major in biology, zoology and psychology as an underclassman at Heidendorf at the age of 16 and graduated with a 4.0 within three years. Throughout his professional career he headed up different genetic and/or behavior modification research departments of the finest universities in Europe and several Ivy League schools in America. Through the years he wrote hundreds of articles and thirteen college medical textbooks on his areas of expertise. Eight books he wrote were never intended for the general public to see because they were written for the elite of the Adamic Society and their worldwide interests. They contain dark secrets gained through the millenniums and knowledge of the most advanced medical procedures and experiments not intended for the masses. Only Von Gunten's most trusted and well screened workers who go through extensive and thorough background checks have access to limited portions of this secret information under his watchful eye. The lower level minions of Ci Mada and the others who work directly with them are then given high security clearances after they are sworn to secrecy. They have been told their work is of vital national security interest. If they disclose classified information, they could end up having an accidental death - off the record, of course.

Fritz Von Gunten picked up where his dad had left off in the development of a super predator. He used his dad's secret research and experiments as a springboard from which he discovered more highly advanced levels of genetic and behavioral research. Without a doubt he would have been awarded the Nobel Prize in Medicine for all the "good" scientific breakthroughs he had achieved in his lifetime several times if it were not for the fact he had been born a Von Gunten. Also, the fact that his greatest medical and genetic research had to be hidden from the general medical community didn't help either. Since World War II, rumors and half-truths had been whispered behind closed doors within the ivy towers of the academic world concerning what his father, Dr. Wilhelm Von Gunten, had been involved in during World War II.

Another reason the Nobel Peace Prize eluded him was the fact that his own name was on about every list of the most radical groups that opposed genetically modified seeds, dairy products, and foods, as well as any tampering with the gene pool of the animal kingdom. Fritz Von Gunten had in the last few years come under fire for the possible deaths of those that had initially come forward with allegations against him and the research conducted at Ci Mada Union Laboratories. However, nothing had been proven to put him or anyone else in the company behind bars. He had a number of allies in the congress and senate, despite all the criminal allegations against him, because the Adamic Society knew how to keep the professional politicians' mouths shut and their palms greased with money under the table. However, many people in the organic and natural foods industries and animal rights activists loathed him, Ci Mada, and everything they stood for. Everyone from independent or co-op organic farmers to retailers in the health food industry saw them as a serious threat to the whole food chain, their way of life and a detriment to the health and well-being of the general public.

Dr. Von Gunten had also created an uproar within certain circles of the scientific community, and there were mixed emotions concerning him and his work. Those that respected his work were of the mindset that he was a pioneer, an Isaac Newton or Leonardo da Vinci, in the field of genetics and the behavior sciences. Von Gunten was viewed by these followers as a ground breaker who bent the rules in new areas of research for the betterment of society. Still others viewed him as pushing and confusing the boundaries and roles of science. He was accused of breaking century old taboos of medicine and trying to play God.

Dr. Fritz Von Gunten is the director of the multi-billion dollar corporation Ci Mada Union Laboratories, which is one of many subsidiaries of Alpine Advanced Electronics (AAE), based in Geneva Switzerland and owned by Wolfgang Martin. Ci Mada is located on the outskirts of Boulder, Colorado.

Boulder, Colorado has been a mecca for decades of radical progressive thought. But Fritz Von Gunten is not without his enemies there. Another reason Boulder was chosen as the site for the building of Ci Mada Union Laboratories is because of a large underground cavern system, not known to the public, that is accessed with secret elevators and a tunnel from the high security area of the basement of the building. The cavern is used as the training facility to test the giant pitwolves and observe some of their behavior. Boulder also provides close proximity to very remote wilderness areas and big game in a more natural setting for test purposes.

Three years ago experiments began 25 miles away in a rugged wilderness Bureau of Land Management (BLM) area of the Rocky Mountains, northwest of Boulder. Initially, it resulted in about 10 specimens escaping into the wild until the height of the fence was raised to 14 feet and electrified. These early specimens had microchips in their collars. Alpine Advanced Electronics had been trying for years to develop a special microchip reader and a chip called the sleeper chip to put into the skulls of Von Gunten's specimens. Prior to the invention of the sleeper chip, Von Gunten had decided to go ahead and chip the animals with the latest technology available for identification purposes. He did not believe at that time that it was possible for the giant pitwolves to escape the confines of the remote wilderness facility. Time would disprove this belief; thus his insistence of the sleeper chip to be developed by AAE arose. This kind of chip would allow the super predators to be tracked by special satellites and drones, and no one could detect the sleeper chip in the pitwolves, unless they possessed the sleeper computer software accessed by a their satellite, drone, or a special hand held microchip reader. After a mishap at the remote facility Dr. Von Gunten refused to use ordinary microchips in his genetically modified beasts, because it was way too risky. Veterinarians and many farmers and ranchers could access the information of giant pitwolves with an average microchip reader if the beasts escaped and were captured or killed. Only in the last six months had the sleeper chip and all related technology been perfected by AAE. As a result the sleeper chips had been embedded in the skulls of all giant pitwolf specimens. Ci Mada was now on its second generation of satellites and drones, working out minor kinks in the system.

An accidental, premature escape of the super predators three years earlier evolved into the urban legend of the giant pitwolf. The mistake had advanced the cause of the Adamic Society's goal more than they had ever imagined. As a result, lately more and more small number releases of the super predators had been occurring in different areas of North America under Von Gunten's direction. He hated the fact that these animals at that time could not be micro-chipped and tracked for data purposes. As of yet, no live specimens or dead giant pitwolves have ever been seen on the internet or TV. Just eye-witness accounts of large, ferocious prehistoric animals with huge fangs that resembled a giant pitbull and wolf made the news from time to time. Bogus accounts also began popping up in the tabloid newspapers, and the news as youth and older people began to make up unbelievable stories about encounters with them in the forest. The story of the giant pitwolf was evolving into a mythical legend.

The fact was that one look at this giant predator or a ferocious growl from it had been known at times to paralyze the average man with fear and oftentimes induce a deadly heart attack. Experiments conducted in the cavern under Ci Mada using kidnapped humans as guinea pigs proved this. Initially when the first ten giant predators were transported to the remote outdoor facility, they were placed inside a ten-foot-high heavy duty prison chain link fenced in an area one mile square. Because the paws of the giant pitwolves were so huge, there was no concern they could climb it. Big game such as deer, elk, grizzly bear and bison were brought in to see what these prehistoric looking predators would do. In all cases, except grizzlies and bison, the average giant pitwolf could easily kill the animals. Grizzlies and bison usually required two pitwolves to kill them in a short period of time. Experiments were also performed on humans. The giant pitwolves seemed to enjoy the taste of human flesh above all others.

On the third night that the pitwolves were there, a security guard was making his rounds in a specially designed humvee by the light of an almost full moon. In the moonlight he spotted a large mule buck deer being chased by the pack of ten giant pitwolves. He had stated that the deer must have jumped the fence and gotten inside. It could not be one of theirs because it had a small rack. It was not a trophy size animal like all the other deer they stocked on the property. His report also said that when the pack chased the deer, the deer barely cleared the fence, leaving the facility's property. But seven of the large giant pitwolves cleared it with at least a foot to spare, the three smaller ones barely clearing the fence. One of them, the smallest, scraped the fence hard with his chest, leaving a bloody patch of skin and hair behind.

When the sun rose the next morning another guard found six black nylon collars, still attached to tracking devices shredded in half on the ground inside the fenced in area. Two days later, three collars were found ten miles away in a cave under a thick forest. Five days later, one of the larger pitwolves with his collar still on was recovered by a team of six Ci Mada high-security subcontractor agents. The agents, all of which were ex-special forces in NETO (Northern European Treaty Organization), had to rappel by helicopter to get into the remote area to search and recover the body of one of the ten pitwolves. It had been dead for two days. Apparently, a hunter had shot three 7mm rounds into a large specimen in non-vital areas.

Four shells were found around the dead bodies of the pitwolf and the hunter. Three were empty, and one had not been shot. It was assumed that in the midst of the fear, adrenalin rush, and chaos of shooting at the animal, the hunter had accidently ejected and wasted his last live round, much to his demise. Bloody tracks of the super predator showed that the giant pitwolf, even though severely wounded, must have charged the hunter, who used the butt end of his empty rifle to try to defend himself from the beast. Large teeth marks pierced the wooden rifle stock that was found split into pieces. Apparently, this had given the hunter enough time to reach for his hunting knife with his right hand.

The partially decomposed bodies of both the super predator and hunter had revealed that the hunter's left forearm had been cleanly severed in half by the pitwolf, biting once through the radius and ulna bones. Evidence had shown the middle-aged hunter, who was identified by the agents as Brad Jones of Boulder, in the midst of the fight had used his Marine Kabar military knife with a razor sharp six-inch blade on the beast. He had stabbed the giant pitwolf in the chest area twice before the beast finally died. It took a total of three 7mm rounds in non-vital areas, a couple hits from the butt end of the hunter's rifle, and two stabbings from his Kabar knife before the beast died. Loss of blood from the severance of the hunter's forearm and shock probably led to the man's death.

Brad Jones' younger brother Lamar who had been hunting with him witnessed the horiffic pitwolf attack on Brad. He quickly ran away from the scene, became disoriented, and got lost. Three days later he came upon a highway - cold, dirty, and hungry from the ordeal - and babbling incoherent words with a wild look in his eyes. A deputy happened to spot him while out on patrol and took him to a nearby hospital. Authorities were able to eventually piece together the basic story of what he told them had happened, but they didn't believe him. Lamar could remember vivid details of the attack on his brother but could not remember any details of where the attack had occurred because his mind was fragmented. His story of a large prehistoric looking creature with large fangs was the first to surface to the general public. Lamar's story spread like wildfire over the internet and television. It was the beginning of the giant pitwolf urban legend and fanned the flames of multiple accounts of fake news about the beast. He is still receiving psychiatric help and counseling to this day.

The bodies of both the dead giant pitwolf and Brad Jones were recovered from the scene and placed in body bags by the agents. Then the site was swept clean of any evidence. Dr. Von Gunten personally oversaw the study of all dead pitwolves and of the body of Brad Jones.

Von Gunten came from a long line of evil and brilliant doctors, scientists, researchers, alchemists and practitioners of black magic. His family members were Luciferians, and some had been upper level Adamic Society members, as his father and he were. Von Gunten had also been involved as a director and consultant in his fields of study for a number of secret government projects. Most of these were of a black ops nature during most of his academic and professional career for both European and American spy agencies.

His father, Dr. Wilhelm Von Gunten, was considered the most brilliant genetic researcher in Europe in his lifetime. Hitler had sent one of his most trusted agents to Geneva, Switzerland at the start of World War II to recruit him to head up a top secret project dealing with genetic research and mind control experiments. He agreed only after half a million dollars in Swiss francs and gold bullion was paid in advance and placed in his Swiss Bank safety deposit box. This was his signing on bonus for joining the German war effort and he was also paid handsomely each month with many perks added. In addition, he enjoyed a carte blanche check for his equipment, supplies, and whatever else he needed for his research. Wilhelm Von Gunten demanded that complete control of the operation be given to him.

When the agent first told Hitler what terms Wilhelm had laid down, Hitler casually replied, "Give the doctor exactly what he wants. He is invaluable to the Third Reich." Only a few hand selected, high ranking Gestapo officers knew of Wilhelm's work and were told personally by Hitler not to interfere with his research. Barbaric and sadistic medical experiments were performed on live and dead Jews, homosexuals, captured Russian soldiers and anyone else Hitler deemed as undesirable, and animals. The code name for the project was Operation Frankenstein. Dr. Von Gunten's research team consisted of some of the finest doctors and scientists in their respective fields from around the world. These specialists were each hand-picked by Von Gunten and sworn to secrecy to the point of death.

Hitler relished and thoroughly enjoyed the evil experimentation Dr. Von Gunten's medical team performed on a daily basis. He eagerly looked forward to Von Gunten's monthly reports and pictures of his experiments sent to him in Berlin each month. During Wilhelm's first year of research, early advanced DNA knowledge was gained, organ transplants were conducted, early successful attempts of cloning on simple life forms were achieved, and mass mind control techniques were developed and eventually instituted by Hitler in his rallies. As time went on, Dr.Von Gunten believed with his whole heart that the possibilities of de-extinction could become a reality and utilized in his research.

In the second year of World War II, Hitler had discussed with Wilhelm Von Gunten his desire for him to create a super predator that could block out pain and stalk and attack opposing armies behind enemy lines. He believed this would cause chaos and strike fear in the hearts of the Allied soldiers on the battlefield, and anyone else who opposed him, and lead ultimately to their surrender. Hitler dreamed of some of his pilots flying over enemy lines and having their crews pushing these animals out of planes in crates by parachutes. He also believed that they could be used to destabilize and cause chaos among a large segment of their enemies civilian population.

Since the Von Gunten family crest had a wolf at the center, he chose a wolf to be bred with the only animal on earth that was game, besides some roosters. Game was the term given to dogs with certain desirable characteristics. They were usually well-muscled and agile, with big heads and powerful jaws, and were willing to fight to the point of death. Some of these dogs, called pitbulls, were seemingly immune to pain. The ones that were game would fight bulls in a ring until they either killed the bull or the bull killed them. These were the only suitable specimens of pitbulls Wilhelm would use in his experiments for creating his super predators. Wilhelm also chose wolves because they had been the subject of countless European folktales of mystery and evil since the dawn of man. Wolves loose in the forest instilled fear into people's minds. Wilhelm practiced selective breeding using only the most highly intelligent, cunning, and largest wolves he could find and trap.

Additionally, in order to raise the fear factor a couple of notches, Wilhelm decided to include characteristics of another fierce animal. He had always been fascinated with the saber tooth tiger and wanted to incorporate its long fangs and size in the creation of the ultimate super predator. Wilhelm Von Gunten had a special agent to purchase the skull of a saber tooth tiger for DNA material to achieve this goal. Wilhelm and his team were close to tapping into unknown biological laws that could in a sense resurrect previously prehistoric, extinct animals from fossilized bones from ages ago. Eventually, the special agent was able to locate a skull of a saber tooth tiger in Warsaw, Poland from an ex-curator of a science museum for $5,000 in gold.

It is rumored that Wilhelm and his wife were summoning demonic spirits for insights and knowledge of how to achieve his goals. A lot of Wilhelm's scientific information was gained by automatic handwriting from demonic beings. A year before the war was coming to a close, Dr. Wilhelm Von Gunten's group of doctors and scientists had successfully created a new species of animal that had reached full maturity and possessed the desired attributes of a wolf, pitbull and saber tooth tiger. Wilhelm had succeeded in creating the first super predator that he would call a giant pitwolf. Due to the research efforts, demonic help, and the expertise of Von Gunten and his team, de-extinction was no longer a fantasy, but a reality.

With World War II coming to a close and the impending arrival of American troops two weeks away, Wilhelm devised a plan with the help of his Jewish wife, Ingrid, to kill all his workers with poisonous mustard gas. Because Operation Frankenstein was so top secret, Wilhelm knew if he took the right steps, no one would ever find out what had taken place in the heart of the mountain in Germany where his secret laboratory lay, a quarter of a mile underground. The thought of being tried and sentenced to prison for horrific war crimes didn't appeal to him.

No one at his secret laboratory knew of the approaching U.S. and British troops, except Wilhelm and his wife. For security reasons, he had kept workers in complete isolation the last month they were alive. In fact, Von Gunten had told them the prototype jets the Germans had been working on were finally functional, the glitches had been worked out, and the war would be over in about a month. German victory was in sight. Five days before the possible American invasion, he told his team that a special night of celebration was called for and that everyone was free to relax and enjoy the victory celebration that night in the cafeteria, with kegs of the finest German beer and wine available for all. The evening came, the celebration began with loud music, and the men began singing. Everyone was laughing and having a good time while they were getting drunk. None knew that they would be entombed in the secret research cave before the night was over. It was a mandatory meeting, and when the last person entered through the steel door into the cafeteria, Ingrid locked it. Then Wilhelm hit a switch that released mustard gas into the room. Within a few minutes, everyone died from the gas. Before he and Ingrid left, Wilhelm wired a very large quantity of dynamite to blow up the large cavern where they had done their research and to seal off the secret entrance into the cave. Once they blew it up, he and Ingrid secretly crossed over into Switzerland where half a million dollars in gold was waiting for them in safety deposit boxes in their Swiss bank, along with another four hundred thousand dollars that had been wired into his Swiss bank account from Berlin during the course of the war.

They traveled light, but not without several suitcases of important scientific papers, DNA material of their hybrid animals, and the saber tooth tiger skull with its huge fangs. The Von Guntens also carried pictures of the horrible and gruesome medical experiments performed on their victims, both human and animal. In addition, they possessed pictures of their massive wolf and pitbull, which were the original stock from which the first pair of super predators pups were produced. Two very large pups produced from the selected wolf and pitbull emerged as a suitable male and female to become the breeding stock from which other giant pitwolves were to be used in the service for Hitler's war effort. The male was named the Red Baron and the female was called Sonja. Red Baron was named after the famous German World War I ace pilot. Wilhelm and his wife smuggled out ten reels of footage of the Red Baron's and Sonja's incredible physical feats. These beasts, like the rest of the animals and humans, were entombed in the heart of the mountain when it caved in from the explosion. The Red Baron weighed about 220 pounds and stood 40 inches at the shoulder, with three-inch fangs. He was four times stronger than any pitbull in their laboratory and could chase down and kill the fastest greyhound dogs that could be found in all of Europe. Hitler had been very impressed with the photos of the Red Baron and Sonja. He was also thrilled to hear of their physical attributes including feats of strength, speed, agility, jumping ability, and fearless aggressive behavior. Wilhelm and Ingrid desperately wanted to sneak out the Red Baron and Sonja from their cages within the mountain but it was too dangerous and risky, and there was not enough time with the advancing enemy troops closing in.

Wilhelm had named Operation Frankenstein in honor of his great, great grandfather, Dr. Albert Von Gunten, who had been a wealthy medical doctor known as the mad scientist of Geneva, Switzerland. He had achieved amazing results with people who were on their death beds. As a result, he had courted the kings, queens, and nobility of Europe with his black magic potions, alchemy elixirs, and ability to hypnotize people. Albert had also been an amazing traditional medical doctor and surgeon for his time. On the other hand, he had conducted countless experiments on cadavers and chained live human subjects. Some said that deep in his basement he had created huge batteries with acid in thick glass containers encased in thick wooden crates to conduct inhumane experiments of electricity on his victims. Rumors had circulated that screams could be heard from the basement of his mansion on days that were Luciferian high holidays, nights with a full moon, and when thunder and lightning were present. His castle- like mansion had been situated on the highest point closest to Geneva. Alongside his house was a three-inch wide copper pole that extended upwards of 100 feet. It was said that lightning had often been seen hitting it.

Inside Albert Von Gunten's three-story mansion, there had been a collection of morbid and occultic objects, paintings and symbols from around the world. On the mantel of his huge stone fireplace was a collection of shrunken heads from the Amazon region of South America and large cone shaped humanoid skulls from Peru and from around the great pyramids in Cairo. These cone-shaped heads had twice the cranium capacity of a normal human and were believed to have been Nephilim in nature. In his large private library he had a collection of four giant Nephilim skeletons with red hair 12 to 15 feet in height from Turkey. The floor-to-ceiling bookshelves housed thousands of occultic books, many of which were bound with real human skins of various colors. Only a small number of trusted friends and a number of high Adamic members had had the privilege of stepping foot in his library. Dr. Albert Von Gunten was the actual person that Mary Shelley used to create her character, Dr. Victor Frankenstein, in her 1818 novel entitled *Frankenstein*. Much of her novel was based in Geneva, Switzerland.

Dr. Fritz Von Gunten hung up on billionaire Wolfgang Martin, the CEO of Alpine Advanced Electronics, based in Geneva, Switzerland. Friend or no friend, Wolfgang is not used to people hanging up on him, especially one who works for him. Wolfgang's company is on the cutting edge of technology for governments, NETO, major banks, and corporations. He dreads calling Marla, for Von Gunten's sake and well-being, so he decides to call on a new rising star in the Adamic Society. His new friend has a little more clout than Wolfgang does, and this friend has a special relationship with Dr. Von Gunten. Wolfgang makes the call and is told by his friend that he will make Von Gunten see the error of his way.

After about ten minutes talking with Wolfgang, Fritz Von Gunten gets a call on his VIP phone. "Dr. Von Gunten, do you know who this is?"

"Yes, Isaac, my boy."

"No! Today you will address me as President Cohen! I'm calling you in the middle of a hectic schedule from my Oval Office."

"Excuse me, Mr. President," replies a startled Von Gunten. "I was not thinking."

Von Gunten quickly realizes he has overstepped his bounds if Cohen is giving him a call. It is time to be more congenial and diplomatic. Cohen wants Von Gunten to sweat it out a little bit and to know his disapproval.

"It seems to me that you are having a problem today following a directive given by our mutual friend, Wolfgang. Maybe it's your age? Maybe you are not thinking clearly?" taunts Cohen in a dramatic, sarcastic tone.

"Well, Mr. President, if you are calling about the previous conversation I had with Wolfgang Martin, I'm sure there was a misunderstanding on his part or possibly a miscommunication on mine."

"That's exactly along the lines of what I was thinking, Fritz." "Listen we all know in the society that you are a perfectionist, but sometimes necessity trumps perfection. We must strike while the iron is hot. The goal is to use the giant pitwolves to play a huge role in relocating some of the masses from rural areas and containing others in large metropolitan areas. The society's council is just trying to capitalize right now on pure raw human emotion, with all the meteorites hitting at this time. We must all be flexible from time to time, Fritz. Remember all the time, money, and resources that the society has given you through the years on your numerous pet projects - no pun intended. Let's just say we are calling in the loan now, my good friend."

Fritz Von Gunten is beginning to loosen up a little bit now. He knows Cohen is smooth talking him, but he is relieved it is Isaac delivering the ultimatum versus Marla. He goes on to say, "Well, it is still good to hear that the funny and mischievous boy that I first met many years ago at his bar mitzvah still has a sense of humor."

"Yes, this is true. Some things never change. Are we clear on what needs to be done, Fritz?"

"Yes, sir, Mr. President. You have painted a perfect picture for me. For some odd reason, I can see clearly now."

"While I'm talking to you, Fritz, the code word for releasing one third of the giant pitwolves from the facilities in North America is *BATTING .333*. In the event of a total meltdown of some sort, which I can't foresee, the password is *CARNAGE* for the total release of all the specimens. The 12 digit number is still the same."

"Yes, this is duly noted," says Von Gunten.

"Only you and I are authorized to use these passwords," declares Cohen, "on our Millennium smart phones for the North American operation. In the days to come, I prefer that you, rather than I, voice activate the password *BATTING .333*. It may be viewed as derelict of duty if you don't. I prefer that you stay in good standing with all high Adamic members. I would hate for some strange fate to befall you if you don't. Dr. Von Gunten, it is a pleasure doing business with you. I have a country to run and people to manipulate, so goodbye, my old friend. You may now call me Isaac."

"Thank you, Isaac. I'm glad it was you who called me instead of Marla."

"Yes, I bet you are."

"Can you do me a favor, Isaac?"

"Possibly. What's that?"

"Please tell my beautiful cousin, your mother Heidi, that I said hello, and I look forward to seeing her at the next Adamic Society meeting."

"Yes, I will do that."

"Thanks. Goodbye, Isaac."

"Goodbye."

Chapter 4

THE GIANT PITWOLF HUNT

7:00:13 PM, Mountain Standard Time, Tuesday, 05/07/20_ _, Ci Mada Union Laboratories, North American Tracking Center, Boulder, Colorado, USA

"Dr. Von Gunten?"

"Yes, Cush."

"Sir, I have some bad news. As of yet, I still have not been able to restore contact with satellite GS 33. I believe the problem is on our receiving end, because we have now also lost contact with our drone, Eyegate TLZ, over Colorado."

Von Gunten, startled a little about the information, clears his throat and says, "Then there must be a computer glitch of some kind in our system. The likelihood of both of them individually malfunctioning at basically the same time would be an extremely rare event."

"Sir, I first had a computer glitch with GS 33 at 6:56:14, but at 6:56:15 there was no signal or visual transmission of any kind, and now the same is true for TLZ. I know there is some kind of malfunction, but I have not been able to pinpoint it. Warren and I are doing everything I know to re-establish contact."

Dr. Fritz Von Gunten can feel his blood pressure beginning to rise rapidly as he hears his heartbeat suddenly pounding in his ears. In a frustrated tone, he says, "A short time ago you said there were problems with GS 33, and now this. What's next? Peter, the Eyegate TLZ drone is the most technologically advanced and expensive drone in the world. I cannot afford for it to malfunction. It could take up to a month to replace it. The TLZ model plays a crucial and vital role in the work we do here at Ci Mada.

Since we just released some new fine specimens into the wild southwest of Boulder last week, it has been supplying me with excellent data on them. Finally after all these years the data that I always dreamed of has recently been at my fingertips but now it is slipping through my hands. TLZ is our backup plan for the northern half of Colorado in the event the GS 33 malfunctions. Why hasn't NORAC called, Peter?"

"I don't know, but that's another reason why I think the problem is on our end. If the GS 33 or the TLZ would have crashed, they would have contacted us by now, because that is their protocol."

"Excellent point! Keep trying to restore contact, and hopefully it's just a glitch that we can eliminate. Have Warren call NORAC to confirm that our TLZ and the GS 33 haven't crashed."

"Yes, sir, Dr. Von Gunten."

Von Gunten goes to his office a short distance down the hall to try to relax and think positive thoughts to offset the anxiety he is feeling and to reduce the possibility of another heart attack like the one he suffered a year ago.

7:02:37 PM. In his modern plush office, Fritz is leaning back in the burgundy leather executive's chair at his desk. Knowing he needs to relax, he is trying to breathe slowly with his eyes focused on the beautiful mountain view outside his window with his back towards his office door. He is surrounded by four walls of numerous and prestigious scientific and academic accolades that he has received over a lifetime. Unconsciously, he repeatedly grasps and releases the salt and pepper hair of his beard with his thumb and fingers when he hears a knock at his door.

"Come in," says Von Gunten, as he swivels his chair around. He is fairly confident that his technical supervisor, Peter Cush, has good news. Instead it's Cush with Warren Jones, who is Cush's technical assistant. From the moment they walk into his office, Dr. Von Gunten knows by their facial expressions and body language it is not good news.

Almost reluctantly he momentarily hesitates, then takes a deep breath, and with uncertainty in his voice says, "Yes, what is it?"

Cush speaks up. "Sir, I'm so sorry. I don't know how to tell you this, but we have a worst case scenario on our hands here at Ci Mada. I hate to inform you, but Warren just got a confirmation from Colonel Murphy at NORAC that both the GS 33 and our drone, Eyegate TLZ, were taken out by meteorites."

The stress of the matter makes the usually calm and confident Director of Ci Mada Union Laboratories in Boulder explode in an angry fit of rage. "%$#*@&! When did this happen?"

Warren, startled by the usually mild mannered Von Gunten's demeanor, stutters at first. "Ah... Ah... Sir, Colonel Murphy says the GS 33 got hit by a meteorite at 6:56:15, and our drone got hit by another at 6:57:26 PM."

Immediately Von Gunten gruffly replies, "Why did it take so long for Murphy to confirm these reports?"

"Well, Sir, he said they don't have any record of where a satellite or a drone has been destroyed by a meteorite, let alone two of them being destroyed within two minutes of each other. He said they were puzzled at first and could not discern what caused them to crash. Murphy thought it was an act of war using lasers or some other high tech weapon system, so he put NORAC on red alert for three minutes. The meteorites were so small that they went undetected initially. He said it was an anomaly, and he had his people triple check their radar, thermal imaging, and data to confirm these facts before notifying us with the exact cause."

Shocked by the horrifying information, Dr. Von Gunten replies, "Wait a minute, Peter. When did this confirmed computer glitch first occur in the satellite?"

"Dr. Von Gunten, it was at 6:56:14."

With both a highly frustrated tone and a shocked look on his face, Fritz Von Gunten asks Peter, "You mean to tell me that after a computer glitch is recorded exactly 1/100th of a second later a meteorite falls from the sky and takes out the satellite?"

"Yes, sir. You can check my screen for the time stamp."

"Yes, yes, I must see with my own two eyes this strange set of circumstances."

He immediately jumps out of his chair, walks down the hall briskly to Peter's computer screen, and validates the information. He then walks to Warren's cubicle next to Peter's to see his information from NORAC. At this point, Von Gunten is wringing his hands and seems beside himself.

Peter Cush, who can't believe what has taken place, says, "Dr. Von Gunten, how is this possible that a meteorite hits a military satellite in outer space 1/100th of a second after it has a confirmed computer malfunction and finishes off the satellite, and then just over a minute later another meteorite picks off the drone counterpart to the satellite? What are the odds of that happening?"

Warren, in a confused state, pipes in, "It just seems too unbelievable."

Now Von Gunten, who hears his heart beating more rapidly and his mind rushing for an answer in this surreal moment, replies, "My first instinct says it is sabotage, at least for the TLZ, like maybe our system got hacked into, or it's some kind of secret laser or advanced ground to air heat seeking missile that hit it and has gone undetected. But it can't be because it would have shown up on NORAC'S screens, so it had to have been a meteorite. Besides, nobody on earth could hack into our ultra-high-tech system and coordinate a highly advanced satellite and drone to collide with meteorites. Peter, did the drone deviate from its usual travel speed or flight path today?"

"Absolutely not, Dr. Von Gunten. I double checked the flight pattern and all the stats on my computer screens."

"Then, gentlemen, with that being the case, we know a meteorite has no guidance system and travels between 25,000 to 160,000 miles per hour, depending on the material type, mass, initial rate of speed, and size. I would almost say it was an act of God if I believed in some higher power, but I'm a firmly devout atheist. As a rational human being and scientist, I am left to believe that these separate events are random occurrences that defy mathematical probabilities and my human logic. In layman's terms, we've had extremely bad luck today."

In public, Von Gunten plays the atheist card to the max, but he is a high level secret member of the Adamic Society and a worshipper of Lucifer. Cush, his long-time trusted assistant, is a lower level member of the society who is trying to climb up the ladder. Warren Jones has no knowledge of the Adamic Society and has always believed Von Gunten was what he claimed to be, an atheist.

Jones, a top, cutting-edge computer whiz, was personally recruited by Cush just two years earlier when Jones was a senior at Colorado A&M in Boulder. His passion, computer programming, was Jones' major in college, whereas, his minor was in statistics. He seems a perfect fit to work under Cush at Ci Mada. Money is his god and he has a dark side. Warren knows how to keep his mouth shut for the low six figure income he is making. Peter Cush has sold him on the half-truth that the United States is undergoing restructuring, due to limited resources and climate change. He has been told privatization of land in rural America must be freed up to allow for more productive farming, ranching, and mining methods to be utilized under the direction of a new progressive centralized government, with Cohen at the helm. Because of climate change, water has become a scarcer commodity and must be protected and selectively rationed to large, controlled urban cities and communities in America. Food and water are rapidly becoming another form of a world reserve currency on the open global market. Governmental possession and control of these and other vital resources is of prime importance for the destiny of America. President Cohen is banking on the fear factor that super predators generate and directives that he and his predecessor enacted as a means of helping to keep the USA in the role as the major super power in the world. Rapid large scale "volunteer" mass migration of rural people and containment of citizens in secure large and moderate sized urban areas is the plan, as handed down to him by the Adamic Society. Jones has bought into the lie as presented to him by Cush that Ci Mada Union Laboratories is a black ops company that is using genetics, technology and the giant pitwolves for the good of America and the world.

"I will make the call," states Von Gunten, "to our headquarters in Geneva, but I know that by this time they have already been notified by Colonel Murphy as to what has occurred. Our people in the U.S. military will soon replace the standard AAE GS satellite that got taken out. Fortunately, several are presently in stock. But the TLZ drone will take some more time.

79

As soon as one can be manufactured by AAE in their top secret Silicon Valley facility, it will be shipped to us. I'm hoping it will be no longer than two weeks tops. In the meantime, Peter, re-commission our previous drone, Eyegate TLX. It must be up and flying immediately. It is not as advanced, but our work can continue."

Peter says, "Dr. Von Gunten, it will take at least a week to test and recheck the drone systems and install the new computer software upgrades. Also it recently got damaged while in storage in the hanger by that airplane mechanic."

Fritz Von Gunten, in dismay, tilts his head forward, as he repeatedly rubs his forehead back and forth.

"Remember, he was working on the company's private jet when his truck backed into it. The fool had it in neutral instead of park when he jumped out of his truck quickly to pick up the paperwork he had left in the jet, and it rolled back and damaged the left wing of the TLX."

Von Gunten screams to the top of his lungs, "Yes, and all the people here at Ci Mada involved with the technical and mechanical aspects of the older drone will work around the clock in two shifts until it is ready to fly! It must be in the air in less than two days! I cannot have work halted because of time, money, and the inconvenience and complaints of my workers! Peter, is that clearly understood?"

Peter Cush knows the pressure and stress is getting to his boss. He responds in a quiet, irritated voice, "Yes, sir, Dr. Von Gunten."

"Sorry. Wait a minute, gentlemen. Please excuse my outbursts of anger. My blood pressure, I know, is extremely high. I, ah - again, sorry. Both of you men are tops at what you do."

Peter replies, "We understand your frustration, sir. We are behind you 100 percent," with Warren nodding his head in agreement.

"Great! As far as the new working conditions, this is the protocol that I was to follow, according to Wolfgang Martin, if for some unknown reason mishaps occurred in our program here. Both he and I never envisioned both a satellite and one of the drones would be incapacitated at the same time over one of our regions. We are dependent on the U. S. military and Wolfgang's Alpine Advanced Electronics to get things moving as quickly as possible. He knows the importance of my work and usually complies with my demands, or should I say wishes. The agenda goes forth above all else. It is so critical at this juncture in time to continually monitor our specimens' whereabouts, their behavior in the wild, and their interactions with man! Gentlemen, I need the data! As a result of the new work conditions, I will enact triple pay for all hourly employees and a special fringe benefit to all salary personnel to be revealed at a later time. Am I clear?"

Both Cush and Jones respond in an upbeat manner, "Yes, sir."

6:45:21 PM, Mountain Standard Time, Tuesday, 05/07/20_ _, Fortress/Double V Ranch, northeast corner of the pasture land, Golden Valley, Clark County, Colorado, USA

Caleb Crawford and John Blackhawk are bursting out laughing as they are teasing their young friend, Forrest Johnson, about how his old western style handle bar

moustache looks. Caleb says the waxed strands of facial hair on both sides are twisted into circles that look too big on his slim face.

John says, "No, they are way too small."

Caleb is laughing so much he can barely blurt out that Forrest's moustache is always uneven. Caleb's remark is sending John into a laughing tizzy. John is laughing so hard that he starts repeatedly slapping his lower right thigh above his knee.

About ten seconds later John regains enough composure to say, "No, no, no! That isn't the case. It's an optical illusion because Forrest always leans to the right with his body."

Now everyone is laughing, including good natured Forrest, as they pull up next to the downed barbed wire fence that they came to repair on the northeast side of the Double V Ranch, also called Fortress. It is a small job, and they should be finished in an hour.

Forrest, the smallest and youngest of the three, is sitting in the middle of the bench seat of the pickup, as he leans forward and looks into the rear view mirror, admiring his handle bar moustache. Then he readjusts the mirror and begins to re-twist the waxed hairs on both sides of the moustache into tight circles in methodical movements. With a little bit of a pretend smug attitude, he says, "By the way, guys, Brenda Lee says it makes me look very manly." Inside the pickup cab, more laughter erupts from the three brothers in Christ, as the vehicle comes to a halt and they begin to get out.

Suddenly, the second Blackhawk opens the pickup door on his side, he quits laughing and the smile instantly vanishes from his face. He senses something isn't right. Maybe it's an Indian thing or maybe it's a gift from God, but it is something he has always possessed, some kind of sixth sense. The people at Fortress have never doubted John about things of the outdoors, but his two best friends, Caleb and Forrest, are always picking his brain to try to figure him out when he has these moments.

Blackhawk had been a very successful professional hunting and fishing guide from Montana. John had guided Caleb's dad, Ricky Crawford, and his uncle, Gary Kirkman, on a number of memorable big game hunts and fly fishing trips in past years. They were also always sending their hunting and fishing buddies to him because Blackhawk knew the way of the woods, rivers, and all creatures in them.

Blackhawk left Montana a year after his family was killed in an auto accident. His best friend had been his wife Dena, a full-blooded Sioux Indian like himself, who had grown up on the same reservation as he had. John came to be born again because of her life, ministry, and prayers. She had been a devout Christian with an evangelistic calling to their people. She dearly loved John, their son John Jr., their daughter Hannah, and most of all Jesus Christ her Lord.

Dena and the children had died one snowy winter night two years previously when they had a head on collision with an 18 wheeler on a slippery, icy road coming back to the reservation from grocery shopping. Her jeep had accidently slid over onto a lane of an oncoming trucker. Blackhawk told Caleb recently that for a full year after the accident, he had lived in a fog of deep, dark depression, and that many a night it almost

FORTRESS: Divinely Protected

caused him to blow his brains out with a pistol. He said the pain was almost unbearable, because no one had ever loved him like Dena and his two kids had. But he knew his family was in heaven and he also was pretty sure he'd never see them again if he did take his own life. It was a chance he didn't want to take no matter how much pain he had to bear.

John went on to tell Caleb that one night around a year ago he had a vision from the Lord in which an angel told him to move to Fortress. The big sky country of Montana was his ancestral home, and its beauty was something he had always loved. But the angel told him, "At Fortress you will be surrounded by true brothers and sisters in Christ who will love you with the love of the Lord. The Lord's presence is mighty upon that place, and his eye never leaves it."

The next day he got a letter in the mail from Ricky Crawford. Both Ricky and Gary knew Blackhawk had been having a rough time, so Ricky wrote to tell him they had been praying for him and felt the Lord wanted him to come and stay awhile with them. A few days later, John took them up on their offer, packed his stuff, and headed for Golden Valley. From the very first minute John drove his 4x4 extended cab truck onto the property at Fortress, he felt a soothing peace and Christ's love among the people there. He also stated that the angel told him that he could trust the Crawfords and Kirkmans, who were the elders of Fortress, because they were special chosen vessels for the end times. This was something John knew in his heart, having known Ricky and Gary over the course of years, but having an angel confirm it gave him extra inner peace about the whole move. What also excited him was that the angel said, "There you will serve God's purpose for your life. God has also told me to tell you, John, that from this day forward you will always know the love of Dena and your children, but all the pain of their loss will be removed. You have been an Indian who has been a hunter, tracker, and professional guide. There you will be an Indian who is a Christian warrior for me. You will receive a special gift of courage to bring me glory. "

Forrest is the first to notice the immediate change in Blackhawk's demeanor and the totally serious and intense look on his face, especially in his eyes. Forrest knows John is in his *zone* and quietly whispers, "What is it, John?"

By this time, Caleb's hysterical laughter has come to a screeching halt when he sees the solemn looks on Blackhawk's and Forrest's faces. While Blackhawk is walking around and behind the pickup, he calmly tells Caleb and Forrest, "We need to grab our guns out of the truck."

Caleb, now in a serious mood, in a low tone asks, "Blackhawk, did you see something?"

"No. Nothing."

As Forrest is reaching for John's and Caleb's rifles on the gun rack on the back window of the truck, he quietly whispers again, "Did you hear something, John?"

"Nothing" is Blackhawk's response.

Forrest is from the Cody, Wyoming area and is 24 years old. He was given the nickname, Space Cowboy, as a boy by his dad because he had one foot in the ways of the old west and the other in the deep mysteries of space. Forrest can break wild mustangs, do blacksmith work, make a braided leather lasso, or bake the best sourdough biscuits you ever tasted in a Dutch oven over some hot embers. He is an all-around jack of all trades in cowboy and early pioneer ways.

On the other hand, Forrest also has a nerdish side and inherited an interest in space from his family, especially his two uncles. Both uncles had worked for USSAP (United States Space and Aeronautics Program) at the same time. One worked at USSAP's Kennedy Space Command Center in Houston, Texas and the other at the Aeronautical Space Flight Data Center in Huntsville, Alabama. Forrest graduated with honors from the University of Colorado with a degree in astronomy and physics.

His dad's older brother, Morgan, was a real rocket scientist who lived in Houston, Texas and had given him a Bowie knife that had belonged to Forrest's great-great-grandfather, Charles Wesley Johnson. Morgan had no children and thought Forrest should be the rightful heir of it. Forrest's dad was the second oldest brother and Forrest was his oldest son. Forrest's grandfather Charles Wesley had been a gunsmith, blacksmith, and rancher in Cody after the Civil War until he died in 1899. The knife Charles Wesley Johnson hand forged in his blacksmith shop was one of a kind, with its beautiful curly maple handle, an S-shaped brass guard, and its speckled steel

Bowie style ten-inch blade with a razor's edge. A very faint mark was located at the base of the blade right above the guard with his ancestor's initials C. W. J. hand-stamped on it. The steel was just too hard to make a deeper impression with the stamps. The original fringed buffalo-hide sheath that contained the knife had deteriorated so severely that Forrest used it as a pattern to make an exact replica. His great-great-grandfather called the metal he used to make the knife space steel because he had seen something strange streak across the Wyoming sky with a trail of white smoke in the middle of the day. Charles Wesley had been coming back from visiting a sick relative in a wagon when he spotted it. It terrified him, but he tracked it with his eyes as it hit and exploded on his ranch property early that afternoon. The only thing he ever made from his space steel was the Bowie knife. The reason was that the metal was extremely hard and almost impossible to work with. He spent endless hours working to forge and bring the blade to a razor-sharp edge. For generations it had stirred up endless conversations with family, friends, and strangers. It was the initial source of his uncles' and Forrest's own fascination with outer space. Since he was a kid, Forrest had been interested in all facets of space, but especially meteorites. His beautiful heirloom Bowie knife linked his past to the course he had set for his life.

Forrest is carrying his modern era Colt single-action revolver in the .45 long caliber on his hip in a custom-made western-style leather holster and leather belt with 12 loops in the back that holds extra shells. Ever since he was 18, when he had a run in with a cougar while riding on his horse on his family's ranch in Wyoming, he never ventured into the wild without it strapped to his hip. He hands Blackhawk his bolt action .300 Winchester Magnum rifle and gives Caleb his Remington pump action .30-06 rifle that was his grandfather's.

Blackhawk motions with his right index finger the direction to which they need to start moving, as he holds his rifle in an upward position. He quietly states, "Something happened on Watson's land," and starts walking in that direction over a downed, diseased pine tree that has fallen and pinned down a 25-foot section of four strands of barbed wire to the earth. The three have come with a chain saw and tools to cut the tree up and to repair the fence.

No sooner do they cross over the downed barbed wire and walk through some knee-high grass than the land dips down kind of steeply and flattens out. There at the bottom lay a huge, dead, heavily muscled black angus bull in a meadow of green grass. It is Pete Watson's prize bull named Big Blackie with his neck savagely ripped open and covered in a pool of blood and flies. It is evident that other cows had been close to the bull, about 100 feet away on one side, but quickly left when the attack took place. Both Caleb and Forrest make mental notes and surmise that it would have been impossible for Blackhawk to have seen the bull. Plus the air had been blowing downwind from the truck since they first got out of it. Neither had gotten a whiff of the dead animal in the air and they shake their heads at each other and shrug their shoulders regarding John's gift.

Pete Watson, a rancher, is a close friend and neighbor. He was trying to upgrade the quality of his herd of black angus with the costly champion bull.

Caleb and Forrest are confused and are trying to figure out how Big Blackie died. Both want to think a grizzly had to have done this to the bull, but one reason they know it couldn't have been a grizzly is because he would have gorged himself on the prime beef and not just killed this animal and left it lying there uneaten.

Blackhawk breaks into their thoughts. "I know you are like me and want to say a grizzly did this, but the signs say differently."

Caleb replies, "Yeah, there are no grizzly tracks, just some giant wolf tracks."

Forrest tells Blackhawk, "I've never seen as many wolf tracks as you have, John, but these tracks seem to be more than twice the size of the average wolf."

Still holding tightly to his .300 Winchester magnum wooden stock around the forearm section with his right hand with the butt end on the ground, John is bent down on his right knee by the bloody dead bull. After analyzing the wolf's tracks, he then stands up and calmly says, "This animal is not pure wolf. Its paw prints are very similar, but they're also way too big. It's some kind of unnatural hybrid. A single wolf would have never taken on this big bull by itself. A lone wolf couldn't attack this massive bull by the neck and rip out a huge chunk of meat that size. It would be impossible. Also, a wolf would eat its kill if possible. This animal didn't want to eat the bull."

"Why do you say this, John?" asks Caleb, who doesn't understand.

"Because we didn't scare it off when we pulled up in the pickup. This blood is not fresh and is drying up, and I estimate this bull has been dead for about 30 to 40 minutes. But what amazes me the most is that this bull never knew what was coming. This wolf-like creature must be really cunning, strong, and extremely quick for this to happen. I am looking at the bull's tracks, and they indicate to me that one minute he was chewing on some green grass and the next a huge beast has sunk its teeth, or should I say large fangs, into the major arteries of his neck before he knew it, and then it was all over. If you guys look right around the bull's body, you'll see some giant wolf-like tracks."

This is evident to them, but both Caleb and Forrest have overlooked a very important piece of information at the scene. John fills them in when he says, "Notice this concerning the tracks. You see the same set of wolf tracks all around the bull's body and one set leading away from its body. But there are none leading up to it."

"You're right, John," says an intrigued Forrest.

"That is until you get over here 25 feet away from the bull's body on this flat area of pasture with a small amount of bent grass blades from this wolf-like creature's paws," explains John.

"Man, I didn't notice that until now," says Forrest.

"Guys, I believe this hybrid wolf is so intelligent that he intentionally was downwind from the bull and had the wind blowing in his face just before he attacked big Blackie, so the bull couldn't smell his scent."

"Wow, I think you're right, Blackhawk. What you are laying out here sounds all logical to me!" says Caleb as he processes John's analysis of the situation.

John continues. "From what the tracks are showing me, I think this beast had only a little running start in attacking the prize bull. This creature got some momentum going and bounced on its prey from 30 feet away. I know wolves and wolves do this."

Caleb, who know John is a master tracker of animals, says, "You are absolutely right, John. You never cease to amaze me." At this point, he is getting a check in his spirit that they are in eminent danger. Caleb tells John to make sure the safety is off on his rifle, and he tells Forrest to unsnap his holster and to cock the hammer on his single-action revolver, because they may not have the ordinary reactionary time to fire at the beast if they see him. Both John and Caleb make sure their rifles are ready. Forrest takes the leather loop off his hammer and cocks it back while in the holster so it is ready to fire.

Blackhawk, in a no-nonsense tone, says, "Whatever this animal is, it doesn't always kill for meat. It also kills for sport. I know of no animal like this, and from all I've seen here, it appears to be the most dangerous animal I've ever encountered in the woods."

Putting two and two together, Caleb surmises, "This must be that giant pitwolf that I've heard a few reports on over the last couple of years. I always dismissed them and thought it was total nonsense."

Forrest chimes in, "Yeah, I remember hearing something about them my senior year at A&M, but I thought it was just another silly urban legend cooked up by a guy named Lamar Jones."

"Not anymore," replies Blackhawk. This animal seems to be game and has pitbull characteristics, wolf characteristics, and that of another animal I'm not familiar with. This would explain why it attacks its prey at the neck. This hybrid wolf makes massive puncture marks. The way Blackie's neck muscles are ripped makes me think that this animal has a huge mouth and big fangs like a lion or tiger. There are no Indian legends of the northwest or elsewhere in the U.S. or Canada that describe a beast like this that roams the forests. This beast is incredibly fast and super strong. Look here, guys. You see what I'm talking about?" Blackhawk points to puncture marks in the open ripped out flesh area of the bull's neck. Both Caleb and Forrest nod their heads in the affirmative.

John adds, "I also suspect this animal is not only highly intelligent but also cunning and unpredictable, so be alert for anything. He may be stalking us at this very moment."

Caleb tells Blackhawk that regardless of what this giant pitwolf is doing they have to track this animal now before it gets too far away. Blackhawk knows he has to track it down and doesn't blink an eye about it. Forrest gives Caleb a thumbs up to count him in concerning the hunt. Even though he doesn't want to come face to face with this beast, he knows what has to be done.

Caleb Crawford is no stranger to danger. Having been a Navy SEAL for 14 years, he had been a Captain with SEAL Team Six, prior to taking early retirement. He had seen plenty of action in some of the most dangerous places in the Middle East and other hotspots of the world. Although he had enjoyed the adrenaline rush of being in tight spots and life and death situations as a SEAL, he had also been trained to minimize any loss of life, if at all possible, for his team members and other military personnel. Caleb has also been the assistant pastor at Fortress since he retired his commission in the Navy eight years ago. He wrestled with becoming a chaplain in the Navy before he entered the Naval Academy. However, the pull to see live action as a Navy SEAL was too strong because it had always been a dream of his. Nevertheless, he often wondered if he had made the right choice. He lived with a lot of regrets and a mild case of Post-Traumatic Stress (PTS) that flared up occasionally.

Caleb knows that a dangerous animal of this nature puts everyone's life in jeopardy in Clark county. He tells both his friends that they need to go back to the pickup and gear up. They all go back to the truck, Caleb grabs his backpack, and everyone throws in anything they can find from the truck that is crucial to this wolf hunt. They find flashlights, a roll of gray duct tape to tape the flashlights to their rifles before it gets dark, Caleb's two-way radio, four water bottles, and all the extra ammunition they can scrounge up in the truck and truck box. They then return to the dead bull. Blackhawk starts tracking the beast, that had headed north. The weight of the beast and the fresh tracks make it easy for John to track the animal for most of the way.

The fact that Blackhawk is a master tracker is one reason he had been a successful hunting guide in Montana. Caleb's dad, Ricky Crawford, and his Uncle Gary, both avid outdoorsman, said John was the best in the business.

Ten minutes later, both Caleb and Forrest are amazed at John's ability to track the wolf hybrid, even over rock. Finally, after about thirty minutes of tracking, they are just coming out of a dense forest of Aspen trees when Blackhawk spots the beast from the pit of hell on a huge bolder 20 feet off the ground about 60 yards uphill from them in a box canyon. It looks like an evil looking prehistoric animal from the dinosaur age. It is heavily muscled, beyond any other animal they had ever seen. It stands four feet plus at the shoulders. It has long, thick fur like a wolf, but its color is totally different. It has brindle coloring of orange and black, or more commonly known as tiger striped, a color found on some pit bulls. This creature from hell has a head larger than the size of a basketball, with a long powerful muzzle with three-inch fangs that remind them of pictures of a saber tooth tiger. It is making blood curdling, snarling sounds at them. Then it tilts it head, looking at them with black, piercing, lifeless eyes. The creature's powerful body is positioned in a devilish stance of defiance on a massive boulder, as if it has been hunting and waiting for them to catch up to it.

What is playing out before the eyes of these hunters doesn't seem real. It is like a scene out of a horror movie that doesn't correspond with reality, only this time it is for real. A cold chill sweeps up Caleb's and Forrest's backs like they've never experienced before. Blackhawk, impervious to fear, slowly whispers, "I'm going to kill this demonic animal."

Caleb, knowing that John is definitely the best shot of the three and possesses the largest caliber rifle, quietly tells John to give them a second. He tells Forrest to slowly move to John's left side as he moves to John's right and whispers, "Everyone get ready. Fire at will, John." Just as John Blackhawk utters the words, "You're going to die," to the beast, the animal leans backward on its two heavily muscled hind legs for a split second and makes a giant leap forward off of the huge rock toward the three men. Just as quickly, Blackhawk pulls his rifle tight to his shoulder and squeezes a round off in the center of the giant pitwolf's chest while the beast is in midair. The animal lands on all fours at least ten yards from the base of the boulder and keeps coming at them, seemingly not phased in the least. John's favorite high-powered bolt-action rifle jams on him, and he is unable to chamber another round into his rifle. Caleb, instantly noticing what is happening, shoulders his 30-06, fires a round, and hits the animal at the base of his lower right chest area, shattering his upper right leg bone. The crazy beast is now on its side about 15 yards away. It keeps trying to claw its way to them while gasping for air with his other three legs on its side. With pure evil in its eyes, the beast is snarling and violently snapping at them with its teeth. As the three men stand before the beast, they look at each other and the beast in total amazement. Its power, strength, speed, size, and large jaws and fangs would have created instant crippling terror in the hearts of Caleb and Forrest had the Holy Spirit had not blanketed them with boldness just before they saw the animal. As a result of this supernatural boldness, Forrest cautiously walks up about eight yards from the wolf and fires one hollow point .45 long Colt slug deep into the animal's neck just below the base of its skull. At that time, the animal draws one last breath and dies.

Before there is time to rehash all that has transpired concerning the giant pitwolf, all three men realize that they need back up. Darkness will soon befall the canyon floor. A small amount of the setting sun's rays penetrates the base of the deep canyon below. Blackhawk's extractor broke in his rifle, which caused it to jam, so they are down to only two properly functioning firearms. Blackhawk clears the jam and he is set to fire off only one round before it jams again. The three of them are concerned that additional giant pitwolves might be in the area. Caleb yells to Blackhawk and Forrest to start making four fires for light and protection from any other pitwolves that might be in the area. Caleb slings his backpack to the ground and digs around in it to find his two-way radio, flashlights, and duct tape. Caleb tapes his flashlight to the underside of his rifle barrel and then hands one to John who does the same. Blackhawk then starts gathering kindling material, grass, small twigs, and leaves to start fires. Forrest is gathering some branches nearby with his hand ready to grab his revolver at any second. Each man is on the alert, constantly looking in all directions while working. Blackhawk, with his rifle right beside him, is ready to use it in an instant. John reaches for the Zippo lighter that he always carries to start the first of four fires.

As he is stands with his rifle ready, looking around doing a perimeter check, Caleb radios into Fortress for help. In raw emotion, he says, "Dad, Uncle

Gary, this is Caleb. Do you read me?"

"Caleb, this is Dad. Is there a problem?"

"Yes, you're not going to believe what just happened."

"I'd like to think it's good news, but from your tone I'm thinking it's not. So go ahead."

"Dad, you know those reports of mysterious giant pitwolves that have been spotted in the rugged northwest sections of the United States over the last year or so?"

"Yeah, and right now I have this hunch it's not an urban legend after all?"

"You guessed it. Blackhawk, Forrest, and I each took a shot and killed one, a real giant pitwolf! It looks somewhat like a cross between a saber tooth tiger, a pitbull, and a wolf. If a person is not born again and sees this thing, it will scare the hell right out of them and they will want to get saved. Blackhawk says it probably weighs between 350 and 375 pounds"

"Wow! Unbelievable! So you guys are okay?" asks a concerned Ricky.

"Yes, sir. We're fine at this point. I feel like you need to know some information about what we got ourselves into before you head our way."

"Sure. Okay. Well go head, Caleb. I'm listening."

"Well, this beast killed Pete Watson's prize bull not far from our shared fence line where we went to repair some damaged fence. At first we thought a grizzly bear had attacked the bull, but Blackhawk was the first to spot the wolf's tracks around the dead bull. He knew it wasn't an ordinary wolf. We were on Pete's property, but I know he wouldn't mind us tracking it since it killed his bull. We kind of knew what we were getting ourselves into, but I didn't want this animal to get away if at all possible. So we tracked it on foot to the southern end of that box canyon on Watson's property. It was about a hundred yards from that small pool of water underneath the high cliff and that huge boulder where Pete and I found those three arrowheads when we were kids."

"I remember Son. I know exactly where you are. I hunted with Pete's dad some years back in that same spot. I hate hearing that about Pete's bull. He's invested a lot of money in that animal. Caleb, I, like a lot of others, dismissed these wild, incredible reports of the giant pitwolves because wolves don't usually get really huge. Reports of timber wolves weighing 150 pounds are the exception and not the rule. A good sized pitbull usually runs between 70 and 80 pounds. I suspect this pitwolf is not a prehistoric animal that is living in remote areas of the country nor a mixed breed of chance. At this point, I believe it sounds like a genetically modified beast. We definitely need to bring this dead animal into Fortress to examine it."

"That's my line of thinking, Dad."

"Caleb, it might have a microchip of some kind that we can scan because somebody has been playing around with the animal kingdom, both from the present and the past."

"Dad, once you see what this animal looks like and how massive it is - especially its head, jaws, and fangs - you'll see how downright scary it is. Also, this beast was extremely aggressive and started to attack us. We each put a bullet in it before it went down. John's extractor broke on his rifle, so it's not functioning correctly. He can only fire off one shot with his rifle if we are attacked, so we are down to my pump action 30-06 and Forrest's .45 long single action revolver for protection."

"Caleb, have you guys made some fires to help ward off any potential giant pitwolves attacking you guys in the area before we get there?"

"Forrest and Blackhawk are working on that as we speak. We've also duct taped flashlights underneath the barrels of our rifles for when it gets dark."

"That's good thinking. I'll be setting up a rescue mission pronto, and I'll tell Gary to get the intercessors praying immediately."

"Great! Make sure everyone knows the total seriousness of the situation. We can use all the divine protection we can get from God through prayer in the meantime. Please grab my AR-10 out of the gun safe and the extra clips on belt."

"Definitely I will, Son. Make sure you keep your radio on and I'll do the same. We'll get there as soon as possible with the Lord's help. I love you,

Caleb."

"I love you too, Dad."

Ricky sees Gary and quickly fills him in about what is going on.

Gary says, "I believe this is definitely a code red event."

He says he is staying behind and setting up an armed perimeter and extra lighting with a small number of men around the buildings at Fortress. In their spirit, they don't believe it is necessary on the property of Fortress, but are going to take some precautions anyway. Gary is going to tell the intercessors and others that Caleb, Blackhawk, and Forrest killed a giant pitwolf and need faith-filled prayer for divine protection to get back to Fortress. He relates to them that Ricky is heading up a team of men to rescue Caleb and the others, that it is a dangerous mission, and they need much serious prayer. They also are told that the men are going to bring this animal back into Charlie's garage to get a better look at it.

Ricky Crawford's main concern is that this dead giant pitwolf may be with a pack not far away. He also knows that the terrain is rugged up there, and that in order to pack this animal out of there they will have to carry it with its legs tied to a pole. Ricky figures two younger stout men, periodically switching out with other men, can get the job done.

Caleb's dad, Ricky, talks with Gary and they work out some more quick safeguards that need to be put into place at Fortress. Ricky then walks over to the workshop on the Double V Ranch. He goes to see Charlie Wilcox, who manages the garage workshop and warehouse. Charlie Wilcox is also a very experienced hunter, and his son Tommy has been on a number of hunts with him.

Speaking with authority, yet with a slight hint of anxiety in his voice, Ricky asks his good friend, "Charlie, are you still working on that four wheel drive pickup?"

His good friend Charlie who has known him for years says, "No, Rick, we're done with it. Tommy just finished putting on the new back right tire. The tread was shot."

"Great! I was pretty sure you guys were done with it. We've got a code red at Fortress."

Charlie shouts, "I knew from your tone something was up. A code red!? What in the world is going on?" Is there a grizzly on the loose?"

"No. Blackhawk, Forrest and Caleb killed a giant pitwolf up in Watson's box canyon."

"You're kidding me. Those super huge wolf like creatures are not a myth or hoax after all?"

Just at that moment Gary rings the bell from the church area for a code red alert on the property.

Charlie says, "This place will be a buzz now."

"Absolutely, Charlie. Now according to Caleb, who just called on the two-way radio, the pitwolf they killed is really huge."

"How big, Rick, 200 pounds?"

"No. Try adding about 175 pounds to that."

"Hey, Ricky, I wasn't expecting that. That's getting downright scary. I wish you were joking, but by the concerned look on your face I know different."

"No. I wish I was joking. But Caleb said that Blackhawk estimates that the beast weighs around 350 to 375 pounds."

"Well, John ought to know. The guy has personally hunted since he was a child. He has guided hundreds of hunters, has seen and dressed out more wildlife, and understands them better than all of us combined here at Fortress."

"Yes, without a doubt, Charlie. So, with that being said, we've got to go quickly and rescue John, Forrest, and Caleb and bring in this dead pitwolf. It is crucial we hurry because Blackhawk's .300 Winchester magnum's extractor broke. So now it works like a very slow reloading single shot rifle. They are down to Caleb's grandfather's Remington pump .30-06 and Forrest's single action .45 revolver for two normal functioning firearms."

"Ricky, don't worry. We are going to get them boys out of there by faith in Jesus' name."

"I agree with you, Charlie. Gary is getting a group of intercessors and prayer warriors together right now to pray for the boys and the rescue mission. It's really dangerous for Caleb and them to leave the box canyon now because other beasts are probably in the area. So they're making some fires for light and protection. Right now I've got to assemble a rescue team quickly so we can get up there and get them out. We've got to bring in this dead giant pitwolf and check it out to see what we're up against."

"You can count me and Tommy in, Rick," says Charlie.

"Thanks. There's just a little bit of sunlight, so we have to move. Charlie, go get your semi-automatic 12 gauge and plenty of 00 buckshot. Where's Tommy?"

"He's splitting some firewood in the back."

"Listen. Grab Tommy and have him bring a high-powered rifle or shotgun. And, Charlie, get about ten Bushnell head flashlights out of the warehouse, with new batteries. That way our hands are free to carry our firearms as we travel through the woods."

"What about Gary, Ricky?"

"Gary is rounding up some guys to stay behind and be armed sentries. He's also getting with the intercessors to pray about the situation. Gary will also spread the news to the rest of the people to be on the alert for other possible giant wolves in the area."

"Meet me in fifteen minutes behind the barn. Bring the four wheel drive pickup. We're all piling in and going to where Caleb parked his truck near our northeast fence bordering Pete's property. I'm grabbing my night vision and thermal imaging scope on my .308 semi automatic rifle, my Colt .45 automatic pistol and Caleb's AR-10 at the Lodge."We'll be on foot for the rest of the trip once we get to that point.

"Ricky, I'll grab Tommy, and we'll hurry over to the barn once we get all the supplies."

Exactly 14 minutes later, Charlie pulls up with his son Tommy in the truck behind the barn. Brother Ricky gets in the front seat, as Tommy quickly slides over to the middle.

Tommy asks, "Brother Ricky, are Caleb, Forrest, and Blackhawk going to be okay until we get there?"

"I believe so, Tommy, but a little extra prayer won't hurt."

"Yes, sir. I've been praying hard ever since my dad told me a few minutes ago."

"We both have, Ricky," affirms Charlie.

"Me too. Let's keep praying in faith."

"Amen, Brother Ricky!"

After Tommy climbs into the pickup and sits in the middle of the bench seat, he and Ricky smile at each other while situating their rifles.

Leon Wilson, who's in charge of shipping out the ministry's newsletters, books, CDs, DVDs, and mail, turns the corner of the barn with two other brothers in the Lord. All the men are heavily armed and have on the head flashlights that Charlie supplied for them. The three men hop into the truckbed with apprehension written all over their faces. Even though the night is cool, Leon seems to be breaking out in a sweat on his face and neck.

Just before they leave, Brother Gary shows up, shakes hands with all the men in the truck, thanking them and urging them to be alert on the trail. Then he says, "We will be praying for you guys."

Everyone replies, "Amen."

As Charlie starts driving away, Tommy asks, "Brother Ricky, do you think we are already in the Tribulation? After I told Leon about the rescue mission, he briefly explained why he thinks this possibly is a sign that the Tribulation may have already started. He said the Bible in the Revelation 6 talks about wild beasts attacking and killing men."

Brother Ricky pauses for a second before responding. "Tommy, in Revelation 6:8 it does mention that wild beasts will attack and kill men. But when we study the Bible, we have to look at in the context in which it was written. If you study Revelation 6:1, you will see that it is referring to the Antichrist. What brother Gary and I believe to be the literal son of Satan will rise to power and manifest himself to the world. He assumes his position of power to rule the world. The following verses in Revelation 6:2-8 give a partial understanding of some of the things that take place after that event. In verse 8 it states that one fourth of the world's population is going to die. They are going to die from the sword, which is war, and hunger, which is the shortage of food. Death is the end result of the second and third seals being released. The beasts that attack and kill people follow those events."

"I kind of remember about you or Brother Gary talking about this before."

"Prophecy has two components to it. One is that the prophetic event has to be interpreted correctly and the other is that it has to be in the right chronological time sequence with all the other scriptures."

"Yes! Definitely!"

"Tommy, Brother Gary and I studied Bible prophecy intensely for years but it wasn't until we studied the teachings of Ryan Cotton, Fortress' own Ms. Frances Cotton's deceased husband, that we learned how to study and understand some deep things in God's Word concerning prophecy and other subjects in the scriptures. It took a frustrated layman who was a retired postman from Arkansas to help us sort through the doctrines and traditions of men from true biblical doctrines of Bible prophecy. I don't have the time now to go into a lot of explanation about his teachings, but ..."

"Excuse me," Charlie, a little confused, interrupts. "Sorry, Ricky. Then are you saying that this giant pitwolf couldn't be the fulfillment of that scripture in Revelation 6:8?"

"Okay, let me try to quickly clarify what I'm saying. The fulfillment of prophecy goes through a process. Depending on the number of these giant pitwolves, they could help to bring to pass that scripture. But, if only five or ten of these beasts exist, then they could not be viewed as some of the beasts in that scripture. On the other hand, if a large number of them exists, then yes, they could be eventually viewed as some of those beasts in Revelation 6:8. What I would like to add is that most of the prophecies that you read about in the book of Revelation and the other books of the Bible don't just happen instantly. In order for certain events to take place, it is a process that takes time. Exactly how long these animals have been around and how many there are of these giant pitwolves is still an unknown. We also must realize that other events in Rev. 6:2-8 must be happening at the same general time period when beasts are killing human beings. All these events have to be coinciding to various degrees. If we do not take all these things into consideration, then we are taking the scriptures out of context - which means you end up performing scriptural gymnastics, contorting the Word of God like some Christian teachers of the Word do - which means the teacher is making the Bible say something it doesn't declare."

"Oh, I get it," says Tommy. "This giant pitwolf that the guys killed may be leading up to the fulfillment of Revelation 6:8."

"Yes, that's it in a nutshell, Tommy."

"Correct me if I'm wrong, Ricky. Then are you saying the Tribulation could still be far away from starting?" asks Charlie.

"No, I'm not saying that. America, as you know, is going to hell in a hand basket. The powers that be in this world are not only letting it happen, but are helping to implode the foundations of this country. The world issues are so great, and our nation's problems are so many and often times complex, that it appears it is beyond the point of no return. The world as we know it can't keep going on. Pandora's box has been opened and the evils of society have been unleashed and are wreaking havoc on our once great land. There is no reversing it unless enough of God's people are humbling themselves and praying. From what Gary and I have observed in the natural, most Christians today are straddling the fence and are trying to serve two masters – Satan and God. So I want to finish with this statement because we're almost there. The true church of Jesus Christ, in these end times will rise up and be supernaturally empowered by the Holy Spirit to live godly lives in the midst of a corrupt and evil generation. This end time church will not compromise the truths of God's Word or quench the Spirit of God. It will be mighty in word and deeds and triumphant in the final days of this present earth. Bro. Gary and I like to call these churches - which Fortress and our network of Disciplemaker churches are a part of - The Remnant Church Movement. So, the last faithful remnant churches found on earth are going to make a final stand for Christ against overwhelming odds in the natural just before He comes back. And you know when He does return, He makes war with the forces of hell and its vast number of human puppet minions and is victorious. "

"Hallelujah!" shouts a fired up Tommy with his dad grinning and nodding in agreement.

"There's the downed tree and fence, Charlie."

"Yeah, I see it, Ricky," replies Charlie.

Still curious, Tommy says, "Brother Ricky, one last quick question."

"Real quick, Tommy."

"I want to know what you think about there being more of these huge pitwolves. Are there more of them?"

"My hunch, Tommy, is that there are more of them, a lot more of them across Colorado, the northwest part of the United States, and other areas of the country."

"In that case, Ricky, all I got to say is so be it. Dear God, let's get this end time show on the road," says Charlie intensely.

"Pull up beside Caleb's truck over there, Charlie. We're here, guys! Let's get ready!" shouts Ricky to the men in the back of the truck through the open sliding glass window.

Chapter 5

FAITH VERSUS FEAR

8:01:17 PM, Mountain Standard Time, Thursday, 05/07/20_ _, Fortress/Double V Ranch, northeast corner of the pasture land, Golden Valley, Colorado, USA

Prior to arriving to their destination of the downed fence area, each man deals with what seems like a thousand thoughts flashing through each of their minds. Only a wide but thin jagged section of glowing orange light from the sun barely remains on the horizon. The light of day is coming to a close. Over an hour ago their lives seemed somewhat normal. Now they are dealing with the fear of not knowing what lies ahead of them, possibly pure raw danger. Just as they pull up beside Caleb's pickup by the pinned down barbed wire, the sun has faded away into the night. As the last man climbs out of the truck, each of their head flashlights are turned on. They are making sure their flashlights don't shine into each other's eyes.

Brother Ricky addresses them. "Brothers, what we are about to embark upon is a dangerous rescue mission. Make no mistake about that. We do have a good amount of firepower and plenty of flashlights to light up our path. If you feel you can't handle it, please feel free to stay in the truck." Bro. Ricky scans his men for any hint or movement of defection.

At the moment, Leon is still sweating profusely and every man is internally wrestling with his own bout of fear. Everything in Leon's flesh wants to throw in the towel and stay in the truck. But being alone and waiting by himself in the truck seems even more frightening than going on the mission. There is safety in numbers. Besides being branded a coward at least in his own mind doesn't set well for him. He knows what the book of Revelation says about cowards. He decides being with the group is the only right and honorable thing to do no matter what the cost of his personal

101

welfare.

At Fortress a deep bond exists between the brothers and sisters in the Lord there. Service and sacrifice to the Lord and to each other is a way of life on the Double V Ranch. Bro. Gary and Bro. Ricky teach that real JOY is Jesus first, Others second, and Yourself third. This is the hallmark of a Disciplemaker Church no matter which one is attended. For most people who visit one of the churches, it is what keeps them from coming back. For the people who join one, it is the glue that keeps them there. If one's personal relationships are superficial, showing no desire for accountability to God or to others in church, then there are plenty of other churches to attend. True *koinonia* exists among the members of Fortress much like that of the early New Testament churches, and Leon loves it. He had never experienced that before coming to Fortress and isn't going to trade that for anything in the world - even if it means his own life.

When the moment is up, all are committed to bringing back their brothers in the Lord to Fortress alive. Ricky still gives them another opportunity to stay behind. "As God is my witness, I will not think any less of you if you stay in the truck." Again, he pauses and waits for a few seconds, as everyone stands motionless holding tight to their decision and weapons, their eyes scanning the area.

Ricky shakes his head and says, "Okay, thank you. Now listen closely! It's imperative that every man keep his weapon pointed down and his finger off the trigger, but near on the trigger guard like this." He demonstrates the correct finger placement on his rifle. "We're all a little jumpy with the news of this dead giant pitwolf and possibly other ones that might be nearby. Point your weapon only if you see one of these creatures, and keep shooting until it doesn't move. Let's go on this mission with confidence in the Lord that He is with us every step of this journey. I know we have all been quietly praying, asking the Lord for help, strength, and protection. Remember, we have people back at the church praying for us at this moment. Let's keep it together, because we don't need any accidents or casualties due to friendly fire in our midst. As we travel to where Caleb, John, and Forrest are, we are keeping our mouths shut and our eyes and ears wide open. Understand?"

All the men agree.

Ricky continues. "I'll take point, and, Charlie, you're the caboose. Everybody, watch for my hand signals. If you see me make a fist, that means stop and do a 360 with your eyes. One last thing. Everyone, check your firearm and make sure it is loaded and the safety is off. He pauses for a second as he watches the men take off their safeties on their individual weapons. Remember, there may be other giant pitwolves. Be on the alert because this animal is a killing machine and more cunning than the ordinary wolf or any other animal for that matter." The men follow his instructions. "Is everything clear?" Ricky pauses for a moment.

Everyone says, "Yes, sir."

Charlie adds, "I think we're ready, Rick, in Jesus' name!"

"Then, in His name, let's move out, men."

As the team journeys to the three men in the box canyon, the earlier orange light of the sun has been replaced with a clear dark night and an emerging full moon. In the minds of the rescue team, this only helps to conjure up creepy images of wolves howling at the moon or viciously attacking a downed prey in their food chain and feasting on its bloody carcass. Some reflect momentarily upon their youth about scenes from a movie where werewolves prowled the forest on a full moon, like tonight, in search of their next victim. But as they start to enter the box canyon, the tall pine trees temporarily hide the position of the canyon cliffs and much of the canyon basin below. Later on, the moonlight dances on a stand of smaller pine trees. As the rescue team hikes through them, they provide shape shifting, shadowy images that want to stoke the fires of each man's fearful imagination. When Leon Wilson, in the middle of the group, hears and then sees what turns out to be a rabbit quickly rustling through the woods, he has to bite his lip really hard to keep from screaming to the top of his lungs from fear surging through his body. He knows it is miracle for him not to squeeze the trigger on his rifle as he tastes the salty blood coming from his lower lip. The noise made by the same rabbit also scares 18-year-old Tommy Wilcox so badly that he pees in his pants. But he isn't about to let anyone know about his embarrassing accident if he can help it.

Twenty five minutes into their mission under the golden canopy of another small area of aspen trees, blurry images of high yellow, reddish, and orange flames produced by four fires could be made out by the rescue team. The fires bring at least a partial sigh of relief for Brother Ricky and the others. He has already lost one son in his lifetime, and the thought of losing another would be almost unbearable. Now the two groups of men are separated from each other by only 300 yards. But the 25 degree angle incline is taxing the rescue team. But they are running on adrenaline and the prayers of those back at Fortress. From a physical and psychological standpoint, the fires provide a sense of added security for each man by the intense heat radiating from the stacked logs and branches and by lighting up a portion of the upper box canyon. Even though Ricky and the rest of the men are a relatively short distance away from the three men, no one on the rescue team dares to say a word. The threat of encountering another ferocious predator along the way is still real as they maneuver through the remaining thicket of trees. This is not a time to let their guard down. Being continually vigilant is priority number one.

As the rescue team breaks through the final aspen stand into a more rocky area, they see the relieved faces of Caleb, Blackhawk, and Forrest grinning from ear to ear. But within seconds, the eyes of the men on the rescue team are locked upon the slain prehistoric looking giant pitwolf. Shock and awe grip their hearts and minds momentarily. Nevertheless, the prayers of the intercessors and saints back at Fortress can be felt by every man in the box canyon and they shake the fear off by the grace of God. During the rescue mission, each man in his own way has prayed, made peace with God, and has come to grips with the reality of his own frailty and mortality. Each man realizes that only God is his ultimate defender and protector in this dangerous situation. Even Leon's extra heavy perspiration has subsided, and a supernatural peace from God alone comforts him.

If not for the prayers of the numerous Christians back at Fortress, the hearts and minds of the rescue team members would be crippled with overwhelming fear from looking at this monstrous, hideous beast. It truly possesses the jaws and claws of death. It just doesn't seem real. By God's grace, however, they are able to cast off the cloak of fear that Lucifer's demons have tried to place on each of them. A fear so great that normally it could have easily immobilized them. Through the supernatural power of Christ, mighty intercessory prayer coming forth from Fortress is defeating the enemy of their souls and his fear tactics.

As the rescue team members embrace their three brothers in the Lord, Ricky takes one long look at the giant pitwolf and knows someone has cooked this thing up in a top secret bio lab. He then starts scanning the immediate area around them for signs of more giant pitwolves. His semi-automatic rifle is an early pre-ban Belgian Fal in a .308 caliber, with a 20 round clip, and a custom 3x9 military grade wide-angle night vision scope. Ricky also has a smaller military grade thermal imaging scope attached to the right of the night vision scope. Like a boy scout, he is prepared on this occasion. Ricky feels led by the Lord to methodically scan the top of the canyon, so he turns on his thermal imaging scope. After a minute, he can't believe it, but he spots four thermal images at the top of the high, rugged cliffs on the northern side of the canyon. He switches to the night vision mode and spots a larger male giant pitwolf seemingly bigger than the dead one in their midst. Ricky estimates this giant wolf to be 400 pounds plus. It is looking down on the rescue team. Ricky assumes he has to be the alpha male. Beside him are three smaller giant pitwolves. The other three pitwolves, Ricky believes, are females that run in his pack. Caleb sees and knows what his dad is doing. His dad makes eye contact with him and discreetly flashes four fingers to him. Charlie, who also senses what Ricky is doing, instantly takes in a deep breath and slowly lets it out, as he realizes how dangerous things truly are at this time. Ricky then notices that Charlie has seen the flashing, so he winks at Charlie, who winks back at him. Charlie, Caleb, and Ricky understand that it's best to keep this matter under wraps.

Blackhawk has been examining his rifle the whole time with his back to Ricky trying to figure out why it failed him. He suddenly turns around, walks over to Ricky, and whispers, "We have to go real soon. There are more of them above the canyon floor." Ricky rolls his eyes in disbelief, amazed at John's uncanny spiritual gifts and insights from the Lord. Instinctively, Charlie and Caleb realize that John knows the pitwolves are above the canyon floor.

Caleb casually walks over to John and whispers, "How did you know that more pitwolves were at the top of the canyon? Because again you're blowing me away with your gift."

"It's real simple, Caleb." Blackhawk grins as he explains with mock sincerity, "I saw them earlier before the rescue team came with the eyes of my ancestors. You know I'm a Sioux Indian. My right eye is like an eagle's eye so I can see far away. My left eye is like a cat's so I can see in the dark. So when I focus them together really hard, I can see far away in the dark." Caleb shakes his head in frustration, as he grins at John and mutters under his breath. John then slides back over to Caleb and adds jokingly, "It's a Christian Indian thing. You wouldn't understand," then walks away laughing quietly.

Brother Ricky calmly and coolly brings the celebration to halt. In a gentle but firm voice, he says, "Gentlemen, we are packing this beast out of here on the double."

While Ricky is talking, Charlie hands Caleb, Blackhawk, and Forrest head flashlights from his small backpack, and the three men secure the lights on their heads.

"Before we go, I want every man to double check his rifle to make sure it is loaded and the safety is off," instructs Ricky to his church members.

Ricky hands Caleb the sling to his Colt LE901-16S, AR-10 with a 20 round clip loaded with .308 rounds that Caleb's wife, Ashley, had given to him the past Christmas. The AR-10 is also equipped with a high-powered Fenix flashlight attached to the left side of the barrel on the forearm piece. Ricky had it on his back as they left the pickup. Caleb has two extra clips in quick release magazine pouches on a GI belt that Ricky had worn around his waist. Brother Ricky couldn't find his GI belt with pouches when he went to the lodge, so he just grabbed two extra clips to his rifle and stuck one in each of his front pockets.

After Ricky shoulders his son's rifle, he directs Caleb, "Now give me grandpa's old 30-06 pump." He checks it over quickly. "Now you just watch our backs, Son."

Caleb breathes a sigh of relief as he checks the AR-10 rifle over quickly, turns on the high-powered flashlight on the rifle, and makes sure it is ready to go.

In Caleb's mind, it is a race against the clock to get back to the property line of the Double V ranch, with four giant pitwolves only 500 feet above them on the rocky cliffs of the canyon. Even though he is a former highly decorated Navy SEAL officer trained in countless hours in the use of the AR-10 and other black rifles, in his mind it doesn't level the playing field against the formidable and unpredictable nature of four beasts from hell at the top of the canyon. Possibly the creatures are coming down rapidly at this very moment to stalk them. His prayer is that they can get safely back to their trucks on the property of the Double V Ranch.

Ricky, hyper-focused, tells Tommy, Leon and his brother Tim, and the newest church member James Thornton to put out the fires while everyone stands guard. He tells the team, "We don't need to take a chance of a forest fire breaking out here on top of this pitwolf situation. A dread of extinguishing the fires runs through the minds of all the men, as Leon, Tim, and James cover the last of all the embers in dirt. Nevertheless, the facts that there are three more men going back to the trucks, more firearm power, flashlights, and the light of the full moon are sources of comfort, as the men prepare to return to their pickups.

Brother Ricky then tells Blackhawk, "Here, John. You take my semi-automatic rifle and these two extra clips. Put one in each front pocket."

"John grabs it with his right hand, admires it, and says, "Brother Ricky, this is a sweet rifle and a good gun to have on a night like this."

"Yeah, I know, Blackhawk, and you're just the man to use it. So now take point so you can put that sixth sense the Lord gave you and go to work. I'm going to be slightly behind you and to the right."

"You got it, Brother Ricky."

"John, I'll pack out your rifle so your movements won't be hindered."

John then hands Ricky his .300 Winchester magnum. Blackhawk knows Ricky checked his rifle, but he double checks it himself to make sure it is ready to fire. He puts the two clips in his front pockets. Ricky runs his left arm and head through John's sling so that his rifle is angled diagonally across his back.

John tells him, "If worse comes to worst, you have one shot you can get off with my rifle. The safety is off."

"Thanks, John. Hopefully I won't need to."

He then tells Caleb, "Son, you take the tail end position and watch our backs for any giant pitwolves trailing us."

"Yes, sir."

"In the meantime, I'll work the front on the right side with Blackhawk. Charlie, you position yourself on the left back side just in front of Caleb."

Everyone is following Ricky's directives without hesitation. Ricky then says, "Tommy, you and Forrest are strong young bucks, so, boys, man up on carrying out this dead beast. Forrest, check out that long medium-sized branch over there by the big rock. It should do the trick."

Tommy walks to the branch and makes sure it is stout. He announces, "Yeah, it's good and solid, Brother Ricky."

"Good. Here's some parachute cord." Ricky pulls the cord out of his jeans pocket to tie the pitwolf by his feet to the branch.

"When we get going, Leon, you and the other men rotate in there often on the pole as a third man and as those boys need a break. Don't talk unless it is absolutely necessary, like when switching out on the pole. Keep it to a whisper. Caleb, if you see or hear something, let us know. Guys, remember, make sure you don't pull that trigger unless you know what you are shooting at. I don't want to do an unnecessary funeral in my church. Also, remember to watch my hand signals and listen for Caleb if he hears or sees anything. Are we clear?"

Everyone responds, "Yes, sir!"

"Then let's high tail it out of here as soon as the dead beast is tied up,"

Within a few minutes they hit the trail back to the pickups. Every man's senses are on high alert with the reality that giant pitwolves might be in the area. Ricky, Caleb, and Charlie know for a fact that more pitwolves are close by because Ricky saw them. But Blackhawk had supernaturally seen them by the Spirit of God earlier before Ricky saw them. Ricky made the decision not to tell the whole group, because it would not be of any benefit to confirm that four other pitwolves had been spotted and in fact it might have negative consequences. After about twenty minutes, drenched in sweat, they quickly get back to the pickups in the cool of the night. Thank God it had been a downhill walk. Tommy and Forrest are especially exhausted from carrying the heavy giant pitwolf most of the way back to the truck compared to the other men. Its body is beginning to stink really badly from the dried blood and rigor mortis setting in. Blackhawk, Forrest, and Tommy pick up the animal and throw it in the back of Caleb's truck. Even though they cover it up with a old canvas tarp, the smell and the flies are all over the dead animal. Nobody wants to ride in the back of Caleb's truck with the dead beast. Forrest, Blackhawk, and Caleb all pile in his truck, glad their hair raising ordeal has come to an end. Before they start the ride back to Fortress, Tommy tells his dad he wants to ride in the back this time with the guys. He hops in the pickup and sits on the right side of the bed of the truck with his left arm on top of the cab and his right hand holding his shotgun. Leon accidently drops some of his ammunition on the ground and picks it up. He is the last guy in the pickup. He sits close to Tommy on the floor of the pickup.

Suddenly Leon smells something and loudly says, "What is that smell, Tommy? It's coming from your direction. It smells like urine."

Tommy, ashamed that he had peed in his pants, says, "Oh, wow! You know, I do kind of smell like pee, along with a bunch of other rotten, funky smells. It's from that raunchy, stinkin' dead monster I helped put in back of Caleb's truck. See, Leon, I've got some its blood on my hands and some other bodily fluids on me from picking up that heavy sucker and carrying it."

"Well, Tommy, no offense, but that animal's blood, bodily fluids and the smell of death is all over you. I have to scoot away. It's making me sick to my stomach."

Just as Caleb and Charlie fire up their truck engines to go back to Fortress, loud howling of at least several giant pitwolves can be heard from a distance. As a safeguard, the men in the back of Charlie's truck instantly point their rifles, shotguns, and flashlights in all directions as they start their return to Fortress.

Tim intensely and excitedly tells his younger brother Leon, "See there, Leon, I told you there were more of the them nearby."

In a tired and shaky though somewhat sarcastic tone, Leon says, "Yeah, Tim, I'm so thrilled that you were right."

Charlie's and Ricky's windows are down and they hear the howls. Charlie yells out through the sliding back rear window, "Hang on tight, guys! We're out of here!"

Before the men get back to Fortress, Brother Ricky radios Brother Gary about the good news. He also tells him that he thinks younger children don't need to see the beast, because they might have nightmares. Ultimately, however, it will be left up to each set of parents as to what they think best.

Minutes pass and the lights from the buildings at Fortress draw ever closer while shouts of "Hallelujah," "Thank you, Jesus," and "Praise the Lord" echo through the stillness of the night as nine grateful men return safely home.

As the trucks roll into Fortress, all the people cheer that everyone made it back alive and in one piece. Wives of the men who went on the rescue mission are crying for joy that their husbands are safe. Caleb's wife Ashley lived for years with the possibility that her Caleb may never return alive from a secret mission. She is relieved he made it back unharmed as she wipes the tears from her eyes. Brother Gary hurriedly runs over and talks with Ricky. Gary then talks to Ricky's wife Melody and Gary's wife Mary Anne for several minutes. The two women quickly leave in a car after they greet the men. Melody is extremely grateful to Lord that everyone returned safely home, especially her husband Ricky and her son Caleb. After celebrating their return a short time, some of the mothers leave with their small children.

Then Bro. Gary tells everyone else to quiet down. Everyone who remains is eager and curious about what the dead beast looks like. Before Bro. Ricky pulls the canvas tarp off the giant pitwolf in the back of Caleb's truck, he raises his hands above his head and tells the crowd they cannot allow smart phone pictures of this animal to get out into the outside world. He informs them that they must get a hold of Sheriff Barnes and see what he says. Bro. Ricky whispers to Forrest, an excellent photographer, to get his professional 35mm camera so they can have photos of the pitwolf for Barnes. Forrest leaves to get it, but not until he gets a warm embrace from Brenda Lee, his fiancée.

Ricky holds his hand up to get everyone's attention and loudly says, "People of Fortress, I want you to know that God has allowed this event to occur tonight for a purpose. Exactly what for I don't know. We have to warn and submit to the local authority about the events of this evening. Unfortunately, the killing of this nightmarish beast could turn Fortress into a three ring circus, which is something we don't want. But Jesus is the Lord of Fortress, so we must all bow our knee to Him at this time and His will on earth. Does everyone understand?"

Everyone agrees except for one young teenage boy. He shouts, "Wait a minute!" A tall thin boy with straight, shoulder length brown hair parted above the middle of his right eye steps forward.

"I got something to say!"

It's Dr. Stanton's 16 year old son, Thomas Joseph Smith Stanton IV. He begins speaking with a haughty attitude. "Everyone knows my dad here, Dr. Stanton. Well, I also want everyone to know I've studied a little biology myself. I've read a few books on wildlife biology and studied wolves. I want everyone to know I'm really sick of all this bogus prophecy hype, fear techniques, and mind control. I have really hated almost every minute living in this cult-like campground because my parents believe the end of the world is coming. Folks, I can guarantee you that the big bad wolf under this tarp is just that – a big bad wolf, nothing more and nothing less. He might be bigger than an average wolf with some kind of disease or mutation that makes him look scary. But, believe me, this whole charade is to manipulate your minds into believing that it's the end of the world as we know it and Bro. Ricky and Bro. Gary have all the answers."

Bro. Gary, full of compassion, glances at Dr. Stanton and his wife Lisa, who both have their eyes to the ground and are ashamed of what their son is saying. Gary knows there is not a nicer and more godly Christian couple than the Stantons, even though they have only been saved about two years.

But their son has been pushing the limits of everybody's patience and grace. It is only because of his parents that Bro. Gary and Bro. Ricky have endured Thomas' sporadic episodes of teenage rebellion. Thomas is at the top of everyone's prayer list at Fortress. But time is running out for Thomas' stay at Fortress.

Brother Ricky calmly asks Thomas if he would like to remove the tarp to let everyone see the animal. Thomas sarcastically says, "Yeah! I would love to prove you wrong!"

Thomas comes forward and grabs the tarp. Just as he is beginning to pull it off the beast, Ricky grabs his right wrist very firmly.

Thomas then yells, "Get your hand off me, you old false prophet!"

Brother Ricky calmly but firmly asks, "What will you do if it is not just an ordinary big wolf?"

In a self righteous, angry tone, Thomas replies, "Well, I would wash the dishes in the cafeteria for two weeks. That's what I would do!"

"Okay, everyone, hear that?"

Almost all of those present nod their heads and a few raise their hands. Brother Ricky instructs Thomas to go ahead and pull off the tarp. As he yanks off the tarp to look cute and to be dramatic, the rotting smell of death that had been trapped under the tarp rolls up into his nostrils and causes him to gasp for air. At the same time the color of Thomas' face instantly grows pale, as he sees the dead muscled up giant tiger-striped pitwolf. All of his senses are in overload. He screams a high-pitched sound like a terrified little girl.

Then he yells, "This thing ain't a wolf! It's a demonic creature! Oh, no, it's giving me the evil eye!" The wolf's head is bigger than a basketball. The massive head and evil looking face are positioned in the truck near the end of the tailgate right in front of where Thomas is standing. The creature's body covered in blood was laid on its right side in the 4'x 8' truckbed in a diagonal fashion due to its size. The genetically modified wolf's left eye is wide open and positioned directly at him. His mouth is frozen in place with a dried white foam around it in a growling position that perfectly shows his three inch bloody fangs. For a full five seconds, the frantic, rebellious teenager completely loses it, almost in a state of hysteria. Completely caught off guard by the reality of what he sees, Thomas runs to his parents' cabin and slams the front door, totally scared and embarrassed.

Shouts of "My God," "Oh, Lord Jesus," "These are the end times," and "Precious Jesus," fill the air. Some women and teenagers cover their noses, mouths, and eyes from the deathly stench and from total disbelief of what they are seeing. A few people are both screaming at the horrific sight of the giant wolf-like animal and laughing at the same time because of Thomas' antics and his reaction to the giant pitwolf. Some men shake their heads toward one another acknowledging the end of days is upon them.

All of Fortress' intercessors are gathered around the truck. They see this giant evil beast as a sign to pray more fervently than ever before. Each one knows if there is one dead giant pitwolf, then there have to be more. It is a major signal along with the meteorites to them that the Tribulation period is quickly coming upon the world and it seems like it might be starting in Clark County, Colorado. These people motion to one another with their prayer signal by placing the palms of their hands together, fingers pointing upwards. One of the most serious minded intercessors of all, 24-year-old Brenda Lee Kirkman, the daughter of Sister Mary Anne and Bro. Gary, feels a strong unction in her spirit to pray fervently about what is unfolding. No sooner has she sensed it than she waves her arm to the other intercessors to head to the prayer chapel. She and the others walk there under armed escort.

Of all the people that have come to be a part of Fortress and all the Disciplemaker churches, the elders Ricky, Gary, and their wives know that those called to be intercessors and the prayers they continually offer are the life blood of the ministry. These elders came to the conclusion many years before that prayer and fasting is the only way for the church to sustain itself and survive in any socioeconomic times, especially during the Tribulation period in the end times. For the Christians at Fortress it seems that intercession at this time on God's prophetic clock is needed more than ever.

The brothers and sisters of Christ gathered around the pitwolf in the pickup are asking the leaders of Fortress what this strange animal means. And what about the increasing numbers of meteorites that have been falling around them in the surrounding counties of Colorado and other states? Does it have prophetic significance? In their hearts they want to be reassured that the promise they have been given that Fortress is a city of refuge and a place of protection in the coming horrific Tribulation period is indeed true. Presently the question on everybody's mind is whether this promise extends protection from wildlife or, in this case, an apparent genetically modified dangerous beast.

Brother Gary decides to address the first two questions, "Brothers and sisters in Christ can I get your attention?" A few of the men and women are caught up in deep discussion and keep talking. He clears his throat and everyone quits talking. He repeats himself. "Brothers and sisters in Christ, tonight my brother Ricky and I are hearing three basic questions about the significance of this dead creature and the meteorites falling around us in the surrounding counties and how they will affect our lives here on the Double V Ranch and our Fortress church family. I will address the first two questions and let Brother Ricky tackle the third one."

"The one question I have heard asked over and over again this evening is whether this giant pitwolf is one of the wild beasts mentioned in Revelation 6: 7, 8. I quote from my Bible, 'And when he had opened the fourth seal, I heard the voice of the fourth beast say, Come and see. And I looked, and behold a pale horse: and his name that sat on him was Death and Hell followed him. And power was given unto them over the fourth part of the earth, to kill with sword, and with hunger, and with death, and with the beasts of the earth.'"

"My answer to the first question is that many times people think that the events just happen instantly in the book of Revelation and the other prophetic scriptures. Sometimes events do happen instantly and sometimes there is a transitioning period or the beginning stages of the events that have to take place first. Tonight just may be one of the beginning stages leading up to the fulfillment of those scriptures. One thing we know chronologically is that the killing of humans by wild beasts doesn't reach its maximum limit until the 4th seal. So with this in mind, realize that the first three seals have to precede the 4th. Now, this dead giant pitwolf may be the first of many more to come. We just don't know the number of them in this area or in the United States at this time. What many of us thought was a myth is now a reality. We also do not have large numbers of other beasts strangely attacking mankind around the globe at this time. But this one beast is not the fulfillment of Rev. 6:8 since one quarter of the earth's population has not died in a short period of time. Since none of us has seen this animal before and most of us didn't even believe in its existence until now, it stands to reason that we are possibly still in the beginning stages that lead up to the Tribulation period. Hopefully, that makes logical and biblical sense."

"The second question on everyone's mind is what about these meteorites falling around us? My first response is, thank God, none have fallen in Golden Valley or Clark County as of this time. Our intercessors and prayer warriors have been praying around the clock concerning this matter which is at the top of their prayer list. Now they have added something else of monumental importance to their prayer list - this wild beast before us and others like it still on the prowl. This terrifying specimen of pure evil and destruction must be stopped dead in its tracks. Our heartfelt prayers are with those in the surrounding counties who have suffered loss. We pray for our fellow citizens of Colorado that have had their lives impacted, no pun intended, by meteorites to varying degrees. We pray for their protection and that they will turn to Christ and away from their sins."

"What we do know is that cosmic forces play a very significant role in the prophetic scriptures of the book of Revelation and Matthew 24 and Luke 21 and other scriptures in the end times. Our own Forrest Johnson is a meteorite expert and has a website devoted to this subject called *Meteorites Impacting Mankind.* He deals with the history of meteorites, a tracking of all known significant size ones hitting the earth on a day-to-day basis, and the future as it relates to meteorites and other cosmic forces involving planet earth. He has done extensive research on the subject from a scientific, historical, and of course a biblical prophetic standpoint. He concludes, as well as Bro. Ricky and myself, that meteorites and other events in outer space play key roles in Bible prophecy as we have touched upon in our books. This is the reason he was first divinely led here because he had read some of our books on prophecy. He wanted to talk to Ricky and me about what's coming. He knows as well as any astute student of prophecy that cosmic forces are going to increase before Christ returns at the end of the

Tribulation. That's just a given fact, so what we are experiencing in Colorado and, to a smaller degree, in other states may be a sign of more to come. We will be having Forrest do a seminar on these things in the very near future."

"The third question which has been heavy on everyone's minds since the prayer meeting tonight concerns the issue of this giant pitwolf and how it relates to this property. We all know that Lucifer likes to play with our minds from time to time. So, Ricky, could you answer the third question and I'm going to phrase it this way in two parts. Could we, the four elders, be wrong concerning Fortress being a place of refuge in the Tribulation period?"

"I'd be glad to address that, Gary. Folks, it's a serious and honest question that begs to be answered. Could Bro. Gary, Sister Mary Anne, my wife Melody, and I have missed it concerning this place having God's divine hand of protection on it? Granted, we are human and do err, but I know in my spirit that we heard from God that He will divinely protect us as long as the people of Fortress are here and we honor him. There is no doubt in my mind whatsoever. This is not a positive confession, but a clear rhema from the Holy Spirit that was spoken to each of the elders' hearts prior to the formation of Fortress. Brother Gary and I are Southern California boys who left the only life we had known. We left successful careers, good friends, and family to come here because we heard the voice of God speaking to our hearts to leave. Our dear wives also heard that same still small voice of God to relocate to Golden Valley on Melody's family land.

Leon Wilson, still a little shaken from the whole ordeal of tonight, shouts out to Ricky. "Bro. Ricky, let me play the devil's advocate for a moment. How do you explain this dead prehistoric looking beast in the back of Caleb's truck?"

Ricky, laughing a little, says, "Leon, let me remind you whose property this dead giant pitwolf was first discovered on and where it was killed."

Leon hesitates for a split second as if embarrassed and says, "On Pete's property. Sorry, Bro. Ricky, you got a good point there."

"Folks, as of now, not one meteorite has hit the property of Fortress, let alone Clark County. Now, I can't make any guarantees on Clark County, but I will promise you the land where our church Fortress is located, the Double V Ranch, is safe. You can rest assured of that or you can call Gary and me false prophets. Now, with that being said, I'd like to say that we are in one of the most remote areas in Colorado. It is true that wolves have been on this property many times through the years. Melody's dad, the Big Swede, and his father, and his father before him killed wolves on this property. Other predators such as grizzly bears, coyotes, and mountain lions have also been on this same ground. That's just a natural consequence of living in this basically untamed country of the Rockies. But this giant pitwolf seems to be right out of a horror movie, like young Thomas experienced a while ago. That's what's got everybody shaken here. In my heart, I know that God will divinely protect this property against this kind of animal or any native predators that start acting weird. What I am referring to is wild predators acting like they are being manipulated by demonic forces. The elders of Fortress are also resolute in the belief that God will supernaturally protect us against evil men that would try to come here and do us harm."

"Why will God preserve the people of Fortress here in Clark County?" Ricky continues. "Because our mission as an end time community of brothers and sisters in Christ includes intercessory prayer, evangelism, and discipleship. These are our three main ministry objectives. But it doesn't end there because we need to manifest our God to a dying world. As the people of the living God, we do this by manifesting His love, His character, the truths of His Word and His power to the lost. And that is something we have always tried to do and will continue to do until Christ comes back!" Ricky shouts, "Maranatha!" Amens are returned in the midst of Fortress members huddled around him and Bro. Gary.

"As I look around, I see almost all the men and a few women are armed here. So we have taken some precautions and that's alright. Tomorrow I plan on taking a thorough flight around this property and the county in our helicopter with Brother Gary and Blackhawk, our wildlife expert, and hopefully Sheriff Barnes. I know there are some other questions, but you'll have to hold them. I know everyone has been in prayer. Please continue in the same mode tonight and in the coming days. A life of prayer is vital to keeping Fortress and the entire Disciplemaker Network of Churches united, strong, and in the center of God's will for our lives. Also please keep this event under wraps until Sheriff Barnes tells us otherwise. Bro. Gary and I are going to meet with the deacons before Sheriff Barnes gets here. One last thing. Please do not venture off the property of the Double V Ranch. You know that barbed wire goes completely around the perimeter of this ranch. Do not step beyond that boundary, because I can't guarantee your protection if you do. I'm dead serious! Make sure your children thoroughly understand this reality. Back to you, Gary."

"Thanks, Rick. For now, for the peace of our church family, you guys are free to carry sidearms or other firearms here at Fortress until we can assess all the facts. In my heart I also believe the Lord has promised His hand of protection on this place. I don't doubt that for a moment. But for the comfort level of our members, I think we should allow people to carry their guns for now. Are you good with that, Ricky?"

"Yes, that's fine for now, but I would suggest everyone please keep firearm safety at the forefront of your minds. Ricky, I know there are things we still need to do, but I think it would be to our spiritual benefit if we held each other's hands as a sign of unity and pray about this evening. I would like Caleb, John, and Forrest to pray about this ordeal tonight and God's continual protection on us at Fortress, but also for the surrounding area of Golden Valley and Clark County."

"That sounds like a winner to me," Ricky agrees.

"Fine then. Caleb, would you please start us off?"

"Yes, of course, Bro. Gary. Dear Lord we know that all good things originate from You. We also know that the Devil came to kill, steal, and destroy. I just see this giant pitwolf as an animal from the pit of hell. I pray that You would keep Your hand on everyone here at Fortress, that your hand of protection and provision would rest upon us. Give us Your guidance and keep us diligent in prayer and about the task at hand for us to complete Your will for our lives and for this ministry. I stand in agreement with my parents and my aunt and uncle, who forsook their former way of life to come here to my grandfather's land to carry out your vision for an end time purpose. Be with my good friend Pete Watson, who's new in the Lord, and his sweet wife Molly, who's teetering on accepting You. Use the loss of their champion blue-ribbon bull in some positive way. May Your will be accomplished in all of our lives, in Jesus Christ' name. Amen."

"Oh Great Creator, Great Spirit, the One and true God of the Universe, I confess to the ends of the earth Your Word is true. I thank You for sending Your Jewish Son to die on a cross to save a lost Sioux Indian boy like me twenty five years ago on a reservation in Montana. Bro. Crawford and Bro. Kirkman are for real Christians who dearly love You. I believe in their mission, but I also know You sent me here on a divine mission to Fortress. I feel Your presence when I step inside the borders of this property and I miss it when I leave this place to go into town or elsewhere. I don't believe for a second that this demonic creature from hell can step on this property at Fortress. Keep Your mighty hand on this city of refuge for these end times so that we can fulfill Your mission for our lives. In the name of Jesus I pray."

"Sweet Lord, thank You for bringing us through this ordeal tonight. I thank you that You can give us victory over our flesh and fear that sometimes wants to grip our hearts. I thank You for my two older brothers in the Lord who were cool and calm under pressure as a giant pitwolf charged us. I thank You for the prayers of the good people here at Fortress praying for us. And I want to thank everyone on the rescue team who bravely ventured out there to the box canyon tonight. All of them are heroes in my mind. That took a lot of nerve and guts to do that. And, Dear Lord, I pray that You would be with young Thomas and that he would know people speak the truth around here, that you are the real deal. Touch his heart. I was just like him when I was his age." Everyone says a loud amen. "In Christ's name I pray."

Bro. Ricky shouts out to the remaining people surrounding the truck, "If you want one more peak at this monster sized pitwolf come on because there are some things that we need to do quickly." Most of the people form a line to get one last glance at the animal, even though the stench is almost unbearable. As feisty, six-year-old Frankie Donovan passes by the dead giant pitwolf, he scrunches up his face, punches the animal in the nose, and says, "You ain't so bad, you big old wolf." Frankie then pulls his right fist up to his mouth and blows on it like he's just knocked the wolf out. He then smells his fist and says, "Pee-yoo! He stinks bad! Yuck! I'm out of here!" Everyone watching just chuckles.

Chapter 6

CI MADA/ADAMIC

When the last person views the wolf, Bro. Ricky announces they are now having a leadership/deacon meeting in Charlie's garage. Gary starts rounding up David Schilling and Max Bruno who are both deacons. They, along with some other men, are armed with pump action shotguns with 00 buckshot and have been escorting some of the members back to their cabins and to the prayer chapel. Ricky tells Caleb to drive his truck into Charlie's garage. Charlie, Blackhawk, and Ashley Crawford, Caleb's wife - a deaconess - walk inside the building and start closing the metal roll-up garage doors.

Ashley is the only deaconess so far at Fortress. She has a degree in accounting and handles many of the business aspects of the ministry. Her dad is Irish and her mom is Italian. She favors her mom with her big brown expressive eyes, olive skin, and dark brown hair which is usually pulled back into a ponytail. She is big-boned and 5 foot, 11 inches tall just like her mom. Ashley doesn't have a model's figure or outstanding facial features, but she is still pleasantly attractive. Her more radiant inner spiritual beauty, leadership ability, and good sense of humor always shine forth to those around her. Both older and younger women are always drawn to her. Having two older brothers, both career officers in the Navy, Ashley was a tomboy growing up, doing whatever they did. Athleticism runs in her family. She achieved a second degree black belt in karate by age 13. Being very athletic and tall had earned her a basketball scholarship to Maryland State University. She homeschools Caleb's and her two teenage boys, Andrew, age 15 and Stephen, 14, and four other children at Fortress. Discipleship and intercession are two things she has become very passionate about, especially in the last five years. She is a cancer survivor and loves the beauty of the ranch and the Rocky Mountain surroundings. But most of all she is thankful for Caleb being around and not halfway around the world always fighting radical terrorists or two-bit dictator regimes. Ashley is a serious Christian who whole heartedly believes in the vision of Fortress and the Disciplemaker Network of Churches.

Fortress is the mother church that her in-laws and the Kirkmans started years ago in Los Angeles. Ricky, Melody, Gary and Mary Anne are the elders who oversee all the Disciplemaker churches. Ashley also endorses whole heartedly the Omega Remnant Church Movement which is a broader base of like-minded churches. The Kirkmans and Crawfords are on the ORCM leadership board that oversees thousands of spirit and truth led churches worldwide.

Bro. Ricky is curious about the weight of the pitwolf. So Charlie pulls out an old farm scale from the corner of the garage. Caleb, Blackhawk, Ricky, and Ashley each grab a leg of the wolf's stiff body and put it on the scale. Charlie works the scale and says, "John, you were right on the money. This thing weighs 372 pounds."

Caleb says, "Charlie, this thing is an antique. Is it accurate?"

"Yeah, I calibrated it myself. These scales are old, but they are accurate.

Gary, David, and Max enter through the side door and see the animal on the scale. Gary asks, "How much does it weigh?"

Ashley shouts, "This big wolfdog weighs in at whopping 372 pounds."

All three respond, "WOW!" in unrehearsed harmony.

"Wow is right," agrees Ricky. "What some of you guys don't know is that the night we were there, I spotted four more of these creatures on top of the cliff's ridge above the box canyon with my thermal imaging and night vision scopes. In fact, one of the giant pit wolves on the ridge looked bigger than this one."

When Ricky says that, it is so quiet that one can almost hear a pin drop in the garage. Everyone knows that the seriousness of the situation has gone up a notch as solemn looks appears on all their faces.

Ricky pauses for a second and then goes on to say, "The other three pit wolves were smaller than this dead one. But make no mistake, they were still very huge and are extremely dangerous."

"Oh, my word!" gasps Charlie Wilcox. "There are some out there bigger than this one!"

Ashley, confident in God's faithfulness, voices . "Dad, this kind of puts us in a very defensive position here at Fortress, but I know God has a solution."

Bro. Gary says, "Ricky, you and I were offensive players in football and we liked to make things happen."

"Yes, that is true," replies Ricky.

Caleb glibly speaks up. "Uncle Gary, as a middle linebacker on the football team at the Naval Academy, my job was to stop the advancement of the opposing team on the field."

"Well, in that case, I'm glad we're all the same team," as Gary smiles. Everyone laughs. Gary then goes on to say, "The point I'm trying to make is God is in control like Ashley said. I'm sure we all can agree on that. Everyone is stressed, so laughter is a welcome relief. So for another stress reliever, Gary decides to lightly pull on Charlie's chain. Having known Charlie for over thirty years and knowing how obsessive he is about keeping track of all his tools, equipment, and supplies in his care, Gary says, "Here is what I propose. Let Charlie sift through the mess in the electronic section of the warehouse and try to find that inexpensive microchip reader."

Charlie, knowing the game Gary is playing, rolls his eyes and acts like he is perturbed. He says in a pretend gruff voice, "There won't be any need for sifting. I know exactly where it is. I'll be back in a minute." Everybody just lets out a big belly laugh this time. Gary and Charlie are always playing some kind of comical routine on one another. Everyone knows Charlie is Mr. Organized and runs a tight ship on the ministry's tools, equipment, and supplies.

Charlie Wilcox had been an old faithful friend and successful general contractor working for Kirkman and Kirkman Real Estate Law Firm in Los Angeles for years. He did not work for them exclusively but had worked for them on numerous projects through the years as they needed him. The Kirkmans had invested heavily in Southern California real estate through the years of economic boom, both residentially and commercially. They had kept Charlie and his crews of workers repairing, remodeling, restoring, maintaining, and building houses and commercial buildings from the ground up. Charlie had tackled everything under the sun from concrete work, carpentry, fine woodworking, roofing, electrical, plumbing, and landscaping, to name a few. He could also repair appliances and any kind of motor. His son Tommy had the same kind of aptitude. Charlie's family, like Gary's and Ricky's, came from Okie roots and had migrated to the greener pastures of California during the Great Depression and Dust Bowl Era. It was a distant, but real tie that bound them together. All three families had originally come from humble circumstances in Oklahoma and had prospered in Southern California.

Shane Kirkman and his son Gary had always been fair, honest, and giving toward Charlie, as he had been with them. Charlie did excellent work and he demanded that from his workers. In 1995, Charlie had almost broken his back falling off a ladder. He had to turn away many jobs and lay off most of his workers until he could get up and moving. In the meantime, Charlie's bills kept running up. But the Kirkmans made sure the family had plenty of food and paid all their bills for four months until he regained full use of his back. The Kirkmans had offered up a lot of prayers for Charlie to regain full use of his back. The Kirkmans never once asked for any money in return. Charlie tried to pay them back several times, but they refused. They just told him to help someone else in need when he could. This is what he practiced on a regular basis, helping and giving to those less fortunate while trying not to draw attention to himself. Gary had led Charlie to the Lord while he, Charlie, and Ricky were fishing off the coast of California near Catalina Island one summer Saturday many years ago.

"From what I remember, Ricky, you told me the one Charlie is getting is just a basic RFID scanner. Any veterinarian supply stores sells them, correct Ricky?"

"That is correct. I also want you guys to know I have a very advanced microchip reader. Max and David built it for me from a copy of blue prints from a certain individual I won't mention. So what I'm about to tell all of you goes no further then these walls." Everyone agrees. "The person who gave me the plans got them off of a Russian double agent working for our government. This double agent ended up dead soon after he handed over the reader blue prints to the person who gave them to me. The plans to this invention were kept top secret. As a top high-tech defense contractor for the U.S. military, my company specialized in a variety of high-grade military electronic technology. We built the advanced reader, but we could never get our hands on a newly discovered very rare metal used in the sleeper chip, along with a plan on how to build it. The rare metal is only located somewhere in the frozen tundra of Siberia. It was crucial to the production of the high-tech chip that we called the sleeper chip. We tried for several years to acquire the rare metal, but all leads eventually dried up, leading us nowhere. Great time and millions of dollars were spent to locate the rare metal, but plans to build an alternative sleeper chip were finally abandoned. Project Sleeping Beauty, as it was known to a highly secretive black ops group within the Pentagon, was laid to rest."

Max, leaning against the garage door, whispers to David, "I can't believe Ricky is talking about that classified information. But that's his call."

In a bit more of an empathic voice, David responds, "Well, I kind of understand where he is coming from sharing this information. I trust Ricky's judgment."

"Oh, me too. Don't get me wrong," whispers Max. "The good news is that I haven't seen that toy since Ricky showed it to me over at the lodge a couple of years ago. And I would love to get my hands back on it. This is so strange because I was just thinking about it last week for the first time in years."

David whispers back, "That is weird. Maybe it was kind of a prophetic thing from the Holy Spirit of what was to come."

"Yeah, maybe so, Dave."

"Anyway, I can't wait to put my hands on it either and check it out again. Because I bet you anything that beast over there has a sleeper chip in it."

Max responds in a low voice, "There's no doubt in my mind it does."

Dr. Max Bruno and Dr. David Shilling had been Ricky Crawford's top two electrical design engineers in his research and development department of his company commonly called SEC. SEC, the Spartan Electronics Corporation, had been the premier high-tech military defense contractor to the different branches of service. Ricky, like any successful CEO in any the high-tech corporation, knew that R&D was the heart of any progressive company. He also knew that in order to stay on top of the cutting edge, you had to have the right people. He knew that Max and David were key to the success of his high-tech business in the defense industry.

Max and David had been friends in college since their graduate assistant days. Both had graduated with PhDs in electrical engineering from Stanfield University in California. Ricky had managed to squeeze in the time to get his Master's degree in Electrical Engineering from University of Southwest California when he first started up his company. But SEC quickly mushroomed into the premier defense contractor in the industry, and he never had the time to complete his PhD. But he was a voracious reader and could quickly absorb technical books. He was able to comprehend and remember complex information he read in electrical engineering, physics, aerodynamics, and other science textbooks. He didn't have a photographic memory, but it often seemed like he did. He had excellent short-term and long-term memory skills. Ricky was on the same academic page as Max and David and exceeded them in certain areas. He also loved to design and work with his hands when he wasn't negotiating defense contracts, golfing, or dining with congressmen, senators, generals, and admirals. All three engineers had numerous patents in the world of high technology. He trusted Max and David completely. They had been more than employees at his company; they were two dear friends. He had personally led them both to Christ, and he had mentored and discipled them in the Lord. Both had been well compensated for their ideas and inventions. They in turn knew Ricky trusted them and had their best interest at heart. He gave them a lot of freedom in the R&D department at SEC, which they loved.

Gary says, "Ricky, did you put that gadget in that maximum high security safe you designed?"

"Yeah, I did, and I need to go the lodge and get it," Ricky whispers in Gary and Caleb's ears. He then steps out of the garage, quickly driving to his house called the Lodge. In the meantime, David and Max are excited to use the basic microchip reader to see if they can get a readout on the beast. They both know that this huge pitwolf is too big and freaky to be the natural offspring of a pitbull and wolf or any other animal found presently in nature. Huge fangs protruding from the animal's muzzle are another dead giveaway. Soon Charlie comes back with the basic model and hands it to Max. Max looks at it for a second and hits a few buttons. He thoroughly scans the wolf three times from the tip of his nose to the end of his tail. Nothing happens, which is what David and Max expected all along. Gary then tells everyone what Ricky is up to.

A few minutes pass before Bro. Ricky comes in and says, "I bet you didn't get a readout, Max, did you?"

"Nope. I wasn't expecting one."

Ricky hands the high-tech microchip reader to David and says, "Let's see what happens now."

David is excited to once again handle the reader but is pretending to be sarcastic, saying, "Yeah, this one probably won't get a readout either," as he winks at Ricky. He then hits several buttons. He starts at the tip of the tail and thoroughly scans the massive body. Just as he reaches the top of the animal's skull, a loud beeping sound is heard. David yells, "Bingo!"

Max shouts, "Eureka! You hit the mother lode, my friend."

Ricky asks David, "What does the read out say?"

"It's just a bunch of random symbols, Russian letters and numbers, until I press the encryption translation code into English on the screen, which is a feature I added to this instrument. It takes a few minutes to break the code. I'll let you know when there is data on the screen." Less than a minute passes by, but it seems like an eternity to David and Max. Everyone in the metal building is silent and waiting in great anticipation. "There," says David with a sigh of relief written across his face. "Now I can read it. Oh my gosh! Ricky, Max, guess who's behind this?"

Ricky says, "My best hunch says it's Ci Mada Union Laboratories with their ties to AAE."

David asks, "Max, how about you?"

"I'm with Ricky. It's got to be Ci Mada, that special black ops type of mad science lab with ties to AAE."

"Yes, indeed it is," affirms David.

Gary adds, "As Ricky mentioned, AAE has ties to Ci Mada Union. It's a subsidiary of AAE, which stands for Alpine Advanced Electronics, owned by the new high-tech guru of the 21st century, Wolfgang Martin, in Geneva, Switzerland."

Blackhawk asks, "Brother Ricky, isn't he that multi-billionaire you were telling me about a couple of weeks ago? Isn't his company at the forefront of international cyber and financial security for major corporations, banks, governments, and the New International Union that's based in Geneva, Switzerland?"

"Yes, he is the one, John. He has also started numerous businesses in other fields, one of which is Ci Mada."

"Then, Bro. Ricky, it would seem Alpine Advanced Electronics somehow got their hands not only on this same type of prototype microchip reader, but somehow also on the special rare metal and developed the sleeper chip."

"This appears to be the case," replies Ricky in a calm but slightly frustrated voice. "My contact within the government said that the double agent that sold him the plans for this prototype microchip reader said it was so far advanced that it would be years before others could develop this level of a reader. The Russian scientist who developed this microchip reader was killed by our agent, only after the scientist wouldn't confess where the reader was. The agent knew the KGB was hot on his trail. The double agent was able to get his hands on all the blueprints and information to this reader. That is what he thought at least. The only prototype reader produced by the scientist was never found. Our agent smuggled blueprints out of Moscow to the individual in our government I knew. He was involved in a secret clandestine group that was heavily bankrolled within our government, and the guys actually wore white hats, figuratively speaking. But all of the individuals in this group either disappeared or died under mysterious circumstances within six months of this incident. My contact decided on my company to develop the reader. He told me he didn't trust anyone else in the defense contractor industry except me. He even lied to his own agency about the whereabouts of the reader plans, saying he never got them. Anyway, the gist of the story concerning the double agent was that he was hunted down by the KGB and they eventually caught up with him."

"What happened to him?" asks Caleb.

"We had reliable information that he popped a cyanide capsule in his mouth as soon as some KGB agents were busting down the door in his apartment in London. He knew he would be tortured for selling the reader plans, then shot to death, or worse, sent to a Siberian gulag to work in subzero temperatures."

Caleb, a little concerned, says, "Dad, I'm kind of surprised you're sharing this information. I mean, I trust everyone here, but I know this has to be top classified information."

"Well, Son, normally I would never even consider doing this under any circumstances. But that secret technology has not only come to our shores in America, but now it's in our backyard. It is connected to genetically-modified beasts that threaten both the livelihoods and lives of people in this community. All the leadership in this room needs to know what we are up against."

"Okay, Dad, I'll stand with you. I understand we are in a Catch 22."

Charlie Wilcox says, "I'm not saying jack about what I've heard so far inside these walls or any more information tonight about this ultra high-tech reader and this secret sleeper chip. My lips are sealed. But I'm a little confused about something. Maybe someone can fill in the blanks for me. Why in the world did this first microchip reader not pick up any kind of signal for the chip in the skull of this animal?"

Max replies, "The reason is because this hybrid wolf has a sleeper microchip located in the thickest part of his skull. Ci Mada put the giant pitwolf to sleep, drilled into the thickest part of his skull, then implanted this advanced chip. Finally, they filled the hole with bone material. That way it is never discovered by unsuspecting scientists or researchers if a dead beast is found. This high-tech chip works this way. It goes into a sleep mode when other types of readers try to activate it. No information is given out to the reader. Originally, we were told only this advanced prototype handheld Russian microchip reader works on it, like we built at SEC. But later we were told that there were future plans for this technology to be used in satellites, cell phone towers, and drones to track people or objects with this special chip."

"The sleeper chip is made of an extremely rare metal called Korak that is found only in an unknown part of the frozen tundra of Siberia. What we have also confirmed is that for some unexplainable reason Korak doesn't show up in x-rays."

"How is this scientifically possible?" enquires Caleb.

"We simply don't know. Leave it to the Russians to be the first to develop this technology. It is also believed Korak is the most highly conductive metal on the face of the earth. All these qualities we have mentioned make it invaluable and help to conceal the sleeper chip from being detected."

Max goes on and states, "I would love to extract the chip in this dead animal and analyze it. If you don't have a reader like we have, it can't be detected unless you literally chop up the animal and physically see it."

"Well, how small is it, Max?" inquires Ashley.

"We suspect it is the size of a tiny mustard seed, from the information we've gathered. But it could be a lot smaller."

"A mustard seed is already very tiny," replies Ashley.

"Yes, it is, and from what Ricky told David and me, the double agent could never get anything but the information you heard tonight on the sleeper chip. The Russian higher ups took many precautions with this research and had another scientist working on the sleeper chip in another former U.S.S.R. country. Our agent said there was a mysterious middle man who was the go between for the two scientists, and only he knew the location of the Korak mine in Siberia. He had a limited secret stash of it hidden somewhere around Moscow. Our agent tried to find out who the middle man was, but couldn't because the Russians were on to him. The value of Korak is incalculable in the high-tech world and may advance technology to unknown limits. Our agent tried to get us more information on the sleeper chip and the mineral Korak, but couldn't. This is the first sleeper chip we've had in our possession."

"Dad, what happened to the agent you knew?" asks Caleb.

"Well, I got some information from a trusted source that he disappeared about two weeks after he gave me the plans for the reader."

"Someone took him out?"

"Ah, I'm not really sure, but I know this. If anyone knew how to hide his tracks, the man I knew was that man."

"One more question, Dad. I want to make sure I understand. You're telling us that nobody outside these walls knows we have the advanced microchip reader?"

Ricky replies in a serious tone, "No, not even your mother nor Mary Anne knows. By faith, that is what I believe because no one has come sneaking around yet for it."

"Well, let's hope to God it stays that way, Dad."

"There! All the data is finally in," announces an excited David. Everyone in the garage crowds around David who is holding the reader to see the computer printout.

Ci Mada Union Laboratories

Boulder, Colorado (Region 1)

GPW#201

GS33

Charlie looks at the screen and says, "Okay, I'm no rocket scientist, but is this GPW#201 standing for what I think it does?"

Max speaks up, "Yes, the third line on this readout, I believe, pertains to the subject or object containing the microchip. So GPW in all likelihood stands for this dead giant pitwolf here, which is number 201."

Charlie is all keyed up. "Lord, help us! Lord, help us! Who knows how many more pitwolves are there after this one? They could've shipped in truckloads of these creatures in the mountains around us. What in the world are we going to do?"

Ashley interrupts, "Guys, let's not get caught up trying to guesstimate the number of these pitwolves. These animals may look demonic and terrifying, but remember, we have a dead one here in our midst. These things can be hunted down and killed. I believe that the land that Fortress is built on will not have these animals step foot on it. We can get pulled in a hundred different directions with what about this and what about that. One day all hell is going to break loose around us on planet earth. The only safe ground for a true Christian to be on in these last days is in the center of God's will. Not every born again Christian is going to be here at Fortress or some other city of refuge. They may be working or living in downtown L.A. or in a New York City skyscraper. But our God can protect and provide for a remnant there also, against all odds, if He so chooses."

John Blackhawk, pumped up by Ashley's mini sermon, says, "Amen, sister. We serve a big God and He can enable us to handle anything the devil can throw at us." He raises his deep voice and adds, "It doesn't matter how many pitwolves there are. I have a bullet for each one of them. I'm also totally convinced in my heart that the ministry of Fortress and the alliance of all our Disciplemaker churches is God ordained. God's glory and power is going to be manifested here and in our other sister churches for all to witness. Let's not faint and grow weary. We all serve an awesome God. Everybody just take a deep breath and put your total trust and faith in the Lord Jesus Christ. Cast all your cares upon Him. Charlie, relax. We not only have your back, but God is watching over you and each one of us here."

Charlie, a little embarrassed about being so emotional, says, "Hey, guys, I'm sorry about that rant a minute ago. You know I have heard end times teachings for years now. Gary was telling me prophetic stuff 30 years ago that just seemed ridiculous at the time. But now, when you see it unfolding before your very eyes, that is a different story. What I mean is, when you have a dead urban legend monster that weighs almost 375 pounds, that's bad enough. Then when you find out that it's been genetically modified into a killing machine with three-inch fangs in its mouth with a top secret microchip embedded in its skull... I mean, that is evil and takes it to a whole new level. It's pretty downright terrifying. But let me declare to all of you that Jesus is my Lord. And I know I serve a mighty God. Whatever lies ahead of me, God will give me the grace to endure it and to be victorious."

Everyone, led by Caleb, says, "Amen, Charlie!"

"We're all in this thing together," continues Caleb. Like John said, we have your back."

"Oh, I'm fine now. The stress of events of tonight had finally gotten to me. I'm thankful for all you guys," says a faith-filled Charlie now.

Brother Ricky clears his throat and says, "Praise God, Charlie! I think all of us are recognizing the Lord's timeline, and there is no turning back the clock. Tonight all of our lives have been changed forever. In Daniel 12:32, the Bible declares that at the end of time the true believers in Christ shall be strong and do exploits. We are this type of end time Christians. I can't say we are the only ones because I know we are not. These end time vessels are scattered here and there across the world. What I know in my spirit is that Fortress is definitely part of God's remnant church in these last days."

"Now, Caleb, given your background as a Navy Seal, will you tell us what GS33 probably stands for?"

Caleb pauses, both hands on his hips, as he looks at the concrete floor for a few seconds. He lightly pats his foot several times before jerking his head up. "Sure, Dad. GS33 is a military designation for a Global Satellite route that is synchronized with other satellites for x amount of passovers in a 24/7 period. They have to do this to prevent collisions in outer space. As GS33 flies over from outer space, it is probably tracking this giant pitwolf and an unknown number of other ones. How wide of distance on land does this GS33 track from outer space? I don't know, but I bet our own Space

Cowboy, Forrest, might be able to shed some light. He has connections through his uncles who work for NASA and is very knowledgeable about the satellite end of the space program. He has some recent military printouts of the Global System Network of Satellites which have the times in which all the satellites fly over North America and Europe. How he got them I have no idea. Forrest is very resourceful. I think everyone knows what I mean. I really believe he can help us. That's the gist of what I know about GS33. Forrest will have to fill us in on the rest."

"Fine, Caleb. When we're done here, see if he has any more information on this GS33 satellite and when it goes over this area of Colorado."

"Okay, Dad."

Bro. Gary says, "Thank God for Forrest. I would like to bring out some information on Ci Mada to fill people in, Ricky, if you don't mind."

"That would be fine. Go right ahead, Gary, because the deacons need to know who we are going up against and I know you have studied them extensively."

"Well, I know that Bro. Ricky, Max, David, and Forrest are very knowledgeable in the field of high technology and science. But I would like to share that in my prophetic research over the years, I was led into many different fields of study and investigation. My curiosity as a lawyer was peaked as I saw the name Ci Mada Union Laboratories in my research. It kept popping up in the areas of human and animal behavior modification, nanotechnology, genetically modified foods, seeds, plants, and animals. As you all know, it's been our ministry's philosophy ever since the elders relocated to the Double V Ranch from L.A. to be as environmentally friendly as possible. We grow a large amount of our own food here on the ranch and like to eat foods the way God intended. So that is why a good portion of our foods are primarily organic or at least as natural as possible, at least as much as we can make them, within reason. We can't restore the whole eco-system back to the time of the Garden of Eden in total purity, but Max and David do a great job heading up the food production with their crops of organic red winter wheat, corn, oats and other grains, as well as the different fruit orchards. As you know, we have a small dairy and raise animals for meat such as bison, cattle, sheep, goats, and chickens. Finally, we have a very large garden and a large green house complex.

You also know we produce and store food for our own consumption, give some to needy families in the area, and we wholesale about 40% of what we produce to several small regional grocery chain stores, mom and pop convenient stores and health food stores in about a 75-mile radius. We do this for jobs for some of our members here at Fortress and for the ministry to be self supportive. Max and David's area of expertise in their previous career was electrical engineering. But since moving from L.A. they have used their great scientific minds toward accumulating a storehouse of natural and scientific agricultural knowledge of productive earth-friendly farming techniques. They are doing a first rate job, and we salute them."

Everyone claps.

"So my studies in prophecy and our goal at Fortress of raising healthy, nutritious, and natural organic foods led me to examine Ci Mada pretty closely. What I found out about them I didn't like. They have been investigated by a congressional house committee twice in just the last three years about various types of genetically-modified foods and alleged bizarre experiments performed on animals and even humans. No evidence of illegal activity has ever been proven. About seven witnesses came forward through the years with damaging information about the company. Eventually five of them either said they had been confused about the facts or that they had fabricated stories about Ci Mada because of some personal vendetta against the management in the corporation. Two of the seven were radical animal activists who were not intimidated and died under different mysterious circumstances before they had a chance to testify. The only thing that came about from the hearings was the issue of what is morally correct or ethically right in regards to altering our nation's food supply. There were a few minor infractions that they violated concerning the labeling of some of their foods. They were slapped with minor violations and had to pay token fees.

No serious investigations of them have ever taken place. No laws were ever passed to stop them or hinder their experiments. Nothing was ever proven concerning them on allegations of bizarre animal or human experiments. Ci Mada has been on a number of animal activists' watch group lists for years.

Ci Mada had their wrists slapped a number of times and paid a few minor fines, but that was the extent of their repercussions."

Charlie speaks up, "Yeah, Gary, I remember you telling me some time back that you and Mary Anne drove up to Boulder and by a divine appointment were able to check out Ci Mada Union's facilities."

"Yes, we went to Boulder for a little mini vacation, and while we were there, we just decided to do a little investigating. Mary Anne and I visited their company on the outskirts of Boulder. It's an incredibly modern facility. They spared no expense in building it. It's located at the base of a mountain that can be difficult to spot from the road. By God's grace, we just happened to be there on a weekend when they first opened up and were giving limited tours to the general public. While there on the grounds, we were greatly oppressed in our spirits. Of course, we never got to see anything they didn't want us to see, but I could feel the presence of darkness and pure evil on the entire property. We had parked near their front entrance behind some tall pine trees. Before we left, Mary Anne and I did some serious warfare prayer against the work there at Ci Mada and all that they were involved in."

"By the way, their logo is a twist off of the medical symbol that you see in a doctor's office. But their symbol is three snakes coiled around a pole. If you look at it just right, you notice the snakes form three sixes, as in 666. Most people don't have a clue what it means when they see their logo. They just think it's a modern version of the medical symbol they've seen for years in doctors' offices. Each coiled snake has an apple in its mouth which is still another hint of their intent."

Brother Gary, in a tongue and cheek manner, says, "Oh, yea by a strange twist of fate their address just happens to start with the numbers 666 as well." Everyone in the garage knows its numerical address is by design and not chance.

Ricky wants to share something and nods to Gary who sees him. Ricky then says, "Ci Mada has an outright Luciferian logo in an abstract form, so most people don't even have a clue what it really means, including Christians. Ci Mada Union Laboratories is but one of many subsidiaries of Alpine Advance Electronics owned by Wolfgang Martin in Geneva, Switzerland. In my opinion, he is a very evil man."

Blackhawk, who is very interested, speaks up, "Brother Ricky, you're telling me this Martin guy owns Ci Mada Union?"

"Yes, John that is true."

"Bro. Ricky, isn't he the guy that was interested in buying your company years ago when you had it on the market?"

"Yes, John, he was chomping at the bit to buy it. But I refused to sell it to him. I didn't trust the guy then and I sure don't trust him now. I wasn't willing to risk my country's national security to some multi-billionaire whose hands I knew were dirty for the sake of the almighty dollar. I knew to some degree then that his company, AAE, had a tremendous amount of capital for research and development. AAE was making huge in-roads into the military electronics and computer fields. For several years it had already positioned itself at the forefront of international cyber and financial security for major corporations, banks, and various foreign governments, including some rogue ones, which didn't set well with me at the time or my board of trustees. Now I know he is behind the creation of this dead giant pitwolf and a whole lot more evil stuff. He has also positioned his AAE company and a long list of other subsidiaries he owns now as leaders in high-tech military weaponry, genetically modified food industry, cyber and financial security, cutting-edge AI technology, and communications. Every country boy knows you don't trust the fox to guard the hen house. I'm beginning to smell something rotten, not in Denmark, but Geneva."

Ashley says, "Dad, you also mean Geneva by way of Boulder."

"Yes, that also applies," states Ricky emphatically with a smile.

David anxiously asks, "Ricky, do you want me and Max to take out that sleeper chip from this animal? We'd be more than glad to."

"No, I know you boys would love to get started on that project, but Gary and I believe we have something more pressing to worry about."

"Yeah, I know," replies Max. "I believe I know where you are going with this."

"I would love to analyze this chip myself if it was another time and place," says Ricky in a slightly frustrated tone. "But Gary suggested to me as soon as the rescue team got back from the box canyon that we needed to get Sheriff Barnes involved in this whole scenario. And I'm in total agreement with him. We both feel, along with Sister Melody and Sister Mary Anne, that we have to include him. I think everyone believes we are safe here on this property, but we have an obligation to our neighbors, friends, and fellow citizens to also consider. We are putting this issue in the hands of our local law enforcement officer. Neither Gary nor I really know the man too well. I personally believe he doesn't know how to take us and that he has had misgivings about Fortress since we first moved here. He has always been a little stand offish to us. But we have to see what he wants us to do.

As we all know, what has happened tonight is really in God's hands at this point. This dead giant pitwolf is on our property now and Ci Mada may have already pinpointed its location to this very garage by a drone or satellite. But they don't know we have this reader. We already have the information we need. Is the chip vital for us to have? No, not at this point. If we take the sleeper chip out of this dead beast and someone tries to come to Fortress to confiscate this beast's body, we endanger people's lives once they leave this property. Gary and I can't jeopardize people's lives for this sleeper chip. It just isn't worth it."

"Ricky, can I pipe in here for a moment?"

"Sure, Gary."

"Thanks. We have to see which way Barnes wants to move on this issue. Again, Ricky and I would advise everyone here at this point to keep your mouths silent about the sleeper microchip in this beast. Nobody outside this garage knows Ricky has this advanced prototype Russian microchip reader. We need to keep it that way. I hope I'm very clear on this point."

He can see from their nods and facial expressions everyone knows the cost if it leaks out. "Great," says Gary. "Let's keep in mind that Sam Barnes is a good sheriff in the most conservative county in Colorado. But he is between a rock and a hard place on this giant pitwolf issue. He can either announce it publicly, 'Hey everybody, we have giant monster wolves on the prowl in Clark County.' Which on one hand is the last thing he needs to do with the county's economy sputtering along and meteorites falling in surrounding counties and states. His other option is to send out under the radar experienced hunters he trusts to track down these monsters and kill them. But they have to be able to keep their mouths shut, which the men in this room I know can do, along with a few other men at Fortress. But if, and it is a big if, this story of the giant pitwolves surfaces several days or a week down the road, there are people in Clark County who would want his resignation immediately.

Charlie speaks up, "But, Gary, this thing just happened. It's dark now and there is no way to safely hunt down these beasts tonight."

"Yes, Charlie, this is true and tomorrow is a pivotal day for Sheriff Barnes and for us, concerning what he wants to do. One of the first things Ricky said to me when he came back from the rescue mission was that he was planning to take the sheriff, myself and Blackhawk up in the morning in the ministry's helicopter and scope out the area for these giant pitwolves, that is, if Barnes is willing. Sister Melody and Sister Mary Anne are on their way now to get Barnes. So let's all be in prayer and see what the Lord wants us to do with this dead pitwolf and the other pitwolves in this area. The Lord can do the impossible! Remember my favorite promise in the Bible?"

Everyone quotes it, "With God all things are possible - Matthew 19:26."

Then suddenly Ashley says, "Dad, Uncle Gary, in the crazy atmosphere of this evening I just remembered that a plane crashed in Overton County north of us at around 7:00 PM this evening. I was listening to the show Dispatch on the short wave radio when I heard about it. Did anyone else hear about it?" Everyone is shaking their heads no. She goes on to say, "Oh, well there were unconfirmed reports it was a drone. It crashed into a mountainside in Overton County and started a very small forest fire. Because it was so rocky, the fire never amounted to much."

Bro. Gary responds, "We need to get more information on that possible drone."

Ashley replies, "Yes sir, I will. I'd like to add that they could not determine the cause of the crash. There was speculation that a small meteorite might have hit it." Gary repeats the same strong desire for Ashley to try to find out some more information on that possible drone. She says, "Sure."

"In the meantime," Charlie says excitedly, "Praise the Lord! Maybe it is possible that God has already been doing the impossible and granting us favor in this matter. Maybe through divine intervention he has knocked out a possible spy drone?"

"Oh yeah!" says Blackhawk in an intense tone. All the leadership is high fiving one another and praising God.

When the celebration dies down, a thought passes through Caleb's mind that he thinks is from the Holy Spirit. "Uncle Gary, you are great at thinking outside the box. Let me ask you a question."

"Well, thank you. I get a lot of help from the Holy Spirit. What's the question, Caleb?"

"Why are these creatures in this area?"

"Excellent question, Caleb. In the natural, my thoughts would be that they either escaped from some top Ci Mada secret lab possibly in a remote area or they are being used for one or more evil purposes. But, Caleb, you have that look on your face like you know something. I've seen it many times before. Do you have something from the Lord?"

"Yes, sir, I do. I think these giant pitwolves serve an evil purpose for Ci Mada or another entity. Thus, the need for the highly advanced sleeper microchip. If their numbers are as great as we think they are, they could destabilize an area and the economy like this county, the surrounding counties, or even a whole region of a state. God only knows where all these possible pitwolves are right now. They could be used to put fear into the hearts of a good percentage of the rural population and cause them to pack up and move. Also, isn't it ironic that these giant predators that have been seen tonight have been spotted near the same timeframe as these meteorites falling? Coincidence? Maybe or maybe not. But I don't think so. Lucifer knows we are here and what this ministry stands for in this end time battle. It makes logical sense that the powers that be could use these genetically modified animals to keep the masses in large cities and the people in the suburbs from venturing outside the perimeters of those cities into the country and forests - especially if they or Lucifer had preknowledge of when these meteorites were going to fall. Thank You, Jesus! The Holy Spirit just brought to my remembrance something that happened some years back when I was still in the Navy."

"What was it?" asks Ashley.

"In the process of just sharing that information, I believe the Spirit of God brought to my memory what someone told me years ago in England, when my SEAL Team was doing some anti-terrorism high-security training there. I had completely forgotten about it until just now. It was during this time, as I was attending a party in the home of a friend of mine, a British SAS Colonel, that I met an old Swiss scientist. While we were conversing alone in a large section of the back yard next to a water fountain, we got on the subject of secret weapons used in WWII. He leaned over close to me and said, 'I shouldn't tell you this, and remember you never heard it from me. But during WWII Hitler had contacted a brilliant doctor in Europe to develop a super predator type animal." He would not reveal the doctor's name to me for fear of his life. He stated that Hitler wanted some kind of terrorizing hybrid dog mixture to be used against the U.S. and Allied forces. He said the doctor and his team finally developed specimens of this hybrid toward the end of the war. But just as it was coming to an end, all the evidence and the specimens developed were buried deep inside a mountain near the German and Swiss border by a massive explosion."

Brother Gary's eyes light up. "Yes, I'm positive you are talking about Dr. Wilhelm Von Gunten. He was a very dark character in the last century and came from a long line of occultic doctors and scientists who were involved in barbaric and inhumane experiments. I ran across some whitewash stories on him but also some rumors on him online but nothing like you just told me. He was the evil father of the Director of Ci Mada Union Laboratories in Boulder who apparently has carried on the family tradition. The Director's name is Dr. Fritz Von Gunten.

Max speaks up, "I don't know about you guys, but from all I've seen and heard tonight I thank God for my salvation. If I didn't know Jesus as my personal Lord and Savior, I would be scared silly."

"Me too," says David. "But thank God that he is moving supernaturally in our midst. God seems to be helping us to sovereignly connect the dots of vital information that is needed at this time. It's definitely a God thing. Caleb, has God spoken anything else to you?"

"Yes, David, just now! Has anyone noticed that Ci Mada spelled backwards is Adamic?"

"No," replies Gary. "What is Adamic? Wait a minute! The Lord just popped something else into my mind. Wow! Adamic as in Adamic Society!"

Ricky adds, "Yeah! I just now remembered something from years ago. I had heard that name before, but it was a long time ago at the airport in Los Angeles. I was waiting to catch a flight to Washington D. C. to present a new radar evasion system for a prototype fighter jet to some top military brass in the Pentagon. I was in an upscale restaurant inside the airport drinking coffee and reading the Well Street Journal when I heard two very distinguished looking Swiss businessmen quietly talking in German and heard them whisper the name Adamic Society. I knew they were from Switzerland because I saw one of their passenger identification tickets on a carry-on bag marked Geneva, Switzerland on the floor next to my table. I was very curious because I took German in high school. I definitely heard them say Adamic Society. The name seemed strange and I wondered what it could be. I tried to research the Adamic Society in the early days of the internet but came up short. I never found any information in books or the internet about it. So I abandoned my research, thinking it was probably just a new nightclub in Geneva."

"Very interesting, Dad. Let me fill everybody in on what I know about the Adamic Society. About five winters ago I was stationed in Germany for some training on hostage recovery from commercial planes. I met an Austrian soldier named Daniel Brubaker in a large bookstore in Frankfurt. He was a retired Captain in NETO who was receiving alternative medical treatment there. Daniel and I developed a close friendship the short time I was there. Three months prior to my meeting him, Daniel had held a top

NETO security clearance. He told me that, before he came down with cancer, he and other highly trained NETO military personnel units had occasionally provided security at Wolfgang Martin's 14th century Swiss castle outside of Geneva - about three to six times a year. Daniel said different world leaders and ultra rich CEOs of major corporations, scientists, and a variety of VIPs would secretly show up there sometimes. The media would announce only one event a year taking place at his castle. Daniel was a very sharp soldier and could speak about five languages fluently. He told me he once overheard a slightly drunk world leader getting into a limo and say in French to one of his top aides that he was tired of coming to these meetings and being under the oppressive hand of the Adamic Society. Daniel pretended not to hear a word the man spoke. He did not even tell his own team or commanding officer because he knew a mole was in their midst that reported to someone way above him. Brubaker's NETO security team was only ever used for outside security of the castle and the surrounding grounds. Martin had a private high-security contractor named Ironshield to provide handpicked elite security personnel inside the castle. He said they were a different breed of highly trained security personnel. All of them seemed to have a strange look in their eyes, as if they were in a drug-induced state, under a spell of some kind, or microchipped zombie-like soldiers. Daniel knew they were composed of various ex-special forces soldiers and were just as trained or more so than his team. They didn't like his NETO team and his NETO team didn't like them. Brubaker said he knew only a little about the Adamic Society. Daniel told me the society was so secretive that the internet had virtually nothing on them. Nothing was ever written about it in books or magazines. He found out rumors circulated quietly in some circles of Europe, that information about the Adamic Society never stayed online very long. It was always removed almost instantly when posted. But Daniel knew with 100 percent certainty that this society existed and that it was pure evil."

"How's that, son?" asked Ricky.

"Daniel had many connections and informants in Europe. One of the people in Rome he knew posted some inside information about the Adamic Society one night, and the next morning he was found dead. Supposedly his death was ruled a heart attack by the police in Rome even though the guy was a competitive long distance runner, with no previous health problems, and was only 29 years old. Daniel's informant had the so-called heart attack the same night he posted some pictures and information on the Adamic Society. The coroner had ruled that he had died around 1:00 AM. His body was found at 8:00 AM by his landlord who had noticed his front door was slightly open. The Italian media somehow failed to mention the young man's apartment had been thoroughly searched and all his computer related equipment was gone. Brubaker's own words were that the Adamic Society was composed of the movers and shakers of this world."

"Son, why would this Captain Brubaker confide in you about this dangerous and evil Adamic Society?"

"Well, he was in stage four cancer, didn't have a family, and was about to die. His alternative treatments were his last hope and his body wasn't responding to them. He just wanted to get this off his chest before he died and thought he could trust me." Caleb concludes, "Guys, I believe tonight the Lord is helping us to realize that Clark County, Colorado is ground zero for a Luciferian showdown between the Kingdom of Lucifer and the Kingdom of God."

"It sure seems that way," says his wife Ashley, as everyone agrees.

"We definitely need the Lord!" interjects Gary. "Incredible! It's just incredible. Brothers and sisters, we are involved in something that is more dangerous than some genetically engineered beast lying before you. It sounds like a story stranger than fiction. As Christians, we live within the world's system. We are just passing through this world as ambassadors for Christ. This present sinful world is not our eternal home. So in reality, this physical world we live in is really the Kingdom of Lucifer, and we are involved in an actual war with it. Before we end this meeting, please let me emphasize that what has been said tonight cannot leave this room. Remember loose lips sinks ships. If you are in agreement, please raise your hand." All the leadership members raise their right hands.

Chapter 7

BARNES, THE LAST OF A DYING BREED

Sister Melody Crawford and Sister Mary Anne Kirkman, as they are affectionately called at Fortress, drive to Sheriff Sam and Sarah Barnes' beautiful log cabin that they had built with their own hands. It is a fifteen minute drive from Fortress and each woman is deep into prayer the whole way. Their husbands, Ricky and Gary, know that Sheriff Barnes has to be notified of the dead giant pitwolf and at least four other ones in his county. The elders are wise to the ways of living in a high-tech society that is bent on knowing everyone's business, so they opted to relay a message to Sheriff Barnes in person. It is just too risky to call him and requires someone he knows and believes to be honest to come out to the Double V Ranch. Melody and Sam have always hit it off and the elders are hoping he is home at this hour.

Unpredictable giant predators attacking domestic livestock and humans is a really serious problem that cannot be ignored. How the Lord is going to work everything out leaves the Crawfords and Kirkmans scratching their heads. They just don't know, but they know the Lord isn't caught off guard and has the answers. All the elders find rest in that fact. The elders also know that telling Sam will make his job a lot harder. A small number of the citizens of his county have already left a couple of weeks ago because of six small meteorites hitting surrounding counties that border Clark County. Most them have not returned as of yet. The rest of the people of the county are already on edge because of the meteorites, the bad economy, and the wrong direction the new president is taking the country. All Sheriff Barnes needs is another round of bad news to further alarm the good people of his county. It can turn Clark County into a huge ghost town. Anyone who knows Barnes knows of his loyalty and sense of duty to the law abiding citizens of his county. The county he loves and has lived in almost his whole life will go up in flames if he contacts any state or federal officials or the media about vicious giant pitwolves on the prowl in his county.

But Bro. Ricky and Bro. Gary have quickly analyzed the situation before they sent Melody and Mary Anne to the Barnes house. Both have surmised that the dead giant pitwolf is the product of a possible secret government research lab. They are confident that the Holy Spirit has previously given them peace that Sheriff Barnes will be an ally that they can count on in the hard times ahead. They have conversed with him from time to time while conducting business in town. Both have always extended the warm right hand of fellowship toward him. He has always been professional, but cold toward them and has kept them at arm's length. But tonight is of a serious nature and they have to meet him in person and get a feel of where he stands. He seems cordial enough and likeable under a rough exterior of a personality. It is Melody who knows him the best of the four elders. She, of course, grew up in the valley. Sam was the captain of the basketball team as a senior when she was a junior. Her best friend at Golden Valley High School was Sarah Young. Sarah dated Sam off and on in high school, but their relationship had gotten serious her last year. She was the homecoming queen her senior year, and Sam was her escort. So Melody knew him very well as a teenager, but decades have passed since that time. They have occasionally bumped into each other in Golden Valley and have had short pleasant conversations. Melody always asked about Sarah and how she wanted to talk to her, but Sam's reply was always, 'Oh, she hasn't been up to par lately. I'll tell her you asked about her.' Things have not been the same between Melody and Sarah since her decision to attend her dad's alma mater in Boulder at Colorado A&M University. When she married Ricky and ended up living in L.A. for a number of years, it put much distance between their friendship.

Melody has wondered through the years that maybe Sarah felt she had been abandoned by her when she left for Boulder. There always seemed to be tension on the part of Sarah whenever they met over the years. Melody always tried to maintain a relationship with Sarah by writing her, sending birthday and Christmas cards, and trying to visit with her when she came into town to visit with her mom and dad through the years. But Sarah always seemed so distant and never her old self, especially since the Crawfords and Kirkmans moved their ministry to Golden Valley some years ago. Why? Melody has some ideas why, but doesn't know exactly. But all the intercessors back at Fortress have Sarah and Sam near the top of their prayer lists.

In high school, Sarah was never one to be interested much in her classes in school, let alone getting a college degree. She had instead focused on getting her MRS. degree by marrying Sam when he was fresh out of Army boot camp at the age of 20. Sarah had lived in only one place other than Golden Valley and that was Fayetteville, North Carolina, where the Green Berets are headquartered. When Sam's hitch was up in the Army, they came back to their roots in Golden Valley.

Neither Sam nor Sarah were raised in the church, so Melody speculates that the whole ministry of Fortress is bizarre to both Sam and Sarah. Melody is one of the elders of the ministry along with her husband Ricky and the Kirkmans. Melody is no stranger to hearing gossip that circulates in the county that Fortress is some kind of "Christian Cult," "Jesus Freak Community," or possibly a "Christian Survivalist Compound." So these names that Fortress is called in the community only add to Sarah's not wanting to have a relationship with Melody and the rest of the people that live on the Double V Ranch. The elders work hard to dispel those misconceptions. They want people to see Christ in them in words and deeds. Sheriff Barnes is one of the men in Clark County they most want to know Christ for the end days ahead.

Barnes is like a stereotype cowboy character out of the Old West in the 21st century. His hair is salt and pepper and thick as is the moustache that covers his upper lip. He carries a Model 29 Smith and Wesson .44 magnum 6-inch revolver in a right-handed Bianchi quick release, medium brown leather holster close to his left hip that is slightly tilted toward his custom handmade leather belt buckle. Time has not diminished his lightning fast draw with his revolver nor his dead aim accuracy. Barnes is a no nonsense kind of guy with a dry wit. Smoking through the years has deepened his already deep voice, and he naturally speaks with great authority. Standing 6 feet 2 inches, he still has a lean muscular build for his age with wide shoulders. Sam always says what he means and means what he says and his body language gives no hint otherwise. Through the years some younger men thought they could take him in a fight only to wake up and barely be able to pick themselves up off the floor, sometimes minus a few teeth. The public, for the most part, likes him and considers him honest and fair. But occasionally, he bends the rules to cut someone a break. He had been a sergeant in the elite Special Forces called the Green Berets during the thick of the Vietnam War. Sam saw plenty of action with two purple heart medals and four bullet hole scars to prove it. After his two tours in Vietnam, he and Sarah moved back to Golden Valley. After returning home, he did construction for a while and honed his old rodeo skills. Two years later, he got into the pro rodeo circuit and made a good living for a number of years as a steer wrestler and calf roper with his partner Lane Grogan before he got into law enforcement. After ten years on the circuit, the rodeo life was taking a toll on his marriage to Sarah. Also a number of aches and broken bones was a major factor in him deciding to bring an end to his rodeo career. Sam knew the rodeo was a young man's game. It was time to hang up his spurs and move on to something a little less physically demanding. Law enforcement seemed like a natural fit for him with his military background. After serving three years as a deputy sheriff to Sheriff Wayne Norton, Norton decided to retire his badge after 35 years of service and talked Sam into running for sheriff. Barnes won in a landslide victory in Clark County.

Deputy sheriffs have come and gone during Sam's time as sheriff but Hank Rutherford, the current deputy, is his favorite. Hank is like Barnes and has seen a lot of action in the Army in actual combat. Patriotism still runs deep in Clark County and both men are hometown heroes in Golden Valley. Hank is his right hand man that Barnes trusts to watch his back or to get a job done the right way. Hank had been an Army Ranger and had done two tours in Iraq between 2001 and 2007. Hank had proven his bravery in Iraq time and time again and received a purple heart medal. He had been an EMT for several years for the county hospital before landing the job as deputy sheriff, which was the job he really wanted. Former Deputy Sheriff Clyde Hopkins had retired due to health reasons which opened up a slot for him. Hank's personality is usually laid back, but he can become intense, given the situation. Rutherford, like Barnes, grew up in Golden Valley. He takes his law enforcement oath, that they swore to uphold to serve and protect the citizens of Clark County, seriously. They also remember the oath they took when sworn into duty in the military to uphold the Constitution and defend the United States against all enemies foreign and domestic. Neither one likes anyone jacking around with their county or country.

Outsiders consider Clark County a redneck and backward county. Those things don't bother Sam Barnes nor his deputy - nor the fact that Clark County is the smallest and poorest county in Colorado because it is also the most conservative. But the thing Barnes is most proud of is the fact that his county has the lowest crime rate of any county in the state. Several pot parlors have tried to open up in Golden Valley and were met with the old school, western conservative mentality that pervaded in the county.

Barnes' mindset represents the values of most of the people of the town of Golden Valley which really make up the bulk of the county. It is also the county seat of Clark County. Sheriff Barnes cracks down on the pot parlors' owners in his jurisdiction any way he can legally or with pure intimidation. Over the years he has basically shut down four of them right after opening. Sam Barnes is totally against illegal drugs of any kind and in his way of thinking pot is still illegal. It doesn't matter that the state has legalized it. But alcohol is a different story. If one of those pot parlors' owners had opened up a new western-style saloon instead, Sheriff Barnes would have been one of the first customers to belly up to the bar.

As Melody and Mary Anne drive up into the Barnes' driveway, Melody honks the hybrid car's horn repeatedly trying to get Sarah's attention. Both see several lights on in the log cabin, but Sarah is not coming to the door. Since moving to Golden Valley Melody has run into Sarah in town on several occasions but she was always in a hurry or on her way to something important, was feeling sick or had to run a special errand for Sam. She always had some kind of excuse to avoid her former best friend. Melody tried to call her many times since moving back, but Sarah never answered her calls. Sarah's car is under the carport and Melody says, "I know she is here. We can't afford for her to avoid us at this time. I'm getting out of the car."

Mary Anne says, "I'm not getting a check in my spirit about the pitwolves so I'll get out with you."

"No," says Melody. "You stay here and pray. In my spirit I feel it's safe, but please turn on the high-beam lights before I get out. Honk if you see something. Hopefully Sarah will get over this childish behavior of avoiding me and answer the door. Hopefully she knows when Sam is getting home."

"Okay, be careful, Melody, in Jesus' name."

Melody gets out of the car, does a complete 360 degree with her eyes, and listens intensely for anything out of the ordinary. At the moment everything seems fine. She quickly makes her way to the house's front door with the brightness of the high beam shining on her back. After several series of knocks on the door, Sarah has still not come to greet Melody. Melody again repeatedly knocks to no avail. Anger rises up in Sister Melody's heart to a level she has not experienced in years. Finally things reach a boiling point in her emotions, and she unconsciously yells Sarah's maiden name. "Sarah Young, you unlock this front door right now before I throw a rock through your front window."

The anxiety of the unusual events of the evening and Sarah's refusal to come to the door cause Melody to get very angry. She reverts back to her early days as a mildly rebellious teenager dealing with her friend Sarah. Sarah has been peeking through the curtains upstairs looking out at the car with the lights on and has kept quiet during the knocking. But when Sarah hears Melody scream out and revert back to the old ways of her youth, a flood of memories rushes through Sarah's mind. She then thinks the whole thing is hilarious and starts laughing hysterically upstairs. She says to herself, "Now that's the old Melody I knew," and starts making her way downstairs yelling out Melody's maiden name. "Melody Vardeman, you throw a rock through my window and I'll tell the Big Swede. He'll tan your hide and you know it." She then comes to the door and slowly opens it to see Melody with a big grin on her face and both hands on her head laughing.

She says, "I know your name is Barnes now and I really wasn't going to throw a rock through your window. I just wanted to have a heart-to-heart talk with my best friend from the days of our youth about a serious matter."

Sarah, giggling hard, says, "I couldn't take any chances by not opening the door. The old Melody I knew years ago had a little mean streak in her at times and didn't make idle threats." Sarah, now getting a little misty eyed, says, "I know your last name is Crawford, not Vardeman, and I only wish I could talk to the Big Swede. I loved that man like a second daddy." Melody is now crying, as is Sarah. They quickly embrace one another like long lost friends.

Mary Anne opens the side door of the car with a blank expression on her face. She's shocked and a little perplexed hearing her best friend of thirty plus years talk like that. Melody is out of character, but a more serious matter exists and Mary Anne is concerned about the possibility of giant pitwolves in the area. Seeing both women outside laughing and exposed isn't a bright idea in her mind. So she shouts out to Melody, "I hate to interrupt, but I'd feel a little better if we could all go inside the house given the gravity of the situation." Sarah Barnes now has a puzzled look on her face after all that just happened and wonders what the woman in the car is yelling about. Laughter on their part is now replaced with a somber mood. Melody, reading the face of her old friend, says, "Sarah, can we go in your house now? We need to talk. It's an emergency situation and we need Sam's help."

"Yes. What is it? You girls come on in. Excuse the mess. The house is not as clean as I like, but I've honestly been a little sick with the flu."

Melody, says, "Don't worry about the house, Sarah. I think you know Mary Anne."

"Yes, I couldn't tell who was in the car with the high beams on." A serious tone now comes forth from Sarah's voice as she asks, "Has someone been murdered at the Double V Ranch?"

"No, no," says Mary Anne. There are giant pitwolves in the area."

Melody adds, "One of them attacked and killed Pete Watson's prized champion bull. And there are at least four more in the county and possibly more."

"What in the world are you talking about? You mean to tell me that the urban legend of the giant pitwolf is real?"

"Yes, they are real and they are in Clark County," replies an intense Melody.

"Good grief, this is all my Sam needs!" says Sarah in a frustrated voice. "The meteorites already have people in the valley jumpy and some have moved away. And now this. Please tell me this is a bad joke."

Melody says, "Sorry. I wish it was, but it is not."

Sarah's facial expression tells a story of apparent rattled nerves. It is beginning to dawn on her that the news stories of those giant pitwolves that she had dismissed as made up were not just a figment of people's wild imaginations after all.

Mary Anne, with a sense of urgency, says, "Sarah, when will Sam get home?"

In a bit of a daze, Sarah slowly comes to, pauses for a moment, and says, "He - ah - he just called and said he was close and that he was bringing over Deputy Rutherford who was interested in checking out Sam's old tractor for his Uncle Burt who might want to buy it." Melody inquires as to when they should arrive. Sarah says they are off duty and they should be here any moment. Sarah, still stunned by what she has heard, subconsciously starts biting on her fingernails which she hasn't done in years. She responds, "In fact, when you girls pulled up I thought it was Sam and Hank at first."

Thirty seconds later, Mary Anne hears Sam's and Hank's vehicles as they pull up into the driveway. Melody tells Sarah that they need to take Sam and Hank to the Double V Ranch so they can see the dead giant pitwolf and so Sam can decide how he is going to handle this situation. With anxiety and curiosity rising within her emotions Sarah says, "Yeah, he definitely has to go. If this beast killed a prize bull, the people in this county will want swift action. I want to go along also to see this giant pitwolf and judge for myself."

"Let's go see them," says Sarah, as the women walk out the front door of the house. The hybrid's car headlights are on high. As Sam and Hank get out of their respective police vehicles, they instantly draw their pistols. For these trained lawmen, it seems like a crime has been committed. Thoughts of a home invasion or robbery of some kind flash through their minds until they see Sarah and the women waving in a somewhat normal manner.

Sam calls out to Sarah, "Honey, is everything alright?"

Sarah responds, "Sammy, dear, things could be a lot better. We all need to get in your dual cab pickup and head straight to the Double V Ranch. I don't want to ride in the back of your police SUV all crunched up with me trying to get over the flu."

Sam, now getting very perturbed, says , "What in the blue blazes is going on over at the Double V, Melody?"

"I'll explain as we head there," says Melody.

Mary Anne adds, "I'll follow behind in the car," and starts walking toward the hybrid.

Sam speaks in a regular sounding voice, but tones of irritation are apparent in his words. "Me and Hank aren't going nowhere until we know what is going on," he declares as he walks to his pickup.

Sarah says, "Sam, dear, there is a dead giant wolf over there at the Double V Ranch. It killed Pete Watson's prize bull. Melody and Mary Anne believe it is one of those giant pitwolves, you know, the kind that was in the news some time back."

Sam, still speaking in a calm voice but with less irritation, says, "Sorry, ladies, I'm not buying into no giant pitwolf story. But, man, I hate to hear that about the bull. That thing was a huge championship bull. I saw it the day after Pete got it. He spent a pretty penny on that thing. Now listen. I don't believe for one second in a giant pitwolf story. A big wolf killing Pete's bull, yes. A giant pitwolf, no way. If I had a nickel for every crazy and bizarre story that came down the pike since I have been sheriff, I'd be a rich man by now. There's a few nutty people in this county that even claim they've seen bigfoot in this part of the Rockies, but no one has brought one in yet, dead or alive. So let me tell the both of you straight up what I think this giant pitwolf is - nothing but a huge wolf with some kind of deformity or mutation. Another possibility is that it is some kind of a big dog like a mastiff, great dane, or Irish wolfhound and wolf mix."

Hank butts in,, "I'm sorry, Miss Sarah and Miss Melody, but I have to agree with the sheriff. No disrespect, but I can't swallow that story either. An urban legend called a giant pitwolf that's twice the size of a large wolf? No, no - I'd have to see with my own two eyes to believe it."

Sam confidently tells Sarah, "Don't worry, Hon, I'm going to get to the bottom of this. Regardless, a killer large feral dog, wolf or wolf mix of any kind is bad news for ranchers in the area, especially when a championship bull is involved." As they walk to the truck, he tells the women that Hank needs to ride shotgun. Sarah and Melody climb in on both sides of the truck in the back.

Before Hank gets in he says, "Sheriff, do you want me to call Travis to let him know wolves are back in the area so he can call some of the big ranchers and let them know?"

"No, don't call Travis yet. Not now. You know I don't trust that guy any further than I can throw him. Let's go check out this call and then I'll see what we need to do."

Travis Perkins is the youngest law enforcement official in Clark County. Travis attended one of the most liberal colleges in the country. He graduated from Davidson University in Denver with a double degree in criminal justice and political science two years before. Plans of going on and getting his law degree at Davidson were put on hold after his break up with his ultra-liberal girlfriend Katy of three years. As a result of that, Travis went into a very deep depression and, with his uncles' persistence, decided to return home to Clark County. Occasionally he has smoked pot since its legalization in 2013 in Colorado and has been successful at hiding it from street smart Barnes and Rutherford. Travis graduated near the top of his class and held many socialist views of life which he has not been truthful about with others in Golden Valley. Katy, as the editor of the *Turn Left and get Right* socialist blog, had influenced him to embrace a far more progressive lifestyle while in college. He has a different world view than Sheriff Barnes and Hank, but he knows to talk conservatively in their presence and in the presence of certain other individuals in the county. But Sam and Hank are on to him and don't trust him. Matt Perkins, the long time mayor of Golden Valley, pulled out all stops to have his nephew Travis hired on as a deputy sheriff even though he and Barnes had exchanged some heated words over it. Barnes agreed to it only after he'd made it clear to Perkins that Travis was mostly going to be doing clerical, secretarial, and janitorial type work. Perkins agreed to it because Travis needed a job and he wanted him to get his foot in the door of law enforcement as a stepping stone to eventually get into local, and hopefully state, politics. Travis is over Katy now and is enrolled for the fall semester at Davidison to work on a law degree once school starts.

Travis believes in big government and the centralization of power. For him, personal freedom is an archaic concept and a hindrance to the best interest of society. Travis lives a lie and is what the Bible calls a double minded man. He pretends to be conservative to those who are in authority to try in time to ascend to power with his own agenda. Travis has political aspirations that his uncle is well aware of and supports. In the meantime, his deputing consists of the night shift Monday through Friday at the sheriff's office. He takes an occasional telephone call at night, does janitorial work, files paperwork, and occasionally monitors and takes care of prisoners in jail, usually for minor offenses. Travis loathes transferring any telephone calls of a very serious nature to Barnes or Rutherford, who alternate nights taking those calls and responding to them if necessary, because he craves power and authority. For the most part, Clark County is peaceful and the citizens law abiding. But if there a serious crime committed, Travis dreams of getting in on the action.

Sheriff Barnes says, "What you can do, Hank, is grab your 12 gauge shotgun and shells and my new AR-15 rifle in my Tahoe and a couple of extra 30 round clips out of my ammo bag. This possible wolf hybrid might have some other feral dogs that are running in a pack with it." Barnes keeps mulling over in his mind if it is a hybrid wolf, how it could have taken on such a huge bull like Pete's and killed it. So he is taking extra firepower just in case.

Hank's intensity level is sky high. He says, "Yes, sir," and grabs both guns and ammo out of their police vehicles. As he gets in the pickup, he says, "It never hurts to be prepared."

"Yeah, it's a no brainer," replies Barnes.

As Sheriff Barnes drives away from his house, he is silent for a moment and grabs his chin. Then in an authoritative tone, he says, "I want to keep this hush for now until we have more information on this big dead wolf or possibly any other ones. It's dark and there ain't much we can do at this point anyway."

"Yeah, you're right, Sheriff," says Hank. "The people in this area are already spooked about the meteorites in the other counties that butt up next to ours. Thank God that ours hasn't been hit."

Melody, in the back seat, quietly whispers, "Amen to that."

Hank goes on to say, "Cattlemen in this county are already hard pressed trying to make a living. Ranchers and wolves, hybrid wolves, or feral dogs roaming the countryside possibly in a pack killing livestock don't mix. This couldn't have come at a worse time."

Sam looks at Melody in the rear view mirror and says, "Melody, I've always considered you a straight shooter. Tell me straight up. Did you see this so-called giant pitwolf with your own two eyes?"

Melody knows where Sam is going with his line of questioning. "No, I didn't, Sam." She decides to keep her mouth shut on the matter and is praying silently. She also wants to reestablish an old close relationship with Sarah. Melody knows that for Sam, seeing is believing.

Barnes says in somewhat of a cocky tone, "Yep, that's what I thought. Okay, until I see something different or out of the ordinary, it is a large wolf or hybrid mix in my mind."

Sarah, in the spirit of compromise, says, "Sam, we'll be at the Double V in a few minutes and then we can all see for ourselves. Right, Melody?"

"You're absolutely right, Sarah," replies Melody with a slight smile.

While Sheriff Barnes drives, he and Hank, by the light of the full moon, are keeping their eyes peeled for any animal activity in the area. Sarah and Melody are talking quietly in the back. Mary Anne is following closely behind them. The conversation in the short truck ride between Sam and Hank is about the wolf and others probably in the vicinity. They are also discussing what to do about different scenarios. Sam and Hank are firm in their conviction that the wolf is a hybrid, or some kind of mutation that has affected the features of a wolf. Sam even mentions it may be a large wolf with an extra heavy coat making it appear like a giant wolf. Hank is of the same mindset as Sam on the giant pitwolf story. He believes there is a natural and logical explanation for the appearance of an extra large distorted looking dead wolf at the Double V Ranch.

In the short trip to Fortress, Sarah whispers to Melody some reasons why she has avoided her through the years, most of which deal with the prestige, wealth, and the seemingly glamorous lifestyle that Melody and Ricky had experienced living in Los Angeles. She finally confesses to her that she had been jealous of her. Another reason is because of their religion and especially their strange commune lifestyle on the Double V Ranch. Melody is led by the Holy Spirit not to talk much but mostly listen. As Sam drives onto the property of Fortress, he is eventually directed by Forrest who is outside the garage/warehouse looking for them. He motions to them where to park and tells them the leaders are waiting inside the garage/warehouse. Mary Anne parks right beside Sam's truck.

Forrest then walks up to Sam's door and shakes his hand when Sam gets out. He also shakes Deputy Sheriff Rutherford's and Sarah's hands as they come around the truck. After introducing himself, he tells them that everyone is glad they are there. He then knocks on the side door of the garage and the new arrivals are greeted by Bro. Ricky and Bro. Gary. The friendly greetings from Ricky and Gary are met with looks of skepticism, curiosity, 'howdies,' and firm handshakes from Sam and Hank. Sarah is genuinely friendly, which catches Ricky and Gary off guard.

Ricky is the first to speak about the giant pitwolf. "Sheriff, Deputy, Sarah, please follow us to the next room. The animal is in the back of my son's truck." As they walk to the next room, the leaders are now introducing themselves and shaking the hands of Sam, Hank, and Sarah. Both Melody and Mary Anne are each holding hands with Sarah who seems to be running a fever again from her flu. From her wide-eyed expression, Sarah also seems to be getting scared because deep down she believes Melody's story of the giant beast. An almost nauseating stench of death has filled the garage even though a back window is wide open and a tarp covers the dead beast. Sheriff Barnes walks over to the tarp and yanks it back. He sees an animal unlike anything he has ever seen before.

Hank's eyes get really large and he says, "Sheriff, we have a big problem on our hands." Barnes, stunned by what he sees, just says, "Yep!" really loud.

Melody and Mary Anne notice that Sarah's body just starts shaking uncontrollably. She says, "Sam, darling, this giant pitwolf is for real! It's for real!" Melody and Mary Anne start trying to comfort her and begin praying for her quietly.

Barnes' pride takes a huge hit by realizing Melody and Mary Anne had been right about it being a giant pitwolf. He turns around slowly, hesitates for a moment, and then swallows a huge lump of pride. He looks them square in the eyes one at a time and apologizes to them for doubting their word. Hank follows suit. Sam then goes over to Sarah and hugs her tightly and kisses the top of head, saying, "Baby, it's going to be alright. We are going to get everyone of these beasts if there are any more in the area. Don't worry!" Melody and Mary Ann quietly offer to take Sarah away from the dead pitwolf to the lodge where all the Crawfords and Kirkmans live and give her some aspirin for her fever. They ask Sam if that would be alright and he agrees as long as there is armed protection. Three deacons leave carrying rifles and shotguns to drive them to the lodge.

Barnes is starting to feel the heat of the hot seat that he is in as Sheriff of Clark County. Hank is feeling the heat also. Barnes, never one to beat around the bush, says, "Now that my wife is gone, I want to tell you all this. I don't want anybody breathing a word about this to anyone outside of this ranch until I give the ok. I need some time to figure some things out. This is an explosive situation and I think all you know this. Bro. Ricky and Bro. Gary, I haven't quite figured you guys out since you moved here. I'm not a very religious person, but I have my own belief in God. Regardless of what you exactly believe, I don't care at this point. All I care about is protecting my county and the people in it - period. Whatever power or sway you have over the people in your church or community, whatever you call it, please use it at this time."

Gary speaks up. "Sheriff Barnes, let me assure you, we are already on the same page as you. We told all our people not to mention this animal to anyone and not to take any pictures of it. Sheriff, this is our home. This community is our community. However we can assist you, we will be glad to do so." Everyone in the room verbalizes that they are in agreement. "Everyone you see in this room is trustworthy. As for everyone else on this property, we will insist that they remain silent on this subject until you direct us otherwise."

Barnes, wanting to believe them, says, "I'm going to have to trust you with that statement because I don't know you guys personally very well. I wasn't the sharpest guy in school, but I wasn't the dumbest either. My momma didn't raise a fool and I have enough horse sense to know this animal is not a regular cross between a pitbull or any other kind of dog and a wolf. Some mad scientist developed this animal. These three-inch fangs remind me of something like a saber tooth tiger. This animal's double muscle look reminds me of the blue Belgium bulls I saw at the Colorado State Fair years ago. Those bulls didn't look real. It was like they ate nothing but steroids. This brindle color of its fur reminds me of pitbulls with the same pattern that I've seen a number of times. Its massive head and jaws are a cross between a pitbull and a wolf, but much bigger. This thing could pass for an animal from prehistoric times. Even dead, this thing will scare the hell out of most people. What concerns me the most is that we have no idea how many more of these animals are out there in the wild."

"I hate to inform you, officers, but there are at least four more of these creatures possibly nearby. The biggest one was a huge alpha male with three smaller females. I believe the male may have been pushing 400 plus pounds. I spotted them up on top of Watson's box canyon tonight with my thermal imaging and night vision scopes when we had to rescue Caleb and the boys earlier this evening," declares a solemn Ricky.

'Well, I'm I not surprised, Ricky,' replies Sam in an angry, sarcastic tone.

"I just knew it! I had a gut feeling that kind of information was coming forth. Sheriff, I have a question to ask these people."

"Go head, Hank."

"Well, I know you guys here at the Double V Ranch raise some cattle, bison, a few horses, and other farm animals."

"Yes, we do, Deputy," replies Ricky.

"Well, I was wondering, do y'all have one of those microchip readers like you can get at a veterinarian supply store?"

"Yes, we have one. It's over there on the counter," says Ricky. "We already tried it on the animal and nothing showed up."

"Well, I'm pretty familiar with them and if you don't mind, I'd like to try it myself." Hank has used the same model before on three expensive registered quarter horses at his uncle's ranch. After a few tries, he gets no response.

Ricky says, "Sheriff, what is your game plan?"

"Well, Ricky, I want to talk to John Blackhawk. I've heard some almost unbelievable things about him tracking animals, understanding their behavior, and being a crack shot with a rifle." Barnes knows John is a Sioux Indian and starts walking toward him. Blackhawk does the same and both shake each other's hand firmly.

John says, "How can I help you, Sheriff Barnes?"

"Well, John, I would like to borrow your services to help track down these animals. Were you involved in tracking down and killing this creature?"

"Yes, sir, I tracked it down and got the first shot in. I shot it once with my .300 Winchester magnum bolt action rifle; then it jammed on me. It was a dead shot to the center of the chest as you can see here," as he points to the bullet hole of the dead beast's wide muscular chest.

"My God!" says Barnes. "With the placement of that bullet and using a .300 magnum, that animal should have dropped instantly."

"But it didn't, Sheriff. I shot that wolf in mid air as it leaped off of a huge boulder and it never missed a beat until Caleb shot it in the right upper leg and shattered the bone. The beast went down on its side still trying to claw its way to us when Forrest Johnson finished it off with a .45 caliber bullet to the base of its skull."

Sam, replies, "Wow! Incredible! I'm just glad everybody is safe. Okay, which one is Caleb? There were a lot of names mentioned when we came here."

"I'm Caleb, sir," as he raises his hand. "My Dad is Bro. Ricky."

"Oh, yeah, I thought you were the one. I should have known with those massive hands that you have like your grandfather, the Big Swede."

"Yeah, you could say it has been my most outstanding feature my whole life."

"Yours are huge, but I think your grandfather had you beat. He had the biggest hands and fingers I've ever seen. He was one of a kind and definitely a character. I really liked the Big Swede."

Caleb replies, "Yes, he was a character."

Barnes hesitates for a second. "I remember Sarah mentioning to me that you were a former Captain in the Navy SEALS."

"Yes, sir, I was," responds Caleb.

"With your background, you may also be very valuable for the task ahead. And which one is Forrest?" asks Barnes.

"He's the young guy that met you outside the building just before you came in," responds Caleb.

"He's the second best tracker after Blackhawk," Ricky adds. "John has been teaching Forrest some old school Indian tricks on tracking."

"That's great to know. I'm going to chew on all this information tonight and come up with a game plan as to exactly what I'm going to do. But, in the meantime, guys, I need to get my wife home soon. I also need to talk to Bro. Gary and Bro. Ricky alone with my deputy before we leave. If some of you guys can discreetly put the dead beast in the back of my truck, cover it up with a tarp, and post a couple guards around the truck until I come out, I would appreciate it. You may also want to park my truck away from the building here to keep people from literally getting wind of it. The smell of death is very powerful."

"I'll make sure it's all taken care of, Sheriff," says Caleb, as he shakes Barnes' hand. Barnes hands Caleb the keys to his truck. Everyone quickly leaves the garage except the two male elders and Sam and Hank.

When it is just the four men, Barnes pauses for a moment, then adjusts his cowboy hat up and down on his head, finally telling Ricky and Gary point blank, "I think Ci Mada Union Laboratories in Boulder developed this animal. What do you guys think?"

Gary quickly replies, "Well, Sheriff, I can say that once again we are on the same page."

Barnes, glad to know that he is not dealing with two country bumpkins, says, "Now I have no evidence at this point. I can't prove it, but my hunch is that it's them. I know a little bit about their history and it seems to point to them as the culprits."

Gary says, "We know it's them without a doubt."

Sam, who is almost beside himself, says, "It makes me fighting mad when someone is messin' around with my county and my people and I don't like it one d#%* bit. But, the microchip reader didn't give me any information that I needed to prove that this is the case."

"I thought for sure that animal was chipped and something would come up with that reader," adds Hank.

"Me too," says Barnes, "But I tell you one thing, boys. I'm going to get to the bottom of this situation if it kills me. I guarantee it!"

Ricky winks at Gary and Gary nods back at Ricky. Gary says, "Sheriff, we felt we could trust you before you came and now we are very confident that we can trust both of you. You might already know that I was an attorney in California and practiced real estate law."

Sheriff Barnes replies, "Yeah, I knew a little about you and Ricky."

"Great! And as an attorney I sometimes had to appear in court with my client. So I never laid all my cards on the table in court at one time. I always tried to keep an ace up my sleeve, figuratively speaking that is."

Barnes' face lights up and he begins to form a grin for the first time tonight. He tells Hank, "I'm beginning to like these boys, Hank, because I've always liked having an ace in the hole to fall back on."

Hank replies, "Yeah! I know what you mean, Sheriff. But where are you going with this, Mr. Kirkman?"

"Well, we know for an absolute fact that Ci Mada is behind the creation of this giant pitwolf."

The usually reserved Barnes is highly curious at this point. "What kind of proof do you have that links Ci Mada with the dead giant pitwolf?" Ricky now interjects, "Sheriff, Deputy, can we have your word that the information that we are about to reveal to you will be kept secret? Your very lives may depend on the both of you being 'tightlipped'.

"You got my word on it," says Barnes with a puzzled look on his face.

"Mine too," agrees Hank.

"Then, gentlemen, follow me. I will show you some advanced technology that Ci Mada has no idea we possess," replies a confident Ricky. "I think you men know that my company was a defense contractor in mostly the electronic aerospace field."

"Yeah, I knew that through Sarah and the Big Swede," says Sam.

"Well, at my former company Spartan Electronic Corporation, we never limited our research and development totally to that field. We were always trying to stay on the cutting edge of a lot of electronic and computer-related fields. So my position and company had some perks that came along with it." He walks into the next room and reaches into a drawer where he has temporarily placed the Russian advanced prototype microchip reader. He says, "Guys, as you know the first reader did not work on the dead giant pitwolf. That's because it is a basic model. They can be purchased at any veterinarian supply store or online. But the model I'm holding works on a basic microchip and an advanced one called an SMR, or sleeper microchip reader. The basic model reader can't detect a sleeper chip because it is advanced secret high technology. It requires a reader like the one I'm holding."

"Can you demonstrate, Ricky, how it works?" asks a very interested Sam Barnes.

"Yes, I can," says Ricky, as he pushes several buttons to start the reader. "Give it a minute and it will pull up the last entry which was from the giant pitwolf which we did not delete." Ricky and Gary then tell Barnes and Rutherford why they can't bring this secret information out in public. Sheriff Barnes' face turns a shade of red from the anger mounting up within him. Hank is biting his lip and his thumbs and fingers are pinching both sides of his hips and he rapidly twists his upper body from side to side and moves around while tapping his right cowboy boot on the concrete floor in a rhythmic motion. He is momentarily glassy-eyed in deep thought. But his facial expressions show a high level of anger. He can't believe what he has seen and heard tonight. Finally, Ricky notices the reader has a digital printout on the screen and shows it to the two law officers. They see the name Ci Mada Union Laboratories at the top of the screen. Barnes and Rutherford both let out a string of expletives in rapid succession. Barnes snatches his cowboy hat off and slams the side of his right leg with it in great frustration.

Sam says, "Please, pardon our French." I know the both of you are ministers, but Hank and I are teed off that a multi-billion dollar corporation operating in Colorado is putting the screws to the citizens of this state, especially here in Clark County."

"You got that right, Sheriff! And that's not even the half of it!" says Hank in a very angry tone of voice.

Barnes, still fuming, says, "I love this state I was born in, but it's changed. So in the end the rest of Colorado can go to pot as far as I am concerned, like it has been literally doing since 2013." In Old West fashion, Sam Barnes has his right hand on the wooden rosewood handle of his well worn and oiled .44 magnum. He's just itching to use it, like he is ready to call someone out at high noon for a gunfight. "They'll have to kill me before I let these creatures from hell and that anti-American no good company bushwack my county. I would kill every last one of their filthy beasts if I could get them in my gun's sight. And I would do the same to every white collar criminal connected to creating these monsters n the first place if I knew who they were and could get away with it. I'm so mad right now I could curse a blue streak for a half hour and never use the same string of curse words twice."

Barnes repositions his cowboy hat on his head and grabs the back of his neck with his right hand for a moment. He briefly massages it in an attempt to loosen up his neck muscles that are tightening and ponders the advanced prototype microchip reader screen. He then poses a question to both leaders. "Does that line PW #201 stand for this dead pitwolf being number 201?"

"Yes, I'm afraid it does, Sam," replies Ricky.

By this time, Sam's face has turned a darker shade of red and the veins in his neck bulge out as if they are going to explode. He raises his flat hand above his head and slams it hard on a sturdy wooden work table in the garage. In a deep strained frustrated voice, Sheriff Barnes slowly asks, "What is wrong with people today? What in the world are people thinking? You can't play around with mother nature because it will turn around and bite you in the backside. God Almighty only knows how many more giant pitwolves there are after that number." The usually reserved Barnes is livid.

Hank says, "Sheriff, we are between a rock and a hard place with this giant pitwolf situation."

"I know," says Barnes. "If I don't tell the people of this county about these animals and try to hunt them without them knowing, it will backfire on me, especially if someone is attacked and killed."

"We can't rule out that these giant predators aren't man eaters either, Sheriff."

"No, we can't, Hank. I need a plan by tomorrow morning as to what I'm going to do. I've got to do something quick or people will be calling for my resignation because I didn't warn them right away that these monsters are on the loose. If I let the media know about this monster from hell and possibly other ones in this county, it will become the center of a media frenzy. I'll have people flood into this county from the federal level on down telling me what and what not to do. People will go nuts and some people will be afraid to leave the safety of their own homes. I'll have everybody and their brother sticking their nose in my business. And I really don't want that to happen. Plus, if I go to the media about this, there might be a mass exodus of people out of this county - good people who are just plain scared out of their wits. Last of all, I can't mention that the dead pitwolf has a special chip in its head because I put people lives at risk because of a super highly secretive technology that an evil, corrupt multi-billion dollar corporation named Ci Mada uses."

Ricky interjects, "Sheriff, one thing is for sure. You can't hunt these beasts at night. It's just impossible to track them and it's too dangerous."

"Gentlemen, I don't have an ace up my sleeve at this point. If I did, I think it just slid into a real deep hole and I can't retrieve it. Maybe you have one-because I sure don't see one at this point. It looks to me like I'm in a no win situation because there is no good solution to this problem."

"Yes, one is always available to us."

"Where is it?"

"It's God, Sam."

"Well, I guess I need someone who is on good speaking terms with the Big Man upstairs. We've been disconnected for some time. So I'm going to have to rely on you guys for some divine help."

"Well, we have a special group of people here who have the ear of God. He can move heaven and earth for us if needed. They were born for such a time as this."

"Who are these people?"

"They are intercessors who pray around the clock here in our prayer chapel."

"Well, I'm not sure exactly what an intercessor is or does. But I'll take all the prayer I can get right now. I never expected that I would be needing your spiritual help, but I do. I really do."

"We all need God's help at this point, don't we, Sam?"

"Yes, I guess we do. Our options seem to be limited at this time." Barnes continues, "It makes me think of that saying that God moves in mysterious ways. There were times I prayed in Vietnam because I thought for sure I wouldn't make it back alive on certain missions. But I always survived. But since then my prayers have been few and far between. We need a miracle and it is dark now. There is nothing I can do. I will be racking my brain for a game plan. So I'd like to get a fresh start early in the morning just before the sun comes up."

Bro. Gary, says, "Yes, you're right, Sheriff, because we are dealing with more than one of these vicious and unpredictable animals. We need to err on the side of caution."

"There is a huge favor I need to ask of you guys," says Barnes in a humble manner.

Instantly Ricky responds, "I would be glad to fly you around in our helicopter and help you scope out the area to see if we can spot these animals."

Barnes, looking somewhat shocked, says, "Ricky, it's like you read my mind."

"That's what I was thinking, Sheriff," adds Hank, who also looks a little shocked.

"I saw the scale over there. Did you guys weigh the dead beast?"

"Yes, Sir. He came in at 372 pounds."

"Gee," says Hank. "So this alpha male you saw, Ricky, was he bigger than this monster?"

"I can't be certain, but I think he is probably pushing around 400 pounds."

Barnes, with his dry wit, says, "Hank, the news just keeps getting better and better tonight."

"Sheriff, I was kind of thinking more along the lines that things are going from bad to worse myself."

Barnes is ready to go and tells Ricky and Gary that he wishes he had gotten to know them sooner and better under different circumstances. Both groups recognize the seriousness of the situation and their mutual need for each other. Sheriff Barnes tells Ricky and Gary that he and Hank need to go and talk some more over this situation and figure out what to do with the dead giant pitwolf. He mentions the need to go to Pete's house and tell him the bad news about his bull. He also wants to patrol the county tonight for any signs of pitwolf activity. Barnes also is concerned about Sarah because she was not doing very well the last time he saw her. As he and Hank shake the hands of Ricky and Gary, he says, "I'll be here tomorrow before the sun comes up. If y'all can be ready, along with Blackhawk, I'd greatly appreciate it. Until then, have your people use extreme caution and

R.E. Crofton

protection moving to and from these buildings. Hank and I are going to head over to pick up Sarah at the lodge, then head on over to Watson's place and break the bad news to them. I'm not looking forward to it, but it's a job that has to be done."

"You want one of us to go with you, Sheriff?"

"No we're fine. Just batten down the hatches here."

"Sheriff, could you do us a favor before you leave?"

"What's that, Ricky?"

"Would you mind if I prayed?"

"No, I guess it wouldn't hurt, because I know now I need some help from the Man upstairs."

"Yes, we do, don't we?"

"Thanks, Sam. Sam and Hank, would you please take off cowboy hats?" As they remove their hats, everyone bows their heads. Ricky prays, "Dear Mighty Lord, we know that You are not caught off guard or perplexed about our dilemma here in Golden Valley with these ferocious giant pitwolves surrounding us. Neither are You confused about what to do with this dead one in the back of the Sheriff's pickup. We look to You who is mighty and powerful and full of wisdom to guide Sam and Hank about what to do tonight, tomorrow, and the following days. We believe Your hand is divinely on this property and You will protect us here. But we are our brothers keepers and we ask for Your mighty hand to be upon the people in this area and be merciful. Our law enforcement officials and the people of Fortress don't want the media and government agencies to converge upon this county and snoop around asking a lot of questions so they can oppress us. Our ace in the hole is the prayers of our people. So we are playing that card now in hopes of victory in this situation. Amen."

"Thanks, Ricky. I appreciate all the prayers. I've never prayed very much before, but I'm just hoping we have a winning hand with you boys covering our backs with prayer. In the meantime, we've got to get rolling over to your lodge to get my better half." Hey Sam if you don't mind can Ricky and I catch ride in the backseat of your truck so we can see you guys off with Sarah.

No problem, just climb in. You sure you boys don't want to ride in the back with that covered dead prehistoric looking beast that stinks to the high heavens. No we're good. Thanks for the ride inside the truck and no thanks to ride outside joked Gary. Ricky rolled his eyes and shook his head in the affirmative.

Chapter 8

THE NEED TO INTERCEDE

During the ride, both Sam and Hank are a little numb from the rapid life changing events of the night. They also are silent during the short ride to the lodge, pondering their next series of decisions that need to be made. Sarah's health also weighs heavily on Sam's mind. Gary and Ricky quietly whisper things that need to be done and the direction for the ministry of Fortress at this time. They see the giant pitwolves as instruments of the devil to strike fear in the hearts of the people there and the surrounding area and to bring outside intrusion into Golden Valley and Clark County in general. Like Barnes, these senior co-pastors of Fortress and co-founders of the Disciplemaker Network of Churches do not want the media spotlight on them as a result of these giant pitwolves. The media usually wants to cast their ministry in a bad light, especially in recent years with a growing anti-Christian population who knows neither God nor His Word nor ways. Their ministry has been painted by the media as a weird religious cult, fanatic narrow-minded bigots, or Christian doomsayers. On the other side of the coin, liberal Christians have also attacked them on their uncompromising view of the world. They view discipleship as mind control and the orthodox biblical teachings as antiquated and not progressive in a world of tolerance and an ever growing acceptance of other religions and philosophies. Pseudo Christians view the God of the Bible as a loving father of unlimited grace and mercy for everyone in the world. God is forgiving and would send no one to hell. Because hell does not exist. One thing is for sure. Given the events of the evening, the time has come when anything short of a miracle would not be enough to solve their problems.

Sam has already made up his mind to pick up Sarah and take her straight home after a short stop before making other necessary rounds of the night. At the top of the list is Pete Watson's ranch to tell him the bad news about his bull. Sam is still contemplating what to do with the giant dead animal. What none of the men know before they reach the lodge is that Sarah has been instantly healed of her fever and other flu symptoms. Another glorious and the most spectacular thing is that she has also just gotten born again as a result of Melody's and Mary Anne's praying and witnessing to her after they left the garage.

As they approach the church's multi-purpose room where Fortress members are meeting for prayer, Gary asks Sam to stop briefly. Sam nods and the truck comes to a halt. Gary rolls down his window and he and Ricky quickly find out the latest information from Leon, Charlie, Forrest, and Tommy who are posted outside as guards. They tell Ricky and Gary that almost everyone is at the prayer meeting in the church building with all the intercessors except Sisters Melody and Mary Anne and three brothers in the Lord functioning as bodyguards.

All five of the church members and Mrs. Barnes are at the lodge. Less than half a minute later they pull up to the well-lit lodge. Three middle-aged men with shotguns, rifles, and pistols are standing guard. They greet Gary, Ricky, Sam, and Hank with grins and tell them there is a surprise inside. Sam and Hank think the incident a little strange with the unfolding of the unbelievable events of the night. As the four men enter the house, they soon find out that Sarah has just asked Christ to be her Lord and Savior. Not only is she saved, but delivered and healed at the same time. Sarah says that, upon finishing saying the sinner's prayer, she instantly felt like a shackle that had held her mind captive for years was gone. She felt a rush of joy fill her soul and great peace that she has never known before. The fear of pitwolves has also left her. After getting saved she tells Melody and Mary Anne that she feels like a new woman. Melody tells her that she is indeed a new woman. In fact she tells her that she is a new creation in Christ. That old things have passed away because she has just gotten saved. Sarah says that she is coming back tomorrow to talk with Melody and Mary Anne about her new experience and that she has a lot of questions. Upon hearing the good news, all the elders begin to praise God. Sarah's salvation is an answer to prayer due to numerous hours spent praying for her soul.

Mary Anne notices that when Sam and Hank walk inside the lodge to pick Sarah up, she meets Sam with a big smile, hugs him, and tells him that she is saved. Sam mishears her and thinks she said safe. He tells her that she is safe and that everything is going to be alright. She says, "No, Sam, honey. I said I am saved." Sam has a shocked look on his face like he doesn't know what she is talking about. Sarah's whole countenance has changed and the word "saved" has thrown the old cowboy for a loop like a wild bucking horse. He seems uncomfortable and wants to get out of the lodge fast. His facial expressions indicate that he is perplexed and confused by her actions and speech. Sam ponders if his soulmate has now found religion at this juncture in her life. He asks if she still has a fever. Melody and Mary Anne tell him the Lord has taken away her 102 degree temperature without any aspirin and that it is normal now, which really makes him even more uncomfortable. Hank seems even more bewildered by what has happened to Mrs. Barnes. Sarah seems odd and maybe a little delirious to him. Her health appears to be normal and she definitely doesn't seem afraid any more. But it just seems like Sarah Barnes has been brainwashed or hypnotized. It just isn't making sense to Hank.

Sam grabs Sarah by the hand and says, "Sarah, lets hurry because there is so much to do." He tells the elders thanks and quickly walks out to the truck with Hank, who is also way out of his comfort zone.

All four elders wave goodbye and Ricky tells the three bodyguards, "You guys weren't joking. Gary and I are very surprised. Thanks a lot, brothers. Almost everybody is at the church, if you guys are still up to it."

"We're good now." The three brothers are praising God for his goodness in the midst of a storm and decide to head to the prayer meeting.

As they walk away with their guns in their hands Gary says, "Blessings to you guys." They repeat the same back to him.

After Barnes, Sarah, Hank and the three brothers leave, Ricky, chuckling, says, "I believe this is just the beginning of God moving in our midst in the realm of the miraculous."

Gary adds, "God is still in charge of this whole ordeal. Praise God, this is exciting."

Melody says, "I can't believe it! My best friend from high school finally got saved after all these years of praying for her. It was worth every minute of prayer asking God to save her."

"I know my faith has been rejuvenated tonight in the midst of some ugly events to believe God for the impossible," says Mary Anne.

Ricky and Gary decide to take the girls in the den and fill them in on what took place in the garage previously. After about 15 minutes of explaining what all took place and what was said, Mary Anne and Melody know that their intercessory prayer time has to be ratcheted up several more levels. It has already taken a more serious tone with the meteorites falling around them in other counties. But the intensity of life is heating up in the end times, and they know it.

Ashley Crawford leaves the church's office at the prompting of the Holy Spirit to talk to the elders about information that she just came into contact with after leaving the garage earlier. She refuses to be escorted by Forrest and Charlie who are armed and were going to walk her to the lodge. As she enters her home, Melody sees her and blurts out, "Guess who just got saved, Ashley?"

"Did Sarah get saved?"

"Yes! Oh, my God, that is great news and we sure need it around here. I've been praying for that woman a long, long time. The intercessors are going to be pumped when they hear that good news. Well, my news isn't as great as Sarah getting saved, but it is some interesting news, I believe."

"Well, Ashley, go ahead and share it with us," says Ricky.

"I went to the church office right after leaving the garage and called a Christian friend that I know up in Overton County to find the scoop on the possible drone that crashed earlier today in that county sometime before 7:00 PM. The friend said that she was pretty sure it was a large high-tech drone but couldn't confirm it from rumors she had heard. Some unusual events had occurred and she was trying to find out the details from a friend who was afraid and keeping his mouth shut. She said that when she found out something, she would give me a call. While I was in the office I also felt led by the Holy Spirit for some odd reason and checked both satellite phones in our office. For some odd reason they are not working."

All the elders' eyebrows are arched up with all the news that Ashley shared. Can it be that God used a small meteorite to knock out a drone that was used to track the pitwolves? It's possible!

"I'm not sure why God wanted me to check the satellite phones." She blurts out, "Maybe a satellite was taken out earlier by a meteorite at the same time as the drone was!" She starts laughing under her breath as she is thinking out loud.

All four elders say, "Maybe," in unison. Hope and faith begin to spring up in each of their souls - like the kind that can come only from the Holy Spirit to believe God against all odds. Everyone is excited what God was up to in Golden Valley and they ponder different scenarios. Thirty minutes later Ashley then decides she needs to go and check on her two boys and the rest of the members in the church building.

Before she leaves, Melody says, "Ashley, I want to break the news of Sarah's salvation to the intercessors and the rest of our members, if you don't mind."

"No problem, Mom," says Ashley.

Once Ashley is gone, Mary Anne and Melody talk to their husbands for input concerning direction for praying about different problems that are associated with the giant pitwolf situation. After about 15 minutes, everyone decides it is best to keep it all very general in nature in the prayer chapel. Ricky and Gary know that the creation of the giant beasts by Ci Mada is a dangerous situation and that it is best that the general population of Fortress knows none of the high-tech secret information that was discussed earlier - not even their wives. However, both women are positive it is Ci Mada behind the development of the urban legend. Gary and Ricky know their wives know this and already have all the information they need. A short time later Caleb comes inside the lodge to the living room where his parents and his aunt and uncle are drinking coffee and talking. He has left his two teenage sons, Stephen and Andrew, and Ashley in the church praying.

Earlier, after leaving the church building, he had checked on Forrest and the other guards and had gotten some more men who had been praying to relieve them of their posts. He tells his family that he and Forrest drove around the ranch in his truck and found no signs that the pitwolves had been on the premises. But they heard them off in the distance howling around the box canyon. He also states that he saw Dr. Stanton, who wants to talk with either his dad or Uncle Gary if possible, even though it is late.

"He wouldn't elaborate," says Caleb, "So I'm assuming it's about the incident tonight with Dad and Thomas Jr.." Gary decides to meet with Dr. Stanton and his wife Lisa. Ricky says that is fine with him because he needs to get with David and Max tonight to ask them if they can help him check over the helicopter before he flies it in the morning.

Caleb also tells the elders that while they were driving around, Forrest was positive that GS 33 was the satellite that the military used in their Global System of Routing Satellites for the area of Colorado that includes Clark County. He stated that his Uncle Sonny had told him that he had found out that the satellite that went over the area of the Double V Ranch always did so at 7:00 PM every evening like clockwork during the summer months. He said he was 100% positive about those details because it dealt directly with Fortress. Caleb also states that Ashley told him about the drone going down in the next county.

Upon hearing this, Ricky says, "Son, Ashley felt prompted by God earlier to check the satellite phones for some reason and they weren't working. So now I believe just before 7:00 PM tonight they weren't working."

"I'm positive they weren't, Dad, just like you said at that time."

"Son, I'm beginning to see the hand of God working behind the scenes on this whole event tonight." The Kirkmans' and Crawfords' faith is rising, knowing that God is working in their midst and for their good.

Caleb says, "First, a drone that was probably tracking these pitwolves goes down around a little before 7:00 PM this evening. Next, a satellite that flies over us like clockwork was also probably tracking those beasts. Here's hoping just maybe it got put out of commission around the same time in outer space. I'm hoping meteorites took them both out for more reasons than one."

"That's what I'm hoping," says Gary as he looks at Ricky and nods.

"Yeah, me too," adds Ricky as he nods back to Gary.

"Well, that would be great if indeed it happened," Mary Anne chimes in, not knowing all the details of the events in the garage but having a general idea and knowing eyes in the sky were not a good thing at this time. "But we can't let our guard down."

"Absolutely not," says, Melody. "We must keep on plowing ahead in prayer for God to continue to work all things for our good."

Mary Anne, who is tired, considers going to bed to get some sleep. But with all that has happened, she can't. She feels led to stay at the lodge and that she will pray more in the morning.

Melody says she is so excited and can't sleep and wants to go the prayer chapel and join the other intercessors and church members and tell them the incredible news of Sarah's salvation. She then says, "Mary Anne, get some rest and you can relieve me in the early morning."

"I would be delighted."

"Thanks!"

Mary Anne tells Melody that she will relieve her in four hours. They are hoping Sarah will come tomorrow to visit with them while Sam is flying in the helicopter with their husbands and Blackhawk.

As soon as the elders go about their different activities for the night, Caleb decides to go to the church and check the two satellite phones in the office. He tests each one to see if they are working, but neither one works. Caleb then hears a knock at the door. It's Blackhawk with Pete Watson.

John says, "Caleb, Pete wants to see you right now."

"Sure," says Caleb. "Come in Pete."

"Thanks, John."

"You're welcome."

"I guess you know why I'm here, Caleb."

"Yeah, I do. I'm so sorry, Pete, about the loss of Big Blackie. I know you had invested a lot of capital into that animal to upgrade your herd."

"Caleb, that is the least of my worries. I mean, man, that is bad enough. But Molly is freakin' out right now. The meteorites were already playing with her head. And this huge evil looking creature just took her over the edge. She wanted to see that giant pitwolf in the back of Barnes' truck and he knew she was upset. Mrs. Barnes said, 'Molly, believe me, you don't want to see it.' I didn't want her to see it, but you know how persistent she can be. She insisted on seeing it. You know how she is, Caleb?"

"Yeah, I know, Pete."

"When she saw it, she screamed bloody murder and yelled, 'Get me out of here, Pete. I want out of this God-forsaken country. It ain't worth it. This place is too dangerous for me and my babies. All hell is breaking loose here. I want to go see my family in Salt Lake City. You can either drive me and the kids or we're flying. Either way, we are going for now until this area is safe again.' Sheriff Barnes, Mrs. Barnes, Hank, and I tried to calm her down, but she refused to listen and said that she was going inside to pack. "

"Pete, again I'm sorry. I don't know what to say other than you do what you need to do. We are praying diligently here for this situation and God is working behind the scenes. What I can also tell you is that we are going to continually pray for you and your family."

"Well, I really appreciate that. I have grown a lot in the Lord in the last year since you first led me to Christ. I've always felt we were pretty good friends. As we were growing up I enjoyed seeing you during some of the holidays and every summer for at least a couple of weeks until you eventually went away to college at the Naval Academy."

"Pete, I consider you a good friend and, more than that, we are brothers in the Lord. Whatever you need us to do for you while you are away from your ranch, we'll take care of it. You can count on that."

"Caleb, that takes a load off my mind. Whew, you have no idea what this means to me. I was hoping you could help me out. I mean, I'll make it up to you guys with money or something. Anything."

"Pete, look at me. Don't worry about it. You just let me know what we have to do on your ranch or house and we'll get 'r done. Main thing is that your wife needs to feel secure and have peace of mind. Think of going to Salt Lake City as well-deserved vacation."

"Yeah, you're right. Well anyway, Caleb, here is a list of the most crucial things that need to be done. And I guess you'll need my keys to everything. I used a permanent pen on the keys by putting numbers on them to match them to the items on the list. I also wrote my in-laws' phone numbers in case you can't get a hold of me."

"Oh yeah, they're the ones that own that big freeze-dried food company called Eden's Best."

"Yes, your dad and Uncle Gary bought quite a bit of their inventory some years back."

"That's right," remembers Caleb.

Pete, smiling proudly, says, "I was able to help them get a better discount than normal on the food. Pete's smile quickly turns into a frown as he says, "I don't think it is going to be an R and R type vacation."

"Why?" asks Caleb.

"Because I'm on my in-laws' blacklist now because I'm a born again Christian. I'm so evil now in their minds. Before I was just a lost soul. Now I'm a bad influence leading their daughter away from the Mormon faith and straight to Hell."

"Pete, it's a time to be a witness for Christ. Okay, maybe it won't be an R and R vacation. Think of it as a mission trip to your in-laws."

"That sounds a little bit more realistic, Caleb."

"From what Ashley has told me, Pete, Molly is really close to getting saved. She has had some good conversations with her and she is so close."

"Well, I don't know about that right now, Caleb, with the news we got tonight. Anyway, keep us in your prayers. I better get going now and pack for the trip. Because I guarantee you if I don't, Molly will take off with the kids without me."

"Okay, Pete." They shake hands and give each other a hug. God bless, be safe, and take care."

"Pete says, "Bye," as he walks out.

Caleb leaves two minutes later and bumps into his Uncle Gary and Aunt Mary Anne who are next to the church office door talking. They are going to Dr. Stanton's cabin a short distance from the church. He says, "Oh, excuse me. Sorry, Uncle Gary."

Gary replies, "That's alright, Caleb. Mary Anne and I checked on the people of the church to see how they were doing. There's a good group in there praying intensely. A few who weren't praying at the time are still shaken up by the whole ordeal tonight. I just felt that, even though Mary Anne is really tired, I needed her to go with me to see the Stantons."

"I'll keep you guys in my prayer."

"Thanks," Gary and Mary Anne respond simultaneously.

A few minutes later, Gary knocks on Dr. Stanton's door. Dr. Stanton, a little nervous but very cordial, invites them in. He and his wife Lisa shake hands and hug with Gary and Mary Anne. "Please come in make yourself comfortable on our couch. Well, Bro. Gary and Sister Mary Anne, I really don't know where to begin. We are so sorry about our son's inexcusable behavior. I mean Lisa and I have done everything we know to raise our boy up in the teachings of the Bible especially after the both of us got saved. Even when we were in the Mormon church, we tried to model good biblical character to our son, Thomas in our own power as we now realize."

Lisa interjects, "He wasn't always wild and rebellious like he was tonight. We have always prayed for our son as devout Mormons and now as devout born again Christians. We love him, but we fear God has marked him now."

"Lisa, we are not sure what you mean," says Mary Anne.

"I'm a little confused at this point," Gary adds.

Dr. Stanton explains, "Thomas has lost his voice. He is unable to say a word or even a syllable since he came back to this cabin after the incident tonight in which he was so disrespectful to Bro. Ricky."

"Is he sick?" inquires Mary Anne.

"No, he's not," Dr. Stanton assures them. I thoroughly checked him out and can find no reasonable explanation other than God has allowed this to happen to him."

"Well, Dr. and Mrs. Stanton, I'm going to tell you something. It's not to make me or Bro. Ricky look superior to anybody here at Fortress. We both put our pants on one leg at a time like every man here. We are content with people using Bro. before our name or Mr. or pastor or just our first name. We don't wear suits and ties unless there is a wedding, funeral, or some other special occasion. But we are really apostles called to an end time ministry. Some people, including some Christians, have a problem with that. So we choose not to make it a problem. But maybe now God is trying to make a way of validating us and the mission he has called us and our wives to, at least to Thomas. I mean that's my line of thinking as a possible explanation for your son losing his voice."

"Dr. Stanton and Lisa, I think my husband might be right in his assumption."

"I didn't know what to call it, but the term validation seems to be an appropriate term as it relates to Bro. Gary and Bro. Ricky and the elders concerning what has taken place tonight. God may have used Thomas as the example to learn from as to how we and others outside this community treat you. And if that is the case, a holy fear is descending on this community of believers as in the early days of the New Testament church. But let me tell you, Bro. Gary, that we have never doubted for one moment that you two men are true apostles of God, have we Lisa?"

"No, absolutely not," replies Lisa. "Bro. Gary, we know that you and Bro. Ricky are two anointed apostles with an end time calling. Tom and I are rock solid on that. We just want to know what God wants us to do or what we should do with Thomas because it is a little scary. He really humiliated us tonight with his words and actions. He dishonored Bro. Ricky, you, this ministry, and God tonight. I just wanted to crawl under a rock and die. I know Tom did too."

"Well, Tom and Lisa, let me tell you something," explains Mary Anne. "I firmly believe that since earlier this evening, all our lives have changed. We are in an accelerated mode at this juncture in time. God is going to take it to a whole new level before He is through. I'm Gary's wife, so I'm not speaking as the co-pastor here, but as an elder. Thomas made a public commitment that he would wash the dishes in the cafeteria for two weeks if he was wrong. Everyone that saw the giant pitwolf acknowledged what he said he would do if he was wrong about the pitwolf. As you know, everyone has been praying for him."

"Yes, we know and we are truly grateful," says Lisa.

Gary adds, "I agree with Mary Anne. I would also add that Thomas would need to publicly acknowledge in a non-verbal fashion true repentance that he is sorry for what he said to Ricky. Maybe God will use what happened to Thomas as an example of the fear of the Lord that we all need to walk in so that we can walk in greater holiness on the property as a church and as the people of the living God. I believe that before Christ returns, there will be people dropping dead like flies who are playing church in the true remnant churches remaining. Purity and holiness will reign in the these churches of God. I don't want to see that happen here, but it is a strong possibility to keep the church pure." Gary pauses, then makes a request. "Dr. and Mrs. Stanton, may I talk to Thomas?"

"Let me ask him, Bro. Gary."

Tom starts to knock on Thomas' small bedroom door, but instead opens it and sees Thomas lying on his bed crying. Tom Stanton is heartbroken concerning the condition of his son and about his actions tonight. He asks Thomas if he wouldn't mind seeing Bro. Gary. Thomas nods his head yes. As he gets up, he grabs a note pad and pen from his desk and walks with his dad to the living room. He shakes Bro. Gary and Sister Mary Anne's hands.

Thomas strains to try to force some words to come out of his mouth, but none come. All he is able to make is just groans and unrecognizable vocalizations. A flood of tears streams down his face. He quickly writes, "I know the Lord did this to me. I brought it on myself. I am so sorry that I have been such a big pain. That animal I saw tonight was not a pure wolf as a thought. I'm asking for forgiveness."

Gary sees the note and says, "That is great, Thomas. I'm glad you are sorry for your behavior. You need to sincerely apologize to Bro. Ricky for what you said to him. You also need to wash the dishes for two weeks in the cafeteria. I believe your problem is not a quick fix. You got yourself into this mess and only the Lord can get you out. The people here at Fortress love you and have been praying for you."

Thomas moves his mouth and tries to say, "I know."

"Thomas, if you can do those two things, I believe the Lord will restore your voice."

He nods to indicate he understands as tears fall on his already wet shirt.

"Tom and Lisa, you guys play a vital role here and in the community. I would like to pray for you as a family if no one minds."

Dr. Stanton replies, "Why of course not, Bro. Gary. We would be honored. Go ahead."

"Thanks. Dear Lord, it is with total sincerity that I come before You and plead in behalf of Dr. Stanton and his wife Lisa for their son Thomas. You have called them to Clark County to be part of this ministry and to help the needy and less fortunate as medical missionaries in this poor county. They are a blessing, and I know they love You with all their hearts. God, only You can take a life and make something out of it. You are the potter and we are just the clay. But would You please help Thomas to repent of his sins and ask Jesus Christ to come into his life and be his Lord and Savior and turn from his sinful ways? Help him to apologize to Bro. Ricky and to honor his commitment of washing dishes. I believe that if he would do this his speech will be restored. Amen."

"Thanks, Bro. Gary and Sister Mary Anne, for coming." They leave as they shake each of the Stantons' hands and hug them tight.

"Charlie, can you do me a favor and clean the windshield off? It looks like a couple birds took some liberties on my windshield, if you know what I mean. I'd do it myself but my back is acting up again, probably from walking up and down that box canyon last night."

"Yeah, sure. I'll get on it, Ricky. I bet it's those same two birds as before. I'd like to ring their necks."

"I believe you're right. Thanks. Sheriff Barnes will be here any minute."

"Sure thing, Ricky. I don't know how I overlooked it. Let me get some window cleaner and a rag."

"Thanks, Charlie. I just topped off the tank so you have plenty of fuel. David and Max got through a while ago with a preflight checklist and told me to tell you that you were good to go. So I think that is when the birds took care of their business."

"Probably."

"So we're good to go after the windshield is clean."

"Great!" says Ricky.

"Melody, while walking with Ricky, says, "I'm so exhausted after the emotional roller coaster last night and praying in the prayer chapel. The intercessors were intensely praying last night. They were all so excited when I told them Sarah got saved last night. But I also told them we desperately need a miracle and that is why more than usual prayed all night."

Ricky replies, "I know, Melody. We really need God to intervene in a big way."

Melody yawns and says, "I didn't sleep much last night. I had too many things racing through my mind."

"Yeah, I know what you mean, Honey. I also prayed a lot last night. Then had a hard time falling asleep. I knew I had to get some rest before flying this morning. We are all running on adrenaline at this point. I do not know

183

what the Lord is going to do, but I know He already has a solution like we told Barnes. Regardless of what happens, Jesus is Lord, Ricky."

"Amen, Sister. I thank God there have been no signs of any pitwolves on our property. Caleb and Forrest drove around the perimeter of the fence again this morning in the pasture and saw nothing."

"Praise God. Ricky, has there been any more howling since last night?"

"No, none this morning."

"Well, that is good news for us."

Over at the lodge now Caleb, Forrest, and Ashley are just finishing up some coffee at the breakfast table. Brenda Lee fell asleep less than two hours ago after praying all night. Ashley mentions the drone that crashed yesterday evening, and Forrest is also interested to find out if any more meteorites were spotted last night in Colorado. He turns on the TV in the kitchen and checks to see if there is a mention of anything on these two events. The local news out of Boulder is reporting live a breaking news story about large meteorites that have hit Boulder and Denver within the last five minutes. Immediately, Forrest yells to Brenda Lee to wake up and Caleb grabs his two-way radio to inform his dad and Uncle Gary of the horrific news. "Dad, Uncle Gary, this is Caleb. Do you copy? Do you copy?"

Ricky responds, "It's Dad, Son. What's going on now? It sounds like you have some more bad news."

"Yes, Dad, I do. Forrest just turned on the TV at the lodge and we are watching live coverage of large meteorites that hit the cities of Boulder and Denver about five minutes ago."

"Oh, my Lord, Son."

"And now the TV station in Boulder is saying about a one seventh of Boulder has been destroyed and an area one eighth the size of Denver has become a waste land. Oh my God, Dad! The news is showing pictures of two large craters and the surrounding area where they hit in each city, where there were once homes, businesses, and schools."

Forrest pipes in, "Hey Caleb, look! They are also reporting at the bottom of the TV screen that eight counties close to Clark County got hit hard with small meteorites last night at different times."

"Dad, you and Uncle Gary always said things were going to happen in rapid succession in the end times. And it is happening, not only in our home state but all around us."

"Yes, we did, Son. And to be honest, since last night it all seems surreal even to me and your mom."

In the meantime, Ashley is in awe of the events unfolding and Forrest is frozen in place as they watch the news. Brenda Lee wakes up out of a dead sleep. She runs into the kitchen where everyone is and is now wide-eyed with the alarming events on the TV screen. Caleb continues telling his dad about the newscast reports that fires are breaking out, gas lines are exploding, electric lines have been severed and are sparking all over the ground, water pipes are flooding the streets, and trash and debris are everywhere. Dust and other fine particles are gently fall back down to earth. A good percentage of people away from ground zero are coughing repeatedly from all the dust that is falling like a gray, black, and brown snow blanketing the ground. Fortunately, the wind in the sky appears to be moving kind of rapidly and it is blowing most of the cloud of dust over the city away from Boulder. People are dead all over the city from rocks and debris that flew through the air and hit them while they were walking or burst through the windshield of their cars while they were driving, or through their house's roof or window while they were asleep and killed them. A lot of the people that survived are in complete shock, walking about aimlessly hoping it is a bad dream from which they will awaken. The number of dead in Boulder alone is estimated to be in the tens of thousands.

Melody graduated from the Colorado A&M University along with her famous father the Big Swede who played football there. She asks Ricky to ask Caleb to find out if the university has survived. Ricky asks Caleb the question and he responds, "Tell Mom it is not in the vicinity of where the impact took place. It should be okay overall."

"Dad, it looks just like some war zones I saw when I was a SEAL. It's seems like another 911 except this time, it's meteorites and here in Colorado. The TV screen shows many people crying and several couples on their knees praying."

"Okay, Son, listen. I've got to go and sound the bell this time for another red alert. You grab Ashley, the boys, and anybody there and head to the church. Don't tell anybody else what you heard until I tell you. Got that, Son?"

"Yes. Alright I've got to go."

Melody overhears the conversation and most of the time she has her right hand over her mouth in disbelief. She says, "Ricky, things are going from bad to worse so quickly."

"I know, Honey. This is what Gary and I had been warning the body of Christ about for so many years. We have taught and preached that things were going to happen in rapid succession."

Ricky now sees Gary coming out of the church where he was visiting with Mary Anne before Barnes arrived. Just as Ricky is going to sound the bell in front of the church for a red alert, Gary looks at Ricky and says, "This isn't about pitwolves. This is about large meteorites."

Ricky, with a puzzled look on his face, asks, "How did you know, Gary? Did you hear Caleb contact us on your two-way radio?"

"No, I forgot mine. It's on my dresser at the lodge. The Lord just spoke to my heart so loud and clear and told me that meteorites partially destroyed large portions of Boulder and Denver minutes ago."

"Ricky, in awe of what God is doing, responds, "That's exactly what happened, Gary. You've heard from the Lord. Now I'm going to ring this bell for all to hear, Ding, Ding, Ding, Ding, Ding..."

Chapter 9

THE HAND OF GOD MOVES

5:53:33 AM, Mountain Standard Time, Wednesday, 05/08/20_ _, Ci Mada Union Laboratories, Boulder, Colorado, USA

Peter Nash is coming back from the company's cafeteria on the ground floor with a fresh hot cup of coffee and doughnuts. Dr. Fritz Von Gunten is going to relieve him at 6:30 AM but Nash is sleepy from working all night. He decided to take a walk and get his morning cup of coffee for a caffeine boost. He has been going over what is left of the damaged electronic debris that was recovered late last night at the crash site of the Eyegate TLZ drone in Overton County. The shipment had just arrived two hours before. Two special small units of security forces composed of the New International Union troops were located in different isolated areas of Colorado. They were at Ci Mada's disposal for whatever reason Von Gunten deemed necessary. One unit was dispatched soon after Dr. Von Gunten made a call to Washington, D.C. and left a message for the President who was unavailable after the downing of the satellite and drone became known yesterday evening. They were relatively close by and left in a semi-truck with a special forklift and special equipment inside. A bogus out of state company name was on the truck and a large unmarked white van with tinted windows for the troops followed behind. He also dispatched one special unit along with four black helicopters and 24 men to the location of the downed plane. They had the area lit up like a Christmas tree with a variety of intense lights and flashlights and combed the area with special metal detectors. Nothing of major electronic or computer importance was intact. It was like a meteorite had been turned into cosmic rocks and dust and obliterated and sandblasted the most advanced and technical electronic pieces away. Some locals who knew a plane had crashed wanted to help in the search and were warned not to intervene in the recovery. They were questioned for additional information and were intimidated and threatened to keep silent about the operation.

The meteorite had obliterated the most important technical components of the drone. There was no doubt that a meteorite had hit it from eyewitness accounts and video footage on smart phones that the special unit of the NIU troops had collected from some of the locals. One local pilot had witnessed it firsthand and gave them an account. Just as Nash pushes the button to the elevator, he sees Dr. Von Gunten coming through the security checkpoint at the front desk area. His boss is a scientist he greatly admires on one hand and on the other hand he often has grown tired of the man and his brash arrogance. He stops and drinks a sip of his coffee and eats a bite of his doughnut to wait for him.

"Good morning, Peter. Have you any good news on the satellite and the drone recovery?"

"Sorry, Dr. Von Gunten, but NORAC confirmed a meteorite took out the satellite. No missiles or laser destroyed it. Also, as far as the TLZ is concerned, it was a complete loss. A number of reports confirmed that it was indeed a meteorite and not any kind of a man made weapon."

Fritz Von Gunten hardly slept last night and is in a deep depression. "That is what I was expecting to hear. How are the developments on our old drone TLX coming?"

"Well, they are coming along more rapidly than I expected. Everyone is pulling together, so there is some good news," replies Nash in a very positive manner. "I met with the hourly staff about the triple pay and there were no complaints. As you know money talks. The salary personnel are excited about the fringe benefits, so morale is high now and everyone is working very hard."

"Excellent! Money does talk loud and clear and is a great motivator. It is a god and people love it. People will jump through hoops for it and anything else if the reward is high enough." Now Von Gunten himself is in a bit more of a upbeat mood. He adds, "Great, I need to have some good news to report to Wolfgang Martin today."

"Peter, you know as well as I know that the oppressive and holier than thou God of the Bible intervened in a big way yesterday. He threw a monkey wrench in our plans with our new drone and the GS 33 satellite, but still the kingdom of Lucifer advances".

"Without a doubt He did," responds Peter Nash, grinning as he takes a quick sip of his coffee. He is at a much lower level in the Adamic Society than his boss Von Gunten, but strongly desires to advance quickly in the ranks. He knows working hard and trying to keep his boss happy is his ticket toward advancement.

Dr.Von Gunten, a lifelong admirer and student of Adolf Hitler, watched every speech he had ever given that he could find on the internet. He also had a section of his personal library with hundreds of books on Hitler. Hitler's use of pomp, pageantry, talk of a Third Reich and his oratory skills to mesmerize a crowd had always fascinated him as a scientist from a psychological and sociological point of view.

 Now Fritz Von Gunten goes into his Hitler mode to an audience of one. "Peter, what we can rejoice in is the fact that the whole world is more under Lucifer's spell and control than ever before in this technologically-advanced age. Our people are in place to continually assault and water down the archaic rules and teachings of the Bible in our society at this time. Soon the Bible and Christianity in general will be totally undermined and forgotten by the masses who are so caught up in to their social networking, music, favorite entertainers' personal lives, fashion, and sports. Our Lord Lucifer and his army of demons along with the Adamic Society have fought a long hard battle, especially against the forces of Christ since the cross at Calvary 2000 years ago. Soon total victory will be ours. Operation Super Predators will play a major role in making this happen. Its ultimate purpose is to strike fear into the hearts of men and to manipulate the masses to want to move to and stay within the confines of large cities. Once we build our own version of the Berlin wall around the perimeters of the cities and work centers, the masses will do our master's bidding. There will be large communal farms, mining, and manufacturing centers in select areas of the United States that will go on uninterrupted. These centers will possess people who are capable in their chosen area and who have conformed to our goals and objectives. Then we will have complete dominion over the masses. The useless bottom feeders, non-contributors, and resistors of our brave new world will be eliminated."

"As you know, Nash, people are like sheep - helpless, needy, and scared. We are going to use these super predators to herd people inside the safe perimeters of the largest cities and work centers. These useful idiots will gladly trade their former constitutional rights for peace of mind and security from these man-eating animals. Freedom will soon be forgotten. The rural ignorant hicks will eventually flee to these armed prison camps for security, protection, and a piece of bread and clean water from the ultimate and most vicious predator and killing machine since the days of dinosaurs. Those inside the secure facilities will dare not venture out into the unknown areas of the countryside, deserts, and forests for fear of death and of the unknown that awaits them. Some of these human sheep are useful and serve different purposes. Those who meet our high standards of physical attributes, work skills, intelligence, and conform to our ways and line of thinking will be allowed to work and reproduce. Through a selective process, of course, this will be allowed. Other sheep like genuine born again Christians are diseased and sick of mind and we must put them out of their misery by eradicating them from the face of the earth. Most of the masses that fill the churches pose no threat to us and will quickly convert to our plans for fear of their own lives. Soon our Anti-Christ, the son of Lucifer, will appear and be revealed in full glory. Father Lucifer himself will install his son upon a golden throne and help him set up his domain under his all seeing eye. The Adamic Society members will rule under the Son of Lucifer with complete power and an iron fist. It will be a glorious time for us, his chosen servants, to whom will be given the keys to immortality and the ecstasy of our favorite vices and primitive instincts."

Unconsciously Von Gunten is reaching a crescendo in his speech and mimicking the look of Hitler in his facial expressions and rapid body movements. "We, the ruling elite, will no longer be constrained from participating in the forbidden taboos of the ridiculous book called the Bible. Christian norms in society will have been forgotten. Anything will go for the ruling elite as our ultimate reward for bowing our knees to the real Son of God. Pandora's box will be opened and we will be liberated to indulge our fleshly desires unhindered."

Peter Nash strokes Von Gunten's ego as usual. "Soon it will be a great day to be alive and see the total elimination of the trinity, angelic forces, all true Christians, and that trashy propaganda book they call the Bible. Oh, how mother earth groans for Lucifer and his Lords to cleanse the world of all the vile Christian garbage by death and total destruction."

Nash goes on to flatter Von Gunten. "Oh, Dr. Von Gunten I want to tell you something before I forget."

"What is it, Nash?

"I loved how you played the part of being a confirmed atheist yesterday. What an excellent cover that is because people will then never expect you to be such a devoted follower of Almighty Lucifer."

"Yes, my pretending to be an atheist through the years has served me well. Acting is an illusion which is a form of magic and I love to play that role."

"Yes, sir, you were amazing and I wanted to laugh my head off when you said that yesterday," laughs Nash. The usually very serious and focused Dr. Von Gunten slowly smiles. "Believe me when I say this that Warren Jones believes that about you, hook, line, and sinker." Von Gunten smiles again, which is a rarity. He is proud that his acting is so convincing. Nash goes on to say, "For a guy who is so brilliant at what he does, Jones has no idea about what our whole operation is about here. I've kept him in the dark like a mushroom, along with all the other workers in our department at Ci Mada Union."

"Peter, you are a good actor yourself," remarks a humored Fritz Von Gunten.

Nash is so caught off guard by Von Gunten's light-heartedness, he lets his guard down and slips up. "Another funny thing about Warren is that he told me in his interview years ago that he used to be a born again Christian in high school, before he went off to college to study computer science." Suddenly Peter Nash wishes he hadn't said that.

Von Gunten instantly gives him a cold stare and says, "That is a borderline violation of our hiring procedures at Ci Mada Union Laboratories and any subsidiary of Alpine Advanced Electronics."

Just then the elevator door opens on the ground floor and out rushes 28 - year-old starry-eyed Warren Jones. Warren has the look of a desperate man and is startled to see Nash and Dr. Von Gunten right in front of him. He quickly maneuvers around them and starts heading quickly outside toward the parking lot.

Peter says, "Warren, come here. You look like you just saw a ghost."

He responds in a shaky and frantic voice, "I might as well have seen one."

Von Gunten, greatly perturbed by Jones' strange behavior, yells, "Warren, explain to me what is going on! Take a minute and quit walking away from us. What's wrong?"

"I can't! I've got to go. It's an emergency! I've got to go and pick up my girlfriend Cindy at the hospital. I told her to meet me outside the emergency room."

Peter is totally confused by Warren's actions, expressions, and speech. Once Warren passes by the armed security guards, he is now sprinting outside the building with Nash and Dr. Von Gunten following him. Nash drops his coffee and doughnuts and is sprinting beside Jones trying to grab his right arm long enough for Jones to stop and explain what is going on. Von Gunten is far behind him walking with a limp from an arthritic left knee. He leans heavily on his beautiful custom-made mahogany wooden cane. It is topped off with a solid 18kt yellow gold replica of the head of the first super predator, the Red Baron. It was made by one of the finest goldsmiths in all of Switzerland. The two heavy set middle-aged armed security guards at the front desk, who are aroused by the conversations inside the building and not fully understanding what is going on, run out following Von Gunten, who is outside. Both guards have their hands on their pistols which are in their holsters unsnapped in anticipation of the unexpected.

Peter says, "Warren, what the %#@* is wrong? Stop for just one &*+$ minute and explain to me what is going on!." He grabs his assistant's shirt sleeve and Warren quickly jerks his left elbow back to break Peter's grip. "Why are you acting all crazy?." At this point Warren is on his motorcycle frantically starting it up.

Von Gunten is highly upset at Warren's bizarre actions and screams at him with his cane up in the air. "I like you, Warren, but I demand an answer or you job will be automatically terminated here at Ci Mada! I swear you will be lucky to find a job pushing a broom when I'm done with you!" Warren starts up his motorcycle and revs up the engine putting into second gear. He tells the four men around him that NORAC has just called and said that there is a 99.9% chance a large meteor is going to hit both Boulder and Denver in a matter of nine minutes. He tells them a voice keeps telling him that another meteor is coming right at Ci Mada and he has to go. Warren also states that for some unexplained reason all of NORAC'S high-tech radar and equipment failed to pick them up sooner and these large meteorites strangely came out of nowhere. That was three minutes ago because it is now 5:56 AM, as he quickly glances at his watch. Warren says, "I'm sorry, I've got to go and try to pick up my girlfriend Cindy who's a nurse and try to get out of Boulder." Warren glances up and shouts at the four men at the top of his lungs, "Look! There it is! It's coming right at us, just like that voice said! I'm out of here!" Warren guns the throttle of his fast street bike and burns a thick black stripe of rubber on the pavement. It produces a squealing sound and a cloud of black smoke is seen coming out of from behind the bike's back tire. He leans his muscular upper body forward over the motorcycle's handle bar and quickly exits the Ci Mada parking lot, accelerating to a speed of over a 100 mph, recklessly weaving in and out of traffic. The security guards run back inside building thinking there is safety in the basement four stories below ground level. Nash sprints to his car only to realize that his car keys are in his long white lab jacket upstairs in the building. He took it off earlier this morning to put on some deodorant and a new shirt that he kept in his locker because the one he was wearing was beginning to stink pretty badly, having been at work for 20 straight hours. He forgot to put the jacket on before he came down for coffee and doughnuts. In total desperation, he starts running after Warren Jones screaming and begging him to stop and give him a ride. He falls to his knees crying like a baby, alternating between that and cursing Warren for not giving him a ride and himself for not having his car keys on him.

Dr. Fritz Von Gunten instinctively knows that the meteorite is coming directly at Ci Mada. Von Gunten even knows that in fact God has it aimed precisely for him. He begins to blaspheme the God of heaven, his creator, and call Him every combination of curse words he can think of in his vile anger. Von Gunten feels his chest muscles are beginning to tighten rapidly from the stress and his high blood pressure. His lifetime of work which has consumed him is coming to an end. In a last act of desperation and complete hatred for the God of the Bible, he slowly reaches into his left inside pocket of his sport coat.. He pulls out his new prototype Millennium smart phone designed by AAE. While his fingers can still move, he quickly punches a 12 digit number. He hears a digital voice state, "Proceed with password, Dr. Von Gunten."

Von Gunten, with every fiber of his being, tries to relax with full knowledge of what his fate will be and says, "CARNAGE" in his regular voice.

The digital voice repeatedly says, "Password is activated and cannot be revoked, password is activated and cannot be revoked... "

Fritz Von Gunten intentionally drops the phone on the pavement but it sustains no noticeable damage due to its hardened titanium lightweight case. In one last act of defiance toward God, Dr. Fritz Von Gunten begins to repeatedly shake his mahogany walking cane with its golden head of the Red Baron at the heavenly meteorite like it is God Almighty Himself. He manages to faintly whisper, "Every dog has its day and one day soon You will bow Your knee to Lucifer and confess with your mouth that he is Lord." Von Gunten feels his chest tightening more and more by the second until the point of suffering a massive heart attack. He collapses on his back suffering a painful back injury in addition to the heart attack. Now struggling for life in intense pain, he slowly kicks his feet while still grasping the cane and barely moving it up and down from his chest at the meteorite. Fritz Von Gunten is gasping for air and his face is turning blue from a lack of oxygen in the Ci Mada parking lot. His eyes are bulging out and directly focused on the incoming meteorite. God keeps him alive until the meteor impacts his body and vaporizes it back into dust from which it came. But his soul is cast immediately into hell where his real eternal torment is just beginning. A massive deep crater is created that extends way beyond the border of the property of what was once Ci Mada's, along with a huge mushroom of exploding tiny particles of blacktop, concrete, steel, glass, plastic, vegetation, and displaced dirt going instantly upward and outward into the sky. Huge chunks to the finest dust particles of debris spew out in a circular pattern at super rapid speeds like an atomic bomb going off hitting and killing innocent people in cars, houses, and buildings in a three mile radius from ground zero at Ci Mada Union Laboratories. Upon entering the earth's atmosphere, several smaller pieces from the larger meteor break off and also hit Boulder creating other mini craters in the city. The number of dead and wounded in Boulder is in the tens of thousands.

6:11:45 AM, Mountain Standard Time, Thursday, 05/08/20_ _, Fortress/Double V Ranch

Outside the Fortress church building in, Golden Valley, Colorado, USA

Sheriff Barnes drives his Sheriff Department issued black and white Chevy Tahoe unto the property of Fortress. He slows down just before he gets to the group of buildings where the church is located. A crowd of people has gathered. His wife Sarah is with him feeling better than she has in years. It suddenly occurs to them that maybe the giant pitwolves have been spotted on the property. Already on edge with some news that Sam just received 20 minutes ago over his radio, he jumps out of his vehicle and tells Sarah to stay put. He starts visually scanning the crowd with his right hand on his revolver by his side trying to discern what is going on. Barnes doesn't know that another red alert has been issued. He spots Bro. Ricky and Bro. Gary in the midst of the chaos. He waves to them and yells, but there is too much noise to be heard. The people of Fortress are frantic and have the attention of their co-pastors trying to ask them questions about what is happening. There is too much noise and confusion and Barnes wants to get to the bottom of this matter quickly. Sarah sees Melody standing in the doorway of the church building. She jumps out of the vehicle, moves quickly to Melody, and they hug each other. Ricky and Gary are trying to get the people to be quiet. Most people are frantic and think some giant pitwolves have been spotted nearby.

Barnes is so frustrated and under so much pressure that in Old West fashion he fires off a round from his Smith and Wesson Model 29 .44 magnum revolver in the air to get everyone's attention. The blast sends out what seems like shockwaves that are deafening and stings the crowd's eardrums. The shot jolts everybody and even babies are silent for a few seconds. Barnes yells, "Okay, now that I have everyone's attention, I want to talk to your pastors. Ricky and Gary, are there any pitwolves on this ranch?"

"No, Sheriff," yells out Ricky.

"Then what is all the hoopla about?"

"Sheriff, Caleb needs to talk to the people in the church to give them some vital information."

"Fine! So if everybody could just please make their way to the church, I would be much obliged." Momentarily everyone is still in shock.

Gary yells out, "Okay, everybody, this alarm is not about pitwolves on the property, so relax. Again, listen. There are no giant pitwolves on the property. Sighs of relief are heard within the crowd. But Caleb does need to talk to everyone. Sheriff Barnes is here on an official visit."

Ricky yells to Caleb, "Son, please take the people inside the church building and share the news with them. We would appreciate it." He winks to him because they both know that if Gary and he stay and help break the news about the meteorites to the people that they would not be able to take Barnes up in the helicopter. Cataclysmic events in Boulder and Denver are going to usher in great sweeping changes at every level of life for the people in America and especially Colorado. Ricky, Gary, and Caleb instinctively know that all their lives are going to be forever changed really soon. But the issue of pitwolves around Fortress and the surrounding area affect them immediately. It has to be addressed right away. As Ricky, Gary, Blackhawk, and Sheriff Barnes make their way to the helicopter, Gary tells Barnes that Ricky has some news that he needs to hear.

Some of the people assembled outside the church are still in their pajamas, mothers carrying babies that are now crying loudly, half-shaven men, and some children who have their index fingers wiggling around in their ears still trying to find relief from Barnes firing off a round. Several small children have their hands cupped over their ears to protect them from another possible blast from his revolver. Teenagers Stephen and Andrew Crawford are walking with Thomas Stanton, who is still mute. Caleb and Forrest both start herding the people toward the inside of the church building to tell them about what happened in Boulder, Denver, and the counties around Clark County.

Brenda Lee Kirkman just came back to the church in a hurry and is waiting outside the intercessors' prayer room after being away for just a few hours. She is crying out and pleading with God in her heart to intervene miraculously on behalf of the ministry of Fortress and the surrounding area, praying for God's will regarding the meteorites and pitwolves. She has not breathed a word yet to anyone about what happened in Boulder and Denver. But now all of a sudden she feels like God is giving her a word for her dad. Francis Cotton and a few others took the morning shift and are still praying in the intercessors' room even though they are very tired.

All the intercessors called of God at Fortress know the price that has to be paid for God to intervene in people's lives and the ministry's vision. Deep intercession always requires a toll to be paid in the form of self denial to their flesh. It comes in the form of sacrifice, obedience, sweat, tears, lack of sleep, continual prayer, and fasting. But for those called to this kind of Christian service, it is worth enduring all the hardships to see people saved, healed, delivered, and God doing the impossible. Since last night, the stakes have gotten higher along with the price to be paid in sacrifice to the Lord.

Just as Brenda Lee gets a word from the Lord, she hears gunfire. Her mind instantly flashes to the worst case scenario, but she does not get a check in her spirit and dismisses it. She knows by faith that the giant pitwolves will never step foot on the grounds of Fortress. She takes a break from prayer. The Holy Spirit prompts her to find her Dad and give him the word that God just gave her. As she rushes through the church building, she sees her fiancé Forrest who just came inside and asks him what is going on. He tells her Sheriff Barnes just arrived and was trying to get everyone's attention because he thought there was a giant pitwolf on the premises. Because the bell sounding a red alert had most people nervous, they were huddled together and loud with a lot of questions. So he shot off his revolver to get their attention to make sure no giant pitwolves were on the property. He goes on to tell her Caleb is going to deliver the latest news about Boulder and Denver to the people and then they are going to turn on the news to watch what was going on in the church.. She shakes her head and says, "It's unbelievable, Forrest, and it makes me so very sad. I want to hear more, but I've got to first tell my Dad what the Lord just told me." She gives him a hug. She then asks him, "Forrest, do you know if my Dad and the others are taking off in the helicopter soon?"

"Probably any minute. now."

Brenda Lee quickly replies, "I've got to go," as she runs out of the building and sees her Dad with her Uncle Ricky, Sheriff Barnes, and John. She runs over to him and says, "Daddy, I need to see you for just a second."

"Okay, sure. I think I have a minute before we take off." They walk a short distance away from the others. He says, "Okay, Honey, what is it?"

Brenda Lee, with her bloodshot red eyes, looks her dad square in his eyes and tells him what God told her to tell him and the others, that God's hand is going to move mightily today to show His strength and power on the property of Fortress. He also says that He will remove all doubt from the people at Fortress that He alone can protect them here by His mighty, outstretched arm. All at Fortress will know that He can divinely preserve His remnant in this city of refuge that He has ordained for the end times.

Gary smiles at her as he sees Ricky preparing to start up the helicopter. He tells his godly daughter, "Baby, I receive and believe that word from the Lord. My spirit bears witness with your spirit that you have heard from the Lord Jesus. Amen."

"Okay, Daddy, I'll let you go now. Before you go I want you to know that I know about Boulder and Denver. I'm not afraid, Daddy. This world is not my home."

"You're strong, Honey. God's grace is sufficient. I've got to go. I love you, sweetheart."

"I love you too, Daddy." She kisses him on the cheek and is led by the Spirit to walk back to the Lodge and not to the intercessors' prayer room. The Lord speaks to her that visitors are coming. Brenda Lee is obedient to the prompting of the Holy Spirit.

Brenda Lee Kirkman is the daughter of Mary Anne and Gary Kirkman. At age 24, she is a very mature young woman, a truly gifted artist, and dead serious about the Lord and the ministry and vision of Fortress and The Disciplemaker Network of Churches. She's responsible for the computer graphic outlay and artwork of all the ministry's books, study guides and booklets, and media outlets. She and Forrest oversee the ministry's teachings and videos being put on the internet, the snail mail newsletter entitled Prophetic Truths, and the increasingly popular prophetic website The Immortals Network, which carries updated, relevant news pertaining to Christians, biblical truths, sermons, archeology, and prophetic information and teaching online videos. Prophetic Times is her dad's and uncle's blog. Her dad or Uncle Ricky usually give the final okay on the work. These duties keep her busy, but she views intercession as a labor of love. Also, she and Forrest are the worship leaders at Fortress. She tries to work 8-10 hours a week at the Good Samaritan Free Health Clinic operated by church members Dr. and Mrs. Stanton in Golden Valley, and was recently engaged to Forrest. So her plate is very full.

Mary Anne and Gary were unable to have children, although they underwent numerous tests, examinations, and treatments. Gary and Mary Anne both have relatives on both sides of their families with similar problems. They had looked into adoption but the Lord always seemed to say no for some reason, they didn't know why. After about three years of trying to have a baby, Gary had finally come to grips with the reality that maybe it was not God's will for them. It took two more years for Mary Anne to accept the fate that maybe being childless was her destiny. Still it was a tough pill for her to swallow since her older sister Katherine had five children before she turned 30. But the Lord did a wonderful thing when he brought Brenda Lee into their lives. They both knew it was a God Thing.

Brenda Lee was the daughter of Carly Burton who grew up in deep poverty in the mountains of West Virginia. Carly was the fifth child of ten born to Brenda Joyce and Carl Lee Burton, a coal miner who died of black lung disease and a two pack a day cigarette habit when Carly was just 17 years old. For her, life had been very hard, but through a chain of events at age 25 she decided to take a chance and move to California for a better life. But even with the move, she found herself still caught up in the same cycle of poverty. By a divine appointment she eventually met Mary Anne who was the Assistant Director of God's Storehouse, a resale store and shelter in Los Angeles, who led her to the Lord. Carly was one of those rare individuals that the Lord calls out of darkness into His marvelous light. From the day she got saved, Mary Anne and Melody, with the power of the Holy Spirit, helped nurture her along. A great transformation took place in her life. But she was also like a beautiful rose that blossoms then quickly fades. The

Lord had laid it upon Mary Anne and Gary's heart to go beyond the norm and help Carly and Brenda Lee in numerous ways. She got her a job as a cashier at God's Storehouse and then she became an assistant manager. Mary Anne always told Carly she'd never seen anyone change as much as she had in such a short period. Carly would always humbly say it was a work of grace. Mary Anne adored Brenda Lee who spoke with the most gentle and sweet voice of any child she had ever heard. There was an anointing on her life as a child. Brenda Lee got saved the same day as her mother Carly. Mary Anne shared the plan of salvation with her and she humbly prayed the sinner's prayer. She prayed with her hands pressed together and pointing upward in front of her chest. As the days went by you could tell Brenda Lee loved Jesus, His word, which she easily memorized, and had an unusual call to prayer at a young age. Both she and Carly were also naturally gifted artists when it came to drawing and painting. With Mary Anne and Melody's help, she was making good extra money painting Christian themes, portraits of their friends and acquaintances.

A year and a half after Mary Anne led Carly to the Lord, she was diagnosed with a fast spreading pancreatic cancer. Within three months, her cancer reached stage four. Another three months later, she went home to meet her Lord and Savior, Jesus Christ. But, just before she died, she asked her closest friend and spiritual mentor, Mary Anne, to not only take guardianship of her daughter, but also to adopt her as her own child. Without hesitation, Mary Anne agreed to do this, because she knew that she and Gary could and would love Brenda Lee as their own flesh and blood. Gary was able to get a will and the adoption documents prepared for Carly to fill it out and sign with her blessing before she died. On her death bed, Carly leaned over and whispered to Mary Anne, tears streaming down her cheeks, "Mary Anne, you and Gary take care of our Brenda Lee. Gary is a good man and he'll be a good father. But there is no one else on God's green earth that I love and trust more than you to raise Brenda Lee. Melody is a very close second, but she already has two boys of her own." Within minutes, she faded off into eternity to be with her Lord and Savior. Carly's death brought a strange mixture of deep emotions to Mary Anne. She was deeply saddened with Carly's early death as a Christian, humbled by her sacrifice of giving her daughter to her and Gary, and elated with the fact of finally having a child for Gary and her to raise as their own.

Gary then runs over to the helicopter to get inside where Ricky and John are waiting for him. As he opens the door to get inside, he says, "Sorry, guys, but I think it was worth the wait. Brenda Lee said that God is going to move today in a mighty way. She said more, but I'll tell you later."

"Amen," says Ricky.

Blackhawk says, "I believe that, Bro. Gary."

Ricky has not yet talked to Barnes or Blackhawk about Boulder or Denver. Barnes has made two trips to his SUV since the crowd broke up. The first trip was for his binoculars. The second trip was for his map of the county. It had fallen out of his back pocket in his vehicle. Barnes, the last one in, buckles up and says, "I'm ready to go, Ricky, but I know you want to tell me something. First, let me get my guns and stuff positioned." He's been trying to process all that he needs to do and, on top of that, he doesn't understand all the religious jargon he's heard since last night. Barnes is hoping the pitwolves have moved out of his county since the call from Hank earlier. He even prayed to God in his mind that today the crew won't see any giant pitwolves in Clark County as they fly over. He is also wondering how he can get back at Ci Mada Union. All night long Sam Barnes schemed and dreamed how to make them pay for what they have done.

Everyone brought firearms today, and they are already loaded in the helicopter. Barnes positions his tactical Remington 870 police issue 12 gauge pump shotgun loaded with 00 buckshot. Six more rounds in a plastic clip are attached to the side of his shotgun. He straps it next to him in a vertical position. He also brought his personal Winchester .45-70 caliber lever action rifle with a Weaver 3x9 scope on a side mount of the rifle with a black nylon bag with plenty of ammo for both guns. The ammo bag is between his feet and he is holding his rifle in a vertical position with his hand between his legs. He is carrying his usual Smith and Wesson model 29, .44 magnum six inch revolver that is holstered on his left side. Three speed loaders with 240 grain JHP rounds to quickly reload are on the right side of his tan custom leather belt. He is taking no chances with the dangerous giant pitwolves. Blackhawk is holding his .338 Kimber Montana custom rifle with a match grade stainless steel barrel with a Leopold Mark 4 M1-10x scope for long distance shooting. He also brought his Savage Hunter Bolt Action rifle in the same .338 caliber with open sights below and elevated rings for a Leopold 3x9 scope for a closer shot which was next to Gary's in the back. He is carrying a Cold Steel Trailmaster 12" bowie style knife that is 1/4" thick with a razor's edge. It is made from Carbon V steel, which is considered the holy grail of the best steel ever used in a production knife in America. He is carrying it on a 1½" thick brown western style leather belt and it is inside the black leather knife sheath that came from the factory. He's carrying it on his right side at his waist with a long thin 3/16" black nylon string tied around his right thigh to secure it. Gary brought his identical assault rifle that Ricky has in the front of the helicopter. Ricky had given him the rifle years before when Gary first became a board member of his defense contractor company SEC. It was a pre-ban Belgian Fal .308 semi automatic rifle with a loaded 20 round clip in it and a Streamlight red dot laser and flashlight. What made the gun so good was that it was extremely dependable. This was why it had been used in 93 different countries at one time or another. Gary had three extra loaded clips in his rifle case next to him in the back of the helicopter. Ricky had removed his custom military grade wide angle night vision and thermal imaging 3x9 scope early this morning and replaced it with the same Streamlight red dot laser as Gary's, It was in the front of the helicopter wedged in next to his seat and ready to go.

David, Max, and Charlie all give him a thumbs up to let Ricky know the helicopter is good to go. Ricky then gives them a thumbs up. They start walking toward the church. Ricky is wearing his Ray Ban sunglasses like he wore in Vietnam and his well worn Vietnam Veteran ball cap. He is eager to start pushing buttons, flipping switches, adjusting controls, and checking gauges. Barnes is riding shotgun, Gary is behind Ricky, and John is behind Sam.

Barnes says, "First of all, I want to apologize for my abruptness in the discharge of my weapon earlier."

Ricky says that is understandable with what just took place in Boulder and Denver.

Barnes quickly responds, "What in the blue blazes are you talking about?"

Blackhawk also says, "Bro. Ricky, what just happened?"

"Wait a minute, Sheriff. I knew John didn't know, but you don't know what I mean either?"

"Absolutely not," replies Barnes.

"I thought you knew and that is why you shot off your revolver," says Ricky.

"No! What the %$#* happened in those cities?" Barnes impatiently fires off without forethought. Suddenly realizing the inappropriateness of his language, he adds, "Sorry, guys."

"They just got partially destroyed by large meteorites hitting both cities," informs Ricky. "One seventh of Boulder is destroyed. A large crater now exists there and a blast zone extends to all parts of the city. The same thing happened in Denver except the damage covers about one eighth of the city."

Blackhawk says, "Forrest said a few days back that he thought possibly a big city was going to get hit in Colorado with all these meteorites hitting our state and around it."

Barnes is stunned almost to the point of feeling numb. It's a surreal moment for him. It's like a flashback in time to Vietnam when some of the men in his unit that he was leading on a patrol heard a mortar round coming in. He yelled for them to take cover. He just happened to be beside a downed large tree. He jumped to the left side of it. When he popped his head up after the blast, all seven of his men were on the other side dead with body parts scattered in every direction. He was the lone survivor. Barnes realizes that he is having a flashback and shakes off the stunned feeling. He says, "I thought you boys were whacked out until last night, but now my whole opinion has changed. Even my wife is different. Didn't you guys tell me that your God always has an ace up his sleeve?"

"Yes, we did, Sam."

"And didn't you say you have a special group here called the intercessors?"

"Yes," replies Ricky.

"Well, does anyone know where the meteorite hit in Boulder?" asks Barnes.

Gary says, "The Lord just told me. I heard the words Ci Mada Union Laboratories was ground zero."

"Ci Mada was ground zero? What do you mean the Lord just told you, Gary?" asks Barnes in a perplexed voice. "Are you psychic?"

"No," says Gary.

"He hears from God," says Blackhawk. "When Bro. Gary or Bro. Ricky gets a word from the Lord, you can take it to the bank."

"I'm sorry, I can't buy that! Guys, that is a bad joke! It's more than I can swallow. That's kind of pushing it," says Barnes in a doubting tone.

"Okay, well let's see if Gary heard from God," Ricky replies. "I'll call Caleb on the two-way radio and max out the volume. "Caleb, it's Dad. Do you read me?"

"Dad, is there some problem with the helicopter?"

"No, we are talking and just haven't left yet."

"Well, great, what can I do for you?"

"Son, do you have the TV or shortwave radio on now?"

"Yes, I have the shortwave on."

"I thought it sounded like you did."

"Caleb, we want to know what part of Boulder was destroyed. Has there been any word on it?"

"We haven't heard a thing as of yet about that. Right now a few of us are in Ashley's office listening to the shortwave radio before I go out and talk to the people so I can get some more facts to prep them before we show the live news coverage on the meteorites on the overhead screen. I told Aunt Mary Anne just a little bit before she went in the church. She is in there now praying with the people assuring them that God is in control with all that has happened. Apparently, some of the other members had just found out. But about three minutes before you called, KABZ in Boulder said that they were going to a live interview with the Fire Chief of Boulder who was standing by which might be taking place any minute now to get the latest information on the situation."

"Okay, great, we'll wait (Pause)."

"Dad, can you guys hear it?"

"Yes, but can you get the two-way radio closer to the radio speaker?"

"Sure, Dad."

"Yes, that is good. We can hear the broadcast better now."

One minute passes and the reporter is waiting for the Chief to get through talking to some of the fire officials. The Fire Chief is finally able to talk to her. *"Hi, folks, this is Dana Williams. We are reporting live in Boulder on a deadly and destructive large meteorite. I repeat, a large meteorite that has hit and destroyed about 1/7th of the city of Boulder and another one of the same magnitude impacting and leveling about one 1/8th of Denver. It truly looks like I'm in a warzone. I'm here with the Boulder Fire Chief Ned Simmons. Chief Simmons, I know a large meteorite hit this city and it looks like an atomic bomb just went off. Dust and debris are still falling down to the earth. I have found it difficult to breathe. Sometimes it is so thick people are literally gasping for air. None of what has happened even seems remotely real. Your department has suffered the loss of some of your own firefighters who have died in this horrendous event. Our hearts go out to all those that have suffered today in this incredible natural disaster. What do you have to say, Chief?"*

"Well, Dana, it is mind blowing at this point. Just mind blowing. I just keep hoping that this is just a bad nightmare, but it is not. It's real. All I can say is that the entire fire department, all of my people, the brave men and women in uniform of the Boulder Fire Department are doing everything they possibly can to fight fires and to tend to the hurt and the needy. I just got a report a few minutes ago that about half of one of my firehouses was taken out by one of the smaller meteorites that hit the city."

"I was not aware of that, Chief. I'm so sorry to hear that. Chief Simmons, there are so many questions I would like to ask you, But the first question that stands out in my

mind now and for our audience is where was the point of impact for this meteorite that hit this city?"

"Dana, thanks for the opportunity to speak to the survivors of this great city and to the people of this state and our country. We have suffered a great, great loss today. It is obvious as one looks around at the devastation. Not only us, but our capitol city Denver from what I have been told. At this point, we must all pool our love for humanity and gather resources to get through this horrific tragedy and we will. In answer to your question about where this meteorite hit, from all the latest information that my department and I have gathered, we believe that Ci Mada Union Laboratories was ground zero for the point of impact for the large meteorite."

"Thanks, Son, that's all I need for now. Wait, that is live on Ashley's shortwave radio, correct?"

"Yes, this is live. It's not a recording from earlier."

"All right, over and out."

"Bye, Dad."

Ricky pauses for a second and says, "There is something else I need to tell you guys. Meteorites also hit eight counties that closely surround Clark County, according to Forrest this morning. I'm sure they weren't very big, but they are still frightening to people in the area."

"Okay! Wow! I'm eating crow again. I wasn't born in a Christian home. Right now I feel like one of those guys who gets blown out of the saddle in a western movie from the blast of both barrels of a double barreled scattergun at close range. That best describes how I feel right now. Twelve hours ago I thought you guys were a bunch of religious do-gooders, weird and nutty. Now you guys are literally scaring the hell out of me. I mean you guys hear from God, you got super high-tech gadgets, you've got God's ear, and He blows your enemy off the face of earth."

Ricky says, "Sam, we are nobody special. We are just sinners saved by grace, who are also vessels that submit to the Lord and He uses us as He wills."

"Well, for the first time in my life, I really believe that the world is coming to an end. For some years now, I just thought we were going through a cycle where society was getting bad, but it would cycle out. But I am coming to the reality that the world at this time is like a stage and the final curtain is being drawn as the final act is winding down. What I want to know at this point is when do you guys hold church services because Sarah and I are definitely coming. Because with all that I have seen and heard in the last 12 hours, I'm on overload. I thought all this religious stuff was a bunch of mumbo jumbo. But Sarah is happier than I can ever recall since she went through this 'saved' experience last night. So I think it's time for me and the big man upstairs to definitely get better acquainted. And I believe it's mostly on my end."

"Well, we are very glad to hear that, Sheriff. You and the Mrs. are more than welcome," declares Ricky.

"That's really great," adds Gary.

Blackhawk says, "You're making a good decision, Sheriff Barnes, that you won't regret."

Barnes says, "I can't believe I just said that. But in the meantime, I got two other reports of four pitwolves spotted near the eastern side of the county, which is not too far from here. Both people thought they saw huge wolves from a distance but weren't sure what they saw."

"They must be the ones I saw last night up top on the box canyon, Sheriff."

"That's what I'm thinking, Ricky," agrees Barnes. "Anyway, Hank went by the office this morning before Deputy Travis Perkins, the Judge's nephew, usually clocks out. Hank took both calls and relayed them to me just before I got here. There's a lot more to that story and I'm going to tell you in just a moment. But, since my cell phone doesn't work out here and my two-way radio's battery 'just conveniently' went out if you know what I mean, I can't take any calls right now. What a shame! Anyway, with Boulder and Denver being hit, the news media will swarm those cites like bees on a flower bed. This just might be the diversion we need that can buy us some time to figure out what to do. Just before I got here, I thought those two calls were the big news until that story got trumped by the Boulder and Denver meteorite stories."

"Yeah, I know God has a plan for us. I firmly believe that God is working overtime on our behalf because of the prayers of the intercessors and everyone else here at Fortress. He took out that evil company Ci Mada in a supernatural way. So it seems like our problem got partially solved, but not completely," states Blackhawk.

Gary states, "I honestly don't know how God is working all this out, John, but I believe He is working behind the scenes for our good. Romans 8:28 declares - 'And we know that all things work together for good to them that love God, to them who are the called according to His purpose.' That is a promise that I have stood on all my Christian life in the good times and the bad."

"Right now, men, I'm leaning heavily on your goodness to get on the good side of God. This whole ordeal is not an easy problem to solve because these giant pitwolves are running through the forest around here and Ci Mada's mother company is still around to pick up the pieces. I want to get in the air real soon here. But let me tell you guys this before we go. When I pulled up in front of your church and saw all the people worked up, I just thought you were giving people some more information about what happened last night, with the ringing of the bell. I had no idea about the meteorites that hit Denver and Boulder. Hank must've not heard about it until after I talked with him on the two-way radio."

"That is right, Sheriff. It just happened a few minutes before you pulled up this morning," declares Ricky. "Caleb had just told me as you pulled up."

"Okay, well that explains a few things. It was my turn to respond to the emergency night calls that can't wait until morning. Hank and I alternate nights if something serious takes place. Most things can usually wait until morning. But we both worked hard last night and we were hoping nothing serious would arise. I was grateful because Travis never called. I took that as a good sign that maybe there were no more giant pitwolves in the area. I wanted to believe that because I already had my hands full. After we left Pete Watson's house last night, Hank and I took Sarah home and then dumped the pitwolf's body five miles over the Wilburn County line in the woods. I'm hoping it can't be tracked to me somehow. But I had to get that dead beast out of the county so Hank and I dropped it over a high cliff from the road. On many nights in Golden Valley, nothing of any importance happens. Well, I got a call from Hank this morning that when he reported to work just before 6:00AM, he found Travis with a lump on the back of his head, a minor cut, and some blood on the floor and Travis was kind of out of it. Apparently, he had slipped while mopping the office floors and hit his head on the metal heater attached to the wall. Hank processed the calls and called about where the two people spotted the pitwolves last night. He called me just before Sarah and I got to the Double V Ranch to give me the details. He was taking Travis to see Doc Coleman at the emergency room to get checked over. Hank used to be an EMT there, so Travis was in good hands."

"Well, we will keep Travis in our prayers to get well," says Gary.

"Absolutely," agrees Ricky.

"Thanks. Also, guys, I've got to get this off my chest because it keeps playing with my mind."

"What is it, Sheriff?" inquires Blackhawk.

"What I still can't get over, I mean it keeps rolling over and over in my mind, is the fact that Ci Mada Union Laboratories was ground zero for the meteorite hitting in Boulder. All the people there went up in a cloud of dust. You may think I'm evil, but I feel justice was served."

"Well, I leave all that up to God, Sheriff. I admit there were some evil people at Ci Mada. But I'm sure there were some good people there also. People who worked as secretaries, janitors, cooks, warehouse people, mailroom and maintenance personnel. Then all the good and innocent men, women, and children that lived within a certain radius of Ci Mada who also died because of the meteorite."

"Yeah, you're right, John. You shed a different light on my way of thinking."

"Sheriff, all the intercessors and everyone else who prayed last night prayed for God's will to be done. If we pray for God's will to be done on earth as it in heaven, then we are in the center of His will and there is no better place to be," replies Gary.

"Well, with all that has happened, I think maybe these intercessors are people that the devil doesn't want to mess around with. I think you guys might have the ear of God. And if that is the case I want to be on the winning team in these end times."

"Praise God, Sam," says Ricky.

Blackhawk says, "Sheriff, we also haven't told you that Caleb's wife Ashley found out that a drone crashed up in Overton County yesterday around 7:00 PM and that our satellite phones are still not working."

"Well, I'll be %$&?8!. Oh, sorry, guys. That slipped. Now I know God is moving in my life. A lot of supernatural stuff is happening around here to be just coincidence. Now I'm curious to find out what is going to happen next? Ricky can you get this thing up in the air so we can get a bird's eye view?"

"It would be my privilege, Sam."

"Great! Let's see if we can first spot any pitwolves around the ranch. Then we'll go scope out the other two locations in the county. I feel bad about what happened in Boulder and Denver, but I have to take care of my own county first."

Ricky readjusts his sunglasses and his ball cap as he starts pushing buttons, flipping switches, adjusting controls and checking gauges again. Barnes has his Winchester 1886 lever action that is chambered for the .45-70 caliber bullet with a side mount Leopold 3x9 waterproof scope between his legs in a vertical position. He firmly grips the barrel of his rifle with his right hand as he hears the blades overhead start moving rapidly. His eyes start scanning in all directions while his body tenses as Ricky takes the helicopter up vertically.

Bro. Gary makes a remark as they are flying off, "As Ricky and John know, Sam, my daughter will sometimes get a word from the Lord. I believe it is a true word. So I'm just going to tell you what she told me."

" Let's hear it," says, Ricky."

"Well, she told me that we are going to see God working supernaturally today on this property and that it will give every true believer the faith to believe that Fortress is supernaturally protected by the Lord."

Everyone shouts, "Amen," including Barnes.

Chapter 10

THE MIRACLE

3:58:18 AM, Mountain Standard Time, Friday, 05/08/20_ _, Rock Top Memorial Hospital, Intensive Care Unit, Rock Top, Colorado, USA.

"That's impossible, Nurse Taylor! You're telling me something that is not in the realm of the possible! I just got through checking out the vital signs of that young man with a brown ponytail and beard in the ICU. That was 20 minutes ago," Dr. Allen says while eating his early morning snack of blueberry yogurt and granola and relaxing for a few minutes in the cafeteria.

"But, Dr. Allen, Sir, what I'm telling you is the God honest truth."

"Now, Taylor, that boy, I believe his name is River, somehow, some way - you're telling me all his vital signs and brain activity are now normal? Sorry, the facts just aren't adding up."

"Listen, Dr. Allen. That young man's condition is now normal. In fact, he is sitting up and demanding something to eat."

"Eat!? I gave him enough sedatives to knock out an elephant. He should be sleeping like a baby with all that medication in him."

"Well, apparently the sedative is not working on him."

"In addition to that, he has a hairline fracture in the front of his skull that induced internal bleeding and made his brain swell. He was having seizures before he came into the hospital and vomiting. He made a horrible mess outside the emergency entrance. His condition was and still is really touch and go at this point. Oh, oh yea?, wait a minute! I know what is going on. Dr. Brighton has put you up to prancing me, hasn't he, Nurse?" Dr. Allen now has a huge grin on his face.

"Who's Dr. Brighton?" asks a puzzled Nurse Taylor.

"Oh, come on! Don't pretend like you don't know him. He's the new orthopedic doctor with the short curly reddish orange hair who just came here from Pueblo, Colorado three weeks ago. He's my new golfing buddy and a real jokester."

"No, I didn't remember him at first. But now I remember. But no, he is not involved. This is not a joke."

"Sure, Taylor, sure."

"Nobody is pranking you, Dr. Allen, especially me. Look at me, Dr. Allen. I'm 46 years old, I'm 5'4" and I weigh 210 pounds and have bunions on both feet. On top of all that my lower back is still a little sore. I over did it last weekend gardening in my yard. Believe me, I've got better things to do than to waste my time and energy on pulling a college type prank on you by walking all the way down here and telling you something in person, then walking back to the ICU. I know it sounds unbelievable. No one sent me down here to try to trick you into believing a made-up miracle has taken place upstairs. I walked all the way down here to tell you in person that one of your patients actually did have a miracle take place this morning in your ICU."

"Nurse Taylor, we go way back. Look me straight in the eyes and tell me that boy upstairs is perfectly fine."

"Dr. Allen, that boy River is perfectly fine upstairs, you have my word on it and he can be released."

"Alright, Alright. After 10 years of working with you, my gut tells me you are telling the truth. My head is saying it's a joke. I'm throwing away the rest of my food. This better not be a joke. As the head nurse in the ICU, you wouldn't be pulling a quick one on me, I don't think. But, I 'm warning you, Beatrice. If you are involved with Dr. Brighton in a prank, then you will be the new head bedpan nurse for the rest of this year in this entire hospital."

"It's a deal, Dr. Allen, on one condition." As they are walking to the elevator to go up to the ICU, nurse Taylor says, "I want you to do a favor for this boy River and his young wife."

"What kind of favor are you talking about?"

"Let this boy's hospital bill be a pro bono case."

"Beatrice, I...I..."

"Then please do it as favor for me."

"Taylor, you're one heck of a good nurse and I depend on you tremendously. Since you first became a head nurse in ICU here at Rock Top I have less stress on me and more peace of mind knowing you take the best care of my patients when you are on duty. All the nurses respect you here. You're proactive and you make sure all the nurses under your watch do their jobs. They know better than to be playing around on you when there are patients in critical condition in their care. And because of that I will do it if a genuine miracle did take place. But just this once mind you. But, I have a question, "Why did you want to me to write River's hospital bill off as a pro bono case? That's puzzling me. I know it's not because he doesn't have insurance, right?"

"You're right that they don't have any insurance doctor, but that's not it. We have patients who are flat broke in the ICU here sometimes, who don't have two nickels to rub together. And I know the hospital has to turn a profit here to keep the lights on. So we work out some kind of payment plan with those less fortunate and struggling financially. You know I've never asked you to do this before. I guess the reason I'm asking this time is because there is an anointing on this young man and his wife's life."

"Sorry, that religious jargon doesn't mean too much to me. I don't understand what you are saying."

"In other words, Dr. Allen, ever since I saw him and got around him when he was wheeled into this ICU I have sensed God's spirit mightily on him. He's special, a chosen child of God. I can't describe it any other way. I just feel God wanted me to ask you to please do the pro bono case for him. I also ran into Amy Choate when I went on my break earlier. She's a close friend of mine and a nurse in the ER area."

"Yeah, I know Amy. She's also an excellent nurse" says Dr. Allen. Yes, she is, anyway Amy said to me she also sensed the same thing going on with the boy's wife. Her name is Starlight. So the point I'm trying to make is I'm a PK."

"What's that?"

"A preacher's kid. I know right from wrong and I've seen some healings and miracles in my life. I was in my Daddy's church my whole life until I went to college. But I've been living for God only sporadically since then. Amy was a very strong Christian until four years ago when her husband confessed to her he was gay and left her for another man. It devastated her and she fell away from God as a result. She told me she was on duty when Dr. Gibson broke the news to River's wife about his condition after looking at his x-rays and checking him over. Amy went on to say that what the young wife did next really blew her away. According to her, Starlight dropped to her knees and started praying for River in the ER openly and not giving a flip what people thought about her. Amy said it was a defining spiritual moment in her life. It really impacted her and she said she came under strong conviction about her own life, her relationship with God, and how bitter and cold she had been toward Him. She said the instant when River's wife fell to her knees and started crying out to Jesus chills went down her spine. She felt overwhelming compassion for the young woman and all bitterness toward God left her heart and mind. Dr. Gibson then had a fit, according to Amy, when the young woman was praying.

Just before Dr. Allen and Nurse Taylor leave the privacy of the elevator, Dr. Allen looks Taylor straight in the eyes and says, "Beatrice, what I'm about to tell you goes no further than you and me. Do you understand? "

"Yes, Dr. Allen."

"That Gibson is a strange bird. I'm not sure what religion he is, but he is also the Supervisor of that new Inter-religious Meditation Center. It replaced our traditional non-denominational Christian chapel that used to be here. I always thought it was a nice place with a peaceful atmosphere. He got some federal grant money to update the chapel, but it couldn't be called a chapel as a result because of some new law. Anyway, Dr. Gibson pushed hard for this new 'religious' center and my buddy, Dr. Nick Gilbert, the Director of this hospital, approved it. I still haven't figured out why to this day."

"Yeah, go figure, Dr. Allen. Anyway, Dr. Gibson lost his vision instantly after getting on to her about praying in public. Nurse Choate said that is why he can't see."

"Taylor, you're telling me he's blind now? Because he got on to this boy's Christian wife who was praying?"

"That's what Amy said. Hopefully his condition is just temporary."

As they leave the elevator and walk to the ICU, both Allen and Taylor whisper to each other. "I'll be honest with you, Beatrice. I don't understand all this religious talk. It sounds like you and Amy are having some kind of religious experience and that's all good. As far as Gibson is concerned, I'm not rushing to any kind of conclusion regarding his eyesight. I don't know all the details. I will tell you this. I believe in God. I know the human body is more complex than any machine man has ever invented. If anybody was to ask me what faith I am, I would say Christian. But if I grant this boy River a pro bono case, then I'm only doing it if there has been some kind of incredible spontaneous recovery that has taken place in River's condition. I don't really believe in miracles, as you call them, in the Christian Bible. I think the writer of the Bible took some liberties by putting them in and to help make the teachings of Christ more interesting. Secondly, if it's a prank, the deal's off. If the first condition is met, I'll authorize a pro bono case."

"Dr. Allen, thank you so much. You're the best!"

"Please stop all the accolades. My head will swell too much and then I'll be in my own ICU."

"Fine, Dr. Allen. I'll stop. Thank you so very much."

A few seconds later, Dr. Allen and Nurse Taylor walk into the ICU and hear a middle-aged female nurse say, "Sit down, young man, sit down. You've got IV's in you and electrodes all over your body."

"But I've got to go to the bathroom and I'm starving," insists a desperate River.

Dr. Allen runs over to River and says, "Young man, my name is Dr. Allen and you hit your head on a metal knob on the steering wheel of your vehicle yesterday. You were in really bad shape when your friends and wife brought you in here to the hospital. You have a hairline fracture in the front of your skull." Suddenly a strange look appears on Dr. Fred Allen's face as he ponders what happened to the swollen bump on River's forehead with a 3/4 inch laceration on top of it. "Wait a minute, Nurse Taylor. This boy is not the same boy I saw 30 minutes ago."

"Yes sir, he is, Dr. Allen," responds Nurse Taylor in a confident voice. "Just check his wrist tag. It says River Jenkins."

"But this young man seems to be perfectly healthy."

"That's what I told you."

"But why didn't you tell me that the swelling and the 3/4 inch laceration is completely gone from his forehead?"

"Would you have believed me?"

River quickly touches his forehead, which is normal. "That's easy, Doc," says River, "Because she knows you wouldn't have believed her."

"That's right, young man," Nurse Taylor agrees. "This is what made me walk all the way down there to the cafeteria to talk to you in person, Dr. Allen."

"But that's medically impossible. I saw the swelling and cut with my own two eyes before I went on break."

"That's what I call a miracle, Doctor, and not a spontaneous recovery," shouts Nurse Taylor.

River Jenkins doesn't know what all the fuss is about because he feels great. He has no knowledge of how serious his injury was earlier. The last thing he remembers was driving down the road with Patrick after leaving the rest area and feeling horrible.

"Doctor, I've got to go use the restroom really bad. Then I'd like to get something to eat if I can because I'm starving."

"Okay, Son, give us a second and we'll get you a urine bottle and pull the curtain so you can go." One of the nurses brings a bottle over to him to use. After River finishes and starts pulling back the curtain, the doctor tells him, "I don't understand the seeming reversal of your condition because there is no logical explanation as to the readouts on the monitors here. They are all indicating your vital signs are normal."

"Then I can go, Dr. Allen."

"Sorry, River, but you aren't going anywhere until another set of x-rays of your forehead is taken and I examine them."

"But as I told you, Doctor, I feel absolutely fine."

"That may be the case, Mr. Jenkins, but you see these x-rays here in my hand?"

"Yes, sir," says River.

"Well, they clearly show you have a hairline fracture on your skull. I also know for a fact that your brain was hemorrhaging. See? Look here on the x-ray."

"Yes, sir."

"If you no longer have a hairline fracture right there, I will release you because I will then have to declare a genuine miracle has taken place here. Until then, you are staying put in this hospital."

"Okay, well I serve a big God who is in the healing business, so you are welcome to take another set of x-rays of my skull. But I believe He has healed me."

"Amen!" says Nurse Taylor.

"Nurse Taylor, I want you to personally wheel him down the hall to the x-ray lab and bring me back the results as soon as they are ready."

"Yes, sir, Dr. Allen!"

Twenty minutes later, the joyful veteran ICU Head Nurse Beatrice Taylor comes in pushing River who's praising God for His goodness. She already knows the results of the x-rays and is smiling as she hands the sealed manila envelope to Dr. Allen. He is almost beside himself believing that he is going to witness a bona fide miracle in the making for the first time in his life. What he soon sees defies his logical mind. He says, "Oh my God! There truly is a God in heaven!" He wants to shout, but says in an excited voice, "I've seen people with stage four cancer automatically go into remission for no apparent reason. I've seen people wake up out of a coma who had been in one for months before. I've also seen mangled cars of people who came in this ICU who were involved in crashes that should have killed them, but they lived to tell about it. But I've never ever seen a hair line fracture on a human skull get healed in just a matter of hours or a swelling and a laceration like River had completely disappear in a matter of minutes."

By this time two on-duty nurses in the ICU have quickly come over. Nurse Taylor has been filling them in with some of the details. They have all witnessed River's vital signs, brainwave activity, and the disappearance of the swelling and laceration earlier.

Dr. Allen says, "Nurse Taylor, this young man has no signs or symptoms of ever being injured yesterday." He tells River, "Rise and walk. You are completely healed. I can't find anything wrong with you."

"River stands up and in a humble and solemn gesture points his right pointer finger to heaven and says, "To God be all the glory for the great things He has done!" Dr. Allen, Nurse Taylor, and all the rest of the ICU staff start clapping their hands in amazement of the true miracle that has taken place before their eyes.

While Dr. Allen works on River's paperwork for his release, River eats breakfast and changes into his clothes. When he is done, Dr. Allen walks with Nurse Taylor, who is wheeling River, down to the Inter-religious Meditation Room to where his young bride and his two friends have been spending their time praying for him and resting.

The meditation room has a welcome book for visitors to sign in on a small oak table. Above the sign in four inch stainless steel metal letters it reads, "THIS ROOM IS DEDICATED TO YOU AND YOUR FAITH." The meditation room has light-colored purple walls highlighted with the different stars in the zodiac in white contrasted against a light blue ceiling.

At the northern end of the room, there is a six feet by six feet black square slab of highly polished granite resting on four black granite pillars that are six inches in diameter and six feet in height. On top of the table are six large white candles burning brightly. New age music continually plays softly in the room.

The six candles produce just enough light to make it possible to see where you are going. With no windows and the overall decor of the room, it has given the three born-again friends an unwelcome feeling the whole time they have been in there praying and resting. But it has not weakened their resolve to pray for River. It has only intensified it. The room has been a giant signal to them - along with Dr. Gibson's ranting and raving, River's condition, and the ordeal back at the rock slide - that almost everything on their rocky road to Golden Valley has been an uphill spiritual battle.

Some of the major religions of the world with the symbols associated with them are painted white on the walls of the hexagon-shaped room. The wall with a cross on it is barely visible. A large cleaning cart with cleaning supplies, a small trash can, broom, mop, and duster basically obscured its visibility. On one wall, it is written, "TO THE GOD WITHIN YOU." Starlight decided to move the cleaning cart with all the supplies in front of it, which hid all the letters perfectly. Since yesterday a janitor has never come for the cleaning cart to use it. Patrick, Starlight, and Emily felt like it was purposely placed there to permanently hide the cross of the Christian faith.

Starlight and Patrick traded off during yesterday and the early morning hours praying for River. Yesterday afternoon Emily started praying once she got past a little hesitation. At first she asked Patrick and Starlight, "Well, how do I pray to God?"

"Just talk to Him like He is your best friend. Just be a little bit more respectful," replied Patrick. She caught on quickly. However, she passed out just before 10:00 PM last night because she was used to having to go to bed early in order to get up and be at work at the diner by 5:00AM most days.

Nurse Amy Choate bought Starlight, Patrick, and Emily a late lunch in the cafeteria and loved spending time with everyone. Amy's faith in God was being revived by the sincere devotion to Christ and childlike faith of

Starlight and Patrick. She was excited that Emily had just gotten saved and was traveling with them to Golden Valley.

Starlight and Patrick decided not to mention the angelic visitations that River and Patrick had received from the archangel Michael. But they did mention the rock slide and how God had used the three bears to get them to stop just before the boulders came crashing down earlier in the day. Also, the story of white mountain goats was the first time she had ever heard of them in the area, and it definitely sounded like to her that the devil had used them to try to kill River, Starlight, and Patrick. The personal testimonies of her new young friends had renewed her heart. Maybe God really does look out for His children and has a way of working all things for their good if they just love and serve Him. Starlight gave Amy a new CD of her and River singing Christian songs. Amy said she couldn't wait to hear it. Before they parted, Amy and Starlight exchanged numbers. Amy stated she wanted to see everybody when River got out of the hospital and would come and visit them at Fortress. She had heard some good things about the ministry and wanted to go to a church service and find out more. She had stopped by last night after she got off work and said goodbye one last time. She said she would be continually praying for River and them.

Normal protocol for doctors is to notify a family member if a patient's condition changes in a really bad way or good one. But, Dr. Allen was beside himself and couldn't wait to make a surprise visit with Starlight and River's two friends about his miracle. He is also brainstorming on how to use this incident to generate favorable attention for Rock Top Memorial Hospital. So as nurse Taylor rolls River into the meditation room, Starlight sees River and shouts, "River, you look great! Praise God!" as she runs over to him and plants a big one on his lips. River is so glad to see her, he hugs her tightly.

Patrick comes over and starts shaking River's hand saying, "God is so good."

River says, "Amen."

Due to all the noise, Emily wakes up and asks, "River, is that really you?"

"It's him, Emily," giggles Starlight. "My River is healed, praise God, isn't he,

Doc?

"You must be Starlight. Yes, I think in this particular case you could say he is healed. It's so good to meet you under these circumstances. Yes, your young husband has a clean bill of health. I must confess it seems to be a miracle. I have checked him over thoroughly and I can't find anything wrong with him." Emily is now beside Starlight with her right hand resting on Starlight's shoulder. Dr. Allen looks square at Starlight and says, "Young lady, in my 31 years of medicine, I have never witnessed a true miracle like your husband experienced."

In the course of the next ten minutes, Dr. Allen gives all the information on River's amazing miracle and the pro bono case that he is granting for all of River's hospital expenses. Dr. Allen also expresses his desire to take their picture and to tell River's story of the bears, rock slide accident, and the rare white goats that caused the accident in the hospital newsletter. Most of all, he wants to share the miraculous healing as a result of their faith, prayer, and commitment. After the pictures are taken, Nurse Taylor tells River and everyone that she and Nurse Amy are going to come down soon and visit them in Golden Valley.

Dr. Allen allows River to get up out of the wheelchair after seeing Starlight and his friends. He calls the manager of the hospital's cafeteria and tells her to put whatever the Jenkins and their two friends want for breakfast on his personal tab. River, Starlight, Patrick, and Emily each have a huge breakfast. By the time they get to their vehicles to drive to Golden Valley, it is 5:45 AM.

"Folks! Folks! Please settle down! As my dad stated after he sounded the code red bell, this meeting is not about giant pitwolves being spotted on the property. They are out there, believe me, but none of us have seen one today. So if you can just relax with that good news for a minute, at least we can move on."

Assistant Pastor Caleb Crawford whispers to his young friend Forrest Johnson who is standing beside him. He wants him to get the big 60 inch plasma screen ready in the church auditorium to show the people the news coverage about the meteorites hitting Boulder and Denver. Forrest starts getting things ready.

Tommy Wilcox raises his hand, "I don't understand, Bro. Caleb. Sheriff Barnes comes in here like a race car driver on his last lap and shoots his pistol off like John Wayne, plus a code red for the second time is sounded since last night. What is going on?"

Caleb glances over at his wife Ashley and she nods as she sits between their two boys Andrew and Stephen. Caleb's mom Melody along with Charlie, David, and Max are at the back of the church ready to minster to anyone who is having a hard time with the bad news about the meteorites. She had just enough time to briefly mention the news of the meteorites to Charlie, David, and Max before coming into the church building. The three are feeling kind of numb as a result.

Caleb says, "Tommy, I'm going to address those things you brought up. Please, everybody take a seat. I know since last evening the things that have happened have seemed unbelievable. We are all experiencing a paradigm shift with our new view of reality. But you guys should know better than 99 percent of all Americans that the end times are going to be a roller coaster ride. It's the worst and best of times for the church of Jesus Christ. Everyone is here because you know what's coming and the Lord led you here. You wouldn't be here if that wasn't the case. A lot of you have read the ministry's newsletter for years and read the books my dad and Uncle Gary wrote. The reality of those things is beginning to unfold before our eyes. They are coming to pass, but there is still a lot more to come. My dad and Uncle Gary are still holding to their guns. I would have to agree with them that the Tribulation has not begun. But we are close, my friends, very close. When the reality that there is no rapture out of this mess dawns on our fellow born-again Christians around the country, many will be devastated to say the least. Repeatedly our co-pastors told you what was coming and what the prophetic scriptures declare. They also warned the body of Christ that things were going to happen fast - boom, boom, boom - like one event after another. But they don't have a crystal ball into the future. They only have a really good understanding of it. No one imagined the existence of a huge muscled-up beast like that giant pitwolf until last night. But it does exist and there are others of them out there. They are probably in the vicinity of the ranch here, but none of us have spotted one since last night. These pitwolves still have everyone shaken up and we were already on edge with the meteorites hitting near here."

"Well then, what is this code red all about, Caleb?" asks Tim Wilson who seems a little grumpy from having to get up before his alarm clock went off and plenty sore from last night.

"Tim, everybody, listen. All I've said this morning was to prep you for what I'm about to say now." Upon hearing those words, everyone is motionless and silent. They sense that an event, some issue bigger than the giant pitwolves, has occurred. "As of short time ago, around 20 minutes I believe, a great tragedy struck our state. Two large meteorites hit Boulder and Denver." Everyone is just stunned by Caleb's words, like a boxer who gets hit with a powerful left hook to the side of the face that he never sees coming.

Lisa Stanton who came in her housecoat and slippers starts rapidly waving her hand, "Caleb, where about in Boulder?"

"Mrs. Stanton, I don't have that answer other than Ci Mada Union Laboratories was ground zero for the impact of the large meteorite in Boulder."

Upon hearing the news, a church member gasps, "Uh... this is getting very serious."

Dr. Stanton stands up and says, "Well, I know where they're located. Ci Mada is located on the edge of Boulder's city limits on the southwest side."

"Okay, there we go. Mr. Stanton has the answer for all of us," replies Caleb.

Ci Mada's destruction has raised a few eyebrows in the congregation because some of the Christians at Fortress are a little more savvy than most Christians about things in the news. Some of the brethren at the ranch have all ready connected the dots that more than likely the giant pitwolves were developed at Ci Mada. Those in leadership are trying to figure out if this means their dilemma is solved.

"What kind of damage did it do in Boulder? What's the number of dead?"

inquires an anxious Lisa Stanton.

"I'm afraid it was off the charts with tens of thousands dead."

Leon Wilson shouts, "Oh, my Lord Jesus!" while others are calling out to God in their own way.

"That's bad, people. That's real bad," says another voice in the congregation.

"Give us a moment. I believe Forrest is working on the big screen to give us some live coverage of the events. Forrest, are you about ready?"

"Finished, Caleb."

"Brothers and Sisters, I would just like to say that Forrest, Ashley, and I saw just a few minutes of this before we came inside and it's unbelievable. Parents, I see some of you out there and if you don't want your young children to see these images, then you may want to leave now. If anyone else wants to leave, please feel free to go."

Anita Garcia leans over to her husband Michael and whispers to him about their six year old son's fever. She raises her hand and says, "Caleb, Johnny has been running a fever. I believe I need to take him back to the cabin to rest. Plus I don't want him to see it."

"That's fine, Anita, by all means. Okay, once again if you want to go, just go. That is fine." Anita grabs her little Johnny and walks him back to their home. "Okay, Forrest, go ahead," says Caleb. Forrest pushes the button to the large plasma TV.

"Again, folks, this is Dana Williams with KABZ and we are reporting live from southwest Boulder, Colorado, maybe I should says what's left of this section of the city. We are talking about devastation that looks like an atomic bomb exploded and left a huge crater with rocks, chucks of metal, debris and dust all around us. We can't even get to the point of impact, which according to Boulder's Fire Chief Ned Simmons was Ci Mada Union Laboratories. In all my years as a reporter, I have never witnessed anything like this in the United States. I have worked hurricanes when I lived in Houston, I've seen destruction caused by F4 and F5 tornadoes when I was with one of our affiliates in Kansas, and I have worked major floods and earthquakes. But never have I seen

anything like this before. The number of dead is staggering and the smell of death is permeating all around us. It's stifling and some people can't handle the smell. I don't know how much longer we can stay at this location. I have heard amazing stories of people surviving rocks and large chunks of concrete and steel raining down all around them. With me is my fellow reporter Tom Littleton. Tom, what do you make of this? How are you processing all this devastation around us?"

"Dana, it's hard to believe what I'm seeing is real. We are two miles away from a crater that is one third of a mile wide and about 120 feet deep at it deepest point from estimated reports. The closest thing I can compare to is when I was a reporter in war-torn Afghanistan and Iraq. I've been told from the Boulder's City Manager Roger Vogt that from looking at city maps from a helicopter, the deepest point of the crater is where the front parking lot of Ci Mada Union used to be. According to his estimates, from what he saw in the police helicopter, about one seventh of the city is severely impacted from the meteorite. He said half of the houses, schools, businesses, and commercial enterprises that were in a mile and a half radius of the point of impact are completely gone or partially blown down. Most of those structures were wooden. The remaining half of buildings have sustained enough damage that they will have to be condemned and torn down. Dana, I want to add that just before I came on camera, I talked with reporter Lannette Washington with our sister station in Denver and she said that conditions in Denver parallel what we are seeing here. Their ground zero is an area known by locals as the Grunge Walk. There were a lot of pot parlors, massage parlors, and tattoo shops in the area along with numerous bars and night clubs. But within a short distance from there was the Denver Mile High Mall, many upscale subdivisions, and a number of public schools. Also Davidson University was nearby and financial and insurance type busin..."

"Excuse me for the interruption, Tom, but there is some kind of a huge dog I believe about 300 yards away from us. I'm trying to make it out. It appears to be dragging a possible dead victim's body."

"Folks, our action van is situated on a small hill and we are looking down from a vantage point. Look to the right, Dana, another huge like dog. Dana, it's so tall I'm thinking it must be an Irish wolfhound. We'll see if our cameraman can zoom in and get a close up of the dog. Just give us a sec..."

"Oh, my God! Zoom out! Zoom out now! What the @#$% is that, Tom!?"*

"I don't know. But those animals are scary looking and muscled up and have huge teeth or fangs two to three inches long that they using to rip into the flesh of that dead man!"

226

"Oh, my God! This isn't really happening, is it Tom?"

"Dana, I think they are the giant pitwolves that we thought were an urban legend."

Dana Williams screams hysterically. Her voice quivers as she says, *"They are for real. Just look at them! Now they are chasing those two policemen who are running as quickly as possible to get into their police car!"*

"Dana, look to the right. Four more pitwolves are running down from the mountains over there! Folks, they are as swift as deer, maybe faster. The crowd of people in front of us are running in different directions."

"Tom, what are you doing?"

"I'm getting in the van! Come on, Dana! Hurry!." Before they can think of moving, six people who were listening to them from below them, jump into the open side door of the van and close and lock the door. Tom jumps down and is banging on the driver's door begging them to open it. They open it and he quickly gets inside. The cameraman Harry, reporters Dana Williams, and Tom Littleton hadn't seen them with their peripheral vision as the six individuals were running to get inside the van to protect themselves from the beasts. Dana keeps broadcasting, but is becoming petrified by what she sees. Both policemen start shooting at the six pitwolves once they run past their car with their .40 caliber Glock pistols, each emptying their clips. But they are so shaken, not one bullet hits one of the four beasts.

Dana is still broadcasting, but she is going into shock and she frantically cries out, *"Harry, are we safe from those monsters?"*

Harry says, *"We are 10 feet off the ground with this extended roof. We're fine. This footage is too good to pass up. Those wild animals can't possibly get up here. We're too high up for them to get to us."*

Dana yells hysterically, *"Tom! Tom?"* Tom Littleton yells from within the van and rapidly bangs on the inside ceiling for her to come down and get inside. But then she sees one of the giant pitwolves at a distance easily jump over a parked pickup's roof by five feet. As result of witnessing that, she is instantly frozen with fear. The pitwolves hear and spot her and Harry and start racing right for them.

Harry, who is now afraid for his life, jumps off the backside of the van and in the process accidentally knocks the camera lens upward. He quickly gets in on the driver's side of the action van using his key. Everyone watching the broadcast on TV sees a hazy, brown sky caused from the dust still settling from the meteorite impact.

Dana's voice is still broadcasting live. She can barely talk from the shock gripping her voice and body. All she is capable of doing is to speak in a soft robotic voice, *"The pitwolves are coming. The pitwolves are coming. The giant pitwolves are coming..."* The KABZ officials then cut the link and the broadcast goes blank. Caleb then yells to Forrest to turn off the TV, which he does instantly.

Everyone in the church who has been viewing the live coverage sits motionless for several minutes. No one knows what to say, including Caleb Crawford the Assistant Pastor of Fortress. A few babies and small children can be heard crying. Words like shocked, scared, frightened, numbed can't even begin to describe what some of them are experiencing emotionally. The people who have been watching the beautiful Dana Williams need no explanation of her fate. It is obvious to them. Caleb decides to sing the old Martin Luther hymn written centuries before under dire circumstances and powerful opposition from the Catholic church during the Middle Ages. The hymn *A Mighty Fortress* was the source of inspiration for the naming of their church.

Caleb leads off singing, "A Mighty Fortress is Our God...," and one by one the members join in.

Chapter 11

THE FORTRESS SHIELD

Once Ricky gets airborne, he flies the helicopter back to the downed fence on the Double V Ranch near where Big Blackie was killed by the giant pitwolf. It looks as if a number of pitwolves, or least some other predators, have indeed gorged themselves on his body last night. Buzzards are feasting on what is left of the rotting prime beef now. Presently, they see no signs of these giant predators. Ricky then flies around the entire perimeter of the property, but again no pitwolves are spotted by the four men. Blackhawk says that the foliage from the Aspen and Ponderosa trees can easily hide the animals. Unless they are on the cliffs or out in an open area, it may be difficult to spot one. Ricky covers the entire Double V Ranch thoroughly, but still no sightings. Barnes, wanting to see some signs of them, suggests the area of Golden Valley where there have been two spottings. For the next hour, Ricky flies over those areas and some other large portions of Clark County. Blackhawk has Ricky fly especially over areas that have streams, ponds, and any bodies of water that they can find, but still no sign of the beasts. With a total of four sightings and one dead giant pitwolf, the urban legend has come to Clark County. Sheriff Barnes is expressing to the others that he is not sure how to handle the whole giant pitwolf ordeal.

Blackhawk says, "Sheriff, we all know that you are trying to do your job to the best of your ability. If you're doing the best you can, you have to trust God for the rest. That's all any man can do. And you have already heard how the hand of God has move miraculously in our behalf. He has done some miraculous stuff and this day is not over yet."

"You're right, John. I really have seen God move like in Bible times. I guess I should be thankful that I'm not the sheriff in the Denver or the Boulder areas because I really wouldn't know where to begin with my city partially destroyed and looking like a warzone. My problem seems small in comparison to theirs. People in law enforcement in the state of Colorado have always snickered behind my back about how small and poor this county is and how conservative and non-progressive it remains. When it comes to this county being small and poor, it is what it is. But I have always been proud of this county being conservative, Old West-minded, and above all else having the lowest crime rate in the state. So I'm just going to trust God like you said."

Ricky is happy to see that God is moving in Sam's life and he enthusiastically says, "That sounds like a good plan to me. What do you think, Gary and John?"

Gary whispers to John to say 'yep.' So they both say, "YEP!" like Barnes does a lot of times. Everyone laughs, including Barnes.

Ricky tells Sheriff Barnes he feels led to swing back to the Double V Ranch before searching any more in the area.

"That's fine," responds Barnes. "Maybe the criminals have returned to the scene of the crime. We have come up dry in those other two areas where I was hoping to get a glimpse of the huge predators." Gary, Ricky, and John are still believing a miracle will take place.

But Barnes is thinking he is ready to land the helicopter. He wants to check on Travis and talk with Hank about putting a plan in place to release the news of the giant pitwolves to the public. As Ricky flies over the northwest section of the property, he sees Caleb's truck and a crew of men working on the downed fence. Some are armed and on guard while the others work. The fence has to be repaired to keep from losing any cattle and bison. The men all wave to each other as the helicopter flies over. Then Ricky feels led of the Holy Spirit to fly to the south section of the property. Immediately Barnes spots four giant pitwolves in an opening chasing a herd of three male and three female elk south of the Double V Ranch fence line. The three male elk are huge and possess massive antlers, and the three females are also rather large. With a hundred and fifty yard lead on the pitwolves, the elk are running straight ahead to the property fence of Fortress which appears to be 300 yards away.

Barnes, in a combination of suppressed fear and a good dose of disbelief, reacts to the sight of the giant pitwolves by saying, "I don't believe it! I've never seen anything like this. The giant pitwolves just don't seem real because they are so big, graceful and fast."

"They're real, Sheriff," replies Blackhawk. "I can promise you that!"

The huge pitwolves are amazingly fast and are covering a lot of ground, their gaining on the elk. It looks like the elk will soon be overtaken by the powerful predators. In what just seems like seconds the six elk get to the fence line on the perimeter of Fortress, they easily jump over the four strands of barbed wire onto the property of the Double V Ranch. Barnes is desperately trying to take a shot at the pitwolves, but the door on the helicopter will not stay open in mid-air.

Blackhawk quickly yells, "Look! The six elk that just jumped the fence are grazing on grass like they don't have a care in the world."

In the back of the helicopter, Gary is praising God. All four of the giant pitwolves have stopped at the fence line.

Barnes says, Well, I'll be %$&#*@. Sorry, guys. I just don't believe what I'm seeing. Ricky, do you?"

"It's hard to believe, Sam."

Blackhawk excitedly says, "Take this helicopter down, Bro. Ricky! Take it down, please. Something strange is going on."

Ricky blindly trusts John's instincts. "Yeah, sure! Give me a second to land this bird." As he is taking it down within the perimeter of the barbed wire fence surrounding the Double V Ranch, Barnes takes off his cowboy hat and makes doubly sure his safety is off on his rifle. He is hoping to get in a couple of good shots at the genetically modified beasts from beside the helicopter. Just a split second before the helicopter lands, Blackhawk jumps about four feet to the ground. Ricky is mentally going through the process of shutting down the helicopter. It all happens so quickly.

Barnes shouts, "What is that crazy injun up to? He is going to get himself eaten alive! He has forgotten his rifle in the helicopter! I'm getting out."

"No, wait a minute, Sheriff," says Ricky, as he grabs Sam's left sleeve.

Gary, in the meantime, jumps out, unarmed also. The ferocious looking pitwolves are running up and down the fence line in both directions as if looking for an opening. Something is preventing them from jumping over the fence and attacking the elk.

Barnes is beside himself. He says, "Those dang fools are going to get themselves killed! I can't have this on my watch."

Ricky, in a surprised voice, says, "Sheriff, don't you see them!? It's the most amazing thing I've ever seen!"

"What are you talking about? See what?" responds a puzzled Barnes.

Ricky just breaks into a prayer, "Dear Lord, You can make the blind see and those that can see blind. Please, open the eyes of my friend Sam so he can see a miracle in the spiritual realm."

Instantly, Barnes, like the rest of the men, sees into a spiritual dimension that few living men or even Biblical prophets of old have ever experienced before. "Oh my God, Ricky! Dear Lord, am I dreaming? Am I losing my mind? Ricky, are you seeing what I'm seeing?"

"Yes, Sam! You're talking about those nine-foot plus tall angels with big, long swords standing shoulder to shoulder all up and down the fence line."

"Yep! Ricky, I would never believe it if I didn't see it with my own two eyes. I just pinched myself real hard, and it hurt, so I know I'm not dreaming. Ricky, I declare to you that I believe that God's Son is not dead. He is alive! I'm leaving my rifle in the helicopter and I'm going to join John and Gary."

"Me too, Sam. Let's take a giant step of faith."

"Yeah, let's do it." All four men are outside the helicopter now taunting the huge monsters, which are desperately trying to find an opening between the angels. Some pitwolves are growling at the men. Some are snarling at the warrior angels which they also can see. The huge alpha male pitwolf that Ricky had seen the night before, runs and tries to jump over the angels. He is in the air about 13 feet, but the angel he is trying to jump over just raises the broad blade of his sword and he hits the side of it causing the beast to fall to the ground. It's as if he has hit a brick wall. He bounces back up and runs away with his tail between his legs. Oddly the six elk are peacefully eating grass like nothing is taking place at all around them.

After a couple of minutes, the biggest and most powerful looking angel of all, named Michael, appears before all of them and tells them the following: "Do not fear. My name is Michael and I'm a servant, an archangel, and messenger of God. He has commanded me to tell you that God's hand is on this holy ground you call Fortress, for indeed it is a fortress not built with human hands. Since the conception of this community of believers, the Spirit of God has ordained that no weapon formed against this church shall prosper. Do not fear these giant pitwolves, for their paws will never set foot on any property of Fortress. Neither fear any man, army, nor any demonic force of hell that comes here intent to destroy you or that try to thwart the will of God. He will not allow anyone or anything bent on evil to destroy you unless you lose your zeal and love for God and cease to overcome. The angelic hosts here will stand guard day and night until the appointed day. These warrior angels under my command were created to do the bidding of God Almighty. The God of heaven declares to you that from the foundations of the world this land has been ordained to be a city of refuge in the Tribulation. Only fear Him who can destroy both body and soul. Walk in holiness and the teachings of His holy Word, the Bible. Many will want to live on this property for numerous reasons. But only a remnant are called to live on this property. If any man, woman, or child tries to live on this land and they are not called of God to be here, then they will die before their appointed time. Brother Ricky and Brother Gary have been called to be end time Apostles. They and their wives are men and women of integrity and truth seekers. They are the elders of Fortress who love God and are chosen vessels, and the Lord is releasing greater anointings and manifestations of the gifts of the Spirit into their lives and ministry. Honor them as they honor God. Walk in brotherly and sisterly love toward one another and pray continually, because love covers a multitude of sins."

Gary and Ricky ask, "When will we see you again?"

Michael responds, "I can not disclose that to you, but I will walk with you through the fires of the Tribulation. Days of discouragement will come, but you must not grow weary. Keep your eyes on the Lord and His promises at those times. The miraculous will be manifested in your lives and ministry.

Do not think more highly of yourselves than you should. You have been chosen by God for the work ahead. As shepherds, your job is to watch over your flock here and abroad continually. Above all else remember this, that the lifeblood of Fortress and its survival rests on your love and zeal for God, His word and intercessory prayer."

Michael, who is walking away from the men, turns around and starts walking back to John Blackhawk. He points his finger at Blackhawk and says, "The Lord Almighty is very pleased with you. There is no fear of men nor beast that resides in you. You fear only God and tremble at His Word and He dearly loves you for it."

"Thank you, Michael, for telling me that," says a very humble Blackhawk.

"Oh, and one more thing, John. The Father told me to tell you that Dena, John Jr., and Hannah are doing fine in heaven and are looking forward to being reunited with you."

"Upon hearing that news, John leans backward and stretches out his arms wide and upward, as to God, facing the clouds above him and says, "Thank you, God, for the kindness You have granted to me this day. Thank You so much! Thank You so, so much!" and smiles continually as he moves slowly around in circles with outstretched arms. Ricky and Gary have never seen John so happy in all the years they've known him.

Michael says, "I must go now."

Barnes, under deep conviction of the Holy Spirit, speaks up and asks the angel to please wait. He says, "Michael, I have been a wicked sinner, hard-headed, and a hard drinking man all my life. As a Green Beret in Vietnam, I took an evil pleasure in killing the Viet Cong slowly with a sharp knife because I was eaten up with hatred and a barbaric revenge in my heart. Will you tell God personally that I believe in Him and want His Son Jesus to please forgive me for all my sins and to be my Lord and Savior? I have been a fool my entire life."

Michael says, "Samuel Paul Barnes, Jr., it is done. God, the Father, heard your prayer just now and He knows your thoughts continually. The Lord Jesus has heard your prayer and has forgiven you. The Holy Spirit of God now dwells within your heart. My fellow angels are rejoicing in heaven as are the ones here on this property as I speak." Michael smiles a big smile at Sam who starts crying.

All angels around the perimeter of Fortress raise their swords and shout, "Hallelujah! Hallelujah! Hallelujah!" praising God in thunderous loud, audible voices. But only the four men are allowed to be privy to the event.

Michael then is no longer visible to the naked eye. He disappears along with all the other angels. The window of seeing into the spiritual dimension closes. But the giant pitwolves are still repelled by the invisible angelic hosts. Barnes falls on his hands and knees in true repentance and cries like a baby for several minutes. Each man with him kneels beside him. They place their hands upon him and pray for him. Eventually Barnes gets off his knees a broken man. He says, "I raised a lot of hell in my day, but those days are over." He wipes his eyes and runny nose several times with his handkerchief. "No man has ever seen me cry since I was a very small boy. I saw a lot of death and hell in Vietnam, but that never made me cry. My daddy used to whoop me with a switch if he caught me crying. After a couple hard rounds with the switch, I learned the lesson. It didn't matter how much it hurt, I was taught not to cry. He believed it was one of the codes of the Old West. But you know what? I'm not ashamed. I feel like a new man. It's like God took a huge weight and burden and lifted it off my shoulders. Something within me internally has changed."

"You have changed, Sheriff! You're a new man. You've been born again. You are a new creation in Christ, like the Bible declares in II Corinthians 5:17. Welcome to the brotherhood of the followers of Jesus," says Blackhawk who hugs Sam tightly and gently slaps his back. Gary and Ricky, rejoicing for their new brother in the Lord, each pat Barnes on the back and give him a manly hug.

Barnes, who still has tears streaming down his face, says, "Well, boys, I guess I'm part of your family now."

Gary, Ricky, and John all say, "Yep!"

They stop laughing when Gary quickly notices the giant pitwolves are running away down one side of the fence. He says, "Look, guys! Ricky, I think they are headed back to the crew repairing the fence. Let's fly over there real quick and watch them see a miracle."

Ricky says, "Quick, everybody inside the bird." The four men run to get inside the helicopter. Ricky soon has it in the air flying to the northeast section of Fortress.

Barnes points his finger and says, "Look at those pitwolves down there. They are going to round the corner of the property. The crew below can't see them coming because of those trees along the fence." Leon Wilson has a shotgun in his hands and has his back to the pitwolves. Leon is about 20 feet from the opening in the fence on the outside of it looking at the area where Big Blackie was killed. Two men are right at the downed tree area of the fence line cutting up the tree with chainsaws. Sometimes their bodies are going outside of the fence line and sometimes inside of it. Three armed men are spread out along the inside of the fence line. The cut logs and branches are blocking Leon from easily getting inside the barbed wire fence. The pitwolves are running so fast that they could quickly be upon Leon before he has a chance to get inside the fence unless he is warned in time.

Gary says, "Hurry, Ricky! Take this helicopter down."

Ricky says, "I'm working on it."

Barnes, Gary, and John are motioning to the men below with their arms to get inside the fence. They are all waving their hands at them. The sun is reflecting off the helicopter's windows and the men below can't really see that they are being motioned to move inside the fence. Ricky is bringing the helicopter down. Blackhawk knows time is running out so he jumps while the helicopter is still 10 feet from the ground. He quickly waves his hand for Leon to get inside the fence. But Leon doesn't see him because he is fumbling around trying to hold on to his cowboy hat that is trying to fly off his head because the helicopter's blades are still rotating. Blackhawk hurdles the barbed wire fence to help Leon get inside. As soon as the aircraft lands, Gary steps outside and motions to the men about the pitwolves coming down the fence line and screams for everyone to not shoot their firearms. Barnes steps out with his 12 gauge shotgun in case everything goes south. Ricky is shutting down the helicopter as quickly as possible. Gary yells at the top of his lungs, "All you men all going to see a miracle."

All the men are confused, but still lower their weapons. The pitwolves finally appear as they run under some nearby low branches which have been obscuring the workers' view of the animals. Leon turns around and sees the demonic looking creatures barreling down on him and John and says, "Oh, sweet Jesus, help!"

The crew members are almost in disbelief of what they are seeing. Leon freezes up with fear and stumbles over the downed tree outside the fence like he has two left feet. John, in desperation, firmly grabs him by the waistline of his jeans and yanks him up in the air and carries him over the logs inside the fence line just in the nick of time. A split second later they would have been ripped to shreds by the savage beasts. Everyone is safe inside the fence line with the angelic hosts protecting them as the pack of pitwolves snarl and growl with their massive fangs at the men. The beasts from hell know they can't penetrate the shield of armed giant angels that surround the property of Fortress and don't even try. The crew knows there is some kind of a supernatural protective barrier between them and the crazed giant pitwolves wanting to get at them. But the men on the fence crew are not privy to seeing the warrior angels. They do know they are being divinely protected and later hear the accounts of what Ricky, Gary, John, and Sam have witnessed.

Chapter 12

THE CHILDREN OF NOAH

Gary and Ricky know that if word leaks out about their members killing a giant pitwolf last night, it could draw a media circus and government scrutiny into their lives and the sheriff's department. This is something they hope and pray will not happen. With two major meteorites hitting both Boulder and Denver, it seems to them that the media will focus the eyes of the nation and world on the two cities' responses to the cosmic crisis. The fact that two other people in the county have spotted pitwolves also eases the stress of the situation and relieves the pressure they were feeling last night. This factor takes some heat off of the people of Fortress. Possessing knowledge of Ci Mada's involvement in the development and use of giant pitwolves is still a potential troubling problem. With a select number of Fortress members knowing of Ci Mada's use of secret technology of the sleeper chip and the reader, it can possibly be a problem if government officials start snooping around Fortress and asking questions. Also if it somehow leaks out that Ricky possesses a sleeper chip reader, it can spell danger for all those at Fortress.

Gary and Ricky know if it all goes south with the giant pitwolf situation, the government doesn't have their backs. Conventional wisdom tells them that political figures were paid off to suppress the truth about Ci Mada's top secret and unethical research and developments from coming out in years past. Big government and Ci Mada are having a private dance together at the ball and the public isn't invited. Avoidance of government involvement is something that Gary and Ricky are trying to avoid at all costs. They like to fly under the radar as much as possible, especially with the growing opposition to true biblical Christianity in the country.

Gary and Ricky, having written and taught on prophecy for years, know all too well what the last days will entail, especially holding the post-tribulation view of the rapture. Neither one was too concerned about the end times years before when they believed in a pre-tribulation rapture. Oh sure, they were fascinated with endless speculation on subjects like who might be the Antichrist or when the Jewish temple would be rebuilt in Jerusalem, what the mark of the beast was and when the timing of the rapture might take place. But they believed most of the end time events wouldn't directly affect them because they would not be around when they took place.

But years ago Gary read James McKeever's book entitled _Christians Will Go Through the Tribulation_ and he told Ricky to read it, As a result, the end times took on a whole new meaning in their minds. It led both of them to do in depth studies of the Word of God on the timing of the rapture. After six months of intensely studying and praying about the subject of when the rapture would occur, they walked away from their pretrib rapture view. Both were convinced it was wrong and never returned to that doctrine again. Coming to this conclusion was an epiphany in their lives and changed the direction of their ministry.

More focused study of prophecy, as well as a lot of soul searching about what the Lord would have them do in response to what He had shown them, would take place over the years. Sometime later both co-pastors and their wives had sensed a move was in the works and a call to full-time ministry before their relocation to Colorado. The two close friends had been balancing their secular careers and ministry fairly well, but God was calling them to a new walk of faith, a new chapter in their lives. This was taking place as both of them achieved great success in their chosen careers. Eventually the timing was right and the Lord led Ricky first to sell his very profitable military defense contractor business. Then He led Gary to sell his highly successful real estate law firm that catered to the jet set crowd of California. Gary's dad Shane had been dealing with some health issues and had already stepped down from full-time practice. As a result of the Lord's perfect timing, the market was good and they both received hefty sums of money for their businesses. Then the Lord had them move to Golden Valley to prepare an Ark for His remnant in the coming violent storm of the last days. Just prior to this time, Melody's Dad, the Big Swede - a former NFL tight-end superstar, had gotten up in years and had become almost totally dependent on her for his physical care. A battle with severe heart congestion was finally bringing this giant of man's body to an end on this earth. After she had been caring for him for several months along with a male nurse, he passed away in his sleep. Sensing the Lord wanted Melody and Ricky to buy the Double V Ranch property from her two siblings for their new phase of ministry, Ricky offered her brothers $ 750,000.00 each for their share of the ranch, the lodge and the mineral rights to the land and the defunct Viking Gold Mine, along with all the buildings, equipment and machinery on the property. Both were glad to sell their shares and run. Her older brother Erik took his money and moved to Las Vegas to work as a floor manager in the glitz and glamour of a casino. Lucas, the second oldest, moved to Key West to enjoy sun, fishing and endless margaritas.

The concept of Fortress had gone through an evolution through the years. First, it was a church in LA. Then it became a mother church to other churches it birthed that became known as the Disciplemaker Network of Churches. Next, with the move to Colorado, the Lord made it clear to the elders it was to be a command center in a spiritual sense, for God's people presently and in the coming Great Tribulation period. In Golden Valley, Fortress was going to become a prototype remnant church, a role model for the Christian church, a place where the lost would see His power and glory demonstrated. Where God the Father, God the Son and God the Holy Spirit would be lifted up, magnified and not man

In the hearts and minds of the elders, Fortress was not about property, buildings and supplies. Fortress was for the called out ones - the *ekklesia* - the Greek word for church. Ricky and Gary had hammered it out for years telling Christians that the word *church* had nothing to do with our western mindset of four walls or a structure. They would teach that the true church is the bride of the Lamb who is willing to follow Him wherever He leads and do His will. These Christians would be the kind who would link arms with the elders to establish a new kind of church in America and around the world. Fortress and the Disciplemaker Network of Churches under their leadership along with other like minded churches across the world made up what the elders like to call the Remnant Church Movement.

Ricky and Gary used various media outlets and held periodic retreats for the members of churches in their network and selected Christians who sincerely wanted to learn more about a deeper walk with God. All those connected to the network of churches, whether pastors, leaders, or laymen, would leave these retreats held in different locations over the years revived, refreshed, and rekindled in their faith and pursuit of God and the lost. Many claimed it was like receiving a powerful, spiritual B 12 shot.

For these modern day apostles and their wives, they also had traveled around the world holding end-time prophetic seminars, revivals, and teaching conferences on the true manifestations of the gifts of the Spirit and what it meant to be a real disciple of Christ in an ever-increasing dark and dying world. Some of those people who came to hear Ricky and Gary ended up supernaturally at the doorsteps of Fortress.

For the elders, the small town of Golden Valley was their Jerusalem and Clark County was their Judea. They had reached out repeatedly to anyone who needed help, prayer, and a word of encouragement. Very little fruit had been harvested locally, but many seeds of the love of Christ had been sown. Although there were times they were discouraged, they had not grown weary. The Holy Spirit had communicated to them that Fortress was to be a church in the wilderness, a city of refuge, a city set upon a hill for all to see in the near future as mentioned in Revelation 12. Fortress was to be a spiritual hospital, a teaching and prayer center where Christians would be healed, trained, and equipped so that they would be strengthened for the days ahead. And at the appointed time, these Christians would go back into the darkest recesses of the world with the glorious light of the gospel to win souls to Christ and wreak havoc on the Kingdom of Lucifer. For the call and cause of Christ, the elders were willing to lay down their lives for God.

Ricky and Gary had never entertained thoughts of being isolationists nor envisioned Fortress as being a hardcore survivalist compound in Golden Valley. It was the furthest thing from their minds. Even though these men were literally multi-millionaires, the things of the world held no spell over their thoughts and hearts. Money to them was simply a tool for kingdom purposes. They had traded their former affluent lifestyles for more simple ones. Gary and Ricky traded in their custom tailored suits for faded blue jeans, pullover shirts and cowboy boots. They and their spouses had always hyper-focused on the will of God for their lives and the ministry to which God had called them, especially since leaving Los Angeles. With the move, their call had taken on a sobering, serious note. They knew time was growing short and all four elders knew their wealth could be erased with a push of a computer button, stolen, or devalued to the point of being worthless in an total economic collapse. Each knew in their heart that their provision of basic necessities of life and protection during the coming evil times would have to come from God. He alone was their real fortress, provider, healer, and whatever else they needed Him to be presently and in the future. Ultimately, they and every Christian in the world would have to come to this realization of total dependence on Him.

Gary and Ricky worked with all the leadership of every Disciplemaker church in the U.S. and other foreign countries in establishing "green communities". This was their code name for cities of refuge. All of the elders had heard this message loud and clear from the Holy Spirit. The Crawfords and Kirkmans had literally sunk millions of their own dollars into making Fortress self sufficient and as "green" as possible. They had also helped financially with some of the Disciplemaker churches that didn't have enough funds to adequately prepare physically for the days ahead. Sometimes two or three churches worked together to pool their resources to purchase land in remote areas outside of cities and suburbia to form these types of future communities. Christians from their network of churches that had the funds or had retired early often worked on the property to try to make them as self sufficient as possible. Others would work on their days off or even take their vacation time to work on the property. Almost all the churches were still located in cities where their rural facilities were used for weekend prayer retreats and special meetings. A few of the churches were already in remote areas due to the location of their founders.

True *koinonia* was a hallmark of every Disciplemaker church. They weren't Christian utopias but a genuine Christ-centered fellowships where love for one another truly existed. Whenever a church service was over, the brothers and sisters didn't scatter like cockroaches do when a light is turned on. People hung out and talked about a variety of topics, not just church or the Bible. People tried to encourage one another and invest in each other's lives, not just after church services but also during the week. In Disciplemaker churches people either felt at home and that they belonged there or they couldn't wait for the service to be over to get out of there. No one straddled the fence in these churches. But grace and prayer were always extended to young believers especially millennials who had come out of the dark things of the world and had a real zeal and love for God. Struggling with sin was understandable for new and old believers at times. Continually playing around with it was not tolerated, and they called brothers and sisters out on the mat for it. All the leadership of the network knew that sin was like a cancer and if it wasn't addressed it only got bigger and uglier.

Accountability to each other was a major factor that led to the purity in the Disciplemaker churches. "Lone Ranger" Christians or feel good, back row Christians quickly found themselves in another church where they could just punch their tickets every time the church doors were open. Rich believers who had visited Fortress or other Disciplemaker churches found out that their financial clout didn't guarantee them the pastor's ear or more attention than an elderly woman on a fixed income was shown. This was something that Ricky and Gary had warned against to all the pastors in the network.

Other big issues that Gary and Ricky always warned the shepherds under them and all the flocks of believers were the teachings of cheap grace, liberalism and, political correctness that were creeping into the church at the close of the 20th century and the start of the 21st century. The official stance of all the Disciplemaker churches was that grace was a safety net in case you fell in your walk from time to time. It was not a trampoline to be used and abused whenever a believer wanted to embrace sin and hold it dear. The bedrock foundation of all Disciplemaker churches was that the Bible was their road map to life. Compromising basic, clear doctrines was not an option because it would lead the flock down a dark road to destruction.

Somehow Gary and Ricky had always walked in the fruit of the Spirit for years and were like heavy anchors that others could hook up to in moments of crisis or when help was needed in a sea of turmoil. Day in and day out they were even-tempered, rock solid Christians with much wisdom gained through study of the Word, prayer, and experience. They inspired all those around them. Young, middle-aged, and older men and women alike sought out their counsel and wise advice. Some of these men were called into the ministry of pastoring a Disciplemaker church as a result of being discipled by them and their love of sowing into their lives. In turn, these men linked arms with Ricky and Gary whom they considered spiritual fathers of the faith. For all these pastors, the things of the world had lost their luster. God's kingdom purposes were the driving force behind all that they said and did.

Friendship for the co-pastors of Fortress began when they were nine years old and played on the same championship little league football team in LA. Gridiron success followed the "dynamic duo", as they were called in high school, which culminated in college. As co-captains of the USWC (University of Southwest California) Spartans, they had led their undefeated football team to a national championship their senior year in the Carnation Bowl against the undefeated Grizzly Bears of Colorado A&M University.

They attained two things early in their lives that others only dream about - fame and fortune. Success would follow them through life because God's grace and mercy was upon them. Both had type A personalities with different gifts, talents, and abilities that allowed them to succeed at pretty much whatever they put their minds and hands to. Each man was driven to succeed balanced with a good sense of humor.

They each made tens of millions of dollars in their individual careers and through investments in early dot.com businesses, start up high-tech companies, and real estate. These best friends enjoyed the finer things of life early in life, but the older they got, the less the things of the world had a hold on their hearts. Jesus became their everything. Now each day for them begins with an hour of prayer and Bible study. They desire nothing more than to carry out His will for their lives and ministry. What they live for is to exalt the name of Jesus Christ, the truth of His word and to carry out His will for their lives.

Gary and Ricky have an amazing relationship as brothers in Christ. And somehow they have been forged by the Spirit into almost one being, kind of like identical twins - different but alike in so many ways. Because they have been best friends their entire lives, they can read each other's body language and thoughts and can almost finish each other's sentence when speaking. Time has erased their need to be in the limelight or have their egos stroked. Both men exude confidence, an inner peace, and a humble spirit gained from a very disciplined and close walk with the Lord.

They continually fish for Christians and network with Christians of their same mindset. Coming in contact with other pastors and laymen with the same beliefs and doctrines, especially of discipleship, evangelism, intercession, and how a New Testament church should function gets them excited. They enjoy encouraging them in their walk. Nickels, noses, and numbers are not their goals as ministers of the gospel. Every American and foreign pastor who has linked up with them shares the same vision of service in a post-Christian era of the 21st century. Some pastors have not officially joined the Disciplemaker Network because they are already plugged into a denomination, but they embrace the apostles' vision. Not every pastor that walks with them is post-trib in their view of the rapture. Ricky and Gary don't sweat it because they know time will reveal the truth of that matter. But each pastor has been given Ricky's book, _Resurrection vs. Rapture - What does the Bible Teach?_ Also every pastor has been given Ryan Cotton's deep but easy to understand theological book that filled in a lot of the pieces of the puzzle for Ricky and Gary earlier in their walk in understanding Bible prophecy. It is called _A Revelation in Understanding the Book of Revelation and Other Prophetic Scriptures_.

But of all the activities and doctrines that are key to the end time church of Jesus Christ, the elders believed none was more vital to the church than intercession. Ricky and Gary continually state that intercession is the life blood of Fortress and the Disciplemaker Network of churches. They know that the very survival and existence of the global Christian church would totally depend on it. This is the source of strength, power, miracles and holiness for all the spiritually mature churches in the Remnant Church Movement.

Melody's and Mary Anne's main ministry as two of the four elders at Fortress and the Disciplemaker Churches is intercessory prayer. It is not a ministry that they chose for themselves. God called them to be intercessors. There is nothing glorious from a worldly perspective about it. It consists of a life of sacrifice and commitment to the Lord with a deep burden placed upon their hearts to pray fervently often when their flesh is weak. Many a meal and hours of sleep have been skipped because the Holy Spirit demanded they fast for an individual or a particular situation or to keep praying until there was a spiritual breakthrough. Melody and Mary Anne have seen many miracles in their lifetime as God has answered their prayers and those of their intercessory teams. But these events have not left the stain of pride on them or the feeling that they are spiritually superior to others who have not witnessed God's intervention of doing the impossible. Instead, it has left them humbled and they wonder why they have been chosen. Both of these sisters in the Lord realized years before that a sovereign God has simply chosen and called them to this kind of ministry. They have been faithful and have obeyed because they realize this is their calling and they embrace it. Both Gary and Ricky know that much of the success that they have achieved both in the secular world and their ministry has been the result of their devout wives faithfulness to intercede in prayer. They also realize that the hand of God is upon them mightily and they greatly respect their wives' spiritual advice and opinions.

I - 24/7 is what Melody and Mary Ann calls the intercession ministry. It kind of sounds like an Interstate highway, but they often say the road they travel is on their knees in prayer. The capitol I stands for Intercession and the numbers mean 24 hours a day, seven days a week. Only the most serious minded and mature Christians who have a burden and are called to a life of prayer are involved in this ministry. Melody and Mary Ann also keep tabs on how the other Disciplemaker churches are doing in the area of intercession and answers to prayer. All intercessors fast on a regular basis sometimes in a variety of ways. Melody and Mary Anne, along with their husbands, give oversight regarding the needs and direction of prayer for the intercessors. At least one prayer intercessor is in the prayer chapel located in the back of the church at all times.

No intercessor is allowed to leave the chapel until another intercessor relieves them. There are exceptions to this rule such as emergencies when someone is sick or injured. So when those times arise, someone from the church will fill in to pray until another intercessor comes.

Often when the intercessor who has been praying for their hour is relieved, they keep praying if time and their energy level permit it. There is never any condemnation if one cannot stay past their hour. Often a I - 24/7 intercessor can be found on their knees often praying for hours on end in their apartment or cabin. The intercessors of Fortress and the Disciplemaker churches never try to draw attention to themselves. They are just functioning as vessels in the service for which the master potter, God, created them to perform. They aren't better than anyone else, but their contributions can't be ignored either. This isn't to say that God doesn't hear or answer the prayers of other faithful members of Fortress or the other sister churches. One doesn't have to be the greatest Bible student or the greatest soul winner to be an intercessor, but just has to have a real burden to pray. It isn't something that can be worked up within oneself by self initiation. Some thought that God had called them to intercession only to shortly realize later that he hadn't.

Over the years some within the greater Christian community nationwide have called Gary and Ricky weird, extremists, legalistic Christians, and survivalists. These names and allegations have never deterred these two men of God from the mandate that God has given them. When it comes to the subject of preparing for the end because of their post-trib views they prefer to be called the children of Noah. Ricky and Gary have often asked the following question to both believers and unbelievers whenever they have a chance to communicate their end time beliefs in regards to preparing for the apocalyptic times: "What would have happened to Noah and the human race today if Noah had not prepared an ark for the salvation of his family and the animal life of his day?' Their response is always that no people would be here today and neither would any animal life. Thus, their reason for all the preparations at Fortress and the other Disciplemaker churches "green communities" is established.

Fortress is the role model of a green community, including water wells and farm animals. They raise a small herd of bison, black angus and Holstein cattle, goats, hogs, and chickens for meat, milk, and eggs. They also raise organic grains, organic fruit orchards, a large organic vegetable garden, a huge greenhouse for produce especially in the winter and an old time smoke house. A small time commercial food processing plant was added on to Charlie's warehouse one year after it was built. The plant is huge and always clean. It contains a large freezer/refrigerator section that stores large amounts of bulk foods, dairy, produce, and various groceries that are rotated on a regular basis so they will not expire.

Church members can and dehydrate fruits and vegetables that are harvested on the property. Beef and buffalo jerky are processed and are very popular retail items. All the retail food is sold under the Double V Ranch Organics label.

Some of the food produced on the ranch is for the needs of the members who live or work on the Double V Ranch. Food taken from the food storage area of the warehouse is replaced and rotated so food spoilage will be at a minimum. About 40 percent of the food produced is marketed for retail which gives some members of Fortress employment. Around 20% is used for the needs of the Fortress church members and for food storage. The remaining 40% is given away to the poor and needy in the county.

Charlie's warehouse also contains a vast array of medical supplies, bleach, dishwashing liquid, soap, personal care items, vitamins, plastic ware, paper plates, napkins, paper towels, and the most important commodity of all - toilet paper. It also contains canning supplies, a large stockpile of wool blankets, subzero sleeping bags, new extreme cold coats, vests, thick flannel shirts, blue jeans, underwear, long johns, diapers, clean used clothing in baby to adult sizes, insulated boots, wool socks, flashlights, batteries of various sizes, various tents, and camping supplies. Most of the things are for those still to come who may not have anything when they arrive.

Because the weather and events in this country started getting strange and unpredictable around Y2K and 9/11, the four elders decided to be ready on all accounts. Besides, Fortress is in the Rocky Mountains and not being prepared for extremely tough winters could be a fatal mistake. With record breaking cold temperatures, continual subzero weather, record snowfall, and severe ice storms continually taking place, Ricky and Gary believe it is better to be prepared than unprepared. Behind the garage/warehouse is the old, but solid, huge barn the Big Swede built when he was a young man. It contains lumber, building supplies, animal feed, hay, tractors and other farm machinery and related tools.

On the Double V Ranch are cabins and a two-story apartment complex where members live and guests can stay when visiting. Most families with at least one or more children live in either a small, cozy two or three bedroom log cabin depending on their needs. Childless couples and singles live in a small, but well laid out, one bedroom apartment. The apartment complex is shaped like a T and single males live in one section, single females in another, and married couples in the other. Several cabins and apartments are always vacant for visiting guests. In each cabin and apartment there is a least one ample size woodstove with a seemingly endless supply of firewood behind the garage and warehouse. All able-bodied men, including Gary and Ricky, teenage boys, and some women, take turns swinging an axe and splitting firewood throughout the year.

On the property a large windmill with 20-foot blades and three smaller ones with 10-foot blades on a higher point of the property a short distance from the buildings, 50 large solar panels, and 100 six volt deep cycle storage batteries interconnected supply almost all their electrical needs. But it cannot support a direct source of heat or cooling for everyone's cabin or apartment continually. So it supplements the existing source of standard residential and commercial electricity. Melody's dad, the Big Swede, had worked two summers during his pro-football off-season bulldozing his property to form a 10 acre lake with a maximum depth of 14 feet. He stocked it with fish, and it contained valuable water for his cattle and bison. A small stream from an artesian spring flows down from the mountain on the far west side of the property. The water is diverted to the lake with an adjustable dam gate that he had installed that controls the depth of the water in the lake and diverts the overflow water into the same stream to help keep the water in the lake from getting stagnant. The elders know this water will be priceless in the days ahead.

Logistically speaking, all four elders know that their "green communities", or cities of refuge, can never stockpile enough food, water, medicine, and basic necessities for their own members, let alone the small number of Christians who will be led there in the coming end times. Each Disciplemaker church will simply do the best they can and will have to trust God for the rest. Each pastor in their network of churches and their members will have to be totally dependent on God to provide what is not available. In order to join the Disciplemaker Network, each pastor has to embrace the vision of his church being a beehive of activity in evangelism, discipleship, and intercessory prayer in the last days and make some physical preparations for the future.

Ricky and Gary often say that evangelism, discipleship and intercessory prayer are the big three building blocks that have kept churches healthy in all types of political and economic turmoil throughout history. Ricky's and Gary's theory is soon to be put to the test in the worst time mankind has ever known in the coming Tribulation period.

These two godly men have been under attack for years by sincere ministers of the Gospel who had previously viewed their post-trib view of the rapture as unbiblical. Some of these ministers presently are beginning to have second thoughts. A few of their most vocal opponents in years gone by have secretly contacted them and admitted that they now thought the timing of the rapture may very well take place at the end of the Tribulation. A number of ministers they did not know have read their books and have researched and prayed about the rapture and are now totally convinced that the rapture will indeed take place at the end of the Tribulation. Two former pastors contacted them and told them that they had lost their churches as a result of taking this new view. They had been voted out by their deacon board or elders.

Many ministers and laymen have contacted them through the years and asked for forgiveness for their hurtful words and actions. In the last few years, the numbers have been increasing. Time is vindicating the close friends' post-tribulational views and actions. Ricky and Gary are both elated and sad at the same time. They are happy because Christians are beginning to see something in the Scriptures that they had preached and taught for decades. But a feeling of sadness also permeates their hearts because they know that time is running out for Christians to prepare in various ways for what lay ahead. Yet even with all they possess, they know their total dependence on their God to supply all their needs according to His riches in glory is paramount. They have always communicated with people that they should study God's Word and pray for an understanding about when the rapture occurs, not just listen to them or believe what they wrote. Both ministers are adamant in telling Christians that they need to be like the Bereans and search the Scriptures for themselves.

They have taught for years that Christians have been lulled to sleep believing in a quick exit from the earth in the pretrib rapture theology developed in the 1830's in England by Edwin Irving (who died shortly thereafter) and John Darby. Darby was one of the key leaders of the Plymouth Brethren. Darby had almost single-handedly recreated modern prophetic thought that he developed and preached and brought to the United States on seven voyages. His message spread across America in the mid-19th century with the help of Dr. James Hall Brookes of St. Louis, a nationally known proponent of a slightly altered version of Darby's dispensational premillennialism. And his protégé C.I. Scofield would later release his first reference/prophecy study Bible in 1909. America was ripe to accept Scofield's refined Brookes and Darby teachings of the pretrib rapture and dispensational premillennialism. It is a fact that from Calvary to the 1830's the post-trib rapture view was overwhelmingly embraced by all Christian denominations. This means they believed in a resurrection of believers only at the conclusion of the Tribulation period. Christians did not believe in pretrib rapture until after the 1830's. But these facts had been quickly forgotten, hidden or condemned by many modern popular pretrib prophecy teachers in the 20th and 21st centuries.

From Y2K on, all spectrums of life in America including the Christian church as a whole are accelerating in a negative fashion. Things are not getting better. They are getting worse, with record breaking high and lows in weather, stock market, precious metals,...etc. New laws are washing away moral boundaries, norms and traditions that were established with and before the founding of the country. Sin is accepted as good and the masses of people are growing darker and more evil in their minds and actions. The wants of different kinds of minority groups are superseding the majority because they have been more vocal and are revolting. It is as if the world is going stark raving mad. One can almost hear the Tribulation Train coming down the tracks hard and fast and Ricky, Gary, their wives, and the adult Christians at Fortress know it. Every man, woman and child in the world is going to board this train for its first and only run called the end of the line. Each will be getting off at their final destinations at different times.

Many American nominal Christians of the 21st century have also been hoodwinked into believing President Isaac Cohen, who was recently elected as the first independent ever to win the presidency and the first Jew to take that office. He professed more moderate overall political and moral views than his opponent during the last election, the ultra liberal presidential candidate from California, Senator Blake Hendricks. For Gary, Ricky, and their wives, he always raised a red flag in their spirits when he was running for President. Cohen seemed to say many of the right things. It wasn't his tone or body language, but there was something about him that made them deeply distrust him. Since he has taken office, they have seen him for what he is - a liar, a complete fraud who is hell bent on destroying the nation. Cohen ran on the Independent platform saying that he would lower taxes and reduce the national debt. He would get military spending under control, yet stand with Israel militarily and economically regardless of the opposition. Well-known economists had endorsed his economic reforms to jump start the nation's economy. Cheaper healthcare for the middle class had caught their ear and had earned him big points with them. Creating better paying jobs from the private sector had caught the attention of the poor. Cohen had long been an advocate of personal freedom and responsibility and less of the U. S. government agencies acting like big brother. These positions had been his hallmark as a U.S. Senator. During his campaign across America, he was able to extend one arm to the ultra political left and the other toward the ultra conservatives in the Democratic and Republican ranks. His magnetic and charismatic personality drew both groups to his moderate Independent position. The fact that he was Jewish was a big political plus with the Jewish and Christian community and key representatives of the liberal media and also the African American community. Women loved him and were infatuated with him because of his movie star good looks, perfect white teeth, the golden tongue with which he spoke, and, of course, the fact that he was single.

During his campaign, Cohen was a smooth communicator who presented himself as all things to all men. Although he is still in the first year of his term as President of the United States, President Cohen is already rapidly doing an about face on many of his campaign promises, economic statements, and the long standing political views which he professed for years. Mature, seasoned Christians are left scratching their heads as to why the masses are not realizing what is taking place before their very eyes.

President Cohen is also increasingly entangling the aid of New International Union foreign troops on American soil with the increasing natural disasters and economic unrest besieging some large cities. He continues the dismantling and downsizing of all American military branches as did his predecessor, in the name of saving the economy. Volunteers from the different U. S. branches of service are being reassigned and sworn into the N.I.U. to serve directly under them in war and humanitarian service. As a result, the N.I.U. pays these former U. S. military men and women much higher rates of pay than what they previously made. There has been a huge defection to serve in the N.I. U. to say the least. These former U.S. military personnel first have to undergo re-education and training at Fort Union which was formerly called Fort Stevens in Louisiana and then they are assigned to tours in foreign countries.

Just recently the increasing number of meteorites hitting the U.S., although small in size and very mild in destructiveness, are making many politically right citizens uneasy as to how he might respond. Cohen's shift of views and policies has brought much dismay to a dwindling number of true Bible-based churches and the conservative minority in the population. Much of what he is doing is totally against the laws of the land.

Any kind of backlash against him is stifled by the media under his strong arm tactics and an ever growing influx of illegal aliens who view Isaac Cohen as a hero and savior. With an exponentially growing population, around four hundred million people in America consisting of about 30 percent who are not U. S. citizens, the middle class is rapidly going the way of the dinosaurs. The once beautiful, wealthy cities in America are becoming dangerous ugly slums, with endless neighborhoods of run down residential homes, littered streets and tall mounds of trash in black plastic garbage bags, empty and burned out factories, and multitudes of homeless people living in tents and cardboard boxes begging for food and money. Prostitution has been legalized in most of the major cities of the country under Cohen's watch and is in the process of coming under governmental control. It is creating the fastest growing sector of jobs in the economy and politicians in D. C. see it as a new tax revenue. Many new laws have been instituted with a swirl of his pen through executive orders issued within days after he was sworn in office, and the process is still ongoing almost on a daily basis. Seemingly America has fallen like a cracked Humpty Dumpty, never to be put back together again.

The World Confederation building in New York was bombed so severely it was condemned two years before. Immediately afterwards a cry went out around the world and world leaders chose Geneva, Switzerland as the new neutral location for a more progressive and powerful type of WC. The role of the New International Union that replaced WC is not only to raise up a powerful peacekeeping force for actual combat in war, but also a large number of troops called N.I.U. Security Forces. The Security Forces of the

NIU are still actual soldiers that are designated to assist countries around the globe in times of natural disasters. At least this was the reason given at first before they were put on the ground in different countries. Natural disasters have shot up exponentially not only in their number but also in their magnitude, since the dawn of the new millennium in 2000. But once each disaster subsides and things return to somewhat of a normal state, the NIU Security Forces never leave. The Security Forces gradually take over local, regional, and entire countries' law enforcement programs and their military without resistance. The government officials and appointed law officials appear to be in control, but in reality the top brass of the Security Forces are dictating to these officials the actions to be taken. Cohen, as the leader of the free world, is the NIU's biggest advocate and supporter.

Chapter 13

ARRIVAL IN GOLDEN VALLEY

"$12,555.27!" shouts Starlight.

"Yes indeed, that's the amount of my little overnight stay at Rock Top Memorial Hospital. If it had not been for nurse Taylor fighting for my hospital bill to be a pro bono case, my three $20.00 gold pieces and all the cash we have would just have been enough to cover the bill."

"Well, River, we would have just had to work out some kind of payment plan. But thank you, Jesus!" says Starlight shaking her head in disbelief and relief

"I had no idea that it would have been so much."

"Yes, we need to praise God for His kindness and for putting Nurse Taylor across our path."

"Starlight, we are almost to the ministry in Golden Valley according to what Patrick said a few minutes ago. You know this trip should've been just a two and half hour trip from Boulder, but with everything that has happened, it has literally taken a whole day."

"You're right. It's been an unbelievable road trip. But it could have been a lot worse with the bears, rockslide, and your hairline fracture. On a more positive note, you and Patrick had angelic visitations from Michael, God provided confirmation by literally putting us on the same page with the books at the campground, Emily got saved, and God healed you and performed a miracle that saved us twelve and a half thousand dollars.. Plus, we made some new friends like Nurses Amy and Nurse Taylor. Given what happened at Rock Top Memorial Hospital, it seems their faith has been rekindled and revived, so I'm excited for them."

"You're right. It does seem unbelievable. It all seems like a long dream that can't possibly be real, but those things did happen."

"Wow, Babe, check out those rocky cliffs over there and the boulders down below to the left. They are so cool! This area should be called Rock Valley instead of Golden Valley. We could do some serious rock climbing and bouldering in this area."

"Well, the only thing that concerns me about that is the kind of animals I saw about two miles back. I don't think they were big dogs. I also think I saw maybe three of those animals, but I'm not sure. But I definitely saw two."

"Well, when I looked where you were pointing, whatever you saw was gone. So I don't know."

"River, they were so fast and seemed huge with striped bodies."

"It was still kind of dark then. You know I'm right, Star. Besides, it was probably just shadows from the trees and the remaining moonlight possibly hitting some big dogs just right. Another possibility is that they were some big wolves. Who knows?"

"Yes, I think you might be right," says a slightly convinced Starlight. Wolves can get big and fluffy with all that fur so it makes them appear even bigger."

"Now you're making sense, Star. Wolves are big and fluffy with a variety of earth tone colors. Think about it, my young bride. We're in the Rockies where wolves are common along with grizzly bears and Bigfoot."

"Get out of here with that Bigfoot baloney, River! I'm not buying into that nonsense," laughs Starlight. "Enough of your joking. Seriously, I've got questions, lots of them besides what I saw back there."

"Like what?"

"For example, I don't know exactly what we are going to do in Golden Valley. How are we going to make a living? Where can we hook up our van for some electricity so we can live in it? I have so many questions."

"Me too, Star. We'll just take it a day at a time because that's all we can do. It's a total walk of faith, trusting God each step along the journey," says River in a serious tone. "I recently heard on a Christian radio program a minister say, 'Where God guides, He also provides.' So we will find out real soon what this whole move from Boulder and this trip have been about."

"You're right, River. I know deep down in my heart and from the Word of God that a Christian's journey in this life is truly is a walk of faith. We have to keep the faith. The word of God says, 'For we walk by faith and not by sight' (2 Corinthians 5:7) and it also says, 'Trust in the Lord with all thy heart and lean not unto thy understanding, and in all thy ways acknowledge Him and He will make your paths straight' (Proverbs 3:5-6)!"

"Amen, Sister, amen! Preach it, girl, preach it!"

"River, pull this tin can of a van over and I'm going to use that milk crate behind my seat that we are storing some of our food in as a soap box and preach to the birds, the bees, and the Aspen trees," says Starlight laughing.

"Sorry, Sister Starlight, you'll need to save that anointing for the people in the big metropolis of Golden Valley." Now River joins in laughing.

"You're so funny, Star. I knew there had to be a reason why I've always liked you."

"Yeah, I tickle your funny bone, don't I?" She starts tickling River on his side and neck with her fingers and he starts laughing really hard. She is making his body jerk around in his seat to the point where he swerves a little bit in his lane.

"Stop it, Starlight! Stop, Star," he says in a half serious tone of voice, "before I have another accident and we both get killed. You want that on your conscience?"

"Well, well." Starlight tilts her head to the right and says, "Umm..." Her eyes are rolled back and her right index finger is touching the right corner of her mouth like she is thinking very intently on the subject.

"Well, what do have to say for yourself, Starlight Weaver Jenkins?"

Starlight pauses for a another second and says, "I'm still debating that in my mind."

"Okay, enough of that nonsense, Starlight. I was wondering about your phone."

"Oh, don't worry about it. While you were in the ICU, Patrick helped me dig it out. It took a while moving all the junk around to find it."

"Did you call Jenny?"

"Yes, and she and Mark are in Fort Collins and will be there a couple of days more. So that is comforting to me."

"Well great, Star."

"Hey, Patrick's a good guy, ain't he, Star?"

"Yeah , he is."

"How's Emily dealing with all that has taken place?"

"Emily seems cool about it. We had a heart-to-heart talk and she said she feels comfortable around us. Most of all, she said she trusts us after what happened back at the diner when the State Trooper came in and validated all we said. She says she has trust issues with her mom and dad and other people she knows. She trusts very few people. Ivan and his wife had been the only people she knew she could trust for a long time. Patrick told her about the angel Michael telling him a fourth individual would join us on the last leg of the journey. She said she is not sure what that is all about. But guess what I found out about her?

"What Star?"

"I found out she has a beautiful alto voice."

"Really?"

"Yeah, and Emily loved choir but dropped out after her sophomore year because she had to work at Ivan's to pay her bills."

"Well, Star maybe that is one major reason why she is to be with us."

"Exactly! That's what I was thinking and to also grow in the Lord. River, all day yesterday, Emily kept saying she felt different. I told her she is a new creation in Christ and old things have passed away. I gave her the analogy of how a caterpillar turns into a beautiful butterfly and it made sense to her."

"Yeah, I always liked that analogy of how Christ changes you into a new creation versus a tadpole into a bullfrog."

"Oh yuk, River. Yeah, I definitely like the thought of being a beautiful butterfly instead of a bullfrog,"

"Yeah, you got that right, Starlight, because some people eat bullfrogs, like those guys, the Richardsons on the show Goose Empire. I don't think they eat butterflies, but I wouldn't put it past them."

"Gross!" Both Starlight and River start laughing out loud.

After the laughter dies down, River says, "Star, do you think Emily likes Patrick?"

"I kinda of get that feeling. He was calling her the kid yesterday and she didn't seem to mind. Right after we left the diner, she told me that she has allowed only Ivan to call her that. They seem to enjoy each other's company. Emily makes Patrick laugh big time. I also think she enjoys his laughter."

"That's interesting to know," says River, nodding his head slowly and smiling.

"Wow, I think we're finally here. Patrick is turning up there on that dirt road and now Emily is getting out and pushing the gate to the inside."

"Hey, Star, look! The kid is waving at us and smiling."

"Stop that, River. Maybe she is happy being with Patrick, but you better not call her that or she might get mad," says Starlight in a defensive tone as she makes a funny mad face and shakes her fist at him.

"Okay, okay, I get the picture." They wave back at her as she gets back into Patrick's vehicle. Patrick starts going down the dirt road. River pulls inside the fence line.

"River, is this the place? I don't see a church," says Starlight. "Are you sure Patrick has the right place?"

"Pat is a pretty sharp guy, Star. It's gotta be."

"Well, Riv, another reason I'm asking is that there was an old wooden sign on a wagon wheel back there at the entrance that said the Double V Ranch and The Viking Gold Mine."

"Starlight, Patrick is motioning with his index finger. Oh, look way over there. I see a bunch of buildings. That one building over there has a cross on it."

"That's gotta be their church building. Hold on, River. I've got to shut the gate. They've got cattle and even some buffalos over there by the tree line of the fence." Starlight jumps out of the van and races to shut the gate and hops back into the van. They then slowly travel down the dirt road taking in all the sights. "River, I can't believe we are here. This place is more beautiful than the UEC Farm and I always thought that place was really special. I'm also sensing God's peace to a great degree here."

"Yeah, me too, you're right, Starlight. This place is very peaceful and look at that awesome lake over there and the cattle and the buffalos. Wow! Check it out. They also have some quarter horses and paint horses running down by the lake. It seems so picturesque with the back drop of the Rocky Mountains behind this little bit of heaven."

"Hey, look! A young woman with red hair is coming out of that lodge-type building. She is motioning for us to come over and get out. Pull over next to Patrick and let's get out to meet her."

As they get out, the young woman says, "Hi, my name is Brenda Lee Kirkman and welcome to Fortress. I've already met Patrick and Emily here. What are your names?"

"My name is River Jenkins and this is my bride Starlight."

"It's so nice to meet you guys on this beautiful day the Lord has made. I kind of experienced meeting you yesterday."

"What do you mean, Brenda Lee?" asks Starlight. .

"Well, let me show you guys what I mean. I'm an artist and the Lord had me sketch this yesterday. She reaches for her left back pocket and pulls out a folded sheet of computer paper. She unfolds and places it on the hood of Patrick's SUV.

"Oh, my goodness! Look! The letter M with Lee next to it," says Emily, as she cups her mouth in disbelief.

"I'm the shamrock because I'm full blooded Irish," says Patrick, chuckling.

"I'm the Star with rays of light coming out from it,' says a bewildered Starlight. "Brenda Lee, you are confirming in our hearts that God wants us here. We are in the right place at the right time."

"And look, everybody. I'm the creek," says River jokingly.

"It's a River," everybody else says.

"I know, I know," laughs River.

Brenda Lee says, "You guys are a lively group. I knew you were coming. I just didn't know when. But when I felt led of the Lord to look out the window just a minute ago and saw two vehicles I had never seen before, I knew it was you guys. Brenda Lee does not feel led to tell them all that has transpired since last night or this morning. She doesn't want it to ruin their initial experience of coming to Fortress. No one is back at the Lodge and she wants them to relax a little before they find out that the world around them is in upheaval. She is curious and wants to find out why the Lord has sent them there. "Why don't we go to the lodge and I'll fix you guys some breakfast."

But everyone says they aren't hungry.

"How about some coffee, juice, milk, or water?"

Everyone agrees to something to drink.

As they walk to the lodge, Brenda Lee says, "With it being so early in the morning, there must be a reason why you are here at this time."

"Brenda Lee, we are here by the miraculous grace of God," says River. As they enter the lodge, they can't help but notice its beautiful western decor. But even more so, an overwhelming sense of peace pervades the entire lodge. The Spirit of God's presence seems to reside there putting the body, soul, and spirit at rest as soon as one enters the door.

Emily says, "I have felt a supernatural peace since I first opened the gate back at the road. It's even greater here."

"We often hear that once people take a minute to slow down from their hectic lifestyle.

Brenda Lee, who is exhausted from staying up almost the whole night praying, begins to explain to River, Starlight, Patrick, and Emily the purpose and vision of Fortress and the Disciplemaker Network of Churches. Brenda Lee tells them about her parents' calling into the ministry, her dad and uncle giving up their successful secular careers, and then eventually moving their ministry from Los Angeles to Golden Valley. She explains the role of Fortress and the Disciplemaker Churches in the end times. River and Starlight are elated to find out that Fortress raises and sells organic produce and food products under the Double V Ranch Organics label and ministers to the local poor people by giving them a portion of their produce and products.

When Patrick finds out that Brenda Lee's fiancé is Forrest Johnson, he excitedly says, "Yes!" while quickly pulling his fist, fingers side up, toward his right side. Brenda Lee then remembered that Forrest has been praying for a guy named Patrick the whole two years he has been at Fortress.

Brenda Lee smiles and says, "Forrest is going to be beside himself when he finds out his former climbing partner got saved and is here."

But, when Brenda Lee felt led of the Lord to explain the recent course of events, everybody's eyes get big as saucers. Frightened, Emily grabs and holds Patrick's hand, who doesn't mind at all. Starlight knows then that she indeed did see a pack of giant pitwolves. Usually a regular jokester, River is completely somber. Later, he and Patrick explain their visions from the archangel Michael, and Brenda Lee knows the elders and deacons are going to love to hear about that. Starlight also explains parts of the trip and the miracle in the Rock Top Memorial Hospital. Emily eventually relaxes a bit and shares how she came to the Lord and was befriended by Starlight, River, and Patrick. Brenda Lee does not doubt their stories because she has the gift of discernment, and Holy Spirit is speaking to her heart that what they are sharing is the truth.

Then Brenda Lee shares what happened in Boulder and Denver and everyone breaks down and weeps continually for five minutes. What they thought might happen has happened, but they all are jolted to the core to hear some of the details.

After about an hour, Brenda Lee decides to take her new friends to see the rest of the church members. They have regained their composure but are still red-eyed. Emily seems to be the most impacted. Brenda Lee has told them about Sheriff Barnes, her dad, Blackhawk, and Uncle Ricky flying around in the ministry's helicopter to try to spot and kill some of those dangerous giant pitwolves. Emily becomes frightened again hearing the story of the giant pitwolves, enough to not even want to walk outside the door of the lodge. Only with repeated assurance from Brenda Lee that God's hand of protection is on the property of Fortress does she find the courage to walk outside the lodge holding tightly to Patrick's hand. As they walk to the church building knowing the giant pitwolves are in the area, a little fear creeps into their hearts, with the exception of Brenda Lee. Using their peripheral vision as they walk, Starlight and River find themselves on guard. Patrick isn't as subtle. He keeps looking over his shoulder scanning the whole area thoroughly. He keeps quietly reassuring Emily that God is in control and everything is going to be alright. At this point, it is just as much for her comfort as for his. Emily is just focused on just getting to the church in one piece. Brenda Lee walks fearlessly pointing out the different buildings on the property. She makes special note of the Double V Ranch Organics food processing plant, which River and Starlight are delighted to see. It is small in comparison to the UEC plant back home. Brenda Lee is proud of the fact that almost all the grains, fruits, nuts, vegetables, and meats raised are organic. She also tries to point out the different grain crops, fruit orchards, huge garden, and the windmills for electricity that are located on the ranch. The four friends are giving half-hearted responses to

Brenda Lee's comments, like "that's nice," "that's great," "yeah, I see it." They are distracted by the feeling that they are on a death march walking to the church with beasts from hell eyeballing them - vicious beasts so powerful they could pounce on their flesh and rip them to shreds. Brenda Lee knows that her new friends in the Lord are intimidated by the giant pitwolves. And the meteorites that hit Boulder and Denver freak them out and almost send them over the edge. If not for the fact that the archangel Michael revealed himself to River and Patrick and God's hand intervened in so many ways, they might be getting into their vehicles and leaving. Brenda Lee senses the fear the four are dealing with, so she peppers her comments about the different aspects of the ranch as they walk to the church with sayings like, "Jesus is Lord," "God's mighty hand protects this property," and "this place will be a city of refuge in the Tribulation."

As soon as they reach the church building, a sense of relief envelops the four friends' souls. Smiles return to their once serious faces because they have made a journey that seems like they have gone through the Valley of the Shadow of Death and have been victorious. Emily releases her tight grip on Patrick's hand causing him to immediately miss the intimacy. The initially faint distant sound of a helicopter grows stronger by the second until it can be seen several miles away and eventually landing on the pad by the garage warehouse complex. Everybody is walking out of the church except Grandma Cotton who's alone in the intercessory prayer room. Forrest is also inside in the sound booth in the church building when he catches wind that President Cohen is going to speak live from the White House Conference Room in a few minutes. It is an emergency broadcast to address the world about the meteorites that had hit Colorado. Caleb knows the president will be speaking and has told Forrest to monitor the news and notify him immediately when he is going to come on. KABZ white washes the death of Dana Williams as delicately as possible. No KABZ reporters are reporting live on the streets of Boulder, except for James Alcorn from his Action Live Channel 12 chopper. All the other reporters are frightened to death of the wild beasts roaming the city and have sought shelter or have been personally impacted by the meteorite strike. The huge meteorite alone has sent almost all of them into a paranoid state, let alone killer giant pitwolves roaming what was left of the streets of Boulder.

As everyone piles out of the church building, almost all eyes are on the two male elders, Blackhawk, and Sheriff Barnes as Ricky lands the helicopter. All of them are giving a thumbs up and a big smile. Caleb comes over and hugs Brenda Lee screaming so he can be heard. "I see we have some early morning visitors."

She yells back into Caleb's right ear, "They have an incredible story to tell of what God is going to do here." He waves to them, but the noise of the descending chopper deafens out all sound around them. Caleb motions to the four friends and Brenda Lee that he has to go to the chopper on the ground now. Melody, Mary Anne, Ashley, and Sarah Barnes spot the new visitors and come over to hug them and try to talk to them, but the words are muffled. Forrest comes out of the church and runs straight to Caleb. Before he reaches the chopper, the blades have slowed and are not producing the deafening sound as before.

He yells, "Caleb, President Cohen will be speaking live from the White House in about two minutes."

Caleb opens the pilot's door and shakes his dad's hand before holding his hand out in front of him to get everyone's attention. He then says, "Gentlemen, the President will be giving a speech any minute now about the meteorite strikes in Colorado."

"I think we definitely need to hear it," says Gary with firm conviction. Sheriff Barnes has been on an emotional and spiritual roller coaster since yesterday evening. He has been in the clouds, but now feels the roller coaster descending at record speed. He knows that everything is going south really quickly, given President Cohen's current track record and the devastation of two major cities in his home state. Barnes, with his 30 plus years of law enforcement experience, has this gut feeling that changes in law enforcement are at the forefront of the coming presidential emergency speech. His soul is torn between wanting to trust God and letting hate and revenge eat him alive.

Ricky says, "Son, we have some incredible news to tell you, but we'll wait until after we hear the bad news we all know is coming." As the men exit the helicopter and hug their wives, Caleb begins ushering everyone into the church building because the President is about to give his speech. All the adult church members and most of the older teenagers have an idea of the mind games that are going to play out on the screen with the new great communicator in the oval office. President Cohen is beginning to show his true colors on the vital issues of the day. He is no longer "middle of the road" in his political views. They have quickly taken a sharp leftward turn since he first got elected. Everyone knows that he is going to spin the events of the meteorites in Boulder and Denver and the story of the giant pitwolves to the fullest degree.

Without a doubt, those who keep up with the news and are informed know that Cohen is going to request the New International Union Security Forces to come and save the day in the state of Colorado. All the mature members know deep down in their hearts that this is a given. It has been the hot topic of conversation the entire morning amongst the Fortress members along with the issue of giant pitwolves in their own backyard. All the events have almost everyone on edge and paranoia rages like a cancer that is trying to weave its tentacles through the ranks at Fortress.

In all the commotion with adults and children moving around and the noise of the helicopter, Patrick doesn't see Forrest as he sprints by to the chopper. After talking for a moment with Brenda Lee's Dad, he spots Patrick beside his fiancée. Smiling, Forrest walks quickly toward them and hugs Brenda Lee while reaching out and shaking Patrick's hand vigorously.

Forrest says, "Patrick, man, it is so good to see you here! I can't believe it! I been praying for you daily for two years."

"Forrest, he got saved," says Brenda Lee.

"I've been saved for around six months, Forrest."

"Awesome, man! That's great. Praise God he answered my prayers! Hey, I want to talk to you, ah... are these some friends of yours?"

"Yeah, Forrest, this is my friend River Jenkins and his wife Starlight and our new friend Emily."

"It's so nice to meet you guys. Listen, we'll have to talk later. The President is going to speak and the leadership here wants us to hear him. As you know, things are hitting the fan prophetically speaking. I'm working the sound booth in the church and I need to hurry and get the big screen TV ready to broadcast the speech. We'll have to talk later, guys. Nice meeting you River, Starlight, and Emily. Bye!" says a hurried Forrest.

"Bye, Forrest," responds Brenda Lee's new friends.

Everyone dreads what is coming as they enter the church auditorium and find a seat just in time to listen to President Cohen's speech.

President Isaac Cohen, the first Jewish President of the United States, is broadcasting live from the White House Press Conference Room to address the American people about the horrific meteorite strikes on the cities of Boulder, Denver and, to a much smaller degree, a total of eight counties in Colorado. He is wearing a traditional religious Jewish cap called a yarmulke in this emergency broadcast . He milks that yarmulke for the most mileage possible whenever it is advantageous to play his religious Jewish card. "Get ready, Mr. President. I'll give you a countdown: 5, 4, 3, 2, 1."

"My fellow Americans, it is with great sorrow and grief that I come before you now. What has happened is unfathomable to most of us in this great country. The news of what has occurred first in Boulder, then in Denver in only a matter of minutes this morning at 5:59 AM Mountain Standard Time is beyond most of our ability to fully comprehend. Eight other counties in Colorado were also impacted by much smaller meteorites, and we are still trying to gather information on their collective damage. Our hearts go out to them. One thing is for sure. All these acts of God have truly shaken all of us to our core."

"If I could be transparent with you, the American people, I would have to admit my faith has suffered as a result of seeing the horrible images and footage of unimaginable devastation that has occurred today. I have just gotten off the phone talking with my Rabbi and offering up prayers on behalf of those who have suffered from these acts of God in Colorado early this morning. The events of the day first began at 7:59 AM Eastern Standard Time when a large meteorite impacted Boulder followed by another big meteorite that hit Denver only moments later. Eight Colorado counties also got hit sometime in between. In all honesty, when I was on my knees praying, I just kept asking the following questions over and over again. 'Why, God, did this happen this morning? What purpose is there for this act of devastation? Why these two major cities? Why did innocent people have to die?' But, then again, I'm Jewish and these are the same types of questions my people have been crying out to God for millenniums, and in more recent times during the World War II holocaust. This June morning started out cool and beautiful. Parents were

267

getting ready to take their babies and young children to daycare or to stay with family members, then heading off to work. Hard working people were finishing up third shifts at factories, looking forward to coming home to their families. Professors and college students were preparing to begin a new school day. Young successful urbanites were running in parks and working out at fitness gyms before preparing to go their respective offices. Average Americans were taking nice warm showers or preparing their breakfasts to start their day. Retired elderly men and women were sitting down at their breakfast tables or their favorite recliners reading obituaries of former co-workers or friends who had just recently passed, not knowing that an act of God was going to add their names to the next edition. Just normal Americans, doing normal activities in the course of a normal June morning, or so it seemed. Then the worst cosmic natural disaster in the recorded annals of this great country struck."

"It has been brought to my attention that the United States Space and Aeronautics Program was tracking this meteorite before it entered our atmosphere. It was believed that it would disintegrate as soon as it hit our atmosphere, as so many do. Instead, as it hit the atmosphere, they discovered it was larger than first expected. They report that it broke into two pieces. Each piece traveled a different course, thus resulting in two cities being partially eradicated."

"Projections by engineers and scientists at USSAP indicate that had the meteorite not broken into two pieces, the total devastation upon impact would have been more cataclysmic. They have pinpointed that the point of impact would have been Clark County in Colorado. It turns out it is the smallest, least densely populated county in Colorado. The entire county would have been a huge crater, according to top USSAP scientists. This would have been good news for the citizens of Boulder and Denver, but bad news for the people of that county".

"As President of the most powerful nation on earth, I'm calling for the nations of the world to lay aside the political, religious, social, and cultural issues that divide us on a continual basis. As a practicing reformed Jew, I am asking for all world leaders to join with me in a united effort to come together as one people. Our greatest threat to our global survival as a collective people is not from our fellow man, but according to the top leading scientists of the world, from the cosmic forces of outer space. What we are now experiencing is a taste of more to come in greater frequency and intensity. The lack of solar flares is causing the earth to cool down running the risk of entering a mini ice age. The false alarm of global warming is replaced by the reality of global cooling that could plunge us into a catastrophic ice age".

"As a small gesture of my willingness to cooperate with both small and great, rich and poor, and free and totalitarian nations of the world - as well as peoples of different faiths, colors, races, and ethnicities - I'm taking off my yarmulke to symbolically represent the laying aside of differences that divide us and longing to link arms with any nation on issues that unite us in our struggle to survive on this planet." With solemn face and misty eyes, President Cohen is giving the performance of his life as he slowly removes his cap. *"I'm calling for the an emergency meeting of the twelve most powerful nations in Geneva, Switzerland. In a united effort, we must enact a plan to survive the coming cosmic chaos that has already started embroiling the world. Before I came on air, I signed into law by executive order, the use of New International Union Security Forces to play an active role in monitoring safety and helping to meet the basic humanitarian needs of the people of Boulder and Denver. I'm also establishing the cities of Salt Lake City, Utah; Colorado Springs, Colorado; and Omaha, Nebraska as Humanitarian Relief Centers. Homeless, destitute, and injured people will be relocated to these cities by buses. We are advising all survivors who have the financial means and vehicles to please remain in the cities of Boulder and Denver if possible. We need you to help rebuild what was destroyed today in an effort to build a better tomorrow."*

"I'm declaring the triangular area between Boulder, Denver, and the eight counties that have been hit with meteorites a hot zone. I have been told that Comet Lucis has a record breaking long coma that surpasses the coma of Comet Ison in 2013. Fortunately, Comet Ison disintegrated when it went around the sun in November of that year and was of no effect. But Comet Lucis has proven to be a bad omen. As the earth's orbit has been continually traveling in the flight of its tail, not only Colorado, but also Russia, China, France, and Australia, have been experiencing the onslaught of meteorites."

"I repeat, if you are not destitute, homeless, or injured and your basic human needs are being met, relocation is only an option, not a requirement. Keep in mind more meteorites striking the U. S. are in the realm of possibly happening."

"I will now take questions." President Cohen points to the Washington Observer's reporter Tim Jordan.

"Thank you, Mr. President. Correct me if I'm wrong, sir, but it seems to me that you are saying that the citizens of the nations of the world, along with their leaders, need to lay aside their political and philosophical differences and come together as one in order to survive these acts of God, as you are calling them, from outer space."

"Yes, in a nutshell, that is what I'm saying. Religion has been the devil's advocate since

the beginning of time, which is why I removed my yarmulke. Religion has provoked and started more costly wars and misery than you or I could count or put a price tag on. Unless we share our knowledge, resources, and manpower to help lessen the blow of economic losses and valuable resources from these terrible meteorites impacting the earth, we may all end up dead or at the least in the poor house."

"Thank you, Mr. President."

Cohen points to Michelle Bourne the White House Correspondent with the American Broadcasting Network. She also covertly works for Cohen via the Adamic Society and does the bidding of the President. *"Thanks, President Cohen. I'm sure the hundreds of millions of people who are viewing this broadcast from around the world are wondering if you are overstepping your bounds by allowing foreign troops to come and oversee the law enforcement officials of Colorado and the dispersion of basic water, food, medicine, clothing, and shelter for those less fortunate and whose lives have been severely impacted by the meteorites."*

"Oh, I'm sure, Michelle, what I'm doing may be perceived as strange or traitorous, but I view the use of the New International Union Security Forces as a united world effort that is a necessary means to accomplish the goal of what I'm advocating. Next week it might be Moscow, Paris, Beijing, Mexico City, Dublin, Dubai, Rome, Jerusalem, London, or our own New York City that gets wiped off the face of the globe by cosmic forces or a natural disaster. God forbid, but it's possible. Let's pool our resources together and aid one another in this moment of crisis."

"Thanks, Mr. President."

"My advisors are telling me I have time for one last question. Yes, how about you, Sid?"

Sid Goldman of the Conservative Voice News speaks up. *"Mr. President, as a conservative and as a Messianic Jew, it concerns me that you have done a 180 degree turn on your stated policy of allowing military troops, let alone foreign troops, to now come into major American cities and dictate to local political and law enforcement officials policy on what they can and cannot do. This whole thing seems to reek of Marshall Law to me."*

"Pure nonsense, Sid. The use of the New International Union Security Forces is nothing more than a goodwill gesture, as I mentioned earlier, basically a humanitarian relief agency effort."

"Then, sir, why does the New International Union's own literature advocate the use of

armor personnel carriers, tanks, and armed soldiers with AK 47's patrolling large sections of destroyed and intact areas of cities during times of natural and manmade disasters. They have standing orders to shoot to kill all who resist or oppose them. From pictures and videos I've seen they erect high towers with armed guards stationed every ¼ miles around large areas or entire cities along with eight feet high chain link fence with concertina wire on top wrapped around three stands of barbed wire. Also they have checkpoints in and out of the areas in times of large scale disasters? Countless high definition surveillance cameras with advanced audio capabilities are placed all over the city.

From all my research Mr. President I've found that once the disaster subsides things never return back to normal. The N.I.U. becomes firmly entrenched into the city and the area evolves into a police state with them at the helm. Jewelry stores, banks, stores that sell firearms, museums with valuable works of art and artifacts mysteriously get looted and robbed under their watchful eyes."

"Sid, don't be ridiculous! They can't be held blamed and become the scapegoat for everything that goes wrong or every crime committed in times of a disaster situation. It is plain and simple from a logical viewpoint that the security forces are needed during the chaotic times of disasters. Peace and safety have to be maintained in times of tragedy and chaos. From the standpoint of just taking care of people's basic needs, it is a logistical nightmare. You just can't do it if people are running around in a state of paranoia, anarchy, looting, pillaging, and doing whatever they want. Order must be maintained and personal freedoms have to be suspended. The state of returning to normalcy take time Sid."

"Yeah, right - Mr. President!" says a sarcastic Sid Goldman loud enough to echo through the press conference room.

In a calm, but very perturbed tone, Cohen responds, *"Can I please get some Secret Service men to escort Mr. Goldman out of here?"*

It is a moment of awkwardness, because it has never happened before in a White House Press Conference for a screened reporter to be kicked out during a live broadcast. This event causes the Secret Service men to hesitate momentarily. Cohen repeats himself in a nasty, authoritative voice. *"Can I get three secret service men to show Mr. Goldman to the door?"* Unbeknown to the nation three secret service men instantly pounce on Goldman roughly placing a white handkerchief over his mouth to muffle his yelling and escort him out of the conference room, the camera man never taking his lens off the President.

"Ladies and gentlemen, this concludes..."

"Mr. President! Mr. President!" interrupts Ms. Bourne. *"It has just come to my attention through a text from a reliable contact in the Boulder City government that the unknown large man eating feral-type dogs roaming the streets of Boulder are not large dogs but some kind of other predatory species that has never before been seen in the public. My source and others are saying that they are giant pitwolves."*

All the reporters in the press conference respond, *"Ah... Ah..."* in concerted expressions.

Ms. Bourne follows their response with, "Two of these so-called urban legends savagely attacked and killed Dana Williams, a reporter for KABZ who was on top of her action cam van, along with fellow reporter Tom Littleton, and her camera man who abandoned her by jumping off their van and getting inside it. Dana was 10 feet off the ground when two of these monsters jumped on her in the air with one going for her throat and the other her side. Confirmed reports coming in are saying that 12 of these beast have been spotted running loose in the city of Boulder. They are man killers and extremely dangerous. I would like to get your comment on that if I may."

"Michelle, let me be clear. The cities of Boulder and Denver are already in crisis mode. Please, for Pete's sake don't add to this already chaotic situation with any more tabloid journalism drama. As a nation, our hearts mourn the loss of Dana Williams. The people of Boulder are already under a great strain. I have no knowledge of any kind of so-called urban legend running wild on the streets of Boulder. Possibly a few dangerous large dogs running loose in Boulder. Maybe a couple of wolves in nearby forests were scared out of their wits from the meteorite and ran into populated suburban areas. Let me see if my national security advisor has been briefed on this possible development. Lou Marino, can you take the microphone and address this issue?"

"Yes, sir, Mr. President. Ms. Bourne, I hold you responsible for even suggesting such a preposterous statement that there is an unknown monster predator called giant pitwolves on the loose in Boulder. As everyone knows, this emergency broadcast was thrown together literally at the last minute because of unforeseen meteorites striking Boulder and Denver. I have not had time to brief the President on this issue you are referring to in Boulder. Besides, presently the details are very few about some large wild dogs or possibly wolves

running down the streets of Boulder. Whatever problem these feral dogs or wolves pose to the city of Boulder, we know the police there will speedily resolve the issue. As you know, there are a multitude of serious issues confronting Boulder officials right now. Our condolences go out to Dana Williams' employer, KABZ, and her family and friends. We are sorry for this tragedy and their loss."

"Mr. Marino, while we have been talking, I have just been notified through my earpiece that a very reliable source in the Boulder area says with 100 percent certainty that these animals are not feral dogs, but are indeed prehistoric-like predators that some have called the giant pitwolf."

"Nonsense, Ms. Bourne, utter nonsense. Please do not add false claims and fear to a city already in a panic mode. I don't have time to debate a fictional creature that doesn't exist. I need to focus on two cities in the United States in complete and utter turmoil. I'm done, Mr. President!"

"Well, I stand by my source 100 percent!" shouts Michelle Bourne.

After Bourne's last comment, President Cohen starts walking off the stage waving goodbye to all the reporters refusing to take any more questions. Michelle Bourne has whipped the seasoned reporters into a frenzy with her comments. Although the reporters are usually well reserved, the events of the day have made them act like gymnasts contorting their bodies, jumping up and down like high school cheerleaders shouting to get the President's attention and response to the possibility of mankiller giant pitwolves roaming the streets of Boulder.

Multitudes of reporters are screaming, *"Mr. President, your response to the possibility of giant pitwolves attacking innocent civilians...," "Mr. President, sir..., I have a question," "President Cohen, will you respond to the claims..."*

Cohen shakes his head and shouts, *"That's all"* and *"No comment"* several times as he briskly walks away from the reporters.

As Cohen walks away from the podium, Haji Patel, the White House Press Secretary, steps up to the podium and announces, *"Ladies and gentlemen, this will conclude the press conference today."* Haji then quickly exits the conference room on the heels of the President.

Chapter 14

THE RESPONSE PLAN

The moment President Isaac Cohen steps out of the White House Press Conference Room his long-time political confidant and Chief of Staff, Tom Williamson, meets him and whispers that Marla wants him to call her right away. After quickly walking to the Oval Office, Williamson says, "Isaac, Marla said that the Golden Level of the Adamic Society on the conference call gives you a thumbs up on your award-winning performance at the press conference."

"Well, in that case, Tom, tell them I want a real $#@&**^! Oscar if it was that good," laughs Cohen.

"Yeah, you're right, Isaac. She also said Lou and Michelle followed the script perfectly."

Glibly, Cohen fires back, "They can be nominated as the best supporting actor and actress, but I'm walking away with best actor, ha, ha, ha."

"Seriously now, Isaac, Marla said she had a team review the recorded live video streaming from the cameras that were inside and outside Ci Mada Union Laboratories. The cameras were tied into Geneva just before they went blank from the meteorite taking out the facility. Marla said that Dr. Von Gunten could be seen outside with his assistant Peter Nash and another worker who was identified as Warren Jones, along two security guards. Jones could be seen rapidly leaving the premises of Ci Mada on a motorcycle. He was Nash's assistant. Nash and Von Gunten were trying to get him to stop and talk to them. Marla said it was clear from the video coverage that Jones was pointing to the meteorite as it was coming in." "Tom did this Jones guy have some prior warning that this meteorite was coming?"

"Yes, he did, Isaac. He was the contact for NORAC at Ci Mada. They had been tracking it and just thought it would disintegrate like so many meteorites do when they hit our atmosphere. It didn't, of course, and they notified Jones as soon as they realized it didn't disintegrate and had broken into two huge pieces. It is believed that Jones was the only survivor at Ci Mada to escape the impact of the meteorite hitting Ci Mada Union. Apparently, this Jones guy was trying to save his skin and sped away on his motorcycle just in the nick of time."

"Okay, what was the deal with Dr. Von Gunten using the password CARNAGE? The old man was a perfectionist and raised all kinds of cain about releasing a higher percentage of giant pitwolves than originally agreed upon. I just talked to him yesterday after he wouldn't listen to Wolfgang Martin. Why would he use the password CARNAGE? Why did he do it, Tom?"

"Well, Marla saw footage of him making the cell phone call from Ci Mada's parking lot. She stated the video footage seemed to indicate that he was starting to have another heart attack, but was able to get it together long enough to make the call to activate the password."

"I think I now know his motive," says President Cohen. "Fritz knew his and Ci Mada Union's time was up, and he was just going for broke. He saw the meteorite coming toward Ci Mada and realized his life's work was all over. He wanted to release all his giant pitwolves. He hated America because of all the Christians in this country. His ultimate purpose was to erase all vestiges of the Bible and Christianity."

"Well, you can't blame the man for that, can you, Isaac?"

"No, you can't, Tom. Lucifer makes it very clear to the Adamic Society members that we overcome by the shed blood of innocent victims, by deception, and by loving our lives. This is how we faithfully serve our master, Lucifer."

"Isaac, you better call Marla now because I don't want to get on her bad side."

"Listen, Tommy, you don't worry about Marla. I can handle her! You got that? You worry about taking care of me," snaps Cohen harshly.

"Yes, sir, Mr. President," replies a startled Chief of Staff.

Marla Wittenhaur is a hybrid, the offspring of a mortal, her mother Julia DeVegaz Wittenhaur, and Lucifer. It has often been said that the eyes are the window to the soul. Marla's eyes are black and lifeless unless she is giving someone who has angered her a cold, deadly stare. Then eyes of pure evil and darkness are activated. There is a literal cool temperature that sometimes precedes her when she enters a room and often lingers long after she has left. Her skin is abnormally cool to the touch.

As the daughter of Lucifer, she possesses supernatural powers that some mortals only dream of possessing. Marla can manipulate people's minds, such as instilling in their conscious and sub-conscious fear, confusion, lust, hate, and a host of other negative emotions. Often she tells people things about their private lives that there is no way in the world she could possibly know. Many times they are spellbound, amazed, or totally horrified with her ability to reveal their unknown secrets, or they are petrified to death of her exposing their deep dark sins to the public. With this ability, she has been known to blackmail individuals to do things they would never dream of doing under normal circumstances.

Individuals who dare to cross Marla Wittenhaur put their lives in jeopardy. A few have succeeded only to meet a slow and painful death. Others have died suddenly of mysterious diseases with unusual symptoms or by strange, freakish accidents. She is the kind of woman who can make a typical type A man with a high level of testosterone feel uncomfortable really quickly. She wields great power and wealth and uses it to her advantage whenever she desires or it serves her purpose. On the other hand, her incredibly beautiful, alluring face and enticingly curvaceous figure can make the most devoted husband eat right out of her hand and do her bidding. Marla always gets what she wants when she wants it. For most of her life this has been the rule and not the exception.

Julia DeVegaz, her mother, had been a beauty queen and the leading international fashion model in the 1970s. Julia had been born into an evil, corrupt and very prominent family of untold wealth and power, based in Madrid, Spain. Generation after generation of the DeVegaz family had been key players in the Adamic Society. When Lucifer summoned Julia to be one of his brides, she eagerly responded to his proposal without hesitation. In order to disguise her pregnancy by Lucifer, she had married Daniel Wittenhaur six months before.

The Wittenhaurs of Geneva were also an old Luciferian family, composed of movers and shakers through the centuries. Their extreme power and influence extended well beyond the borders of not only Switzerland, but throughout Europe, spilling into other continents. Daniel Wittenhaur was the leading member of the Swiss Parliament and had close VIP connections and big business interests across the globe. Unknown to the public, he and his wife Julia were the major stockholders of Alpine Advanced Electronics and all of its numerous subsidiaries.

Marla has an outstanding and impressive resume'. She graduated first in her class from Harver University in Massachusetts with a double major in accounting and marketing. She also obtained an MBA from Harver Business School, again graduating at the top of her class. Upon graduation, she went to work for her mom's brother, Senor Maximilian DeVegaz, who is the CEO of DeVegaz Worldwide Enterprises. Under his tutelage for eight years as the Vice-President of Operational Affairs, she learned how to ruthlessly eliminate competitors and to efficiently rule a huge business empire with an iron fist.

Upon completion of her uncle's training, she was given the huge responsibility of running the Wittenhaur business empire from Geneva. With her amazing mind and endless energy she is a master at multi-tasking. Not only does she oversee the business aspects of the Wittenhaur family, but coordinates Adamic Society affairs along with the New International Union Security Forces based out of Geneva. Wolfgang Martin is now simply the talking head of Alpine Advanced Electronics. Since Marla's return to Geneva, she is now calling the shots and Wolfgang is still going about his daily routine and attending to business. But he clicks his heels to the demands of Marla now. Because of his devout service to Lucifer and his wide range of friends who are VIPs and Adamic Society members, he has become a high profile messenger and errand boy for the society. Now, due to the nature of his business, he flies in and out of countries on a weekly basis conducting business for the society per Marla.

Each night, right at midnight, new directives are emailed to Marla. Where they come from cannot be traced. Even she does not know who sends them, but she knows they are directives from Lucifer. This is her agenda for the next 24 hours and is to be followed to the letter unless there are disruptions. If there are changes, further emails are sent out to her. Since her coronation ceremony as the highest ranking high priestess in the Adamic Society Golden Level, rapid changes have been happening in the world. Lucifer is on the verge of revealing his son to the world. He is going to be the fulfillment and the crowning jewel and pinnacle of achievement for endless centuries and millenniums of work for countless Adamic Society members.

President Cohen is so upset at Williamson, he almost pulls his customized .45 caliber automatic pistol out of the middle drawer of his beautiful mahogany desk and points it between Tom's eyes. But he doesn't do it because he can visibly see Tom Williamson is shaken to the core already. Instead, for several moments he ponders calling Marla Wittenhaur. She doesn't like to wait, but Cohen wants her to know he is the recognized leader of the world, so he waits for ten minutes and reviews the directives she sent him about using the New International Union Security Forces in Colorado and the new Humanitarian Relief Centers.

Of all the men on the face of the earth. only Isaac Cohen intimidates Marla. He is extremely handsome and he appeals to her basic instinct of lust. But she sometimes overrides this lust for a greater one of power. Besides being handsome, Isaac is very charismatic, intelligent, witty, and oozes confidence - all of which she loves. Her cravings for power are exceeded only by his. All of her supernatural powers are useless around him and she doesn't know why.

Cohen finally calls Marla in Geneva on the hardened phone line in his Oval office. He says, "Hi, Marla."

"Hello, darling. So nice of you to quickly return my call."

"I called as soon as I got the message."

"Oh, I bet you did, Isaac. Listen, Isaac, my team and I have been examining the facts of these meteorite strikes, and what we have noticed is that for some strange reason a little county in Colorado keeps coming to our attention. This county, the smallest and poorest in Colorado, is called Clark

County. It has also been brought to my attention that it is the most conservative. Something supernatural is taking place there on the part of our archenemy."

"Well, I know from the speech you emailed me today, Marla, that a small hick town called Golden Valley was the precise original destination of the huge meteorite, according to USSAP, before it split in two and hit Boulder and Denver."

"Yes, that is true, and smaller fragments also hit eight counties around Clark County."

"That was kind of odd, I thought. What else can you tell me about Golden Valley and Clark County?"

"Well, Isaac, the GS33 satellite went down yesterday apparently taken out by a small meteorite before it was going to go over that section of Colorado. And Ci Mada's Eyegate TLZ drone first encountered a glitch north of there and was shortly taken out by another meteorite. Then on top of all that, Ci Mada Union was ground zero for the huge meteorite that hit Boulder."

"That's all interesting, Marla, but unless we are talking about a huge rebel army base camp or enemy jets in Colorado, I'm not too concerned because I can take out any threat in Colorado with a snap of my fingers. Besides, the release of all these giant pitwolves at once may be the greatest thing old man Von Gunten did for the society. These pitwolves and meteorites will have people begging for peace and security in no time. Yes, it's definitely a great time to be alive if you are on the side of Lucifer."

"Yes, this is true, again, great speech and acting today. I will keep you abreast of any new developments in Clark County. Hail Lucifer!"

"Hail Lucifer!" replies Cohen.

****

Ricky, Melody, Caleb, Gary, and Mary Anne are all sitting in chairs on the church platform when the emergency broadcast ends. It is a very somber moment for all the people of Fortress. It is something along the lines of what they have expected for years. Still, shockwaves roll across the people's minds and hearts about what had transpired and it is still only beginning to sink in. Ricky and Gary look at each other, and Ricky points to Gary to talk first to the congregation. His body language and facial expressions reflect this somber occasion. He begins by saying, "Well, brothers and sisters in Christ, our work seems cut out for us. Yesterday evening started out typically. Yet, since that time, all hell has broken loose around us. But a lot of miraculous things have happened also. From this moment on, we are in a period of acceleration toward the beginning of the Tribulation. The stage is being set for a dictator to come upon the world and to be endued with supernatural power from on high. In fact, you may have heard a leading candidate politically just now. He may have thrown his hat in the ring, in a sense, for that position. Cohen is a smooth talker and you have to read between the lines of what he is saying and not saying. Am I making an absolute forecast concerning him? No, I'm not, just an observation of what I heard. The anti-christ is coming really soon," says Bro. Gary, as he grasps his mouth several times with the fingers and thumb of his right hand. "As you heard, President Cohen is going to utilize foreign troops on American soil to oversee this so-called humanitarian relief effort for our fellow citizens here in Colorado as well as in centers in Utah and Nebraska. According to their track record, once these Security Forces come in and establish a foothold, they will not leave. Bro. Ricky, John, Sheriff Barnes, and I did not see the earlier KABZ footage, but we heard what you saw. I can also promise you that there are more of those giant pitwolves in Colorado and elsewhere. How many? Well, all we can do at this point is speculate. The threat is real. But there is hope, because we are on God's side. God has supernaturally promised to protect us against the giant pitwolves and all invaders on this property. He revealed His powerful arm of protection today to all of the four men who went up in the helicopter. Charlie, Leon, and the others working on the downed fence saw a glimpse of what we saw. God is alive and He'll protect every God-fearing person on this property. I cannot claim that promise for anyone off of this property. I repeat, especially to all the parents of youth and children, please listen. Do not allow your children to venture off into the woods outside of Fortress. Their very lives are at risk. So much more could be said at this time, but I think if you are like me you are completely physically exhausted and mentally drained. My daughter is motioning that we have some visitors with us. Please greet and welcome them and allow the elders some quality time with them. Ricky, how about if we have another meeting tonight, say around 6:30 PM, to share about God's divine protection for Fortress?"

Ricky nods in approval.

"Ricky, before I close, is there anything you would like to share?"

"Yes, real quick, everyone. If you are like me, you had to bite your lip while listening to President Cohen. As a former Navy pilot and Vietnam veteran, my blood was boiling. The America I knew as a boy is gone. Over the passage of time, the foundation of this country has been eroded by evil, powerful, and wealthy people. I have to remind myself of what Ephesians 6 says, that our fight is not against flesh and blood, but against principalities, against powers, against the rulers of the darkness of this world, against spiritual wickedness in high places. Make no mistake, people of Fortress, that the war is on. It is on! It's a spiritual war – one in which we cannot beat our enemy with guns and bullets. We will defeat the devil, his anti-christ, and his false prophet, his unholy trinity, by marching on our knees in prayer and the power of God. We will share with the church tonight what we saw today. Let me reiterate what Bro. Gary said. No giant pitwolves or invaders are a threat to the people of Fortress. But there is a stipulation - we have to keep doing what we have been doing. Basically, the only thing we are going to ratchet up is prayer and intercession here at Fortress. God Bless all of you. Okay, Gary, I'm done."

"Thanks, Ricky. I will close in prayer and then everyone needs to return to their regular tasks and jobs at Fortress if you can. The events since last night have been overwhelming. If you can't, then take as much time as you need today with your spouse, family, or by yourself. Any of the deacons will be glad to pray for you. Dear Father, much could be said. Unlimited questions arise and fears mount in our minds if we are not focused on You. We are soon to be in the Tribulation. We rejoice in the fact that You are our help in a time of trouble. You alone are our mighty fortress in a time of need. Help us not to fear men nor wild beasts who are only able to kill our bodies. Help us to fear only You who can kill both body and soul. You are the solution to all of our problems. We look to You for peace and joy. Your Holy Word declares that the joy of the Lord is our strength. So please, let us walk in it as we all carry out Your will for our lives today. Amen."

281

Barnes hurriedly approaches Gary and Ricky. "Guys, I've got to go. I know Hank and the mayor sent me tons of text messages during our flight. I just radioed Hank and he told me Tony Sanchez spotted a pitwolf on his sheep ranch on the east side of Golden Valley. And Hank also said four other surrounding counties have spotted giant pitwolves roaming in them. So I think we are off the hook, unlike what we thought last night."

"The Lord seems to have worked it out to our advantage," says Gary. Sam, if you need to deputize Blackhawk, Caleb, Forrest, or anyone else, just let us know. We'll try to help you with the giant pitwolves."

"Well, I appreciate that, but I'm sure the mayor wants to put in his two cents. I've got to find out some more information first before I involve anyone here, especially after all we have seen and experienced in less than a day's time. Before I go, I want to say you guys know those large feral dogs that are loose in Boulder are giant pitwolves. Even though we didn't see the news coverage, I just know they are. That national security advisor Lou Marino was lying through his teeth. He couldn't tell the truth if he had to."

"We know, Sam. It was plain and simple he was lying."

"I really don't know what to do at this point. I'm sure the mayor will want a town hall meeting for the citizens of this county to come to. We might have to end up in the high school auditorium to address all the people."

"We understand, Sam, and we want you to know that Sarah is free to stay with us. We'll take care of her."

"Thanks. But, I want her to ride back with me to the house so we can talk and get a bite to eat. So much has happened to me and so much is going on right now. I really don't know what else to say other than I'm going to trust God."

"That's all any of us can do, Sam."

"I just can't believe all that has taken place. But I've got to go. I'm going to tell Sarah goodbye now. Where is she?"

Melody responds, "Sam, it looks like she is talking to John Blackhawk over there."

"Probably wanting him to join your sheriff's department with all his tracking and hunting experience," suggests Caleb. He would be a good man to have if you need him."

"One thing before you go, Sam." Ricky leans over and whispers in Sam's ear asking whether it's okay to share later in the evening that he got saved today. Sam whispers back to Ricky to leave out that crying bit. He doesn't want that to get around the county. Ricky assures him it won't.

Barnes says, "I've got to go. I'll be in close contact with you guys and maybe talk to Blackhawk later." Everyone tells Sheriff Barnes goodbye before heading over to quickly greet and shake hands with Brenda Lee's friends.

The church members are respectful and allow the visitors time with the leadership, even though everyone has tons of questions to ask them. Almost everyone trusts Ricky and Gary with their lives. The only holdout has been Thomas Stanton, Jr., but the Lord is working on his heart.

Brenda Lee and Forrest briefly talk with Starlight, River, Patrick, and Emily after Bro. Gary closes in prayer. Then the church family quickly introduce themselves to the new visitors. The four friends are amazed how friendly everyone is towards them. They are also blown away and thankful that they were not in Boulder this morning when the meteorite impacted the city. Still a sense of guilt floods the newcomers' minds. They all know they would have died this morning had God not intervened in their lives. Each one was in tears as the events were retold during the president's speech. Brenda Lee was dazed, amazed, and even caught off guard hearing about the meteorites and the diabolical giant pitwolves roaming the city. She had prayed intensely all night for God to intervene in the dead giant pitwolf incident. By all appearances, it seems that God is diffusing the situation for Fortress. Although she is not privy to the inside information of Ci Mada Union Laboratories positively being involved, she pretty much knows without a doubt they were involved in the creation of the giant pitwolves. And God wiped the company off the face of the earth as a result of it.

In a strange kind of way, she temporarily struggles with a sense of guilt that both innocent and evil people have died as a result of her and the people of Fortress praying for God to move in their situation. Brenda Lee simply has to keep putting these thoughts back into God's hands and rest in the fact that He is sovereign and just.

Everyone at Fortress ponders where they are on God's prophetic time line. Is Cohen the anti-christ? Are their freedoms going to be suspended? Has the Tribulation officially started? What all is going to take place in the U.S., Colorado, and Golden Valley? But most of all, what is God going to require of them in these last days?

River and Patrick are both totally stunned with all that they have experienced. Nothing in their short Christian walks has prepared them for all the bad news they have been hearing. But the reality that they have been chosen to have an angelic visitation from one of the mightiest angels in the Bible to forewarn them is what blows them away the most. 'Why were they chosen?' is what each one has been asking himself the whole trip to Golden Valley. It has quietly nagged at them in the deep recesses of their minds over the span of the day. For some unknown reason, God chose to reveal himself to them in a unique way. Both feel unworthy knowing that friends and acquaintances have died back in Boulder. Both are also confident God will provide what they need when they need it in the journey He has chosen for them.

Emily feels strongly she has a new lease on life. She feels for the first time in a long time that someone loves her greatly and that Person is God. The love of God has been shed in her heart from the moment she got saved. She knows she has experienced the forgiveness of her sins at the moment. But at this time the Holy Spirit is all over her like a comfortable, warm blanket on a cold Rocky Mountain night. The Holy Spirit is also melting away different fears that have plagued her most of her life. Even guilty thoughts of not dying in the meteorite strike are leaving her. She knows beyond a shadow of doubt that God rescued her from the jaws of certain death and hell by not allowing her to go to Boulder yesterday. Emily feels as if God is orchestrating her life and she has a purpose and a destiny. Ivan back at the diner is going to be upset with her, but she knows she has done the right thing by coming to Fortress. No longer does she feel alone. She feels a strong connection with Starlight and River, and she really likes Brenda Lee's spirit. Patrick makes her feel special. She secretly likes him and he makes her life enjoyable in the short time she has known him. And she make him laugh too. Just as a butterfly emerges from a cocoon, a new Emily is beginning to come forth.

For Starlight, something strange started to happen during President Cohen's speech. The whole time while he was speaking, the words *music evangelism and revival, music evangelism and revival...* kept ringing loudly in Starlight's heart. Hell has broken loose, but music evangelism and revival are consuming her thoughts. The three greatest gifts God has given her are her salvation, River, and her voice. How is she going to use those gifts to combat giant pitwolves, thousands of homeless people, and a despot President who wants to overthrow her country with foreign troops? Something from deep within in her spirit is crying out to let God know her life is His to do whatever He wants with it.

Starlight feels she is at a crossroads in life and is desperately trying to make sense of it all. There has to be a reason for her and River to be alive. She has to have a purpose or something to protest. It is embedded in her third generation hippie genes. She knows that she found Christ six months ago. He set her free from a bunch of baggage in her life that had accumulated over her short span of 19 years. But from what the archangel Michael told River, music evangelism and revival are the main reasons they are at Fortress. Exactly what that means she doesn't know, but she is determined to find out. Paying the price on her knees in prayer is something she is willing to do to get the answer. She doesn't want to make something happen in the flesh. It has to be a God thing.

After all the church members all greet the new visitors she stands in front of her four new friends, and says, "Well, I don't know about you guys, but it definitely seems that God's divine providence has brought you here, and not Boulder, at this appointed time."

Forrest quips in, "Of all the generations born throughout history, God has chosen you guys, Brenda Lee, myself and every God-loving Christian for such a time as this. We have a mission to live out the Gospel to those around us and those we are going to meet. Welcome to Fortress! It is not a Christian survival compound or a cult. It's simply a church with a threefold mission of discipleship, evangelism, and prayer. If we as Christians focus on discipling new converts, evangelizing the lost, and praying continually with our eyes and hearts focused on Christ and his word, we can't go wrong biblically. And we love to praise and worship God here."

"Preach it, Forrest! Preach it! says Patrick, as everyone smiles.

"You know how I can get now, Pat," says Forrest grinning.

"Oh, believe me. I remember, Forrest. And you're a big reason why I'm saved today. Thank you, brother."

Brenda Lee smiles and says, "My Forrest is one of our resident soap box preachers and he loves to share the Gospel. Hey, if you guys don't mind, follow me. I would love to introduce you to my mom, dad, Uncle Ricky, Aunt Melody, my cousin Caleb, and his wife Ashley up there on the stage. They are our main ministers here."

Smiling, Brenda Lee and Forrest go over to the stage with their new friends and introduce them to her family who had been talking to one another and answering some of the questions of their church members. Ricky and Gary, recognizing Emily from the diner, remember her name and say, "Hi, Emily."

She smiles and replies, "Hello, Bro. Ricky and Bro. Gary. It's good to see you two again." Brenda Lee introduces everyone and there is a time of shaking hands and greeting.

Finally, Brenda Lee says, "Dad, Uncle Ricky, Mom, and Aunt Melody, I know you guys are really exhausted, but my new friends have a really awesome testimony about how they ended up at Fortress. If not for the grace of God, they would've all been in Boulder this morning. It all started with both River and Patrick who had angelic visions from the archangel Michael and he told them to come here. All I can say is that these guys are legit. I spent some good time with them picking their brains and getting to know their hearts before we came to the church. After all that has happened, they have a lot of questions. Their heads are spinning, but they are really fired up about the Lord."

"When you mentioned the archangel Michael, my ears perked up. I think we are all very curious," says Ricky.

"Bro. Gary and Bro. Ricky, it's an honor to meet you. I don't know exactly why we are here, but we believe God sent us here," says River humbly.

"Let me tell you, River, the Holy Spirit in me bears witness with what you are saying. I believe you, Son, and we have made provisions for those whom God has sent to us. Once we hear your story and you hear ours, it will make more sense."

"Then it's settled," says Melody. "Let's all head over to the lodge where we all can relax while you fill us in on all the details of your journey here."

"Mary Anne and I will make some fresh coffee and some homemade chocolate chip cookies. Are you guys up to it?" asks Gary.

"Chocolate chip cookies are my favorite snack! In exchange, I will tell you everything I know and then some," says a giggly Starlight.

"We have ways of making people talk," says Mary Anne in a funny, spooky voice. They all start laughing as they head for the lodge.

Chapter 15

INEVITABLE CHANGE

A month has gone by since the meteorites impacted and destroyed large sections of Boulder and Denver. Much has transpired not only in Colorado, but in the nation as a whole, and most of it is not for the better. Rock solid freedoms once guaranteed in the Constitution and Bill of Rights are being eroded and chiseled away on a daily basis. Churches by the thousands all across America are closing their doors due to their members falling away from God and the lack of giving. Many of these pastors have abandoned their pulpits never to return again, disillusioned with God and confused by what's happening in the world around them.

Caleb Crawford has just finished running and opens the door to the timber frame and river rock lodge that his grandfather had built. Just then the antique Swedish-made grandfather clock in the living room strikes six o'clock. The century and a half old clock chimes six times in rhythmic successions, an old familiar sound he has known and loved since his childhood. It still keeps almost perfect time, a testimony to the quality of old world Swedish craftsmanship of a bygone era in which men possessed great skills, artistic abilities and took pride in their work. The chimes echo through the house as they always have. But this time the familiar sound brought a flood of old memories about his charismatic grandpa, the former All Pro tight end with the Los Angeles Stars whom he affectionately called the Big Swede. Caleb just ran four miles called "The Trail" on the property, just as his grandfather did years before to get in shape for each NFL season.

Because he had been a giant of young man in his day as a teenager, he had earned the nickname the Big Swede. He was the kind of guy you either loved or hated. The man could talk some smack in his day, but he was almost always in a good mood and was either making you laugh, laughing himself, or the both of you would be laughing. Caleb reminisces for a moment on how much he loves and misses that big old man.

In the meantime, sweat is dripping off Caleb's large six-foot-two frame like melting icicles hanging from the Rocky Mountain cliffs when springtime finally arrives in Colorado. Ashley comes out from the dining room with a hand towel for her husband. He says, "Thanks, Ash," in a sweet tone.

She replies, "You're welcome."

Caleb follows her back into the dining room. I can't wait for your twisted ankle to get better so you can run with me."

"Me too. My body is feeling a little sluggish."

"Is that wonderful smell what I think it is?" asks a hungry Caleb as he wipes down his wet body with the towel.

"Yes, it is. I just got through setting the table for us to eat."

"But, I'm all sweaty."

"Well, it's not the first time I have smelled your body all sweaty. Besides, the food is still piping hot and I'm starved."

"Yeah, so am I, honey."

"Grandma Cotton just made us your favorite meal - homemade southern fried chicken, fried okra, purple hull peas, garden salad, cornbread in a cast iron skillet, mashed potatoes with homemade brown gravy, and sweet tea to celebrate our anniversary."

"Bless her heart. She is so sweet. Where is she?"

"She is fasting. It's her time to intercede in prayer at the church."

"God knows I love her to death, and her cooking is out of this world," responds Caleb. "I've eaten at the best restaurants around the world being in the Navy. But nothing compares to Grandma Cotton's home cooked meals. She has the magic touch when it comes to pleasing my taste buds."

"The lady is not only a saint, but she also knows how to fix southern home-style cooking at its finest. I have watched her cook and tried to follow her recipes to the letter. It just doesn't come out the same."

"Yeah, I know," says Caleb with a teasing smile.

"Watch it, boy, or you're going to be in the doghouse," says Ashley, smiling back at him.

"Ashley, had you ever eaten fried okra before Grandma came to Fortress?"

"Are you kidding? No! My momma is Italian and probably has never seen okra or purple hull peas. My mom didn't ..."

Ring, ring...

"Who could that be?" says Caleb, who's kind of perturbed that someone is interfering with his favorite meal. "I'll go check." As he opens the front door, his eyes light up when he sees his good friend Peter Watson. First, he shakes his hand really firmly before grabbing him by the neck and hugging him. Then he hugs Pete's wife Molly more gently.

Ashley sees Pete and his family including his mother-in-law, she believes. Ashley says, "We have been praying really hard for you guys. Come on in and relax," as she hugs everyone, especially her friend Molly and their two children.

Caleb, in a friendly tone, says, "In fact, we were just going to sit down and eat so everyone head to the dining room table."

"No, no, we don't want to impose on you guys," says Molly. "My mom is with us and everything."

"Nonsense," insists Caleb. "We are all heading to the table while the food is still hot. There are no if, ands, or buts about it. There's plenty of Grandma Cotton's food to go around. She doesn't know how to fix a small meal."

"Well, if you insist, Caleb," reply Pete and Molly.

"Oh, I'm sorry, Caleb and Ashley. I have forgotten my manners. Excuse me. This is my mother-in-law Evelyn Good. We have been through an ordeal."

"Pete it's okay!" assures Mrs. Good. "I have heard a lot of nice things about you, Caleb, and your wife Ashley and your whole church. I can't believe all that has happened to my family and me." She starts to cry.

"Mommy, I'm hungry," says little Peter, Jr.

"Me too," says his younger sister Nicole.

Ashley says, "Molly, why don't you and I fix the children's plates and feed them in the dining room and talk while Caleb ministers to your mom in the living room. Pete can fill him in with what is happening in Salt Lake City."

At this point, Molly breaks down and starts sobbing. "Yes, Ashley. Thank you so very much. I'm sick to my stomach. You can't believe how much I have missed you and my church family here. But I know the kids are hungry for a good meal and some milk, which they love, if you have it."

"Sure, we have plenty of milk and whatever they or you want."

"Mom, you okay with that?"

"Yes, feed the kids. I know they're hungry."

"If you need me, Mom, I'll be in the dining room with Ashley and the kids."

"I'll be fine, dear, with God's help. Please fix their plates."

After the wives are through preparing the children's plates and their own, they begin to eat and talk. Their husbands and Mrs. Good are relaxing in the living room. Caleb is trying to get to the bottom of what has taken place in her life and with Salt Lake City becoming a Humanitarian Relief Center over the last month. Various rumors have surfaced and left everybody speculating as to what is actually taking place in the capital city of Utah.

Mrs. Good is a little apprehensive about sharing with Caleb. Pete has to reassure her. "Mrs. Good, you can trust Caleb. I've known him and his family since I was a boy. I would trust him with my life. If there is one true blue American left in this country who will continually put his life on the line for God, country, and family, it is Caleb Crawford. He's the former Navy SEAL I was telling you about."

"Well, I...I...I'm scared for Frank."

"Who's Frank?" inquires Caleb.

In a shaky voice, Mrs. Good responds, "Pete, if you trust Caleb, then I do." She starts crying and blowing her nose on some tissue she pulled from her purse. "It's okay, Pete. I know I told you to promise not to tell anyone what Frank told me, but we're out of Utah now and I release you from that promise. Why don't you just tell your friend what's happened ? I'm just too emotional right now."

"Okay, thanks, Mrs. Good," replies Pete.

"Relax, Mrs. Good. You are safe here," reassures Caleb.

"Thanks."

"Now what's the story, Pete?"

"Well, as you know, when Molly and I left here, she was really emotional. In fact, she was a basket case. With the small meteorites hitting the counties around us, she was already stressed big time. Then when Big Blackie was found dead with his throat ripped out by that giant pitwolf, it really freaked her out. That was the icing on the cake."

"Oh...God...Oh...God..., Pete!" interrupts Mrs. Good. "If the evil foreign military taking over in Salt Lake isn't bad enough, I'm out here in the middle of the sticks with some type of prehistoric predators on the prowl. God help us all!" Mrs. Good, whose personality is high strung even in good times, is on the verge of hyperventilating. Caleb, with his extensive medical training as a Navy SEAL and real life military experiences, recognizes her condition. He quickly reassures her repeatedly that she is absolutely safe on the property at Fortress. After a few minutes, her breathing is not as rapid and she appears to be more relaxed. Caleb knows she can't handle the harsh reality of the conversation, so he grabs her left hand with his left hand and pats the top of her hand with his right hand gently. He encourages her to go ahead and try to eat something and that Pete can fill him in on the details.

Ashley can't help but over hear Caleb trying to calm down Molly's mother. So she comes into the living room and says, "Mrs. Good, when is the last time you had homemade fried chicken and cornbread?"

"It's been a good while."

Well, let me tell you something, Mrs. Good. We've got some homemade southern fried chicken in the dining room that a dear sweet little old lady right around your age made."

"Well, I usually eat baked chicken because it's healthier, you know. And cornbread is loaded with carbs and oil. But tonight I think I'm going to live it up and kick calories to the curb."

"Yeah, you have to let your hair down and smell the roses every once in a while. Now follow me. Delicious southern cooking awaits you."

Mrs. Good lightens up and leaves the room to eat. "Pete, it appears you have had your hands full," whispers Caleb.

Pete leans over to Caleb and says in soft whisper, "Believe me, you don't know the half of it."

The conversation then resumes in a more normal tone once Mrs. Good is completely in the other room. Caleb asks, "Pete, what has happened in Salt Lake City since you left?"

"Well, my family and I never made it to my in-laws' house. My father-in-law, Frank, called me right after the news broke on the meteorites hitting Denver and Boulder. We had been driving all night. Fortunately, we were near a cell phone tower a hundred miles from Salt Lake City when I got the call. I had to tell him we had decided to make a surprise visit, and then he shocked by us saying not to come to Salt Lake. I just couldn't tell him that the giant pitwolf killed my champion bull. Frank said that he drove Evelyn to their mountain retreat cabin, which is about 60 miles west of Salt Lake City, and had to leave her there all alone. He couldn't stay there because his freeze-dried food company was coming under the control of the N.I. U. because Salt Lake had been designated a relief center. He had to be at his company. Apparently, they want him to step up production of his freeze-dried foods and other products for their needs. He was highly upset about that because he feels they have commandeered his business that he has invested his whole life into. Frank had called me thinking we were in Golden Valley and wanted me to come and pick up Evelyn and take her back to Golden Valley. His gut feeling was that things were going to take a turn for the worse in the city, and many Mormons weren't going to go along with Cohen and the N.I.U. mandates."

"How was Molly dealing with all this, Pete?"

"Well, to be honest, at first not good, not good at all. She had about three panic attacks the first 24 hours after leaving here, but thank God not around her mom. I was praying for her and my mother-in-law continually. Then the second day at the cabin, when we were alone in the basement, I told her she needed to turn it all over to God and accept His Son into her heart. And you know what she said, Caleb? It shocked me."

"What did she say?"

"She said, 'You know, honey, you're right. I do need to accept Jesus Christ as my Lord and Savior.'"

"Praise God, Pete!"

"So I led my wife in the sinner's prayer and she got saved. She said a peace came into her heart like she had never experienced before. After that Molly was able to keep it together for the most part. She was trying to be strong for her mom and the kids. She started doing a lot of praying and claiming the promises of God over herself, me, and her family. I began to see a different kind of Molly emerge."

"That's the best news I've heard in awhile. Thank You, Jesus. Ashley and I have prayed many an hour for you two, and God has answered our prayers. I want to know how Mrs. Good has been dealing with the stress of this ordeal."

"Well, Caleb, when we got to their log cabin, Evelyn was nervous and pacing the floors waiting for us. She told us that Frank had driven her away as soon after the news broke about the meteorites destroying Denver and Boulder. The instant he knew Cohen wanted Salt Lake City to be one of the Humanitarian Relief Centers, he started loading up all their valuables in a specially designed hidden heavy duty safe in the floorbed of his SUV, some family albums of pictures along with two large emergency go bags in their new GMC Yukon, and covered up the stuff with a blanket and suitcases with Evelyn's clothes and makeup bag. Before he left the city, Frank topped off his four custom gas tanks that hold a total of 90 gallons and drove her to the cabin. He left her there and then quickly headed back to Salt Lake in the old pickup he keeps in his garage. Evelyn said Frank hated doing that, but he felt he had no other choice. He didn't want to leave her in the city if something was going down. Frank knew he couldn't permanently leave because he felt the Security Forces would hunt him down. Caleb, the man knows how to not only make freeze-dried foods, run the business, but he can also service all the machines himself."

"Your mother-in-law appears to be having a hard time with all these changes in her life."

"That's an understatement, Caleb. Evelyn was so paranoid that giant pitwolves might be in the vicinity around the cabin. But Frank did some fast talking and convinced her that there were none in the state."

"Wow, your family and Molly's parents have been through a whole lot. So that explains why you were driving the Yukon and Molly was driving your truck."

"Yeah, Molly's dad is from the old Mormon pioneer school and has been saving up for tough times with tons of bulk and freeze-dried foods but also in gold, platinum, silver, cash, and some expensive large diamond jewelry."

"Let me guess. You have his stash in the SUV, right?"

"Yea, most of his valuable assets."

"How much are his assets worth?"

"Evelyn says, from what Frank had showed her, around $1,300,000.00 worth of precious metals, diamonds, and another $200,000 in cash."

"Pete! You've got to keep your mouth shut about that!"

"Yeah, that's another reason she wanted to know she could trust you. We took as many back roads as possible to get back here to Golden Valley. I drove under the speed limit the whole way."

"So, Pete, you got paranoid yourself transporting all that precious metal, jewels and cash, didn't you?"

"You bet I did, and it's not even mine. I've done nothing wrong or illegal. But the whole trip I felt like a criminal who was trying not to get stopped by law enforcement or New International Union troops. The last thing I wanted was to try to explain why I'm using my in-laws' SUV as an armored truck transporting $1,500,000 in valuables and cash."

"Where are you going to put all those valuables, Pete?"

"They are going in a vault. You're not seriously going to put all those valuables and cash in that old, outdated Golden Valley First National Bank's vault, are you?"

"Ain't no way I would do that, Caleb. I'm going to put it all in an earth vault."

"What do mean? Oh, you are going to bury it?"

"Yeah! Caleb, I've got only two years of college, but I have a PhD."

"I know what you're talking about, a post hole digger. That'll work. Just make sure you tell Molly where it is, just in case something happens to you. And bury it about two feet deep off in a secluded area."

"Well, I'm telling Molly, and I'm looking at the other person I'm going to tell when and where I decide to bury it."

"Okay, well you know I'll keep my mouth shut."

"I know."

"What's going to happen to Molly's dad?"

"I can't say. My guess is the Security Forces are watching his every move and are not letting him leave the city. Putting together some things I've heard, I was told his name is on some kind of list, and he can't leave Salt Lake City. Evelyn told me Frank got a call within 30 minutes of the meteorites hitting Colorado telling him his freeze-dried company would be under the control of the N.I.U. troops. Frank was ordered not to leave Salt Lake City and to contact every worker and tell them the same. He broke the first rule, but quickly returned to Salt Lake. Frank had already been told by a close Mormon friend high up in some government department in D. C.

that this scenario would play out in the event of some kind of national emergency. Devastating meteorites had not be factored into the scenario. But Frank had pretty much been gearing up for years in the event of a national emergency for some type of Marshall Law."

"Were you able to sneak into Salt Lake City while you were there and try to see him?"

"No, that was not an option. Caleb, I'm no Rambo and I'm not you. I had Molly, my children, and my mother-in-law to consider. Within a day of the meteorite strikes, Cohen allowed 1000 Security Force soldiers to fly into the city's airport. Salt Lake was crawling with soldiers and other N.I.U. officials. Plus, with all that has happened, I didn't like leaving my family alone in a secluded area. On day two, they had armed soldiers with AK 47's patrolling the streets of Salt Lake and stationed at checkpoints in and out on the perimeter of the city. There were armed soldiers around the perimeter in about twenty makeshift metal towers that sprung up over night."

"What I did do to find out some information was drive my father-in-law's Yukon minus all the valuables with Utah tags down to a large truck stop ten miles from the cabin about six times over the last month. I pretended that I was a local and ate some meals and drank a lot of coffee there at the counter. I struck up some conversations with various truckers but only a few gave me bits of information about what's going on in Salt Lake. I paid out $1000.00 to four truckers who were Christians and were careful with their words. Once they knew they could trust me, they each gave me the same basic information I've told you. Which confirmed the stories they told me."

"So what kind of information can you tell me, Pete, concerning what's happening in Salt Lake?"

"Well for one the city is under Marshall Law or Dominion Law, as the Security Forces like to call it, and now there are around 20,000 troops there and growing daily. About one week after Boulder and Denver got hit, they started building a thick heavy duty 15-foot chain link fence around the perimeter of the city and the airport just as fast as they could. It extends way beyond the city limits and they are about finished with the basic structure."

"Initially they told the people of Salt Lake it was for their protection against the giant pitwolves that had been spotted in the area. And that was partially true, but they also had another ulterior motive, as we know. They also started building a tent city for all the displaced citizens coming in from Colorado on school buses."

"Since you've been gone, Pete, I've heard reports and read emails that giant pitwolves are popping up all across America for some unknown reason. About ten people have been attacked and killed by them in various states."

"That's true, Caleb, and as far as I know, not one pitwolf has been killed and not one has been seen on the TV or internet as of yet. And I believe that the powers that be don't want any live or dead ones shown. Because it makes them more mysterious, mythical and more scary.

Molly and I haven't told a soul we saw a dead one. And let me tell you this, Caleb. I talked to three other truckers at the truck stop that have personally seen these monsters from hell from a distance while traveling across the U. S., and they all said it made the hair on their necks stand up. Almost all truckers across the country are traveling in convoys now and are heavily armed for protection against these beasts."

"I believe that. So, Pete, is there anything else you can tell me about these relocation centers?"

"Well, as you know, Cohen said it was to relocate people from Boulder and Denver - only healthy people that basically lost everything. What I was able to piece together from the truckers I talked to was that people with severe injuries were taken to another location to be executed. The Security Forces brought in special tractor trailers that looked state of the art medically speaking, and trucked the really sick and severely injured out of Boulder and Denver. The foreign troops shot them and buried them in undisclosed mass graves or caves somewhere in the Rocky Mountains."

"Oh, Lord, we must be at the start of the Tribulation. It seems I'm reliving my Navy SEAL days all over again in a third world country with a two-bit dictator at the helm. Except this time it's in my own country."

"Caleb, the real reason these relocation centers were chosen was to turn them into three huge N.I.U. Air Force bases. And they are doing it! Apparently, the N.I.U. wanted to have military bases for a stronghold in the center of the country. They are flying in Russian, German, English, French, and Chinese jets and huge aircraft carrying massive amounts of N.I.U. troops, military hardware, weapons, tanks, vehicles, supplies, and more."

"Well, what have the people in Salt Lake City, Colorado Springs, and Omaha done in response to this military takeover in their cities? We've been given a lot of fake news as to what has been going on."

"Well, some people revolted at first and were either eliminated or have never been seen or heard from again."

"No trial and hearing for the citizens of any of the cities?"

"No, that doesn't exists anymore under Dominion Law."

"Well, what are you going to do about your father-in-law?"

"I don't know. It seems there are no options other than praying and that has been what we have been doing this past month. He is between a rock and a hard place."

"We'll have our intercessors and other members to seriously pray about his situation."

"Thanks, Caleb, but you can't tell everyone the whole story."

"I know. Well, Peter, after a month you have come in here and cheered me up with all your positive news. I'm just joking, kind of, but anyway there have been lots of miraculous things that happened right after you and Molly left. It will take a while for me to fill you in on all the details."

"A thought just occurred to me. Why don't you and your family stay in the big three bedroom cabin that we just finished a couple of weeks ago? There is plenty of room for all you guys and all the furnishings are brand new. Everything you need is already in there. I know the elders need to hear what has happened on your trip to Utah. I think they will be back here soon."

"Yeah, that will work. I'm spent. I know Molly has been lonely and could use fellowship and encouragement. She loves her mom, but also enjoys spending time with Ashley, who is so positive and has a gift of encouraging people. I'm sure Evelyn is also enjoying talking with Ashley. The two basically shut themselves into the cabin for fear of missing Frank if he came and because of the threat of giant pitwolves. Caleb, it sounds like a great plan."

"Pete, did you just hear that?"

"Hear what?"

"Caleb?" Pete quickly puts his hand on the holster of his Colt .45 automatic with the extended 10 round magazine that used to be his dad's. "What are you talking about, Caleb?"

"You mean you didn't hear it?"

"No!"

"Grandma Cotton's fried chicken just called my name."

"Oh, boy! You got me! You got me good. My heart is pounding. I'm thinking giant pitwolf! I owe you, Caleb."

"Yea, I know. I deserve it. I just couldn't resist."

They both laugh and smile at each other, appreciating their friendship over the years. Caleb is a little over a month older than Pete. They had played and hung out together every summer, Thanksgiving, and Christmas when Caleb's parents had come back to visit his grandparents in Golden Valley. But Pete saw very little of Caleb once they graduated from high school, each went to college, and Caleb served in the Navy. But their friendship resumed pretty much where it had left off in high school after Caleb took early retirement in the Navy and he and Ashley moved to the Double V Ranch.

"Let's go get some of Grandma Cotton's southern gourmet cooking."

"Caleb, you know I bet Mrs. Cotton could teach that cook on TV, Samantha Dane of New Orleans, a thing or two about southern cooking."

"Yeah, I bet she could."

As they walk to the dining room, Caleb says, "You'll never believe who got saved the day after you guys left."

"Wally down at the gas station?"

"No, not yet. Sheriff Barnes and his wife Sarah got saved."

"What?! Are you serious? Did you just say what I think you said?"

"Yes!"

"Unbelievable! I wouldn't have guessed them in a million years. Wait 'til Molly hears about this. That must be one of the miracles you were telling me about. Oh, by the way, Caleb, Molly's mom is also really close to getting saved."

"Praise God, Pete. I'm so glad to hear that, bro. You know God is making things happen in these last of the last days."

"Yeah, definitely. When Sam Barnes gets saved, that's big news in Heaven."

Ashley sees Caleb and Pete come in the dining room and says, "It's about time you boys got in here while there is still some fried chicken left."

Mrs. Good declares, "Peter, this chicken is absolutely delicious. It puts my fried chicken to shame and also my mother's. I thought I knew how to fry chicken."

Pete, Jr. says, "Daddy, look how much chicken I ate. I'm eating like a big boy."

"Daddy, this chicken is yummy," giggles Nicole. "I'm a big girl. Look at my little chicken leg. All the meat is in my tummy."

Pete responds, "Yes, I know I have a big boy and big girl. You guys are eating good and daddy is proud of both of you."

Molly is dry-eyed for a change. She had been crying off and on for the last month, but has found some peace since she got saved a month ago and is progressively getting better. She looks at Pete with loving, expressive eyes and says "I'm thankful to be back in Golden Valley with good friends, neighbors and my mom."

Pete pauses for a second, and with a humble heart, says, "Yeah, I know what you mean, Molly."

"Well, Molly, we are glad you, Peter, and your family are back here in Golden Valley. Aren't we Caleb?"

"Yes, thank you, Jesus."

"Okay, on that note, boys, get it while it's still a little warm or you guys can fix your plate and nuke it in the microwave," says Ashley. As Caleb and Pete pile the food that is left over onto their plates, everyone is talking and enjoying each other's company. Watson's children seem to be getting tired.

After thirty minutes, Caleb and Pete finished off the rest of what was truly a delicious meal. There was just enough for everyone to have an enjoyable supper. There are two big pieces of the pecan pie left that Grandma Cotton had made. Caleb tops off his piece with real whipped cream and Pete is just enjoying his plain. When Pete finishes his last bite of pie, Molly mentions that she wants to take Caleb up on his offer of spending the night in the new cabin. Pete says it is fine with him, and Mrs. Good says she feels at ease on Double V Ranch.

In fact, she says, "I can't explain it, but for some reason, I have been more at ease here than I have in over a month and maybe in my entire life. There is peace here. I don't know any other way to explain it."

"You're right, Mrs. Good. God's peace resides here in this Lodge and on this property."

"Amen, sister." Then Caleb says, "Pete, let's get your family situated over at the cabin. Then you and I will come back here and wait for the elders."

Pete says, "I'm cool with that. As everyone piles in the vehicles to go to the cabin, Ashley says, "Here comes Grandma Cotton."

Everyone, including the sleepy Watson children, says, "Hi, Grandma."

She graciously smiles at them as she waves and says, "Well hello, everyone."

Molly dear, I'm so glad to see you back in Golden Valley," as she gives her a big hug.

Molly wipes some tears from her eyes and says, "It's so good to see you, Grandma."

"Mrs. Cotton then gives each of the Watson children a kiss on the top of their heads. She walks over and gives Pete a big hug, and says, "I'm glad God protected you and your family, Peter. You guys have been in my prayers daily."

"Thanks, Grandma."

Mrs. Good asks, "Is this the dear sweet lady you told me about? Is she the southern gourmet cook?"

"She is the one, Mrs. Good," replies a grinning Caleb.

"I've just got to talk to you, Mrs. Cotton, if you have some time. Molly and I have been cooped up in my mountain retreat for a solid month."

"Why, I'm free as a bird right now. Where are guys going now," smiles Mrs. Good? "Please call me Evelyn," says Mrs. Good.

"Well, you can call me Frances," says Mrs. Cotton.

"Here, we'll ride in the back of the Yukon together and let Peter and Caleb drive us over to the cabin where we are spending the night. Molly, her children, and Ashley can go in the other vehicle."

When they get to the cabin, Pete and Caleb unload everyone's suitcases into the cabin. Molly and Ashley are tucking in the kids and Evelyn is talking Francis' ear off in the living room. But Grandma Cotton doesn't mind because she thinks Mrs. Good is funny. And she is enjoying talking with someone from her own generation.

Caleb wants Molly to come back to the lodge to talk to the elders. He asks Ashley to watch the children until she comes back. Ashley says she doesn't mind taking care of the children and is looking forward to it. Pete, Molly, and Caleb walk back to the lodge once Caleb convinces them that Fortress is completely safe from giant pitwolves.

When they get to the lodge, they each pour themselves a glass of sweet tea and Caleb begins to tell Pete about all the miraculous things that have taken place since he left. Pete's eyes get big and he can't believe all that has happened. The angelic protection of Fortress blows him away. But Sheriff Barnes getting saved just doesn't even seem possible. He says, "If Sam Barnes can get saved, there's hope for anyone."

After about an hour there at the lodge, Ricky, Melody, Gary, and Mary Anne arrive in the ministry's hybrid car. They ate supper earlier over at the Barnes' house. After shaking hands and hugging the elders, Pete sits down and retells the story of what happened in Utah and what he has learned. None if it is shocking to the elders. It just confirms some things they already knew about the N.I.U. Security Forces and have suspected the whole time since Cohen first revealed his plans of using the foreign Security Forces to establish relocation centers in Salt Lake City, Omaha, and Colorado Springs.

On a happier note, they are all excited and glad to hear the good news that Molly has gotten saved and that she is grasping that the end times is upon them and is trying to deal with it. They also conclude that Frank Good is a very knowledgeable and resourceful guy. But he is in a difficult situation. If he just abandons his freeze-dried company and somehow sneaks out of Salt Lake, the N.I.U. will just track him back to Golden Valley. Prayer seems to be the only solution to his dilemma. Pete offers to pay the elders for helping him out feeding and taking care of his livestock while he and his family were away. But they refuse to take any money and say that he and Molly are neighbors and part of their church family. They would not hear of such talk.

Ricky wants to bring up a point with Pete about his ranch. He says, "Pete, Melody and I have known you since you were a little boy. You and Caleb have been good friends since you guys were kids. Melody was friends with your mom and dad when they were living and went to school with them. Bro. Gary, Caleb, and I have previously discussed this with our wives and we would like to extend an offer to you. Now, you don't have to accept it. We think it is a solid proposal to only benefit you."

"Well, what are you getting at, Mr. Crawford?"

"As you know, Pete, things are getting pretty crazy in this country. We don't fully see all that is going to transpire, but what we do know is that God has promised His divine hand of protection on this property. That we are 100 percent sure of. We also were told not to fear any man, any army, nor giant pitwolves, because no one with ill intent or any pitwolf is going to set foot on this property. God has told us through the archangel Michael that it's not gonna happen."

"Yeah, I understand. Caleb and all of you have told me that. But what are you getting at?"

"Well, our proposal to you and Molly is that we would like to lease your property to us for $1.00 for a year."

"Why exactly would you want to do that, Mr. Crawford?"

"Because then it would officially be part of the Double V Ranch, which is property upon which our church Fortress is built. We believe that the angels will protect you, your family, and livestock as a result of us leasing your land - because technically it would be part of Fortress."

"Well, that sounds fine, but who ultimately controls the day-to-day operation of my ranch?"

"You do, Pete. You call all the shots and reap all the financial rewards. All we are doing is offering you God's protection."

"So what are the stipulations to this lease?"

"You just have to keep serving God, praying, and doing His will."

"It's that simple? Caleb, you never told me how many cattle have I lost to those giant pitwolves since I left."

"I decided to leave that to my dad to tell you."

"How many, Mr. Crawford?"

"Pete, you have lost three cows and two young bulls besides your champion bull Big Blackie."

"How many cattle, horses and bison have you guys lost, Mr. Crawford?"

"None."

"Well, it would appear I would be a dang fool if I didn't take you up on your offer. I know I can trust you. If I can't trust you folks, I don't know who I can trust. But first let me see the contract and I'll talk it over with Molly and we will go to the Lord in prayer."

"Peter Watson, you don't need to talk this business deal over with me. In my spirit I know the Lord wants you to sign on the dotted line."

"Well then, it's a no brainer."

Pete, who is kind of shocked by his wife's words, says, "I guess you guys know now who wears the pants in my family. Does someone have a pen?"

"Here," says Caleb as he hands him one and bursts out laughing. Then everyone else joins in laughing, including Pete, who starts looking around the room at everybody, rubbing his nose with his right index finger.

Gary suddenly walks out of the room, only to reappear almost immediately. "Peter, here is the contract I drew up. But listen closely. There is one more major stipulation in the contract."

"So what is the second major stipulation?"

"You can't let people know that your land is protected by God Almighty, because it would be like putting a neon sign on your property that would attract everybody coming down the pike. There are severe consequences for anyone who is on your property with evil motives. Right now we are trying to keep this supernatural protection under wraps until the appropriate time."

"I understand, Mr. Kirkman. I sincerely just want to do God's will in these last days. My hope and faith is not in the three year supply of freeze-dried food in my basement my father-in-law gave us. It's not in my livestock, my water well, or my guns and ammo. It is simply being in the center of God's will for my life and His will for my family's. My land is God's land. I'm just a steward of it. So just show me where to sign."

"Peter, we're just trying to look out for you, Molly, and the kids. You guys are family."

"I know, Mrs. Crawford. All you guys are too."

"Ricky says, "Son, why don't you close this time in prayer?"

"Okay, Dad. Dear God, I thank you for Pete, Molly, their children, and Pete's mother-in-law, Mrs. Good. We also ask that you intervene in Mr. Good's life and work it out so he can get away from Salt Lake." Molly starts dabbing her eyes, along with, Mary Anne, Melody and Ashley. "You can make a way where there is no way. Help Pete's family readjust to being back in Golden Valley. Give Pete and his family peace as they return to their ranch. Amen."

"Well, we've got to get going now, guys, because we're just plain tuckered out. Both Molly and I have been on an emotional roller coaster these last four weeks."

Molly speaks up and says, "I never thought I would be so glad to be back in Golden Valley, but I am."

Pete and Molly say goodnight as they wave to everybody. Everyone waves back. Caleb walks them outside the house and Pete and he shake each other's hand firmly. Caleb says, "Pete, you guys sleep in tomorrow if you can."

"Oh, believe me, I will try," says Pete laughing.

"That is, if the kids don't wake us up," says Molly, who is now smiling..

"Alright, good night," waves Caleb. Pete and Molly wave back as they walk to the cabin where his family, Ashley, and Grandma Cotton are.

As Caleb enters the lodge, he sits on the couch in the living room and says, "Well, I'm glad Pete and his family are back safely."

"Yeah, agrees Melody, "But I feel bad for Mr. Good."

"We'll definitely pray for Pete's father-in-law, Frank, and his mother-in-law, Evelyn," says Mary Anne. "And ask God to intervene in their behalf."

"Amen," says Caleb. "On another note, I'm dying to find out how the meeting went with Sheriff Barnes, Mrs. Barnes, and Mayor Perkins."

His dad replies, "The meeting went better than expected. Mayor Perkins is beginning to see the handwriting on the wall regarding this country and his own county."

"Well, Dad, it's about time he figures out that so-called progressive change isn't always for the betterment of society. We all know he voted for Cohen."

"Yeah, but he confessed to us he is so sorry that he ever did. He has decided to allow us to hold an evangelistic meeting in the Golden Valley High School gym."

"That is wild. Thank you Jesus!" shouts Caleb.

"As you know, Son, after meeting with the Mayor, Sam Barnes told us at supper that he has been sharing the gospel with the Mayor, his once old-time political adversary," explains Ricky. "Perkins is actually beginning to do a 180 in his way of thinking; so is his wife."

"It is very apparent God is working in their hearts," says Mary Anne.

"I can't believe it," smiles Melody. "But my best friend from high school is finally saved after all these years and she has been sharing Christ lately with Linda Perkins, whom we couldn't stand when we were younger. She mentioned that at supper tonight and I almost couldn't believe my ears. Linda Perkins use to be Linda Reynolds who was a senior when Sarah and I were freshmen in high school. She always came across very uppity. She walked around with her nose in the air like she was better than everybody else. Thank God, He has mercy on us," laughs Melody.

"Well, I know two former All-American football players from USWC who years ago strutted around and thought they owned the campus," laughs Gary.

Then everybody except Ricky starts laughing. He somehow maintains a straight face and says, "I have no idea who you are referring to, Gary." Then Ricky joins in laughing loudly and everyone laughs even harder.

After the laughter dies down, Caleb says, "It's hard to believe Mayor Perkins is changing."

"Not really when you consider that his nephew Travis Perkins is in Boulder working as a Liaison Officer with the N.I.U. Security Forces," says his Dad.

"What? You're kidding me. This is the first I heard of where he was or what he was doing since he resigned a month ago as a deputy under Sheriff Barnes," replies Caleb. "Did you guys know anything about this?"

"No, none us of knew, Caleb. Sheriff Barnes just found out tonight himself," informs his Uncle Gary. "Remember he just up and left shortly after the severe headaches stopped. He was the subject of a lot of jokes by some of the townspeople because he fell and knocked himself out on the heater and was found on a bloody floor in the Sheriff's office. He was viewed as incompetent because it happened on the same night other people spotted the giant pitwolves. A couple calls went unanswered because he was unconscious."

"Even Mayor Perkins didn't know until a week ago where or what he was doing. He just showed up last Saturday at noon at his uncle's house. He told the mayor he got a new law enforcement job with the N.I. U. and was given the weekend off from training. He had a fraternity brother from the former ultra-liberal Davidson University in Denver that helped get him hired. His buddy is a supervisor with the U.S. Civilian Liaison Officers Division of the N.I.U. Security Forces for the three new relief centers."

"It doesn't sound good working for the N.I.U. Security Forces as a Liaison Officer."

"It isn't," replies Ricky. "You function as a buffer between the N.I.U., civilians, and the local law enforcement officials. He basically helps smooth out disputes people have with the Security Forces."

"In other words, Dad, he whitewashes everything for the Security Forces and puts a spin on what they do."

"Yeah, you got it. But now Travis claims, according to his uncle, that he really regrets taking the job. His frat brother pushed hard for him to get that position that pays twice what he was making here as a deputy sheriff.

Travis really thought he was climbing the career ladder by taking the job. Mayor Perkins said at first it was just too tempting for his nephew to turn down the money. He was also lured by what his friend called the prestige of the position. I'm sure another factor was that he wanted to get away from this small sleepy county as quickly as possible. Plus Travis thought he could really help the people of Boulder recover from the disaster with his new job." ⁎

Gary replies, "On top of all that, he now feels he is in over his head and he can't get out. According to his uncle, Travis now knows that most of the politically left views that he secretly held while a deputy sheriff were a bunch of lies and now he feels like a Benedict Arnold. He can't tell his uncle much of what he has secretly learned in his new position or the details of the things he has done as a liaison officer because he took a oath. As a result, he doesn't sleep well most nights. All Perkins knows is that his nephew is doing things that go against his conscience. At one point in our conversation, the Mayor said that Travis is now afraid for his life because he realizes how dangerous the job is. He is also afraid of the general public who are increasingly hating liaison officers like himself. He doesn't trust any of the Security Forces soldiers, of which none are Americans."

"Travis does seem to be in over his head if that is the case. I know as Christians we need to be careful what we say about other people. All my years in the military told me that I couldn't trust that guy. Maybe now his eyes have been opened to some truth," says Caleb.

"I agree, Caleb," says Ricky. "We were all saying the same thing in the car coming back here to Fortress. He always seemed to talk conservatively the limited times I talked to him, but I always got a check in my spirit about him." Everybody is nodding their heads in agreement.

Gary speaks up, "Now on to a more positive note, Mayor and Mrs. Perkins are drawing closer to the Lord and seem just about ready to get saved. So we know there is hope for their nephew. Matt got teary eyed and wanted us to keep Travis in prayer. I told him we would definitely be praying for him here at Fortress. So everybody put him on your prayer list. Melody and Mary Anne, make a note of that for the intercessors."

"That is good news, Uncle Gary. I'm also curious about the upcoming evangelistic prayer meeting in the Golden Valley High School gym."

"Well, Caleb, we are tentatively shooting for two weeks from this Friday at 6:30 PM. So that gives us a little time to get the ball rolling and let people know about it."

"Son, the elders are requesting that everyone at Fortress, not just the intercessors, really bathe this event in prayer."

"That is so true," says Mary Anne. "God is working in this county and the Perkins' lives without a shadow of a doubt. Just think about it for a second. Matt Perkins in his former liberal mindset would have never allowed us to use the high school gym a month ago before all these latest developments took place. You do know Caleb that Perkins is the President of the Board of Trustees for the school district? No, I didn't know that. But, now he is a desperate man. He is under great conviction of the Holy Spirit, and on top of that he knows this town's and this county's very existence and preservation are at stake."

"You're so right, Aunt Mary Anne. Desperate men sometimes take desperate actions, and Perkins is desperate."

"That describes Perkins perfectly," replies Gary. "Perkins said that if more and more people keep moving out of Clarke County because of the meteorites and giant pitwolves, it is going to become one big ghost town."

That statement cracks Melody up. "That is funny, but so very true."

Gary smiles and says, "Now let me quote him verbatim. 'Ghost towns have no need of a mayor.'"

"One thing I have to admit," says Caleb, "is that God deals with every person in a very unique way. Anyway, praise God! First Sheriff Barnes comes over to the light and now Perkins and his wife seem to be headed in the same direction."

"Amen," replies everyone.

"Hey guys, I just remembered," blurts out Mary Anne. "I'm sorry to change the subject, but I just remembered Starlight gave me our mail before we went to see the Mayor earlier. Then there was the Sam and Sarah thing this evening. I was in such a rush to get ready for the meeting with the Mayor earlier today I forgot to go through it. Check out this letter. I just read it while everyone was talking. It's from Dr. Ken Hagman of The Rapture Watchman Hour TV program."

"Oh, no! What's he saying now? I'm the anti-christ," jokes Ricky.

"And I'm the false prophet," snickers Gary.

Ricky is just shaking his head side to side, "Here we go again."

"No, no, not at all! Listen guys, just the opposite. He says he was wrong on the timing of the rapture."

"Say what?" yells Melody in almost complete disbelief.

"You heard me correctly, Melody."

"Hagman is apologizing for twenty years of calling us every dirty name in the book for our post-tribulation view of the rapture. Ken has finally seen the light after calling my Gary and your Ricky false teachers, wolves in sheep's clothing, false prophets, false shepherds teaching unbiblical heresy, and a host of others slanderous names."

"Well, read us some more, Mary Anne. I'm dying to hear exactly what he said," requests Melody enthusiastically."

"Well here it is.

Dear Bro. Ricky and Bro. Gary,

I am sending this letter, that I wrote with my own hand, to you with much fear and trembling. I did not feel an email or phone call was the appropriate way to communicate with you. I'm asking for your forgiveness after two decades of opposing you at every turn of your ministry's journey. Recently I spent a week alone at our lakeside house in north Alabama. I shut myself up to reexamine the Scriptures on the timing of the rapture and other prophetic events. Things in our once great country are in a nose dive and I felt like the rapture should have already taken place some time ago.

Never in my wildest dreams would I have believed these events unfolding before our eyes would be happening in my lifetime. Since I was a child sitting under my grandfather's teachings on prophecy in his church I never envisioned that the church would still be here at a time like this. Then again I never imagined I would be cautiously walking around at my lake house with a 12 gauge riot pump shotgun loaded with seven rounds of 00 buckshot in my hands just to take the trash outside. Why? Because these dangerous, giant, genetically-modified mankilling wolves have been spotted in the state forest nearby.

Much has rapidly transpired since the meteorites struck and destroyed large portions of Denver and Boulder, the arrival of foreign N. I. U. troops, the establishment of humanitarian relief centers (military bases), and endless rumors of those demonic-like giant pitwolves all over the country that have sent a chill down most people's backs, including mine. My purpose in coming to my lake house was to read several of your books, and to poke holes in your theology and to reaffirm mine. Deep prayer for God to show me His truths concerning the matter was also on the agenda.

Two days after arriving here, I had an epiphany when I remembered President Cohen mentioning, during his speech a month ago, that Clark County Colorado was the original destination of the huge meteorite before it broke in two. That really got me to thinking. From different news stories I've seen, it seemed really strange to me that eight counties were hit by smaller meteorites that are around or close to Clark County. Yet not one meteorite hit Clark County. Then it dawned on me and I remembered reading about you guys relocating your ministry there from LA some years back. I just kept thinking and asking myself why would Clark County be spared from God's wrath? I used to loathe the post-trib view you would teach when I heard you on the radio or internet because I believed it was false. As horrible as it sounds, I just thought, 'God, why have You spared that county that contains that ministry that has opposed me, Your servant?' I also kept asking Him why the rapture hadn't occurred yet. Plus, many other why questions were popping into my mind. My life had been way too busy for years so I just decided to get away and alone with God to find some answers. During this special time alone with God, He revealed things in the Scriptures that I had never seen before. It was like I put on a new pair of prescription glasses and could see things clearly and in more detail. Scriptures literally jumped off the pages to me like a three-pound bass on the bank of my lake. I was able to connect dots concerning the prophetic Scripture like I had never been able to do before. After devouring your books with the way you logically laid out the Scriptures and the background of the development of the rapture, I couldn't find any holes to punch in your prophetic theology. Finally, I concluded that the pretrib rapture is a doctrine I can no longer teach and preach. As a result of my new position on the rapture, I stand to lose everything. But I will now preach and teach until my dying breath that the rapture occurs at the end of the Tribulation and not before.

Your brother in Christ,

Sincerely,

Ken Hagman

P.S. May God have mercy on me for all the pain I have caused you!"'

"Oh, my goodness! I don't believe it! I just don't believe it!" says Melody. "I thought when Sarah and then Sam got saved, God had performed two of His biggest miracles. But this miracle has just superseded that!"

"You said it, Mom. I remember while at the Naval Academy that you said Dr. Hagman was the most antagonistic person to Dad's and Uncle Gary's end time ministry. Now, he is like a Saul who has had a road to Damascus experience."

Mary Anne replies, "Let's hope he can make up for lost time because the winds of change are indeed blowing in this country. Gary, you and Ricky need to call Ken Hagman and tell him thank you for the apology. He probably would really appreciate it. He sounds like a broken vessel who could use some encouragement."

"Absolutely, Mary Anne!" says Gary.

"Definitely!" agrees Ricky.

"He is two hours ahead of us in Birmingham, Alabama so it's too late to call him tonight. But we can try to call and get hold of him tomorrow," explains Gary.

"Yeah, I'm really looking forward to talking to him," says Ricky. "It is truly unbelievable that someone like him who was a staunch dyed-in-the-wool pretriber has jumped ship to our view of the rapture. This is big news, but I really want to switch our conversation back to what we were talking about earlier this evening. Praise God for some very positive news. We'll have to put that conversation on speaker so we can all hear it."

"Okay, now I would like for the elders to meet with Brenda Lee and

Forrest tomorrow, as we briefly touched upon in the car coming back here, and then meet with Starlight, River, Emily, and Patrick about their role in worship at the upcoming evangelistic and prayer meeting in the gym," instructs Ricky.

Melody quickly adds, "Ricky, don't forget about our grandsons, Andrew and Stephen, because they are also on the worship team."

"Sorry, I meant to include them. Mary Anne told me earlier that she would tell Brenda Lee about the meeting at 8:30 in the morning, but wouldn't give her any details. She also said that she would tell the others to meet us around 9:00AM, if you guys agree. After the meeting Mary Anne can tell Brenda Lee to design the flyers to get out to the people in the community." Everyone agrees on the times and the flyers.

Ricky concludes the meeting. "Well, guys, we've had a big day with huge surprises from our new friend Dr. Ken Hagman and confirmed information from Pete about Salt Lake and the two other relief centers in Colorado Springs and Omaha. We have another big day tomorrow meeting with the worship team to further plan for this evangelistic and prayer meeting in the high school gym. But I'm exhausted now and a little bit hungry. Son, I heard through the grapevine that Grandma supplied you and Ashley with a great anniversary dinner tonight."

"Yes sir, she did and it was delicious!"

"I heard it was a southern fried chicken feast tonight. Did you and Pete save me a chicken leg?"

"Seriously, Dad?"

"A piece of pecan pie?"

"No!"

"A small piece of cornbread?"

"S-o-r-r-y!"

"Okay, it doesn't hurt to hope and ask, Son. Thank God we already ate." Everyone laughs because Ricky loves Grandma's cooking just as much or more than Caleb does. When the laughter subsides, Bro. Gary leads everyone in prayer about the coming special event in the high school gym.

Chapter 16

BUTTERFLY EMERGES

Brenda Lee knocks on the door to the conference room before slowly opening it to the waiting elders seated where they usually discuss important ministry decisions and take turns counseling people. Inside the relatively plain room is a beautiful, ornately hand carved, Victorian-style antique redwood table along with ten matching chairs from the late 1880's made in San Francisco. It was purchased from an estate sale of one of Gary's former clients who was multi-millionaire. Bro. Gary's dad had purchased it for his conference room in his law practice in the 1960's and Gary could not part with it when they moved from California. The four elders are gathered around talking about the weekly emails that Melody sent out to all the pastors of the Disciplemaker churches in their network. Each is sharing how they feel God is going to do something special in Golden Valley at the meeting, but they don't know exactly what.

As Brenda Lee and Forrest arrive, they aren't sure why the elders want to meet with them. Mary Anne never told them exactly what it would be about. Although the elders have always been very friendly, encouraging, and helpful to Forrest even before he became engaged to Brenda Lee, they have always intimidated him because of their successful backgrounds and the great wealth they had accumulated. But people never know it if they meet the elders on the street because they are ordinary, down-to-earth Christian people who have attained extraordinary success. But even though they have been successful by the world's standards, Forrest holds them in even more awe as a result of their Christian walk and because he knows they are chosen vessels for the end times. As a result, he regards the Crawfords and Kirkmans as spiritual parents whom he doesn't want to displease.

Forrest is hoping the meeting won't last too long because he has to relieve

317

John Blackhawk at the sheriff's office. Both were sworn in as temporary deputy sheriffs under special provisions with the county. Barnes needs John and Forrest because of their animal tracking abilities and because they came face to face with a giant pitwolf and contributed to its death.

Their hiring was also spurred on because Travis Perkins and Hank Rutherford had both abruptly resigned for totally opposite reasons. Sheriff Sam Barnes normally would have counted it a blessing if Travis had quickly resigned from his post. But it couldn't have come at a worst time, especially when Hank handed in his resignation less than a week later. It was like someone sucker punched Sam in the gut. He never saw it coming and took it hard, really hard. Not only was Hank Rutherford his right-hand man, but more importantly, he was like a son to him. He had already lost his only child, a son, years before. Samuel Paul Barnes, Jr., who was just like his dad in so many ways, died an early death from a swimming accident at age 10.

Sammy, as he called him, was the spittin' image of his father at the same age. Through the years, Sam had clung to the bottle for comfort and relief many a night when the pain of the loss was too much for him to handle. Since he got saved a month earlier, God Almighty had miraculously delivered him from a lifetime of sporadic hard drinking and nightmarish PTSD flashbacks of war and painful memories of his son. All desire for alcohol completely left him. Since Hank had joined the sheriff's department, he was a close substitute to Sammy Jr. Both Barnes and Hank had served in the Army and seen plenty of action. Both were hometown war heroes. Hank and Barnes shared similar interests, tastes, and values. That was until Barnes got 'religion,' as Hank put it. He knew Barnes was changing. He just wasn't the same guy. Hardnosed Sam Barnes was morphing right before his eyes into a Jesus Freak. Sam's change felt like a small, jagged stone in a nice comfortable pair of cowboy boots on a long walk - a feeling Hank hated.

But what really set Hank off on a different and more radical course was the fact that four days after a large part of Boulder got blown off the face of the earth, he got a call from his old Army buddy Keith Brown. Hank and Keith had been highly decorated Army Rangers serving side by side. They had seen a lot of fighting and had been in many tight spots in the Middle East. Keith lived about 20 miles outside of Boulder. His brother Brian lived in

Boulder and had been severely injured while working out at a crossfit gym close to his apartment when fragments of the meteorite blew in the windows of the gym from the point of impact at Ci Mada Union Laboratories, which was three miles away. He had received multiple injuries and cuts as a result of the impact. They were serious, but not life threatening with the right medical attention. Brian's girlfriend Lori was also working out in the gym but had gone to talk to one of her friends in the locker room when the meteorite hit. She had been protected from any injuries. Initially, she said was able to get Brian to the hospital, but it was so overwhelmed with victims in far worse shape on top of their regular patients. Doctors and nurses were almost in shock themselves and the hospital floors were covered in blood. She basically had to beg for some alcohol, gauze, tape, and towels to try to keep Brian from bleeding to death from glass cuts on the outside and inside of his body.

Brian's condition was beginning to stabilize until the first wave of N.I.U. Security Forces arrived and started clearing out all the new medically fragile patients and loading them into thirteen state of the art medical semi-trucks to take them to other nearby cities to treat the victims. Loved ones and friends were confused by the commotion. Lori was opposed and vocally spoke out against moving Brian and the other patients from the hospital. But once an AK-47 was shoved in front of her face by a soldier screaming in an angry foreign voice and motioning for her to get back, all she could do at that point was cry and not speak out. According to her report, she later found out from a nurse that Brian was wheeled away in a wheelchair by a N.I.U. soldier in complete shock, confused and scared, as he was shoved into another group of semi-trucks that were unmarked, dirty and crowded with the rest of the very sick and seriously injured patients.

Keith had told Hank that within four hours after the blast the first wave of 600 N.I.U. Security Forces soldiers had been flown in on commercial 757 planes that were heavily armed with a bunch of gear into the Rocky Mountain International Airport in Boulder, which was still intact. Also, U.S. C-130 cargo planes began landing later on that night, and in the days that followed, carrying more troops, armored-type vehicles, and tons of supplies. Upon their arrival, the N. I. U. declared Dominion Law, which was basically Marshall law. Many freedoms and rights were not only suspended, but were no longer in effect. Local law enforcement officials were up in arms over the ordeal. The Boulder Chief of Police got a call from Governor Benton and was told to have his police department stand down and obey all directives given by Colonel Krasnov, the head of the Boulder N.I.U. Security Forces. Benton told the Police Chief that President Cohen had just signed executive order F66666 into law before he called which gave all acting head representatives of the N.I.U. complete jurisdiction over all civilian and political officials elected or appointed in a city, state, or region where Dominion Law had been authorized by the N.I.U. headquarters in Geneva.

It was rumored that Keith's brother was shot and killed by Security Forces soldiers because of his severe injuries. His brother never made it to a hospital or even a morgue in another city. Lori said N.I.U. personnel would never give her a direct answer where Brian was taken. Keith believes from what he was able to piece together from Lori and other people in Boulder that Brian was probably shot and killed and his body dumped in an unknown cave, pit, or mass grave at some unknown place in a remote area of the Rockies. That's the N.I.U. Security Forces' track record of helping the seriously injured or diseased by committing human atrocities worldwide. For them it is cost effective to deal with the badly diseased and severely injured in this manner in countries where they have been sent.

Hank's friend Keith had been on vacation backpacking and camping with his wife and another couple who were friends in the Rocky Mountains with no cell phone service. After the backpack excursion, Keith found out what happened and he sneaked into Boulder and did some reconnaissance with his friend and two other ex-vets. He has since formed the Mormon Brotherhood. It's an underground movement that appears to be gaining numbers in the region. MB is a radical Mormon militia group that opposes the N.I.U. troops on American soil. No armed confrontations have taken place up to this point. Only accumulating information, secret meetings, rallying men to their cause, and stockpiling weapons and supplies are all that have taken place so far.

About a month has passed since Starlight, River, Patrick, and Emily first arrived at Fortress. Changes have been happening very rapidly in the world, the United States, and what used to be a very peaceful little county in Colorado where they live.

"Come on in," welcome Gary and Ricky in a friendly tone, waving their hands, motioning them to come into the room. Forrest respects and trusts Bro. Gary and Bro. Ricky. They set his heart at rest with their body language, smiles, and manner of speaking. "We just want to talk to you guys and share with you some things the Lord is laying on our hearts," says Bro. Gary.

"Hi, everybody," says a happy Brenda Lee. Forrest, her fiancé', nodded his head, smiled, and waved his hand. "What's this meeting about?" asks a curious Brenda Lee.

"Honey, your father and I and your Aunt Melody and Uncle Ricky have been discussing the purpose of River, Starlight, Emily and Patrick at Fortress in regards to music and worship."

"Oh, that's what this meeting is about? Forrest and I have discussed it several times over the last few weeks. And we are perfectly fine handing over the worship during our Sunday morning and Wednesday night services to them if you want us to."

"I'm in total agreement with Brenda Lee," says a more relaxed Forrest. He feels at ease once he thinks he knows the purpose for the meeting.

"Not so quick, Brenda Lee and Forrest," says her father, Gary, in a casual tone. "This meeting is more than just discussing music and worship as usual. We'll get to that point in a minute, but first let me explain. All the elders feel that we don't want to hand over the worship team and service to Starlight and River, at least not yet."

"Daddy, Forrest and I are fine with whatever you guys want us to do. In the last month I've really seen all four of our new friends really blossom in the Lord," says a perfectly content Brenda Lee.

"Starlight and River are not only very talented musically," replied Forrest, "But they have a special anointing whenever they sing. Starlight's voice is angelic to say the least."

"Oh, there is no doubt that they are definitely gifted and anointed in the area of singing, especially Starlight," replies Gary, "And that River is an incredible guitar and harmonica player."

"But there is more to the picture than meets the eyes," continues Mary Anne in a motherly tone. "You two are more like spiritual mentors to them. You guys are discipling them in their walk. They need that accountability at this stage in their walk with the Lord. All of them are very young in the Lord, especially Emily, and we want you to continue to be good examples of Christians to them even though you guys are just a few years older. Both of you have been walking with Christ for years and you know the ups and downs of the Christian walk."

Melody interjects, "Don't take this the wrong way. You two have done a great job leading praise the last two years. We have no complaints. We want you both to continue to lead the worship team with Brenda Lee singing and playing the tambourine and you playing the electric guitar Forrest. But the Lord is showing the elders that our worship and praise team should take a new direction here at Fortress, as Gary alluded to earlier."

"What do you mean, Sister Melody?" asks a puzzled Forrest.

"Well, I'll let Gary fill you in."

"Thanks, Melody. What we want to tell you, Forrest and Brenda Lee, is that we want to turn our worship team into a part-time Christian band."

"A Christian band, Daddy?" asks a bewildered Brenda Lee. "I'm not following your train of thought."

"Me either," says a confused Forrest.

"I can see the looks in both of your eyes, like what in the world are the elders talking about? It's really very simple. As you know, there were people who packed their bags and left here because of the meteorites. A few are still leaving because of the giant pitwolves. Some of those people were just plain scared to death. Numerous ranchers and farmers have found dead cows, bulls, hogs, and other livestock either savagely attacked with their necks ripped open and left alone or their bodies picked clean. Even people's dogs have suffered the same fate. The old time hardcore country folks around here have stayed. They're the descendents of tough-minded, resilient pioneers who blazed across the country around a century and a half ago in wagons and on foot and settled in this wilderness area in hopes of a better future. These people are of the same stock as their ancestors who endured Indian raids, blizzards, droughts, grizzly bears, and wolves attacking their livestock. Because of the events of our day, most of these people are in survival mode, just like their ancestors were years ago. They are desperate and are hanging on, hoping for a better tomorrow. The ones that are staying have family members and friends moving in with them for economic and security reasons. Some of those that came back to this county were from Boulder, Denver, Colorado Springs, Omaha, and Salt Lake City."

"Daddy, I didn't know some people were moving in to Clark County."

"Me either," quips Forrest.

"Gary, I would love to share this news with them if you would allow me because I am so excited about it."

"Sure, Melody, by all means."

"Thank you. Listen, guys, some people are actually moving here from around the region. It surprised all of us yesterday, especially the mayor. My old friend Sarah Barnes knows so many people and she probably knows better what's going on in this county than anyone. We both used to love to gossip in high school and get the scoop on what was going on in people's lives. And she told us this information during the meeting yesterday with the mayor. We were all surprised. Apparently, the people that have come here witnessed firsthand the horror and destruction of their cities and could not bear to be under Dominion Law. They decided to take their chances here with smaller meteorites and giant pitwolves rather than with N.I.U. Security Forces. That's what I wanted to share."

"Thanks, Melody. That's good news." Gary grins as he says, "I'm glad you gave up gossiping years ago."

"Yes, God did deliver me of that awful habit."

"Thank God, yes, He did," pipes in Ricky.

Gary shakes his head and laughs a little. "Anyway, Honey, as both you and Forrest know we have tried to reach out to this community before in numerous ways in the past and we were not very successful. But on God's prophetic time clock, we feel these people's hearts are ready to receive the message of the Gospel given what has taken place. The elders here are sensing that these people are more open to the Gospel than ever before and that something big is going to break out in the supernatural here in Clark County. We also believe in our spirits that there are other places in this country where the Lord is working overtime on people's hearts for this last great harvest that is still to come. We have talked with each other and know things are converging at this juncture in time. Time is running short and we want to be in on that action. We feel the Lord may have us send out this Christian band with other disciples from time to time to evangelize the lost. All the elders agree the worship team's music is very anointed and your music can be used to soften the hearts of unbelievers so they can receive the truth of God's Word and be saved."

"Honey, in all my years of being a Christian, I have never heard more anointed worship than here at Fortress."

"Momma, that means a lot coming from you."

"Wow, I knew we were pretty good, Mrs. Kirkman, but I didn't know we were that good. I'm humbled."

"It's the truth, guys," affirms Ricky.

"So this idea of the Christian band is for evangelistic purposes," replies Forrest, shaking his head back and forth. Praise God! I'm sensing that God is in this concept of starting a Christian band to help win the lost. Music evangelism is one of the buzz phrases that Starlight and River have talked about, along with revival since they got here."

"I'm beginning to like the idea of a Christian band more and more," says Brenda Lee.

"Gary, I'd like to share some details with them if you don't mind."

"Go ahead, Rick."

"Brenda Lee and Forrest, we are planning to hold a special meeting in the Golden Valley High School gym."

"Yes, Jesus!" shouts Brenda Lee.

Forrest holds his hands up and says, "Praise Jesus!"

"Yes, praise Jesus. So what I want the both of you to know is that this meeting is not just for evangelism but also a time of prayer for the community. You see, people in this county need to get saved today and they need hope for tomorrow to keep going in the midst of this time of crisis. So we also want this meeting to be a call to prayer for the people of this county to seek God for their needs. God loves Clark County and none of us are here by mistake. What the elders are proposing is to use the worship team and give it a new name and have you guys perform in the Golden Valley High School gym. It's the only building in the county that could hold a thousand or more people. We hope to launch you off into other cities in the near future."

"Have you guys mentioned this to the Mayor yet?" inquires Forrest.

"We officially proposed it yesterday to him and he okayed it. We just have to rent the high school building to use it because it can't be a school sanctioned event. But that is trivial and such a small amount of money."

"You know I hear from God at times very clearly. This is one of these times. I sense in my spirit that God is going to exceed our expectations at this meeting. I sense that strongly."

Everyone says, "Amen."

"Are we good then, everybody?" Everyone present nods and smiles. Gary then closes in prayer.

"Starlight, what's wrong?"

"I, ah, I, don't feel like we are doing what God called us here to do."

"What do mean, Star? Everything is going as good as can be expected in this mixed up world. Look, we're in the center of God's will. Look at the nice apartment we're staying in. It sure beats living in the van. We have jobs here and it's not like we're free loading off of anybody. The food is great here and its natural and organic. This place is a real Christian utopia surrounded by the beautiful Rocky Mountains."

"I know, I know all that, River! We're still doing music, singing, and writing great new songs. I know it seems like it's about as good as it can get. The Christians are for real here and they really love Jesus."

"Then what is it, Starlight?"

"Remember what the archangel Michael told you about coming here?"

"Well, he said a number of things. Oh, you are referring to the part about music evangelism and revival."

"Yeah, that's it River! Remember the day we arrived, the Holy Spirit kept saying music evangelism and revival over and over again in my mind while Cohen was talking?"

"Yeah, Star, I remember clearly now. Everybody in the church was getting blown away by what the President was saying about the meteorites, reports of giant pitwolves, and the coming changes, and you got some kind of a word from God on music evangelism and revival. Yeah, I remember. I just think we need to be patient and the Lord will bring it about in His time."

"You're right, River. I need to just wait on the Lord."

"You can't rush God. He runs on His own timetable. I just want to see God move in our lives."

"Sorry, Starlight, but we better get going to meet with the elders."

"Riv, what exactly did Forest tell you last night about this meeting?"

"He didn't know what it was for. All he said was that we were to meet with the elders at 9:00 AM. That is all he told me and we have to get moving."

"River, I hope we're not in any kind of trouble."

"Nah, we're cool. I don't think so. We both work hard at our jobs here. We're not causing any problems and we get along with everybody."

"Yeah, that's true."

"Riv, would you please grab my denim jacket on that rocker? It's a little nippy outside this morning."

As they step out of their apartment, Starlight says, "Hey, look up there in the sky." Instantly in a state of wonder, she points to the eastern sky. "It's so awesome to see that majestic bald eagle effortlessly gliding high above the earth against the back drop of a beautiful blue sky over the golden valley with an amazing, blazing orange sun casting down rays of warm sunlight for all of creation to enjoy."

"Starlight, that is really cool! You are so poetic, just like Moonbeam and Jane."

"Well, I'm glad Jane had a few good qualities and gifts to pass down to my Mom and me."

"Yeah, let's hurry before we're late for the meeting."

As River and Starlight briskly walk from their end of the apartment complex, they see Emily coming out of her section of the apartment. Patrick comes out of the other end of the complex rubbing his right eye, still trying to wake up. He shares an apartment with Forrest, who just left for work. As he runs to catch up with Emily, he waves to River and Starlight. Patrick yells, "I don't want to be late."

River yells back, "We don't either."

Emily grabs Patrick's hand as they start running to the meeting with the elders. Starlight and River start running to beat Emily and Patrick to the church as all four start laughing. When they enter the church building, they have to catch their breath before teasing each other as to who won the race. Then they walk to conference room, hesitating outside the door.

River asks, "Does anyone know what this meeting is about?"

"I have no idea," replies Emily. Patrick volunteers that he too has no idea except that Forrest and Brenda Lee finished meeting with the elders just ten minutes ago and he was in the shower when Forrest had to bolt for work. Just then Andrew and Stephen Crawford, the youngest members of the worship team, show up. They are Caleb's and Ashley's sixteen-year-old twins and they prefer to be called Andy and Steve. Only their grandparents and aunt and uncle call them Andrew and Stephen. Andy plays the keyboard and Steve plays the drums. Andy is older by two minutes and always reminds his brother of this fact. They seriously love the Lord, but they are also some serious pranksters. Everyone says hi to them as River is about to open the door to go inside.

Andy stretches out his hand and shakes his head side to side, whispering quietly, "Don't do that. You don't know the protocol."

Steve, who has no idea what Andy was referring to, plays along and says, "Do you want things to go from bad to worse?"

Andy tells everyone, "Give me some room." River, Starlight, Emily, and Patrick, looking puzzled, stand back. Andy comes to the door, puts his ear on it, and tells the group to watch and remember the protocol.

Steve tells everyone with a sad voice, "Everyone, my brother and I will try to smooth out this terrible problem."

Andy then knocks on the door, opens it slightly so only his mouth can be seen in the opening, and says in a very soft voice, "Grandma, Grandpa, Uncle Gary, and Aunt Mary Anne, I know everyone on the worship team is not worthy to come before you except Stephen and myself, but may we all approach your thrones as humble servants?"

Ricky jokingly yells out, "You clown, Andrew, get in here. Come on in everybody." The elders burst laughing as they know Andrew and Stephen are up to their old tricks.

Andy and Steve had everyone going for a second. All the elders tell the worship team members that they will have to watch themselves around Andy and Steve. Everyone thinks it is funny, but no one laughs louder than Starlight. She thinks what the twins did was hilarious. After the laughter dies down, Melody and Mary Anne take the lead in sharing the vision of Fortress and the need of a new emphasis on reaching out to the people of the county and even the surrounding counties with an evangelistic meeting and time of prayer. As the two women share the vision of the Christian band, Starlight, River, Patrick, and Emily can do nothing but cry as details of what the vision entails is explained. All four of them know that they were snatched from the jaws of death for a reason. The ultimate purpose of their being there is being revealed to River and Patrick just as archangel Michael had shared with them. God's timetable is now for His purpose of their being there to begin to sprout. They know greater things are still to come from the Throne of God. Steve and Andy take in the moment solemnly and are humbled and moved with compassion for their older worship team members. And in their young teenage hearts, they know deep down for the first time in their lives that they are a part of something much bigger than themselves.

The elders tell the worship team how they are all in agreement that their Christian band will play a significant role in the coming meeting. The timeframe is given for the event and they are told much effort is needed in getting the word out to the people in the area. When they are finished sharing the vision, Starlight says that she has been praying endlessly for this kind of opportunity to minister outside of the church building. She shares that God has answered her prayer and this confirms to her why River, her, Emily, and Patrick were brought to Fortress. Mary Anne asks the worship team what they think their Christian band should be called. All the worship team members feel led by the Holy Spirit to allow Starlight to decide the name of the band.

Starlight says, "No, I don't want to be the one. Brenda Lee and Forrest are the worship leaders and they aren't here."

Mary Anne says, "Starlight, I know my daughter and Forrest very well and they would not have a problem with you naming the band."

"Okay, Sister Mary Anne. I'll take your word for it. In that case, I choose Butterfly for the name of our band because a butterfly represents the Christian's new birth

"Then Butterfly it is," announces Mary Anne.

Steve says jokingly, "Aunt Mary Anne, you know if I had been asked to choose a name for the band, I would have come up with a different name."

"What would you have chosen, Stephen?"

"I would have chosen Bullfrog."

Everyone says, "Nah!"

He then goes on to say, "It's the same kind of concept of transformation."

Again everyone says, "No!"

Melody says, "Stephen honey, I don't think we want to have a Christian band whose name begins with bull in cattle country. It could lead to a number of off color jokes, if you know what I mean." Everyone laughs, shaking their heads in agreement

Later on that morning, Ricky and Gary place a long distance call and finally get in contact with Dr. Ken Hagman. He is truly taken back by the call and friendliness of his two former archenemies. Hagman profusely apologizes for his behavior of how he treated them and their ministry over the course of more than two decades. Humbled by the whole experience, Dr. Hagman confesses that his TV show, *The Rapture Watchman Hour,* has been canceled due to his financial partners lack of backing because of his new position on the timing of the rapture. Ricky and Gary repeatedly tell him that the past is water under the bridge and the blood of Christ has wiped his slate clean. Hagman, all choked up with the dramatic changes in his life and ministry, confesses to his two new friends that his wife Lynn of 32 years has left him. She could not handle all the financial pressures and humiliation of his new view on prophecy. Even his son and daughter, distraught by the sudden changes, are not returning his calls. While still on the phone with Hagman, Gary whispers to Ricky about flying Hagman up to Golden Valley to encourage and minister to him. Ricky nods in full agreement.

Gary says, "Ken, I just talked to Ricky and we want you to come and stay with us in our lodge for a week during our upcoming evangelistic and prayer meeting."

Ken says, "I would love to sit down and visit with you guys. I just can't do it financially and I'm battling depression."

Immediately the Holy Spirit speaks loudly into Gary's heart to give him $40,000 of his own personal money. Gary then says, "Listen, Ken, the Holy Spirit just spoke to my heart and said to give you $40,000."

Astonished, Dr. Hagman says, "You can't be serious! Have you talked to anybody associated with me or my ministry?"

"No, we haven't talked to anyone down there in your neck of the woods. Why do you ask, Ken?"

"Because to be frank, just before you called, my CPA told me that I needed exactly $40,000 to settle all my accounts and to have money to live on for the next two months while I shut down this ministry. I haven't seen God move in my life in a divine appointment like this in a long time. If you would be willing to give me that amount of money, I would be eternally grateful. I'll hop the first plane for the week you want me to come up there and visit with you and Ricky."

Ricky, who is on the other line, says, "Gary I'll split the money with you for Ken."

Gary says, "Thanks Rick, but I'm supposed to do it."

"That's fine then," replies Ricky. "Well, Ken, we would love to have you come visit with us. I think we will have a great time together. We actually share many of the same prophetic beliefs, especially now. Maybe your wife would be willing to come."

"Ricky, I know the Lord works miracles, because a financial one just occurred from one of the last people on earth whom I thought would do it. But my wife may need a bigger miracle."

"Ken, we are so glad you see what we see in the Scriptures. Ricky and I have a lot to do now, but I'll have my wife Mary Anne call you back in a few minutes and work out all the details of wiring you the money and getting you a ticket or tickets to fly up here. All I can say is bless you and the new ministry God has called you to. Ken, we are going to go now, but you, and your wife, and your ministry are in our prayers."

"Again thanks, Gary and Ricky."

"Goodbye Ken."

"Goodbye."

"Ricky, would you have ever believed before that Dr. Ken Hagman would be coming to visit with us?"

"Never in my wildest dreams would I have even dreamed that would be possible."

Melody and Mary Anne sat in on the conversation, remaining quiet the whole time. Melody, her eyes closed and her hands interlocked as they lay flat on her head, is stunned by the whole conversation. The Holy Spirit is removing years of pent-up anger and bitterness toward Ken Hagman that, unknown to her, had been stored up in her heart from the years of false accusations he had hurled toward their ministry. Mary Anne's personality has always allowed her to easily forgive and forget wrongs done to her throughout her life. She is eager to get in contact with Hagman to wire him money and to get him and his wife a plane ticket. She hopes by getting a ticket for his wife that she might come and that it would be a time of restoration for her and Ken. The $40,000 her husband is willing to give Hagman never phases her. Money and material objects have never meant much to her personally. But she does enjoy using it as the Lord directs her and Gary. Gary, Ricky, and Melody are all in agreement with this view of the things they possess.

Mary Anne is the first to walk out of the conference room to make arrangements for Ken Hagman. As she opens the door and walks away, she bumps into Pete. He says, "Mrs. Kirkman, I'm so sorry. I should have been paying better attention."

"Oh , Peter, that's okay. I'm partly to blame because I wasn't looking where I was going either. Peter, I thought you were going to sleep in this morning with Molly."

"No, I tried, but I was just itchin' to get back to work. I'm convinced that I'm safe at least on your property and mine that your leasing from me."

"Well, praise God for that."

"Yes Ma'am, well, anyway, I have a trailer load of alfalfa hay that I figured Max and David could use. I couldn't find them so I thought they may be over here around the church office."

"No, they're not here. I believe they were looking at buying two or three goats for milking on one of the local ranches."

"Well, that's okay. I'll just ask Charlie where to drop off the hay. I just picked it up from a friend of mine and decided to give it to the ministry here for all that you guys have done for Molly and me while we were away."

"Pete, you don't need to do that, but I know everybody will appreciate the kind gift."

"Oh, it's no big deal. It's the least I can do for taking care of my place and livestock." .

"Pete, that is what true Christianity is all about - living out the principles and commandments of the Bible and taking care of each other as brothers and sisters in Christ."

"I know that now. But to be honest, I never saw it demonstrated until I met you guys when I was a kid, and especially since you guys moved here to Golden Valley. If giant pitwolves killed all my livestock and I had nothing left, it is nothing compared to my salvation and my wife's salvation as a result of y'all's love and demonstration of the gospel."

"That's true, Peter. Our salvation is priceless."

"I reckon I'll be going now, Mrs. Kirkman. Again, tell everybody thanks for all you've done."

"Oh, I will Peter. Bye now."

"Bye."

Chapter 17

THE GOLDEN VALLEY REVIVAL

Over the next two weeks a great amount of effort goes into getting the word out to the community and beyond. Brenda Lee designs some beautiful flyers and small posters that get handed out, mailed out, and put up around the county and surrounding areas. The up and coming Golden Valley Revival meeting, as the locals begin to call it, becomes the talk of the area. People are very nervous with the giant pitwolves on the loose and the other issues facing Colorado and the nation as a whole. Scary things are going on and the people feel vulnerable in so many ways.

The country folks of Golden Valley and all of Clark County are ready to call on God's mercy. Divine help from above is on everybody's minds as the only solution to their overwhelming problems. Everyone at Fortress makes numerous phone calls to let people in the area know of the meeting. Starlight contacts Nurse Amy and Nurse Taylor about the upcoming event. Both are excited about the revival and are definitely coming. Emily contacts Ivan who is still upset with her for leaving him, but says he and his wife will come to make sure she is alright. Even Emily's mom promises to come, but Emily is not going to hold her breath. But Grandma Cotton says she will pray especially hard for her to come and get saved. Emily does find great comfort in knowing that. Hope in the hearts of the people in Golden Valley is beginning to rise. But there are evil forces clamoring to put an end to the wind in people's sails of hope.

"Officer Perkins, please take a seat," Colonel Krasnev says firmly and authoritatively in slightly broken English with a strong Russian accent. He is in charge of the N. I. U. Security Forces in Boulder, Colorado. Krasnev, an iron fisted, highly decorated war veteran of numerous conflicts around the globe, has called in the young Liaison Officer from Clark County. He wants Travis Perkins to do some ground work spying on the future Golden Valley Revival and events that will unfold there. Marla had contacted Krasnev personally to find someone from the area to investigate the strange phenomenon of divine protection over Clark County and an uncommon kind of church located on a ranch in Golden Valley heading up the revival. Perkins is the logical choice for the mission.

By this time Ricky Crawford's and Gary Kirkman's names had popped up on the radar in Geneva from research done by Marla's minions. What caught her eye was that these Christian ministers not only lived in Clark County, where no smaller meteorites had struck, whereas counties around them had all been impacted, but their actual address was the town of Golden Valley - the exact location where the huge meteorite should have hit, obliterating not only the small town, but most of the county itself off the face of the earth, had it not split in two and hit Boulder and Denver. It was of great interest to her that both of these ministers had written and taught extensively on supernatural events taking place in the end times. Crawford's previous background as head of the technological cutting edge defense contractor company Spartan Electronic Corporation also caused her to raise her eyebrows.

Since the irreplaceable Dr. Von Gunten and Ci Mada's North American headquarters had literally gone up in smoke, Marla had added another task to her full plate. She oversaw what could be salvaged concerning the data on the giant pitwolves in the North American operation. A partially dual system for the data had been put into place in Geneva long before Fritz Von Gunten's demise and the destruction of the Boulder headquarters. It was a backup system that mostly dealt with the tracking of the super predators by satellites, drones, and planes. But before the meteorite in Boulder, Von Gunten had almost always called the shots on the worldwide operation.

Ironically, even in his death he called the shots and it hadn't backfired. The very thing that Von Gunten would have never done in life, he did in one last act of defiance to God, whom he hated with every fiber of his being. And the funny thing was it was achieving greater results than he had ever envisioned. Plus, only one giant pitwolf, #231, had been assumed dead as of yet, according to the data Marla had available. His whereabouts was an unsolved mystery. The batteries in the giant pitwolves' sleeper chips are activated by movement. And #231 sleeper chip has not been activated since May 7th, the day the TLZ drone and GS 33 satellite were taken out by the meteorites.

The urban legend had come to life and kept 99 percent of all hunters from hunting. But there was that extreme 1 percent out there along the highways and byways of the country seeking fame and fortune by trying to kill one of these monsters. Unfortunately, more and more of these hunters were coming up missing where giant pitwolves had been officially spotted. Most people who liked to live life on the edge and craved outdoor adventure stayed out of the woods once these animals were spotted in a given area. The film footage of the giant pitwolves in Boulder shot by Dana Williams' cameraman mysteriously disappeared the same day she had been attacked and killed, which led to numerous rumors and conspiracies.

Fear had swept across America like a death plague with the release of all the super predators. The masses of people were beginning to beg for peace and safety. This was the desired effect for those in the highest levels of the Adamic Society and exactly what they wanted to hear.

Marla's scientists and number crunchers who actually monitored the day-to-day data of the giant pitwolves saw normal patterns of activity and movement of the animals. Von Gunten had not completed all the behavior modification studies and changes in his genetically-modified beasts that he had wanted to achieve before his untimely death. But a plus for the Adamic Society was that his super predators were animals that predominately ran in packs. They were highly intelligent and learned from each other and an understanding of their environment was continually increasing. But there was a phenomenon of an unknown origin in Golden Valley, Colorado, and it was brought to Marla's attention by one of her staff members.

One of the most disturbing facts of all to her was that all the data , thermal images, and infrared photos from planes, drones, and satellites showed the super predators never penetrating the property lines of the good-sized ranch called the Double V Ranch. Also an adjacent neighbors ranch owned by a Peter Watson had no activity since the second week in June. For the month prior to that time super predators were active on the property. A number of the super predators often circled the properties, especially at night but never stepped on these two properties. She suspected either high technology or angelic protection was preventing them from going on those two properties and this she didn't like.

Travis is more intimated by Krasnev than he ever was of Sheriff Sam Barnes on his worst day when he was a deputy back in Golden Valley. Immediately his heart pounds hard in his chest and the palms of his hands become clammy, as he perspires heavily. Perkins forehead is now breaking out in beads of sweat. He has to know if he has done something wrong. He says, "Sir, if I may have permission to speak, I'm curious as to why I'm here."

The Colonel is silent for a moment and reads Travis' body language and demeanor like a book. He sees that the anxiety is killing Travis. Then Krasnev slowly grabs a cigarette and lights it with the lighter from his shirt pocket, as he relishes in the fact that Perkins is squirming like a worm on a hot summer day on a blistering sidewalk. The Russian Colonel's eyes are cold as ice and a slight sadistic grin forms on his face. He then closes his eyes and takes a long drag on his cigarette, holding the smoke for a few seconds in his lungs before slowly blowing it across his desk in Travis' direction. He responds to Perkins' question by saying in a somewhat friendly tone, "No, of course not. I have read your profile and reviewed your work as a Liaison Officer for the N.I.U. and I am well pleased."

Surrounded by a cloud of smoke, the young officer coughs a few times, then subconsciously lets out a sigh of relief while loosening the firm grip he has on the ornate mahogany arm rest of the antique chair where he is sitting. Two others just like it had been "borrowed" from an exclusive antique store in Boulder by the Colonel who had seen them while out on patrol and wanted them. The store had been partially destroyed by the blast of the meteorite impact. The owner was trying to salvage what he could of his inventory and he protested the Colonel's outright theft. Later he was taken away in the evening hours by several Security Forces soldiers under the cover of night never to be seen again.

After another very long drag on his cigarette, Krasnev repeats the process of blowing smoke toward Officer Perkins and says, "Let me cut to the chase, as you say here in America. After reviewing your profile and job performance, I have chosen you for a special mission."

"Yes, Sir. What will it entail?"

"You grew up and lived in Golden Valley most of your life, correct?"

"Yes, Sir, except for the time I attended Davidson University, which of course was almost completely destroyed by the meteorite. Only the sewage disposal plant survived."

"Yes, I know. How ironic," replies the Colonel as he quietly laughs.

Travis is more nervous now than he has ever been in his life and is not following protocol. He asks Krasnev, "Has the Mormon Brotherhood Militia formed there now, Sir?"

"No, something far more dangerous is taking place there."

"I don't understand, Sir."

"Passive resistance which needs to be halted. Also, some kind of strange phenomenon is protecting that county from which you came."

"Really? I'm confused. What do you mean? What do you want me to do, Sir?"

"Your job is very simple. We want you to go back home on paid leave. Check around and see what the people are doing to keep these giant pitwolves at bay. If anything out of the ordinary is taking place, report it to me directly. Also, when they hold this Golden Valley Revival, as it is being called, I want you to record it. You will wear these glasses. Don't worry. They have the same prescription that you are wearing now. We checked your medical history. These glasses have a microscopic camera lens embedded in the frame. Flip this switch on the side here, then these glasses will video record the entire service."

"Sir, all you are asking is for me to find out if anything out of the ordinary is taking place in Clark County and record this revival meeting? That's it?"

"That's it, Officer Perkins, along with the names of all the religious leaders of the revival."

"It will be my pleasure, Sir."

"Oh, and by the way, I have decided to give you a promotion to Assistant Supervisor of the Liaison Officers in this city."

With excitement in his voice, Perkins says, "Thank you, Sir. I appreciate your confidence in me and the promotion."

"You're welcome and here are your glasses. Guard them with your life."

"Yes, Sir."

"And one last thing, Perkins. You must fulfill your mission and report directly back to me once this religious meeting is over. I am granting you a five day pass that begins three days prior to the meeting and ends two days after. This is a paid vacation on us, on your new pay raise scale as a Assistant Supervisor of Liaison Officers in Boulder. Gather all the information you can. Is that understood?"

"Yes, Sir. Thank you, Sir."

Travis Perkins leaves Colonel Krasnev's office feeling ten feet tall. Pride swells up in his chest and he feels for the first time in his life that he is going places. He knows Fortress is behind this Golden Valley Revival, but there is no love lost for them. His own parents had a religious experience in Las Vegas while on vacation. Some man named Brother James was preaching on a soap box on the strip. Travis' dad told his much older brother Matt that he and his wife had gotten saved on their vacation years ago. Matt Perkins liked to say they got religion of all places in Sin City. Two years later when Travis was six, they decided to go on mission trip to San Francisco to a poor section of the city and witness to the lost. After a month there, they were robbed and each was shot several times and left for dead in a back alley. Travis blamed God his whole life for their deaths and never cared anything for Him. His Uncle Matt had raised him since his parent's death and had been like a father to him.

Finally the day of the Golden Valley Revival arrives. Nurse Amy Choate and Nurse Beatrice Taylor from Rock Top Memorial Hospital are making their way to the Golden Valley gym under tight security. Mayor Perkins and Sheriff Barnes don't want an incident with giant pitwolves so they had a temporary high chain link fence installed around the parking lot. A number of people are temporarily deputized for the event and heavily armed. As

Nurse Amy is stepping up on the curb, she gets a glimpse of a ruggedly handsome, powerful looking American Indian. He is a deputy with a long black ponytail hanging down his back. His features make her stumble on the curb and she falls to the concrete sidewalk.

John Blackhawk, not noticing her before, races to her aid and helps pick her up off the ground. He says, "Are you alright, Miss?"

As her eyes lock with his, something seemingly mystical and spiritual happens inside of Amy and John. She blurts out, "Yes, I am going to live thanks to you." What she says seems odd at the time.

"Well, I'm glad you're okay," John says in a sincere tone as he holds onto her left arm a little longer than normal and peers deeply into her eyes as if he is looking into her soul for answers as to who this woman is. John instantly knows from God that this woman has not just randomly stumbled into his life. He feels a strange and unusual connection to her. For the first time in a long time since his wife died, feelings of attraction for another woman are beginning to bubble up and come to the surface. The attraction he feels toward Amy is something that transcends her outer appearance even though she is attractive to John. No, it is something in the woman's soul that hold's Blackhawk's intrigue. As Beatrice grabs Amy's right hand, she is unaware of a spiritual connection that her friend Amy and Blackhawk are experiencing. Nurse Taylor tells Nurse Choate they have to hurry and thanks the officer. As Amy walks away, guided by Beatrice's hand, she continues looking back at Blackhawk and he continues to stare at her. A few seconds later as Amy is going to enter the high school, she waves to him and he back to her.

Although John has never seen her before, he knows if he runs after her and asks her for her name and number, she will give it to him. But he has a post to man as a Deputy Sheriff and John is all about duty and honor. Besides, it just isn't his style. As Blackhawk mans his post, he begins to pray for Jesus to be Lord of his life in every way. He prays, "Great Creator and the Author and Finisher of my faith, may Your will be done in my life and in this woman's life. Amen."

As Beatrice and Amy enter the gym, area they spot Sarah Barnes wearing a volunteer badge and ask her if she knows where Starlight Jenkins is.

Sarah says, "I just saw Starlight." She asks the woman if they are friends of hers and Beatrice gleefully responds, "Yes, we sure are!"

"Well, in that case, follow me." Sarah takes them to her in what is becoming a packed gym. "Starlight, look who I ran into."

"Oh, Mrs. Barnes, thank you so much."

"You're welcome. I now have to find my Sam. Have you seen him, Star?"

"I think he is talking to Caleb about security. Oh yes, there they are to the right of the stage in the back."

"Thanks, Starlight. Goodbye, girls."

"Thank you, Mrs. Barnes," reply Beatrice and Amy. All three women wave to her.

"Ms. Taylor and Amy, I'm so glad you made it to the Golden Valley Revival."

"Girl, I wouldn't missed this for the world. Just call me Beatrice."

"Ah, okay, Beatrice," smiles Starlight. "Be patient with me because it will take me a little while to get used to saying it."

Amy says, "We wanted to come and see you sooner, Starlight, but we ended up with the overflow of injured people from the meteorite impacts." She then whispers to Starlight that they are the ones who left town before the N.I.U. Security Forces came in the city. "So we have been swamped working tons of overtime. Where is your miracle boy, Starlight?"

"Oh, Beatrice, I think he and some of the others are working on the wiring for the sound system. I know he is looking forward to seeing you guys."

"I know I can't wait to see him, but in the meantime, where is the nearest restroom?" asks Beatrice.

"It's down that hallway under those banners over there."

"Thanks."

"Starlight, you guys started a revival at the hospital."

"You didn't tell me that, Amy."

"There is so much to talk about. River's miracle got everyone thinking about God. So Beatrice and I started a Bible study at the hospital and about 10 people are coming to study God's Word. The whole atmosphere at the hospital has changed."

"What about Dr. Gibson?"

"Well, his eyesight returned and now it's pretty apparent he is anti-Christian. A lot of the higher ups in the hospital want him gone but haven't got sufficient grounds yet to fire him or to move him out of there."

"Well, Amy, how are you doing, spiritually that is?"

"Things are going great and God is so real to me now. I have been studying my Bible and praying a lot and listening to Christian music. I also have been listening to your and River's CD all the time, especially your song *Amazing Grace*. It still gives me goose bumps."

"Well, glad to hear God is moving in your life and in Rock Top."

"Starlight, I know the meeting is about to start, but I hope you don't mind me asking you this. Can you tell me about that Deputy Sheriff outside who is Native American?"

"Oh, that's John Blackhawk. He's a full-blooded Sioux Indian and is single."

"You read my mind, Starlight."

"He is 100 percent sold out to Jesus and is straight as an arrow, pun intended."

"That is so cool. My dad is half Sioux and he grew up in Canada. That's where I got my black hair and high cheekbones. I sure didn't get it from my mom who is full-blooded German with blonde hair."

"I hope you're not just physically attracted to him."

"Well, to be honest that doesn't hurt. But it goes well beyond that. I fell, Star, and he came over and picked me up. We stared into each other's eyes. It seemed like we had this deep connection. Maybe it's just my imagination, but it seemed so real."

"Well, I'll introduce you after the meeting and let God do His thing."

"Thank you so much."

"Hi, Amy. So glad you could make it."

"Hi, River. I am excited about tonight."

"Me too. Hey, we'll have to catch up with you after the meeting and talk. Is Nurse Taylor here?"

"Yes, along with some other staff from the ICU."

"Great! We'll definitely get together later. In the meantime, Starlight, Caleb said Brenda Lee and Forrest want everybody in the band to get together to pray for tonight. I'll catch you later, Amy. Love you."

Love you too. Bye, guys, and may Jesus be Lord of this revival."

"Amy, was that River with Starlight?" asks a disappointed Beatrice who is breathing harder than usual as she approaches.

"Yes, it was."

"Oh, shoot," says Beatrice.

"Oh, don't worry, Beatrice," replies Amy. "River definitely wants to see you. He and Starlight will meet with us and the staff after the meeting."

"Praise Jesus, I just love that River and Starlight." Beatrice then notices someone. "Amy, look over there. Is that Dr. Gibson?"

"Oh, my goodness, it is him! What is he doing here? Beatrice, he saw the revival flyers and has a vendetta against Starlight, River, Emily, and Patrick and also for our own revival breaking out at the hospital."

"Listen to me, Amy. That fool has already been blinded by the Holy Spirit temporarily. He ain't got enough sense to know that if you play around with fire you're going to get burnt. Gibson better just back his big old booty on out of this gym while he is still in one piece."

"Without a doubt," quips Amy who continues in a laughing manner, "Beatrice, you have a unique way of speaking the truth."

Travis Perkins has been staying at his uncle and aunt's house the last few days and is asking a lot of questions around the area and about the coming revival meeting. He is finding out that his uncle's and aunt's views on life are changing. In fact, his uncle had okayed Crawford and Kirkman to hold their revival meeting in his old high school, which he can't believe. It is totally weird to him that his old hard-nosed boss had some kind of religious experience. And now his own family is coming under the same spell of the Fortress Cult. Another completely strange and ironic thing is it seems from what his uncle was telling him that Barnes and his uncle are on friendly terms. The only religious news that Travis has heard from his old liberal buddies in town is that members of Fortress are burning more incense, chanting, praying, and claiming more than ever that the end of the world is near. All of his friends have been thinking that the coming Golden Valley Revival is a huge joke.

In the meantime, Travis has had a complete turnaround on his view of his job and the N. I. U. Security Forces since his last visit home and his new promotion. He's got more clout and authority than ever and he is getting high on it - literally. Pot is looked upon by Security Forces higher ups, the same as cigarettes. What you do when off duty is your business. He also definitely feels safer from giant pitwolves in the big city than in the little town where he is from. High fences and barbed wire along with troops walking around with automatic high caliber rifles may be intimidating, but the threat of monstrous beasts attacking you basically becomes zero.

Finally, the day of the big revival comes and Travis is wearing his activated spy glasses and is one of the last people to enter the slightly darkened gym. He sits in the back row of the gym to get more of a panoramic view. He feels uncomfortable and out of his element in a religious gathering. In addition, he resigned his deputy position under humiliating terms and is now viewed by some as a traitor working for the N.I.U. Security Forces. Regardless of how uncomfortable he feels, he has his orders from Colonel

Krasnev who intimidates him to the max, to say the least.

Travis spent the previous day relaxing and trying to explain to his uncle that N. I. U. Security Forces measures at times may seem drastic but are needed in chaotic conditions when disasters strike. His uncle told him that he had been rethinking his liberal ways. Matt Perkins had been extremely upset with his nephew and told him point blank the N.I.U. had pulled the wool over his eyes. He also told him he was full of bull if he swallowed everything the N.I.U. Security Forces told him hook, line, and sinker. Matt Perkins told Travis he was not only fighting for the survival and existence of Golden Valley but Clark County and the welfare of its people. Finally the morning of the revival Matt Perkins admitted to his nephew that he needed divine help to keep it all together.

Before the revival meeting begins Mary Anne, Melody, Grandma Cotton and some other intercessors are in the girls' locker room praying fervently for the meeting. Everyone else from Fortress is either busy with their children or doing some task in or outside the gym. At 7:00 p.m. sharp Caleb Crawford announces, "Ladies and gentleman, my name is Caleb Crawford and I am the assistant pastor of Fortress. We are a Christian church located on the Double V Ranch in the southwest portion of this county. We are so glad that all of you could attend this revival meeting. On behalf of Fortress, I want to thank Mayor Perkins, Sheriff Barnes, and the Golden Valley School District for making this occasion possible tonight. There are many issues facing us today individually, as a community, as a state, and as a nation that our forefathers never experienced. We are here to offer you hope and help in a time of trouble. If you take away a man's sense of hope, he has nothing to hold on to when life becomes hard. Hope is like an artesian spring in a barren desert. Hope helps to sustain you when the tough times hit. Without hope you will dry up, wither, and perish. My dad, Ricky Crawford, and my Uncle Gary Kirkman, the co-pastors of Fortress want to extend the hand of fellowship to anyone who wants to give Jesus Christ a chance to prove who He is and what His holy Word, the Bible, are really all about tonight. They have with them on the stage a Christian minister who had previously opposed them every step of the way in their ministry for 20 plus years. The Lord has reconciled the three men miraculously." There was a small number of people in the audience who were familiar with Dr. Ken Hagman who couldn't believe their ears. "I could say a lot more, but I will leave that to these three godly men on stage tonight. In the meantime, would everyone please bow their heads while I pray. Dear God, tonight is special night because tonight is to honor you and to lift up your Son. Please grace us with your prescience and power tonight for all to see and experience. We praise you and bless you. In the name of Christ. Amen.

Now everyone is in for a treat to hear Fortress' own Christian band, *Butterfly*, perform some of their songs and renditions of old hymns. Without further ado, here's Butterfly. Everyone starts clapping. Starlight walks to the microphone with her long blonde hair shining under the lights and snapping around like a whip from her excitement and eagerness to perform. She smiles really big with her pearly white teeth as she looks over the audience and makes sure everyone in the band is in place and ready. Starlight is in an upbeat mood with much conviction in her tone as she thanks Brother Caleb. She then tells everyone, "Butterfly's goal tonight is to honor our Lord and Savior Jesus Christ. We are not here just to entertain you, but to help bring you into the throne room of God to experience His presence. She goes on to say, "Because in His presence, you will experience His joy, peace, hope, and love." We will now sing *Amazing Grace*. As *Butterfly* begins to worship in song, the Holy Spirit instantly sweeps over the entire audience like a mighty rushing wave. Old boot-leather tough ranchers and farmers and their families succumb to the strong but gentle presence of the Holy Spirit and eventually begin to weep uncontrollably. A seemingly holy sovereign work of God is taking place before everybody's eyes. But in reality, is the result of endless hours of intercession by holy saints on bent knees pleading for the hearts and souls of the men, women, and children of Clark County and the surrounding counties. Travis Perkins is beginning to become restless in his seat. From a distance, he can see his uncle and aunt begin to wipe the tears from their eyes. Beatrice Taylor is quietly thanking Jesus over and over again. Her friend Amy has her hands over her face crying out repenting of previous unconfessed sins as her makeup is smeared and running down her face. Emily spots Ivan near the front with his wife's head on his shoulder wiping her tears with a tissue. Tears are streaming down his face. Emily, seeing her mother, Cindy, in the fourth row, almost loses it on stage where she is singing and playing the tambourine. Cindy appears not to be totally or even partially stoned for a change, which is a miracle in and of itself when she is not working. To her daughter's surprise, she is repeatedly wiping her eyes while waving to Emily.

Mrs. Good is also wiping her eyes with a clean handkerchief her son-in-law Pete handed her. She repeatedly tells her daughter Molly, "I don't know why I'm so emotional. I've heard the Tabernacle Choir sing this song many times before in person."

Molly leans over and says, "Mom, it's a work of the Holy Spirit that God is doing in your heart."

Dr. Ken Hagman, who's in complete awe, leans over and tells Gary that he has never in his entire life felt the conviction of the Holy Spirit so heavy on him.

Gary says, "Me either." Gary whispers to Ricky what Ken said, and Ricky replies that he hasn't either.

Originally Ricky was going to preach tonight with a message on evangelism and the need for prayer. He had been praying and preparing a message for a solid week in anticipation of this meeting. But God has other plans for the night and tells him so. As *Butterfly* is leading the people in the gym into a time of deep worship, the atmosphere is supernaturally and spiritually charged. Anticipation of what is coming next is on everybody's minds, and no one knows really what to expect. A Holy reverence toward God overrides the fleshly desires and sinful thoughts of the masses. After 45 minutes of the band bringing a bit of heaven down, Brenda Lee and Forrest sense the Holy Spirit wants the band to stop. So they nod to each other and the other members of *Butterfly*. As the last song comes to a close, the members silence their voices and instruments. There is complete silence in the gym and nobody is moving.

After a short time, Ricky quietly walks over to Gary and says, "You are supposed to take the ball tonight and run with it."

Gary never flinches because he has sensed they same thing. He approaches the podium with no planned message, but he has a strong unction from the Lord. Gary is usually more reserved than Ricky and usually likes to just teach. But tonight, as soon as Ricky turns the meeting over to him he feels a strong desire to preach instead. The anointing of God is all over him like a thick, warm oil. He just knows for a fact that the Holy Spirit is going to move in a big way tonight. After an hour and a half of some of the most anointed fire and brimstone preaching, along with a dose of end times prophecy and pleading with the masses to follow Jesus, Gary wipes a steady stream of sweat from his forehead, face, and neck. It seems the fear of God has gripped the whole congregation. Some of the bodies of the young and old alike are shaking from the fear of the Lord that is upon them. Gary walks to Ricky and is preparing to pass the spiritual baton to Ricky for the altar call. Many in the gym are wailing because they know if they die now they will go to hell and they are scared. Ricky was originally going preach tonight and Gary was going to give an altar call when the Holy Spirit halts him again dead in his tracks.

Without a doubt he hears the Holy Spirit say loud and clear in his spirit, "No, let Ken do it!"

Ricky instantly turns to Dr. Ken Hagman and says, "Brother, I have never heard the Holy Spirit speak more loudly or clearly than just now. He told me that - you are the one to offer an invitation to the people tonight to accept Jesus Christ!"

Ken Hagman, always articulate and never at a loss for words, looks stunned momentarily. He points his right index finger to his chest like he can't believe what he has just heard. Ricky gets out of his chair nodding his head yes and whispers into Hagman's left ear. The former host of *The Rapture Watchman Hour* has his well-worn KJV Bible, one of the trademarks of his show, in his left hand and grabs his dress pants in the middle behind his back along with his belt and gives it a quick, strong tug. He walks slowly but confidently to the podium while Gary sits down still wiping the sweat dripping from his face. Ken Hagman carefully places his tattered, black, fine leather-bound Bible squarely in the center of the vintage solid oak podium. Ken takes his time looking down at his Bible, hesitating for a moment, then rocking his upper body back and forth over the podium numerous times, he prays silently. He then grabs both sides of the podium and gradually leans back. He is both empowered and humbled by the Spirit of God at the same time for the task ahead. After he scans the whole gymnasium for several seconds, he begins speaking as a broken man with great conviction - not the glib and polished speaker as he usually appeared on his TV show. It takes much effort on his part to spit out the following words. "Of all the people in this gym, I am the most unworthy person to give this altar call tonight." He wipes several tears from the side of his right eye. "But I will comply with my spiritual brothers' wishes and more importantly the Holy Spirit's desire." After five minutes of sharing a salvation message from his heart and numerous scriptures, he pleads for the people to surrender their lives to Christ and to ask him into their hearts and receive eternal life. He says, "If that is you, please stand to your feet now. Don't wait another moment. Do not hesitate." At this point almost everyone in the gym stands to their feet. It seems as if the only exceptions are those that are already Christians. Travis Perkins is intentionally resisting and wrestling with his own reasoning as to why not to stand up. Chief of those thoughts is fear of what Colonel Krasnev would say and do to him. But it literally takes everything within him to remain seated.

No sooner does this happen than Hagman turns around quickly with a look of astonishment and confusion in his voice as he whispers to Ricky and Gary, "Didn't I make it clear as to what I wanted the audience to do if they wanted to accept Christ? Am I dreaming or something?

Smiling, Gary replies, "Ken, they heard what you said. They all want to get saved. Relax and proceed with the invitation. Then Dr. Hagman leads the entire congregation in the sinner's prayer. Again silence fills the school's gym as the masses stand with tears running down their solemn faces. Upon completion of the prayer, Ricky walks over and pats the shoulder of Hagman, who is staggering under the reality of what has just happened. Almost everybody in the gym got saved.

Ricky whispers to Hagman, "Ken, I think what just happened qualifies this as a real revival."

"Ricky, I didn't really do anything special. This is a God thing."

"Yes, indeed, Ken. It is a God thing. I need to borrow your microphone. The Holy Spirit is prompting me to do something."

"Sure, Ricky." Hagman then walks over to Gary, who is just shaking his head in pure joy of the amazing move of God he is witnessing.

Ricky announces, "Mayor Perkins, would you please come up here? I see that you and your wife are two people who chose to ask the Lord into your hearts amidst a sea of people tonight who decided to accept Christ into their hearts." At this point, Travis is almost beside himself realizing that the outcome of this revival will not be good for his uncle, his fellow townspeople, and himself. His uncle by blood had replaced his dad and his aunt was like his mom. He could not and would not betray the two most important people on earth to him. He then secretly takes off his glasses and turns the switch to off.

"Please come up here and share about your decision tonight to accept Christ." Matthew Perkins always loves to be in the limelight whenever possible, but the strain of all the events the last month has taxed the limits of his health. His blood pressure has skyrocketed, even with his medication, and the lack of sleep has taken its toll on him physically. As he and his wife walk up the steps to share their testimony, he collapses and drops to the stage floor like a rock.

Immediately, his wife screams, "No, Matt! Not now, Matt! No!" Caleb Crawford is nearby and no sooner has he started checking him over than Dr. Gibson rushes on stage and declares he is a medical doctor. Caleb immediately gives him access to the mayor. Mrs. Perkins, in an almost hysterical shaky voice, volunteers the information that Matt had forgotten to take his blood pressure pills today. "On the way to the gym tonight, he remembered he had forgotten to take them. But he refused to turn around and get his pills." Her husband didn't want to be late and he had insisted that he would be just fine. But now it appears that his heart has stopped and Gibson is performing CPR to no avail. EMTs have rushed on stage with an AED machine, but Matt Perkins cannot be resuscitated. What has been an unbelievable event is finishing on a very tragic, sad note. Dr. Gibson, after several valid attempts to resuscitate him, still cannot detect a pulse. There is nothing else that can be done and the doctor officially announces that Mayor Perkins is dead.

During this time, having seen his uncle fall to the floor, Travis Perkins runs from the back of the gym to the stage and is looking over the lifeless body of his dear uncle. Deep depression descends on Travis, as a knot forms and begins to tighten in his stomach.

Ricky Crawford, sensing God's presence and power all over him like he has never known, says in an anointed, authoritative voice, "Yes, the mayor is dead; yet he will he live again." He ordered everybody to stand back and see God raise this man from the dead.

By this time, Sam Barnes, Forrest, and Blackhawk have made their way to the stage. Everyone in the gym is standing in total disbelief about what has just occurred. Dr. Gibson, with hate and anger rising up in his heart, screams loudly, "I have officially declared that this man is dead. Please stop with the mindless religious theatrics!" He orders the EMTs to remove the mayor's body from the gym.

Starlight rushes over to the doctor, grabs him by the arm, and says, "Dr. Gibson, stop! Before you regret it! God will not be mocked!"

He responds in a nasty, low voice, "No, you stop, young lady and get your hands off me now! What happened to me at the hospital had nothing to do with your fictional, so-called Christian God judging me. It was purely a medical condition that caused my temporary blindness."

The EMTs start to pick up Matt Perkins' body when Sheriff Barnes, his teeth flaring, orders them with a deep growl, "Back off, boys! Let Brother Ricky do his thing."

The two EMTs look at each other, shrug their shoulders, and step back two steps, leaving the mayor's body alone. Travis is trying to console his grieving aunt the best he can under the circumstances. His mind is in overload and it all seems surreal to him. Gibson frantically screams at the EMTs to remove the body from the gym, but the two hometown EMTs don't budge because they know better than to cross Barnes.

Ricky, under the divine direction of the Holy Spirit combined with firm conviction and faith, loudly proclaims, "Mayor Matthew Perkins, I order life to come back into your lifeless mortal body now in the name of Jesus Christ of Nazareth. Your heart is healed in the name of Jesus. Arise, for your appointed time to die has not yet come." Everyone in the congregation looks at each other immediately because they know in a few seconds Brother Ricky Crawford is going to be either a hero or a zero to them. Suddenly, Matt Perkins' eyes begin to flutter rapidly, and then within seconds they are wide open. From a lack of oxygen, his body has turned a shade of blue, but now miraculously his skin color is quickly returning to normal. All the people on the stage, except Ricky and Gary, are startled and take a step backward in total disbelief. Dr. Ken Hagman, with his Baptist background, can't believe what he is seeing. Travis almost trips and falls over his aunt's foot because of the miracle that he sees.

Travis' aunt says, "Matt, you're alive," and faints, her body going limp in her nephew's arms. The whole congregation gasps as a holy fear of the Lord seizes everyone's heart. No one is more startled than Dr. Gibson, who falls straight backwards for no apparent reason and hits the stage with a loud thud. He now seems to be motioning with his hands that he cannot see nor talk. As the EMTs quickly begin attending to him, they keep looking back at the Mayor moving around, which is scaring them to death.

People across the gym are experiencing a range of emotions and thoughts. Some people are saying this really must be the end of time. There are comments like, "No one will ever believe what happened tonight unless they were here."

Others, freaked out because the mayor had turned blue, ask each other, "Did you see the mayor's freaky blue skin? He was deader than a doornail."

An atheist who came to the revival just because of all the hoopla is now saved and is heard saying, "I never ever thought I would see a miracle like this tonight of a man being raised from the dead. It's right out of the Bible."

An older woman and follower of Dr. Hagman announces, "If Dr. Hagman has joined up with Fortress, then these ministers must be of God."

Wyatt Banks, the all star running back and captain of the Golden Valley High School football team, and his girlfriend Bobbie Jo Morgan, captain of the cheerleading squad, both know the mayor is really risen from the dead and this is no act. Wyatt declares to all his teammates, Bobbie Jo's fellow cheerleaders, and other friends seated nearby that he is going to start living for God because He has proven He is real to him. All of their friends are in 100 percent agreement.

Burt Collins, the biggest rancher in the area and a close friend of Mayor Perkins, put the Golden Valley Revival meeting into perspective with his comment to his wife. Burt, who has a reputation of being an ornery cuss, turns to his wife Emma of forty-one years and says, "Honey, I have literally had the hell scared out of me tonight. We're gonna start going to Fortress for church starting this Sunday morning."

Emma, also shaken to her core, says, "I second that motion."

When Mayor Perkins finally stands to his feet, the congregation erupts into thunderous praise, whistles and handclapping. Wyatt Banks goes berserk and starts yelling at the top of his lungs, "God is real! God is real! God is real!" repeatedly. Immediately, his classmates join in, followed by the whole gymnasium. For about five minutes, the people in the gym are in a frenzy shouting praise to God for His supernatural miraculous power and this life-changing, unforgettable night. Ricky tries several times to quiet the people down.

Finally Gary comes over, smiles, and says, "Let them go, Rick."

Ricky smiles back and nods. After a while, the shouting subsides and Ricky raises his right arm motioning for silence. He is finally able to talk to Matt Perkins, who has been hugging his wife and nephew.

Ricky announces to the crowd that he wants to ask the mayor what happened. Everybody immediately gets quiet. Ricky says, "Mayor Perkins, exactly what happened to you a few minutes ago?"

The mayor, in a subdued and humbled way, replies, "Well, Brother Ricky, I asked Jesus Christ into my heart to forgive me of all my sins and to be my Lord and Savior like Dr. Ken Hagman explained it to us all. Then, when I came up here on this stage, I suddenly felt an excruciating pain in my chest and then fell flat out dead, with no more pain. If you have any doubt, let me tell you, make no mistake about it. I was dead."

Ricky then asks, "Did you experience anything, Mayor Perkins, while you were dead?"

Perkins pauses for a second, then says, "All I know is that I came up out of my body, I guess in a spirit form, and looked down on my dead body. I saw the EMTs and the doctor working on me. The next thing I knew, I was in heaven."

"You were in heaven, Mayor?"

"Yes, Bro. Ricky - heaven, without a doubt. It was no dream. It was as real as you and the other people in this gym."

"Tell us, Mayor, what it looked like."

"I'll try to describe it, but I just won't do it any justice. Anyway, I always thought I was blessed to live in Golden Valley because this place is so beautiful. But heaven makes this paradise on earth look like a dump. Heaven is so much more beautiful and peaceful. I just can't describe it with colors, words, or pictures. It's just breathtaking."

"Mayor Perkins, who did you see there?"

"I saw Jesus and He just emulated love, kindness, compassion - everything good. He told me He loved me and was glad I had accepted Him into my heart before I had a heart attack and died. He said that you, Bro. Ricky Crawford, had been told by the Holy Spirit to call life back into my dead body. Jesus said the Father wanted you to do this because I had to go back to Golden Valley. There was more work to be done here. I told Him, 'Jesus, I love it here. I don't really want to go back to earth, but if You want me to go, I will. Because in my mind I knew my wife, my nephew, and the good people of this county needed me. The next thing I knew, I was looking up from the floor at you, Bro. Ricky."

"Wow, this is incredible, Mayor, just incredible." Praise to God fills the gym for several minutes. When the people settle down, Ricky asks, "Gary, do you have a question for the Mayor?"

"Mayor Perkins, I have a question that's on everybody's mind. Are you afraid of death now?"

"Absolutely not! I look forward to it now. For my whole life up until this point, the thought of death scared the dickens out of me. Not any more at all."

"Wow, Mayor, that is good news to hear for all of us who have accepted Jesus," declares Ricky, who then starts shouting, "Hallelujah!" repeatedly. Everybody starts clapping loudly, and shouts of 'praise the Lord' and 'thank you, God' could be heard echoing in the gymnasium.

It is a night that will never be forgotten for all those that that are there. The meeting keeps going until a little past midnight, as Ricky and Gary have decided to pray for people's individual prayer requests. Also, Caleb and Ken Hagman keep praying for the needs of the people, along with Melody, Mary Anne, Ashley, Brenda Lee, and Grandma Cotton who were standing in line next to the men. The band members of Butterfly are praying for the young adults and teenagers in the crowd at the opposite end of the gym. River and Starlight immediately bond with Wyatt and Bobbie Jo, who seem to be the ringleaders and who have so many questions about God and the Bible. Emily leads her own mother to the Lord and Patrick leads Ivan and his wife in the sinner's prayer. At first they resisted Ken Hagman's pleas and invitation to accept Christ. But now that they have seen the Mayor raised from the dead, it has blown away all their doubts and reservations about accepting and following Christ. Caleb also begins sharing the Gospel with Travis who is under great conviction of the Holy Spirit and also the fear of man in regards to Colonel Krasnev. To his uncle and aunt's delight, he can no longer refuse to taste and see that the Lord is good and gets saved. The masses keep standing in line and no one is willing to leave the gym before talking to a minister or someone from Fortress and asking for individual prayer.

God's Spirit has moved mightily upon Amy Choate's heart during the service. She has repented of sins in her life and rededicated herself to Christ during the invitation. But she has another agenda to fulfill before she leaves for the night. She feels awkward about it, but she wants to meet the deputy who helped her when she fell down outside the gymnasium earlier. Even with all the miracles she has seen tonight, the deputy has also been in the midst of her thoughts. Something deep within her heart has convinced her that her fate is intermingled with his. As she approaches Blackhawk, fear of rejection begins to plague her mind. Her imagination is running wild and negative thoughts begin to creep in like a bad CD repeating the same line over and over. Is she just physically attracted to him for some reason? Is it because he is an Sioux Indian like her dad? Although her dad was only half Sioux, she had inherited his high cheek bones, raven black hair, and a light shade of red skin. She had always admired these features of her father, whom she loved dearly. Or is this thing that she is feeling something of a

355

more spiritual nature? Amy just has to find out the truth. Finally, she gathers enough nerve and decides to go for broke. She eases her way over to John in the crowd and introduces herself to him.

Unknown to her, Blackhawk has been thinking similar thoughts of why he felt instantly attracted to her. When he recognizes her, a small smile graces his rugged face. As they shake hands, Amy thanks him again for helping her up from the sidewalk before the revival started. It's an awkward moment for Blackhawk and he comes across a little stiff and shy. He is grappling with a variety of emotions flooding his soul and thoughts of Dena. He loosens up a little and tells her his name is John Blackhawk and that it was his privilege to help her. Amy presses on through the tenseness of the situation and allows her radiant and gentle personality to emerge. She tells John that she is a nurse at the same hospital as the doctor who had tried to resuscitate Mayor Perkins earlier. She apologizes for his behavior.

John simply states, "It is what it is. There is no need to apologize for the doctor's behavior. His own tongue speaks what is in his heart. The Bible declares that out of the abundance of the heart the mouth speaks." Amy, not sensing rejection from him and impressed with his spirituality, also recognizes an inner strength and peace that emulates from him. She now feels comfortable and protected around him like she can trust him. Blackhawk loves her shiny, straight, black hair that is parted in the middle and hangs down past her shoulders. He also enjoys her friendly, attractive face with the warmth of her brown eyes and the sincere soothing sound of her voice. They make his knees feel weak and heart beat strong. The only other female that had ever made this happen to him before was his dearly departed sweet wife Dena when he first met her when they were teenagers. He knows there is more to Amy Choate than just another pretty face. Amy tells John that she is a nurse and friend of Nurse Taylor, who left earlier to follow the EMT's ambulance to Rock Top Memorial Hospital to admit Dr. Gibson. Amy also says she is a friend of Starlight and River and talks about the revival at the hospital that started there with River's miracle. In their conversation with one another 30 minutes has flown by before either one knows it. During their conversation, Caleb Crawford intentionally walks by John and Amy twice when he has a moment between praying with people. He winks at Blackhawk who sees him, but pays him no attention. As the night is coming to a close, Sheriff Barnes comes over and tells Blackhawk he needs him to take the Frank's family home, whose SUV isn't starting. Amy is able to get John's email address just before he has to leave unexpectantly.

Sheriff Barnes is a changed man since surrendering his life to Jesus six weeks earlier, and tonight has taken him to a whole new level. Until recently, the Mayor was a huge pain in his neck. Perkins has been under strong conviction of the Holy Spirit for the last two weeks. But tonight, in a matter of minutes, he has surrendered to the Holy Spirit, gotten saved, died, gone to heaven, come back into his body, and is again alive. The events of tonight have finally allowed them to bury the hatchet. Their long-time feud is officially over and Perkins and Barnes have embraced each other as brothers in the Lord. By 12:30 AM all the ministers, Butterfly band members, and everyone who came to the revival meeting are exhausted, sweaty, packed up, and ready to leave. But inwardly, they are energized because their faith has been rejuvenated. Little do they know what will soon follow.

After the revival meeting Travis Perkins travels home to his aunt and uncle's house in their dual cab pickup. Travis had worn the glasses given to him by Krasnev to record the event. He had been on an emotional roller coaster during the revival right up until he got saved at the meeting. After accepting the Lord into his heart, he became more relaxed and noticed he was no longer wringing his hands. In addition to that, thoughts of "I'm dead man" or I'm a dead man walking" are no longer continually running through his mind. Peace like he has never known is flooding his soul. He knows that Colonel Krasnev will not be happy with the results of the revival. Neither will he like it that his uncle was at center of attention at the end of the night. But Travis has concluded these events were beyond his control.

No one had any idea how successful the revival would be, including Ricky Crawford and Gary Kirkman. And since Travis' uncle was miraculously raised from the dead, Travis knows he cannot go back to Boulder to his old job as a liaison officer. What exactly the future holds for him is uncertain, but in the midst of it all, a gentle peace is slowly washing away his fears and anxiety. The fear of death is leaving him as he listens to his uncle and aunt talk about their experiences all the way home. Upon entering the house from the garage, his Uncle Matt lets it be known to his aunt that he needs to talk to Travis alone. She says she understands. After going to the home office, his uncle closes the door behind him. Young Perkins does not know exactly what to expect. His uncle tells him, "There is something I didn't tell anyone tonight about going to heaven."

Travis ponders what he means by that for a second and says, "Well, what was it, Uncle Matt?"

What Mayor Pekins is soon to reveal to Travis is a huge jolt to his mind and is hard to process. "Travis I want you to hear this alone and straight from my lips. Listen, son. I saw your mom and dad!"

"You saw my mom and dad in heaven?"

"Yes, and they looked the same as the last time I saw them. Each appeared to be around 29 years old and were so happy and peaceful. They know you are saved and told me to tell you that they love you."

"Uncle Matt, wait a minute. This I know for sure. You were dead. I saw it with my own two eyes. Your face turned a shade of blue."

"You think I was dreaming, don't you Travis?"

"I, I, can't say for sure, Uncle Matt." Tears begin to stream down both cheeks. "But, I would give anything to see them. I think you had some kind of out of body experience. I just don't know."

"Travis. Listen, son. All your life you have known about my glass left eye."

"Sure, but what is your point?"

"Look at it now!"

Travis studies it for a moment, looking puzzled. He says, "It looks different, Uncle Matt, like...ah..."

"Now, Travis, move your hand back and forth."

Oh, my God, you are tracking my hand with your glass eye! How is that even possible? You are moving it. Wait a minute, your eye is real, isn't it?

It's freakin' real! I've got chills running up and down my spine. I can't believe your left eye is freakin' real! God performed two miracles for you tonight, didn't He, Uncle Matt?"

"Yes, He did, Travis. Now will you believe me when I tell you I saw your mom and dad?"

"Yes, Uncle Matt, I believe you! There is a real God in heaven! There's no doubt that He is good! I believe you! I believe you were in heaven and saw my parents. I have hope now that I will see them again."

"You will, Travis, my boy. You will. I promise you!"

Chapter 18

COUNTING THE COST

It is 2:20 AM in the morning at the lodge back at Fortress. All the elders, Caleb Crawford and his family, Brenda Lee and Forrest, Grandma Cotton, and Ken Hagman are still up. Everyone is exhausted but on a spiritual high and can't go to sleep yet. Hagman is trying to sort through all that has been taking place in his life and his head is spinning. He just wants to be alone at this time. He has retired to the guest bedroom for the night. The rest of the Fortress family is pumped and celebrating what God did earlier in the night in the gym. Everyone is reliving the unbelievable events of the night when the landline phone in the lodge rings.

.

Somewhat surprised, Melody says, "I wonder who is calling our private number at this late hour. Very few people have that number."

Ashley says, "I don't know, Mom, but I'll get it." She walks to the nearby kitchen and picks up the phone.

A frantic voice with a delicate southern accent on the line says, "Hi, my name is Lydia Hagman. I am so sorry to call at this extremely late hour, but I cannot reach my husband on his cell phone. May I please speak with Ken if he is available?"

"Can you just wait one moment, Mrs. Hagman?" asks Ashley, as she places her right hand over the phone's speaker and shouts, "Can someone knock on Dr. Hagman's door and tell him his wife is on the phone?"

Ricky knocks on his door and says, "Ken, it's your wife on the land line. You can take the call on our office phone down the hall."

Hagman, who has been awake reading his Bible and praying, says, "Thanks, Ricky." Still dressed, he walks down the hall to the office. He picks up and phone and immediately says, "Hi, Honey, I love you." Lydia Hagman had not returned any of his calls or emails since he decided to come to Colorado. It had deepened the wedge between them that seemed to be polarizing their already strained relationship.

In response, Lydia says, "I love you too, Ken." Mrs. Hagman states that she doesn't understand all that has happened in their lives. She knows God is working in their lives and she is just confused. She tells her husband of the incredible footage of the Golden Valley Revival she has just witnessed tonight on VideoAlbum. A close friend of hers had sent her a link of the revival along with a startling call about the revival and Ken's role in it. After talking with her friend and viewing the revival footage, she tells him that she is totally astonished and amazed about the peoples response to Ken's altar call in the revival. So she decided to call her husband even though it is so early in the morning. She tells him that so much change has taken place in such a short time - the reversal of his life long view of the timing of the rapture, the loss of his prophecy TV show, and now trotting over halfway across the country and staying with former prophecy teachers he had vehemently opposed in the faith.

Also, with Isaac Cohen at the helm of the presidency and the ferocious giant pitwolves on the loose, it was enough to send her over the edge. But now that she has seen that almost everyone in the gymnasium got saved in the Golden Valley Revival meeting, she knows God must be mightily at work in Colorado. She begs Ken for forgiveness and for reconciliation because in his time of desperate need, she fled to her brother's house in Atlanta. Hagman's pride has long deserted him by now and he gladly accepts her apology. Dr. Hagman then apologizes to her and asks her to trust God for all the abrupt changes in their lives. He reassures her that God is indeed in charge of their lives as long as they surrender to His Lordship. As the conversation comes to an end, they are talking to each other as if they are on their first date. God's fan of forgiveness is helping to rapidly rekindle the flame of their love for one another that was in the process of dying. Then after about half an hour, Ken tells Lydia to stay at her brother's house for now until he knows exactly what the elders of Fortress want to do in the coming days. Before he hangs up, he tells her he loves her unconditionally and she tells him the same. Ken then tells her that he will be in close touch with her and keep her abreast of the latest developments. After Ken hangs up with his wife, he goes and tells his Fortress friends that God has done a great miracle in his marriage. They are so glad to hear the good news. Then Hagman drops a bombshell on everybody about the revival being on VideoAlbum and how 325,000 people have already viewed it.

At 8:02 AM Eastern Standard time the day following the revival, President Cohen signs an executive order making it a federal crime for certain local, state, or federal buildings or property to be used for religious meeting purposes other than funerals and short sermons performed by federal authorized chaplains at the different levels of government and the military. This new law also extends to any organization, institution, or school system that receives any kind of federal money, grants or aid. Since the devastating meteorite impacts on Boulder and Denver, he has been signing new executive orders at an alarming rate. The majority of Americans are either too apathetic or too caught up in their own busy lives to notice numerous changes in the law. Only true Bible believing, born again Christians who know the signs of the times are keeping tabs on the rapid changes regarding new laws affecting their religious and other former constitutional freedoms.

Never once in the signing of the executive order does Cohen mention the Golden Valley Revival as the reason for the executive order going into effect. But every believer who has a chance to view the revival on VideoAlbum knows exactly why the executive order has been signed into law.

At around 8:30 AM the next morning Caleb Crawford is reading his emails. The second one he opens from a Disciplemaker pastor has a link on the new law. Caleb is the first to tell his dad and uncle the unbelievable news. Both Ricky and Gary immediately know the revival has struck a nerve with the powers that be. They also know there will be further retaliation for the move of God in Golden Valley. So their course of action is to call an emergency conference telephone meeting with all the senior pastors of every Disciplemaker church in the country and around the globe and as many of the churches' leaders as possible at 10:00 AM their time. Gary gets Brenda Lee to send out an email to all Disciplemaker pastors and to follow up with a call. As the Crawfords and Kirkmans meet later in the morning for the conference call, they decide to include Ken Hagman in the group. His contribution is God ordained, and now he is entrenched in a spiritual battle that links them together.

The two landline phones in the church have been ringing off the hook all night and there are too many messages to count. Endless reporters want interviews, multitudes of Christian ministers and layman from around the world want to talk to the leadership, and there have also been some very nasty and mocking comments left on the answering machine and emails. Brenda Lee calls and talks to all the Disciplemaker pastors that she can get a hold of on the semi-private landline in the office of the Lodge and leaves messages for the rest.

Earlier that morning when Ashley showed up at 6:30 AM, still exhausted from the late night revival meeting, she listened to a huge backlog of phone messages. Most of the general questions ranged from, "Did Mayor Perkins actually die?" and "Was the Mayor really raised from dead?" A large percentage of the calls people left dealt with the question, "Did almost all the audience really get saved?" Others asked, "Was this the beginning of a national revival that has broken out in Golden Valley?"

Also, earlier in the morning Caleb made some rounds on the property and found a total of five people trying to drive onto the property. He locked a chain around the gate to keep strangers from driving on the property. Because some were more persistent and tried to walk on the property, he had to call Sheriff Barnes, who came out and had to stand guard at the entrance to Fortress with Blackhawk and Leon Wilson standing guard. Charlie and Tommy Wilcox are also on duty walking the grounds of Fortress. In addition, Barnes has three new acting deputy sheriffs safeguarding the mayor's house. One is former Deputy Sheriff Glen Stump who's in charge, whom he has a lot of confidence in and trusts. He had gotten sworn in for security prior to the revival in the high school gym. Sarah rode over to Fortress earlier with Sam for her protection and well being and is now helping Ashley take phone calls in the church office. Ashley has just finished putting Gary's, Ricky's and Ken's comments on the revival from last night on the Fortress website at about 7:30 AM. Brenda Lee also came over to help out with answering some of the thousands of general emails concerning the revival. By 9:15 AM, because of the high traffic Fortress' website has been receiving, it is experiencing some glitches. Ricky has his high tech friends, Max Bruno and David Shilling, working frantically to upgrade the level of the ministry's website so it can handle the unprecedented hits.

In the midst of this chaos, one of the most important things that the elders and Hagman are focusing on is trying to reach the newly saved in the area with the basic tenets of the Christian faith. They have concluded that a massive mail out of Gary's small booklet entitled *Getting to Know God and His Word* is needed to arm the citizens of the county with some basic Christian doctrines. It will help them lay a solid foundation of orthodox Christian beliefs and answer a lot of people's questions about God and their new Christian faith. They also want Caleb to head up a visitation program of church members to personally meet and greet everyone who came to the revival and filled out a visitor's card, giving them the ministry's latest newsletter and a free Bible if they didn't already have one.

The Golden Valley Revival far exceeded what they had even hoped for or even imagined. Unless Fortress launches a concerted effort, the newly saved will be like sheep without a shepherd and will scatter. The elders aren't going to let this happen come hell or high water, but at the moment, they are swamped with important decisions to make.

Grandma Cotton has been gently given her marching orders by Melody and Mary Anne earlier to recruit any able-bodied person who had a free moment to pray about the situation at hand. She recruited Mrs. Stanton and Leon Wilson's wife DeDe who are leading intercession in the prayer room with three other people in there. Grandma is going to lead a second group in prayer at around 11:00AM to relieve the first group. Everyone else is tied up with jobs and other responsibilities on the property.

From 10:00 AM to 10:45 AM the elders have their emergency meeting with almost all the Disciplemaker pastors and all the leadership at Fortress except for Blackhawk and Forrest. It is a short meeting where Ricky and Gary emphasize the need to be vigilant and tell their pastors that not only is God on the move, but so is the devil. Gary closes out the meeting by telling them, "Don't get sidetracked and don't lose focus. Keep majoring on the things we have always focused on and God will bless you and be pleased."

They are also told about the new executive order Cohen passed in an "unofficial response" to the Golden Valley revival. They are told that the elders believe revivals will break out in their churches, so be ready for an unprecedented move of God. All the pastors comment that they are really excited about the Golden Valley Revival and so are their members that had already heard about it. Some had even seen it on VideoAlbum and were blown away. Each senses and agrees that revival will soon be coming their way and all definitely know that stronger governmental and demonic opposition against the work of God will ensue.

When the meeting is over, Ricky tells Caleb and Ashley to oversee the answering of people's calls and emails. The elders, along with Ken Hagman, decide they need to shut themselves off from the world in the conference room to seek God's wisdom on how to proceed. Gary suggests they all pray individually and try to get the mind of God. After one hour of solid praying, Gary asks Melody first what the Lord is speaking to her. She says Starlight's and River's names keep coming in her mind for some unknown reason. Mary Anne has a surprised look on her face as she agrees.

When Ricky's time comes, he says, "For some odd reason, I am impressed by Holy Spirit that we need to go get Starlight and River and bring them to the meeting."

Gary says, "I've thinking about them, about when they first came here and what their purpose is for being here. How about you, Ken?"

"Well, you guys know I'm not from a charismatic background, but I've been seeing images of a star and a long flowing body of water flashing through my mind, but it didn't make sense until now. All I can say is who am I to question God being God?"

"Well, Ken, we're all glad to know that God has been moving in your life in new ways." Amens can be heard from everyone.

A knock is heard at the door and Max and David pop their heads inside. Max says, "Guys, we're sorry for bothering you, but we just found out that the video of the Golden Valley Revival has been removed from the VideoAlbum website. David and I were watching it after taking care of our overloaded computer network system in the church office when the screen just went blank. Now you can't pull anything up about the revival on the internet. It's like it never happened last night."

"Well, I'm not surprised," says Melody in a sarcastic tone with a slight smile on her face as she shakes her head. "The devil is up to his old tricks."

David speaks up, "I'm sure Cohen had one of the people in his administration call about the revival and put just a little heat on the VideoAlbum people and that was the end of the story."

"No doubt," says Ricky in a perturbed voice, "But we will still have the victory in Christ. Something great has been set in motion here in Golden Valley last night by God and the devil is highly upset. Thanks guys, for the heads up."

"Okay, Rick," is heard from both Max and David as they leave.

Melody says, "Well, I think we have our work cut out for us, but I know the Lord is on our side. The other bit of good news is that it seems clear that the Lord has confirmed it in all our hearts that we need to talk to River and Starlight. They may know what our next step in the Lord is going to be. I'm going to go get them if we are all still in agreement." Everyone says yes! Within fifteen minutes, Starlight and River return with Melody to the conference room. They are spiritually pumped from last night. Both assume that the elders want to talk to them about the revival last night from talking with Melody. She didn't want to guide them in what to say when they came to meet the others, so she kind of made chit chat with them. Melody allows Starlight and River to go in first. When Starlight enters, she looks radiant like she is glowing and flashes a pretty white smile before saying, "Good morning. I guess you guys were like us and had a hard time sleeping last night." Everyone says good morning.

Ricky is the first to individually address her and says, "Yes, we were all having the same problem, Starlight."

As Starlight and River sit down, River speaks up, "I still can't get over the events of last night. I heard earlier this morning from Bro. Caleb that we can't use the high school gym anymore and that 570,000 people have seen the revival on VideoAlbum."

"Yes, both those things were true just a while ago, River, but the last number we heard was 1,280,000 people have viewed it as of thirty minutes ago. About twenty minutes ago Max and David told us that VideoAlbum removed the revival video. and that it is no longer available."

"Oh, wow! That makes me so mad. God was at work last night in the gym in a big way. Why was the video taken down?" asks a highly upset Starlight who's brilliant smile has vanished instantly.

"We don't know exactly. All we know is that it was taken down by some powerful people who had the VideoAlbum personnel to remove it and try to snuff out the effects of what happened last night."

"That's not right! That's just not right!" shouts Starlight.

"I don't care who they are. We can't let them do this and get away with it. What happened last night was an amazing, powerful move of God," announces River in a frustrated, angry tone.

"You're absolutely right, River," responds Ricky. "And God impressed upon all our hearts to bring the both of you here to give us some insight as to what we need to do in response to that situation. So let me ask you guys, what do you think God would have us to do in response to VideoAlbum taking that video down?"

River spoke up, "I feel like in my spirit that God wants us to have a bigger revival and pull out all stops."

"Yeah," says Starlight who's highly irate and ready to get radical. "Let's have an event called Woodcross!"

"What are you talking about, Starlight?" Melody asks smiling, very curious as to what she means.

"Ah well, it just popped into my mind. I just kinda blurted it out."

"Then the Holy Spirit must have just put it there," laughs Mary Anne.

"Well, I guess what it means," replies a less agitated Starlight, "is what Woodstock was to the liberal young people of America in 1969. Let's make Woodcross be a spiritually defining moment for our country, a bigger event than even the Golden Valley Revival."

"Well, Starlight, you know what happened last night was a big time miracle," declares Melody smiling.

"Oh, there's no doubt about that, Sister Melody. What each of us saw and experienced was the supernatural power of God being released like none of us has seen before. But because of the times we live in, I think that was just a taste of more to come. Kind of like on the Day of Pentecost when 3000 people got saved, it was just the beginning of something that grew and got a lot bigger."

Gary speaks up, "What our young brother and sister have said rings true in my spirit. I believe we have heard from God through them today. Last night was just a start of something much bigger that is to be birthed here in Clark County. If the Lord is in this, then I believe Fortress becomes a launch pad for a great move of God that reaches to the far ends of the earth."

"Amen," replies Mary Anne. "I know for a fact that Starlight and River want to see a great move of God like the rest of us. I have seen them both bombarding Heaven with prayers and tears for hours in the intercessor's room for God to move in a mighty way here in Golden Valley. They started doing that as soon as they got here." Mary Anne asks Starlight, "What do you propose that Woodcross be or consist of?"

"Well...ah, I know. Let's build a giant wood cross out of two huge pine trees on this property, then hold a huge revival on the property somewhere and with the Lord's help start a true Jesus Revolution in the 21st century."

"I love River's and Starlight's radical idea," says Ricky. "How about you, Ken?"

"It sounds real sweet to my ears, Rick."

"How about you girls?" asks Ricky.

"It sounds great and radical to me, Ricky!" says a fired up Melody. "I believe River and Starlight are speaking the mind of God concerning this matter."

"Count me in," adds Mary Anne.

"What do you think, River?" asks Gary.

"Well, in the words of my hippie grandfather, I say it sounds really groovy."

Everyone snickers and says, "Groovy!"

Ricky enthusiastically says, "Gary, Melody, Mary Anne, Ken, and I know we are all on the same page about this Woodcross Revival. Again, I believe in my heart that the Golden Valley Revival last night, as crazy as it sounds, was simply to lay a foundation for something bigger and better that the Lord wants to do, like Starlight declared. Woodcross has to take place here, right on this God ordained ground. With that being said, let's not forget that our adversary, the devil, is going to up his game. We must be spiritually on guard and ready because the forces of hell are going to come against us with a vengeance like we have never seen before. We've already seen a taste of that with Cohen's new executive order and the removal of the Golden Valley Revival video from VideoAlbum.."

"Bro. Ricky, can you tell Star and me more about that new executive order as far as what it all means?" inquires a surprised River. "Caleb didn't have time to fill me in with all the details." Starlight has a curious look on her face.

"Oh, sure guys. Let me fill you in. Cohen signed into law this morning through an executive order that any government buildings on the local, state, and federal level that receive federal money basically can't be used for religious purposes, except for authorized funerals with federally approved chaplains to perform the services. We all know that as a public school, Golden Valley High School receives federal money. So that eliminates us using that facility again."

"Bro. Ricky, I'm surprised how fast things have developed overnight," states Starlight.

"Well, apparently the signing of this executive order was a very low key event this morning. We have a Disciplemaker pastor who has a connection in D.C. and we got an email from him this morning from him. We also found out it will be more publicized later this afternoon. So, Starlight, when you mentioned using the Double V Ranch for holding the Woodcross Revival, it rang true to my ears."

"It sounds like the revival got under Cohen's skin and got him peeved," remarks River.

"Yes, him and some others of like mind with power and great influence. Well, now, let's get back to our game plan." Ricky turns to his friend Gary of many years and looks him square in the eyes and says, "How about you, Gary? Are you ready to host Woodcross?"

Gary staunchly replies, "100 percent! Absolutely!"

Ricky then asks Mary Anne, who confidently says, "I know I was born for such a time as this!"

Ricky then slowly turns to his wife Melody who says, "It's full speed ahead!"

He looks at Ken, who says, "Bring it on!"

Ricky then looks at River and says, "How about you, River?"

River, with a commanding voice, says, "There is no turning back now!"

Finally, Ricky looks deep into Starlight's blue eyes and she says, "Bro. Ricky, I have decided to follow Jesus. There is no turning back. The world is behind me and the cross of my Savior is before me."

Melody asks, "Honey, how about you?"

"I say, let's follow God's lead and get His end time show on the road so He can display His great power and glory and that multitudes will be birthed into the Kingdom of God."

"Starlight, I'm curious. What are you are thinking now?" asks Gary.

"I feel like painting, Bro. Gary."

"Why painting?" inquires Gary.

"It's something I told River some time ago that I wanted to repaint the peace sign on the outside of the tire cover on the back of our VW van with a painted white cross and now have it say 'Give Jesus a chance' on top of the circle and the word Woodcross at the bottom of it!"

"That sounds groovy to me, Starlight," laughs Ricky. For the next half hour the spiritually on-fire elders, Ken Hagman, and young radical Christian couple relive last night's miraculous revival meeting and discuss some of the steps that need to be taken care of before Woodcross can become a reality. They also talk about buying the old huge tractor supply warehouse off of Main Street in Golden Valley and using it to hold teaching classes and services for the new Christians in the area.

Later after the meeting with River and Starlight, Mary Anne and Melody explain to Brenda Lee, Ashley, Caleb, and Sarah about the new revival. Everyone is ecstatic about preparing for another bigger revival and getting the huge tractor supply building for a new church facility. Caleb, who had been in the building many times with his grandfather, the Big Swede, years ago, knows it has great potential.

Everyone loves Starlight's idea of a giant wood cross being erected on the property. Brenda Lee gets really excited. When she hears the story of Starlight wanting to repaint the back of their van's tire cover with a cross instead of a peace sign with words, 'Give Jesus a chance' and Woodcross, she loves it. She thinks it is retro and really catchy and decides to incorporate it into her posters and flyers. Melody asks Sarah to round up any available help to start making envelopes with Christian materials for those that attended the revival. The last thing they will put in them are the flyers of The Woodcross Revival as soon as the elders set a time and give more details to Brenda Lee to complete the layout and make copies.

At 1:00 PM, the elders make the hard decision to disclose that Fortress is divinely protected and that giant pitwolves are no threat to anyone who attends the Woodcross Revival. They also want to put in all their announcements, flyers, and posters a warning. The warning will consist of telling the general public that they are not liable for the health and welfare of anyone or any group who decides to come to Fortress and try to disrupt and oppose what God is doing there. The elders also meet with Caleb, Ashley, and all available deacons about Woodcross and the things that need to be ordered and put into place for the upcoming revival.

Ricky, Gary, and their wives finally disclose to Hagman all the details about the archangel Michael and the people of Fortress who have interacted with him and have seen miracles and an army of warrior angels that surround the property of Fortress. Initially, Hagman has a hard time digesting the disclosure of all the angelic intervention that has taken place and can't believe his ears. But he knows for a fact giant pitwolves aren't on the Double V Ranch where the church is located. Everyone who lives at Fortress, works on the property, and goes to church here are totally at ease on the property. Off the property this is not the case because he has even seen the elders scanning their surroundings constantly in search of the savage pitwolves. Under the weight of evidence of what he knows and has seen, he finally comes to the realization that his Baptist theology can't explain all that is taking place in Golden Valley. Dr. Ken Hagman knows from years of studying Bible prophecy that strange and supernatural things are going to take place in the end times on the part of God dealing with His people and world and the same with Lucifer. Hagman, on the other hand, always thought he wouldn't be around to see it take place. He simply decides to just trust God and to again revaluate his biblical understanding of the Scriptures. One thing Ken Hagman knows positively is that Ricky and Gary are very godly men with sharp minds who walk in integrity. They have not only won his respect but also his trust, unlike some men he has known in the ministry. He leaves the meeting when it is done and has a long conversation with his wife, asking her to please come to Golden Valley. She agrees wholeheartedly.

At around 5:00 PM in the afternoon, Brenda Lee and Forrest again meet briefly with the elders. Then, just before dinner, they meet with the *Butterfly* group members down by the lake in the lighted gazebo. They tell them that since last night a number of churches, including some very big ones, have contacted the ministry and want them to come and perform. All the band members are already floating on a cloud and can't get over what happened last night. Brenda Lee and Forrest announce to the group that they are going to be praying about what the Lord wants them to do along with the elders. But, in the meantime, they are staying put because there is something very huge planned on the property. All the band members are wondering what it could be. River and Starlight are busting at the seams, but they have been asked not to say anything until Brenda Lee and Forrest reveal it to the band. Starlight has been especially so excited that it has been hard to contain it all day long. Forrest stresses to everyone in the band to pray harder than ever and to keep practicing their instruments and songs. They also disclose that the elders are planning a bigger revival meeting on the property in two weeks called The Woodcross Revival, with a giant wood cross and they will be performing there. Brenda Lee tells the members that River and Starlight came up with the idea and that she and Forrest are beyond excited about it and are so proud of everyone. She then goes on to explain to the band that thousands of people could be coming. At first all the band members think it's a really cool idea.

Then Emily starts weeping quietly, then start bawling very loudly. Her whole life she has felt she has been in a dark dungeon and now God has thrust her into an undeserved position of honor. She was lost and now she is found - a formerly depressed, petite, poor, friendly, pretty girl from a little town called Mountain Top, Colorado. She was once bound for hell but is now saved and a citizen of heaven. Orphaned by a dead-beat dad and a drugged- out mom the last few years of her teenage life, she has now come to know her Heavenly Father through her Lord and Savior Jesus Christ. She was a waitress in a declining run down diner two months ago, and now she is in a Christian band that has been cast in the national spotlight literally overnight. She is now surrounded by a multitude of people who really love her. In the short time she has known Patrick he has been her soul mate and the best friend she has ever had. He reaches out his hand to hers and grasps it firmly. Emily holds his hand and continues wailing before the Lord, baring her soul before Him. She quietly speaks the words, "I'm so unworthy, Lord. I am so unworthy," continually. Patrick is also feeling unworthy and is feeling the weight of responsibility on his shoulders as a good soldier of Jesus Christ. He and River were given a glimpse of the other dimension in which God operates along with His messengers, His angels. Why he was chosen by God to have the archangel Michael appear to him and reveal supernatural things has often run through his mind. Now he is a part of something divine in nature and God ordained. He trusts the elders of Fortress and their vision. He knows *Butterfly* is a major reason he is here, and of course, Emily whom he secretly loves but has never told her. What happened last night was a cause much bigger than himself. He didn't want to blow it and decided last night as the Spirit of God fell that all glory belonged to God and to Him alone.

The Holy Spirit falls on each member one by one and in a short time they all begin to cry. Weeping for sins presently and secret sins of long ago forces them to wash them in the blood of the Lamb as they silently confess to Him. Steve and Andy dreamed of fame in their young foolish teenage hearts last night at the revival as supernatural events started to unfold. Now God begins a surgical process of removing those foolish desires by the power of the Holy Spirit. Each member of *Butterfly* feels the Holy Spirit all over them like a jumpsuit. The Spirit of God is squeezing the dross of their sins out of them like a person squeezes toothpaste out of a tube. Steve and Andy cry unashamedly as they lie prostrate on the floor of the gazebo. They cry so hard and so long that they become like dead men. When all the crying subsides, Brenda Lee checks on her younger cousins. They have not fallen asleep, but the Holy Spirit has done such a deep work in their hearts from that day forward they are never as silly minded as before, and they take their walk with the Lord more seriously than ever.

A mighty revival is coming and God will not share the glory with anyone.

Forrest tells everyone in the group that he shares Starlight's vision that Fortress could be at the forefront of ushering a huge spiritual awakening in this area that could impact the United States and possibly the world. He tells the group, "You know as well as I that this ground we are standing on is holy ground. Brother Gary, Sister Mary Anne, Brother Ricky, and Sister Melody set something in motion years ago that was God ordained with their biblically-based ministry, church, lifestyle, teachings, and the Disciplemaker Network of churches. You all know you are here because of a divine appointment. *Butterfly's* purpose is to help people to experience the refreshing presence of God and to praise Him at a level they have maybe never known before. We help set the stage for our ministers to teach and preach and for the presence and power of God to fall on the people who have assembled." Even the usually wise cracking brothers, Andy and Steve Crawford, are silent for a change and are listening intently to the wise words that Forrest is speaking to the band.

Emily had started the time of weeping they all had experienced and had been growing by leaps and bounds in her new faith. Now bold in the Lord, she says, "I think we've got the devil on the run and I'm loving it."

Patrick is amazed at Emily's boldness and how much she has grown in the

Lord, leaving him both shocked and proud of her. He feels ever more confident that he is exactly where he is supposed to be concerning the Lord's will for his life. His parents were really relieved when they found out their only child had not been killed when the meteorite destroyed a large section of Boulder. They begged him to return to the safety of their home in an upper class suburban area of Philadelphia and continue his studies in pre-med at the University of William Penn. He refused and dared only to tell them a small portion of how he ended up in Golden Valley. Telling his parents about his visitation from Michael the archangel and other miraculous events would be a big mistake. Both his unchurched mom and dad are convinced their son has lost his mind and has been brainwashed by a cult. He sent a text to both of them early this morning hoping they had seen the video last night somehow and would call him. But, as of yet, he has received no response. He continually prays for them and is grateful that Emily has linked arms with him with a deep burden to pray for them.

Brenda Lee, who learned from the time she was a small child to be sensitive to the Holy Spirit, feels Starlight and River need to say something. "Starlight, River, I feel God wants you guys to share something with the band."

Starlight says, "Yes, thanks, Brenda Lee. I want everyone here to know that River and I love each and every one of you. We have never had such good friends as you. In fact, you guys are the brothers and sisters we never had. It is truly a privilege to be here in Golden Valley for such a time as this. That's all!" She starts crying and leaning over on Brenda Lee's chest, as Brenda Lee gives her a sisterly hug.

"We are all thankful that you and River are here, Starlight" She gently pats Starlight on her shoulder. Brenda Lee then asks River, "Do you have something to say, River?"

"Yes, I do. I feel in my heart that *Butterfly* is a team effort. Everyone has a role to play and to make a contribution. What happened last night was a group effort and not just Starlight's amazing voice. There are a lot of great Christian bands in this country with incredible singers and musicians. But our little group has something that no voice coach or music teacher can teach and no one can manufacture.

"What's that?" asks young Steve Crawford.

River replies, "It's the anointing of God on our music. It transcends our natural ability to play music and to sing."

"That's exactly what my grandfather said last night talking to my Dad after the revival," remarks Andy. "That's it. He told my Dad that the anointing breaks the yoke. The anointing of God is what this band has on it."

Forrest quips in, "I hate to go, but as you know we have been having issues at the entrance of the church property. I'm sorry, but I need to get back to my deputy work for Sheriff Barnes." Everyone says goodbye to him. Brenda Lee shares some more with them and closes out the meeting in prayer.

Later on in the evening, Brenda Lee's mom asks if she has the time to email all the Disciplemaker pastors and ask them to please try to attend the Woodcross Revival that they have decided will be held two weeks from today on Saturday at 1:00 PM. All their plane tickets would be paid for along with their spouses and the money would come out of Ricky's and Gary's own pockets. They just need to confirm if they can make it. The elders had come to a consensus that travel may soon be restricted and this might be the last time they can meet as an alliance of churches.

Just as Bro. Ricky and Bro. Gary have suspected, all the phone calls coming into and out of Fortress are being closely monitored and reviewed by the Cohen administration and probably the Geneva headquarters of the New International Union. Ricky believes his old rival in the high-tech arena, Wolfgang Martin, has the technology to eavesdrop on Fortress' communications. The reality of the situation is that it is true.

Any significant new developments coming out of Golden Valley were reported to Marla who would relay the message and directives to General Hagel at the N.I.U. Security Forces Global Command Center in Geneva. It was no secret to anyone high up in the military industrial complex that the former Spartan Electronics Corporation's CEO Ricky Crawford was a devout, born-again Christian. That was common knowledge, along with the fact that he sold his business for a rumored 100 million dollars and financially rewarded long-time employees. Upon selling his business, he went full time into ministry with his best friend, high-powered real estate attorney Gary Kirkman. Wolfgang had once met Kirkman with Crawford at a defense contractor party in Washington D. C. and had known he was a major stockholder and Board of Trustees member of SEC. Martin also knew that both of them gave him the creeps and made his skin crawl. They were the two most no-nonsense Christians he had ever been around. These two Christians gave him bad vibes and he couldn't stand being around them any length of time. With all that had taken place around Clark County and Golden Valley, Martin had earlier arrived at the conclusion that they were tied in with the God of the Bible and He was the source of supernatural protection over Golden Valley and Clark County. They were interfering with the plans of the Adamic Society.

At 4:33 PM Mountain Standard Time, Colonel Krasnev receives a phone call from his commanding officer General Hagel at the New International Union Headquarters in Geneva, Switzerland. He says, "General Hagel, so good of you to call me, sir. To what do I owe this great honor and pleasure?"

"Cut the sucking up, Krasnev. We have a mission for you to complete and if you fail the Adamic Society you will be counting icicles inside your prison cell in the summer time in Siberia."

"Yes, General," replies Krasnev in a seldom heard nervous tone.

"Krasnev, have you reviewed the plan we sent you half an hour ago concerning what your men are to do when this Woodcross Revival takes place in Golden Valley?"

"Yes, I'm thoroughly familiar with it. The plan will be carried out to the smallest detail."

"It better be because higher ups in the Adamic Society want to eliminate this Christian Revival virus in Colorado from spreading. The flame of Christianity was dying down in the United States and now this outbreak of religious fanaticism and mass hypnotism has people believing that dead people can come back to life."

"Yes, I know, General. You are right."

"Krasnev, it has taken the society decades to try to eliminate God out of people's lives in America and to try to get them to focus on the pleasures of this world. Your mission, Colonel, is to cut off the head of this Christian snake in Golden Valley. When this occurs, the rest of the snake's body will die. This cult or church or whatever you want to call it there has to be eliminated. Their prayers have to be stopped! Krasnev, there is too much at stake. We are hoping that this so-called revival will bring together many of the highly religious and radical Christian vermin, young and old, so we can put them out of their misery, if you please, all at the same time. Your job is to kill every infected Christian man, woman, or child there and have your men stack their dead carcasses to the ceiling in unmarked semi trucks and dispose of them in an old abandoned rocky quarry with caves 75 miles west of Golden Valley on the map I have emailed you. Krasnev, have I made myself perfectly clear?"

"Yes, General. I will not fail you in this mission."

"I promise, Krasnev, your head will roll if you screw it up. Are you sure you know, comrade, what the Adamic Society expects of you?"

"Yes, sir, I understand clearly."

"Then goodbye."

"Goodbye, sir!" For several minutes Colonel Krasnev ponders the demands placed upon him. He knows there is no second chance for him if the mission fails. In addition to his mission, Krasnev has a personal score to settle with Travis Perkins who resigned his position by texting him as of 1:30 AM last night. He wants to personally give Travis a 9mm 115 grain FMJ bullet from his pistol right between his eyes the next time he sees him, but only after watching him beg for his life.

The night before The Woodcross Revival *Butterfly* band members have been practicing for two hours at the church when Brenda Lee and Forrest decide to call it a night. "We are sounding great," says Brenda Lee in a confident manner.

"I think *Butterfly* will be in top form with these new songs River and

Starlight just wrote for the revival meeting," notes Forrest.

"I believe we are sounding good," says Patrick with a smile.

"I believe so too," agrees Emily.

Andy has changed a lot since almost two week ago, but he still likes to joke around. He confidently says, "We might be too good!"

"How is that possible, Andy?" asks an inquisitive Emily.

"Well, we might knock them dead like we did the mayor at the last revival."

Quickly Steve quips in, "You have to admit, my brother has a point. We don't want to be liable if someone dies and is not raised back from the dead."

"I tell you who's going to be dead if they keep it up," grins Forrest at the boys while waving his right fist at them. They both just laugh back at him.

"Hey, Brenda Lee, did your dad or Bro. Ricky ever figure out who released that video of the revival on VideoAlbum?" inquires River.

"No, they haven't."

"Well, have they found out who took the video off of the Internet?" asks Starlight.

Brenda Lee speaks seriously, "No, but somebody high up with a lot of clout, power, and money didn't want it on the Internet."

"You got that right," says Patrick with a little disgust in his voice. "Because it got at least 1,280,000 plus hits before it was yanked."

"I still can't believe it went so viral in such a short time," says Emily, smiling.

Forrest adds, "What happened at the Golden Valley Revival in the gym was truly miraculous and incredible. But tomorrow is going to be another very interesting day. I'm just wondering what the Lord could possible do to equal that revival or to surpass it?"

Chapter 19

BAPTISM OF FIRE

At the break of dawn on the morning of the Woodcross Revival, Caleb decides to get in a quick run on 'The Trail' as his grandfather called it at the Double V Ranch. His running has become inconsistent with the planning of two revivals basically back to back. This run is not just another run to try to maintain his exercise routine but really more to just try to clear his head and enjoy the beauty of nature around him. The threat of giant pitwolves attacking him on his run is non-existent because of the angelic protection that surrounds the hallowed grounds of Fortress. This greatly eases his mind. It is a privilege most American running enthusiasts can only dream about at this time. Casually venturing into the woods for most Americans has become a thing of the past as giant pitwolves are being spotted all across the United States. Actual citings of the dangerous predators combined with ever-increasing rumors have created an almost mystical creature in the minds of most people. Caleb knows the evil eyes of one or more of the genetically modified beasts are possibly lurking in the forest possibly on him during the run. As a child, Caleb always viewed Golden Valley as a very special place. Especially the Double V Ranch, not just because his mom grew up there and his grandparents lived there. But, also because of its breath taking beauty. It has always made God seem more real to him than any other place on earth. Also, because prayer goes forth on the property 24/7, there is a peace unlike anywhere on earth that he has encountered. With his dad, Uncle Gary, Sheriff Barnes, and Blackhawk encountering the warring archangel Michael on the property, it only reinforces what he believes about the land of his forefathers. As the assistant pastor of Fortress, he is doing a lot of the grunt work for his dad and uncle. But for the two men he respects and loves the most in the world, it truly is a labor of love.

His main job for the Woodcross Revival was to oversee the building of the 100 foot high cross and erect it on the rocky area of the Double V Ranch. Two old, tall ponderosa pines were felled, cut to size, one piece 115 feet long the other 40 feet, then debarked, notched with a chainsaw and four holes drilled. Charlie Wilcox found the perfect spot to dig a two-and-a-half-foot-wide hole with an auger and extension on the back of a tractor. Still a lot of the work was done by hand widening the hole. River, Patrick, and Charlie's son Tommy also took turns expanding the hole 15 feet down with shovels. It took a total of eight days to do all that plus hoist the 40 foot log up horizontally into place and secure it with four one-and-a-half-inch bolts three feet long, washers and nuts, a long one-inch steel cable wrapped around both pieces in an x fashion and secured. A total of five yards of concrete was needed to secure the base of the cross. The biggest cost factor was the need for two 40-ton all-terrain cranes and the biggest cherry picker they could find to enable Charlie Wilcox and his son Tommy to secure the poles into place with bolts and nuts. The cranes were needed to stabilize the massive cross while concrete was poured and some large rocks placed into the 15-feet deep hole. Four one-inch cables and pre-poured concrete anchors with steel eye hooks also helped secure the cross and stabilize it. It also took a full day for the concrete to set up properly. When the wood cross, which was 100 foot high and had a 40 foot cross piece, was finally stabilized with additional supports bracing it at its base, everyone at Fortress clapped and cheered. Everyone who saw the huge cross thought it looked awesome and was inspired by it. Another of Caleb's tasks was to find huge generators and powerful lights to rent and enough fuel to run the lights way into the night if need be. This equipment was finally delivered yesterday and put into place. The other important job was to find 100 portable potties to rent because they were not sure how many people would show up. After many trials and tribulations, they were delivered and set up yesterday after lunch.

Although Caleb loved growing up in Southern California, this family property in Golden Valley has always been a place where he had roots going back four generations. He feels a kinship to the land and it always seemed like home when he visited here on holidays and vacations in the summer growing up. As he runs, he begins to dwell on the fact that the only thing missing in his life is his older brother Joshua who was two years older. Joshua always excelled at everything naturally. Caleb had always looked up to his older brother. Joshua was blessed with pure raw athletic ability and a very high IQ. Caleb worked hard at achieving success both on the football field and in the classroom. But athletics and academics for Joshua always came easy, real easy. In his senior year of high school Joshua made 1st Team High School All-American as a tight end and many believed he was headed for NFL greatness. He was 6' 5", naturally strong and powerful at 250 pounds, fast and agile just like his grandfather, the Big Swede. In school he excelled with a 3.92 GPA with hardly ever bringing a book home to study in upper level courses. When it came to catching the football, his abnormally massive glue-like hands never once fumbled in a high school game. But a freak knee accident in a pickup game of basketball after the football season in high school derailed any hopes of that dream. His two favorite college football teams, USWC and Colorado A&M, rescinded their offers of scholarships upon hearing of the nature of his injury. In the end, he chose the Air Force Academy's offer of appointment and set new sights on being a pilot like his dad. He had attained a pilot's license at the young age of 16 which had made his dad proud. But halfway into the academy, for some unknown reason, his eyesight changed and he no longer had 20/20 vision to be able to fly in the Air Force. Raised in a strong Christian home, Joshua had believed if God closed one door he had a reason to and that he would open another one. Joshua then set his sights on a career in military intelligence. It was this career path that would eventually lead to his mysterious death or disappearance as Ricky always referred to the incident. After serving as a senior Air Force intelligence officer who rapidly achieved the rank of major, he was recruited to use his skills in other capacities. He worked with various U.S. intelligence agencies specializing in anti-computer espionage. During his last assignment Joshua never revealed who the agency was, or rather he couldn't. Even with all his military and political connections, he could not get any leads to crack the case. The last time Ricky had seen Joshua in person he was able to squeeze out of him that his work entailed some kind of Russian sting operation on the West Coast. Two weeks later Joshua's black mustang was found 100 yards below the road and hidden by the tree line of a rugged north California mountainside. No guard rails on the two-lane mountain highway had added to the hardship in trying to find him. When the car was discovered the passenger side door was barely hanging on and completely open, with Joshua's blood smeared all over the interior bucket seats. His driver side door was caved in from the car tumbling down the mountainside. Also found were three bullet holes in the broken glass window of the driver's side. Had Joshua been executed by Russian agents? Was it possible that Joshua's wound or wounds were superficial and he fled the scene for his life and had been in hiding? Was Joshua still alive after the accident and removed from the car at gunpoint, or was he in a daze and wandered off into the woods and died? Four days of heavy rain before the car was finally found had washed away any physical traces of tracking him. It had also washed away any hope the Crawfords had of locating their son. After trying every conceivable way of finding him and exhausting $350,000,00 in a six month search, Melody and Ricky placed the ordeal in God's hands. The disappearance of Joshua had haunted the Crawfords for years.

While running on the trail, Caleb is in deep thought about his brother when about halfway through his run, he is startled. Not since he laid eyes on his first giant pitwolf back in the box canyon has he been taken aback by what he has seen. Standing in the middle of the trail is a 10 foot angel in a flowing white robe. He instinctively knows he poses no threat to him, but on one hand he wants to bow down to him but decides against it. Caleb stops running and freezes waiting for the angel to speak.

The angel, radiating love, peace, and joy, says, *"Caleb, my name is Gabriel and I am here to give you a message from Almighty God the Father of all those who have repented of their sins and have believed in His Son Jesus. He has sent me here to tell you that He knows your thoughts and has heard the prayers of the saints at Fortress and in Golden Valley and across the globe. The purpose of this coming revival is to help those who have been chosen in this last generation on earth to stand firm in the Lord. Tomorrow they will receive a baptism of fire to strengthen them for the hard times ahead. Only those who stand firm will be baptized by fire. Your enemies will experience the strong arm of the Lord. Woe unto them who oppose the one and only true living God and His anointed ones. I must go now in order to carry out the sovereign will of God."*

"Wait! Wait, Gabriel!" shouts Caleb. Immediately he kicks the ground in frustration with his running shoe and says, "I wanted to ask, what did you mean God knows my thoughts? What do you mean stand firm and baptism of fire?" But the angel Gabriel vanished in an instance. Still frustrated but armed with fresh revelation from God, Caleb quickly runs to tell his parents and his aunt and uncle the news.

"Starlight, it's Amy."

"Hello, Amy. It's so good to hear your voice."

"Yeah, the same here. Starlight, I know today is a really big day and you have a million things to do. But I wanted you to know I've tried to get over to Fortress since the revival meeting in the gym. But quite a few medical personnel have resigned lately because of the continual overtime we are having to work at the hospital due to the high number of those injured by the meteorites. It has been extremely physically demanding and emotionally draining to say the least."

"Well, that's okay. I understand, Amy," responds a sympathetic Starlight.

"But, Starlight, God is moving in this hospital in a wonderful way, especially the last few days. The hospital is so different now, especially since Dr. Gibson resigned due to health reasons."

"Amy," asks an inquisitive Starlight, "Did he ever regain his eyesight or speech?"

"No, it appears the judgment of God fell on him and there is no reversing his situation this time I believe."

"That's scary, Amy, but I think we all know he brought it upon himself."

"Yeah, I know, Star. You tried to stop him at the Golden Valley Revival. But on a more positive note, a small number of people have been saved here and are growing in the Lord."

"That's the kind of good news I like to hear, Amy. Praise the Lord!"

"Yea, I'm enjoying going to work now days even though the hours have become seemingly unending."

"Hey, Amy, before I forget there is something that has been bothering me for some time."

"What's that, Star?"

"Is it true some of the badly injured in Boulder and Denver were taken away to some place and still haven't returned?"

"Yeah, I've heard something about that, but I'm not sure. I think it is just a rumor. But what I can tell you is that everybody who was injured in the meteorite strikes that I've met either drove or had someone drive them to our hospital from Boulder. No ambulances ever brought anyone to our hospital, which I thought was kind of odd. All I know is our hospital is filled to capacity."

"Amy, I'm going to pray for extra energy and peace for you and the staff."

"Thanks, Starlight. We all can use it."

"Sure, I promise. Amy, I read in your last email that you said you might not be able to come to the revival. I hope you can make it today."

"Oh, I'm coming, believe me. I was finally able to work it out. I traded being off today with a friend who needed to be off another day."

"What about Ms. Taylor? Is she going to make it?"

No, she can't make it. She just came down with an inner ear infection yesterday and her balance is off. She said her head is continually spinning and she has a hard time walking."

"I wish she could make it. River and I love you guys so much."

"She's upset she can't make it, but she has vertigo and her stomach is queasy."

"Well, I understand. Tell her we will be praying for her here at Fortress."

"I will tell her you guys asked about her and are praying for her."

"Amy, you're not also calling concerning the email you sent me about John Blackhawk, are you?"

"Well, I kinda… am. Yeah, now that you mention it."

"I thought so."

"Starlight, I emailed a letter to John. Has he said anything to you or anyone about me?"

"No, but Forrest told me John had told him he felt a strange connection to you, like a moth to a flame."

"Well, I like hearing that, but I was hoping he would email me back. What's the deal with John?"

"Amy, John doesn't go for all the mushy stuff. He truly loved his wife and two kids. And I think for one thing, he feels guilty about having feelings for another woman for some reason, even though she died a couple years ago. Amy my suggestion to you is to take it slow or you'll push him away. He is about as strong a Christian man as you are going to find. Forrest said Blackhawk is fearless and doesn't crack under pressure. But maybe this connection he feels for you scares him if that makes any sense. My advice to you, Amy, is just to approach your relationship with John slow."

"Star, for someone so young, you make a lot of sense. Well, I've got to go and get ready to come to Woodcross. I am so pumped, I can't wait. God is going to doing something special today. I just know it! God bless you girl. Love ya!"

"The same here, Amy. Looking forward to seeing you today. I'm praying today for you guys and the whole service."

"Thanks, Star! Bye."

"Bye, Amy. We love you, Ms. Taylor, and all our Christian friends there at the hospital."

Emerging from the bathroom after taking a shower with his robe on, River inquires, "Star were you on the phone with someone?"

"Yeah, it was Amy and she is coming."

"Cool. How about Ms. Taylor?"

"No go. She has vertigo."

"Star, that's not funny."

"I wasn't trying to be funny. That's just how it came out. You know I love Ms. Taylor."

"Yeah, I know. She is a blessing."

"Guess what, River?"

"What?"

"John Blackhawk is attracted to Amy."

"Yeah, I knew that."

"You what?"

"John told me he feels a connection to her, but he is dealing with some stuff."

"I didn't know you and John were that close."

"Oh, yeah, and John is cool with a great sense of humor. Besides, us ponytail boys have got to stick together."

"Oh, get of here, River, with that ponytail boys stuff. Wow, then what I told Amy was right on."

"What stuff was right on?"

"That Blackhawk probably is attracted to her, but is still dealing with some issues with the death of his wife."

"Yeah, Star, that's it in a nutshell. Oh, I forgot to tell you that the elders want to meet with the band for about 30 minutes of prayer before the revival begins. Hey, by the way, Star, I've been getting a lot of comments in town about the cross on the back of the van and about giving 'Jesus a chance.' Hopefully people will turn out. I hope people believe the flyers, posters, and announcements that no giant pitwolves will come on this property, or no one will show up. Isn't strange not one news crew has come out here to do a story on Woodcross?"

"Yeah, you're right. I hadn't even thought about that. But Ashley told me she has gotten emails from as far away as New Zealand and Norway that people are coming."

Fortress has become a beehive of activity, especially with the arrival of almost all of the Disciplemaker pastors and their wives, along with some seasoned intercessors, church leaders and close friends of the ministry. Fortunately for them, they are able to house most of them in the new barn, as it is called. It is a new, huge metal building that originally was going to serve multiple purposes. The inside of the basic structure had just been completed with plumbing for water just as spring arrived. It is providing livable conditions with ac and heat in half of the building. It has two good-sized male and female locker rooms with five sinks and five toilet stalls in each and a functional moderate-sized kitchen area and den like area with basic furniture. The rest of the barn is wide open space and empty. The elders had also kicked around the idea of housing people during the Tribulation in the building, but they didn't advertise that possibility. A local contractor and his crew had been brought in just after the Golden Valley Revival to help speed up the process and put the finishing touches on it. At the moment, it was housing about 120 people each night who were sleeping in sleeping bags that many had brought, pallets of blankets, cots, and air mattresses and whatever other kind of bedding they could find. Ricky and Gary told everybody at the last Wednesday night church service that the brothers and sisters staying in the barn were roughing it. Everybody just laughed and agreed. But no one complained and everyone had the joy of the Lord. There was a spiritual electricity in the air full of anticipation as to what was going to happen. The intercessors were pleading with God to have Heaven invade Golden Valley with His presence. The elders met with all the pastors and their wives individually and the intercessors as a group to inform them of what was coming in these end times and to encourage them that God had saved His best wine for the end times for His children. A bond of unity has been manifesting itself days before the revival and everyone senses that they are truly with their brothers and sisters in Christ waiting on God to manifest His power and glory.

Chris Gilbert, who is Lydia Hagman's younger brother, is a commercial airline pilot based in Atlanta, Georgia. He decided to take some vacation time and fly his sister in his personal small aircraft to Clark County to witness firsthand what was spiritually going on in Golden Valley. He had accepted the Lord as a teenager and had been a faithful Christian up until he completed college. Then he then enlisted in the Air Force and became a pilot. After flying on a number of missions in Iraq and Afghanistan and seeing much of the dark side of war and humanity, his heart had grown lukewarm to the things of God. But, after watching meteorites striking down all around Clark County on the news and Ken's altar call at the Golden Valley Revival on VideoAlbum and the majority of the audience getting saved, he had to see firsthand what God was doing in the Rocky Mountains. After seeing, hearing about, and experiencing the refreshing presence of God on his first day at Fortress, he recommitted his life to the Lord. He had connected with Caleb, a former veteran like himself, who shared his testimony of rededicating his life to the Lord, and it impacted him tremendously. His sister Lydia Hagman was also a changed Christian woman from two weeks prior. The moment Lydia Hagman stepped out of her brother's plane, she felt the strong presence of God that had enveloped Golden Valley since the last revival.

At first she thought something was wrong, like maybe it was just the higher altitude that she was experiencing. She soon realized that God's presence was manifesting all over Clark county. She would soon discover God's presence was the thickest at the Double V Ranch. When she saw her husband Ken at the little airport in Golden Valley, he seemed like he did when she first met him as a freshmen in college. Ken was on fire for the Lord at that time, continually walking in the joy of the Lord and evangelizing students all over the campus and the city of Tuscaloosa. At that time, God seemed so real to him. Upon arriving at Fortress, Lydia instantly felt a kindred spirit to Melody and Mary Anne and instantly fell in love with them as sisters in the Lord. They had welcomed her with open arms and were genuinely glad to meet and talk with her. She was shocked how genuinely friendly the people at Fortress were to her.

Finally the time came, and at 10:00 AM the day of the revival, the leadership at Fortress started allowing cars and buses to come onto the property. There was a long steady line of vehicles coming onto the property. Signs were posted, "If you oppose God's work here, enter at your own risk." Six cars carrying loud hecklers with posters quickly turned around and left quietly as soon as possible. The fear of God had come upon them leaving them deathly afraid to drive onto the property. Each of the six drivers somehow managed to do a three point turn and quickly sped away. At noon, a young man wearing a loose fitting navy blue hoodie with a plain tan ball cap, brown hair partially over his ears, dark sunglasses, and a thick beard walks from behind a long line of cars with his head down. His right hand is firmly gripping his .45 automatic that is hidden in the right pocket of his hoodie for fear of the giant pitwolves that might be in the area. As he walks toward Sheriff Barnes, who is at the main gate, the veteran lawman's hands are also tightly clutching his 12 gauge pump shotgun that's pointed down. The threat of giant pitwolves outside the Double V Ranch is an ever present danger. Barnes instantly recognizes that it's Hank Rutherford, his former deputy who had gone rogue towards the N.I. U. Security Forces.

Barnes, with a hint of excitement, says in a low tone, "Hank, long time no see."

"So you spotted me right away, huh, Sheriff?"

"I'd know your bow legged walk anywhere, sober or drunk. I spotted you a mile away."

"Yeah, well, I figured you might, Sam. It's really good to see you. On a more serious note, I came here because the Mormon Brotherhood has found through one of our contacts that a convoy of N.I.U. Security Forces is coming here for the second revival, and it's not for Sunday School."

"I don't doubt it, Hank!"

"I...I... came back to see if I could persuade you and Mrs. Barnes to leave before things hit the fan."

"Thanks, but nope! Hank, we're staying. My powder is dry, but my trust is in God Almighty. Hank, we know that we know that anybody who comes here to stop this move of God is going to wish to God they were never born."

"Sheriff, you know I couldn't swallow all this religious mumbo jumbo junk a few months back. But what I do know is that something happened to you at the Double V Ranch the day of the big meteorite strike. When you came back to the office you were a different guy. You said you got saved and that you just couldn't tell me some stuff. It freaked me out. Sheriff, you even looked different after that helicopter ride Mr. Crawford gave you."

"Yes, I am a different man, Hank. My old self died that day. I was born again like it talks about in John chapter 3 of the Bible and made into a brand new man."

"Exactly what that means, Sam, I don't know. But one thing I've got to admit is that I saw that revival here in Golden Valley on VideoAlbum before it was taken down. I just don't know what to make of it, with Mayor Perkins and all. You know I was an EMT and I'm totally convinced he was absolutely dead. He was a dark shade of blue and I saw that doctor administered the AED machine four times."

"You're right, Hank. Perkins was dead and there was no coming back in the natural. I'd put my hand on the Bible and tell you straight up he was dead as you can be. I know it's a hard pill to swallow, but I guarantee you what you saw is the real deal. God is alive and He is doing supernatural stuff right here in Golden Valley."

"I can't, Sam. I just can't buy into this Bible and Christian stuff. I grew up Mormon to some degree when I did go to church as a child."

"Well, I understand, Hank. I've been praying for you, Son."

"Sheriff, I didn't think I could persuade you to leave. I wish I could talk more, but if you can spot me than others can too and my cover will be blown real quick. I've got to go before somebody else spots me. Just between me and you, Sam, if something is going down right here in my hometown I'm going to fight to the last bullet and then with my bare hands if need be. I swear to God I'll do it. Me and the Mormon brotherhood will be keeping a close eye on this revival. If the N.I.U. Security Forces show up here and start something, then my fellow soldiers and I are going to wax them. I promise you that, Sam. I've got to go, so take care, Sheriff, and take care of the Mrs.," as he extends his hand to shake Barnes' hand.

"Take care, Hank," replies Barnes with a sadness in voice.

As he firmly returns the handshake, he says, "Don't worry about anybody on this property if they come here with good intentions. God help them if they don't." Hank Rutherford quickly turns around with a tear in the corner of his eye as he walks back down the road past some buses until his profile is no longer visible.

At 10:15 PM, Barnes reports to the elders all that Hank told him, but he does not mention to them that Hank is the source of the news. The elders seem unphased and not worried about the news. They are 100 percent resolved that God will fight their battle however it is going to play out with the New International Union Security forces. Masses of people keep streaming unto the property as the time passes. About 30 minutes before the start of the revival the leadership of Fortress gathers with the band members for prayer. When the prayer concludes members of *Butterfly* do one last test of their instruments and equipment. High tech engineers Max Bruno and David Shilling are working with the band finishing up testing and fine tuning the sound system and video recording equipment. Originally, Ricky was the one to present the message today since he didn't do it last time. He has thoroughly prepared and practiced his message repeatedly beforehand. Shortly before the start of the revival he senses something is not right in his spirit. He goes to Gary and says, "You must be the one again today to present the message."

Stunned, Gary replies, "No, not me. The anointing is not on me to deliver a message today."

Ricky, a little confused, turns to Ken Hagman and says point blank, "Ken, is God speaking to you to share the message?"

"That's a big no, Ricky! I would be afraid this time. I'm not the one."

All of a sudden, Caleb approaches Ricky from behind and says, "Dad and Uncle Ricky, I just felt strongly impressed to ask you by the Holy Spirit if I could share a little bit today before you get started with your message."

"Well it's funny you mention that because your Uncle Gary, Ken, and I were just talking about that same subject. You take all the time you need, okay, Son?"

"Great, Dad! I appreciate it." He walks away to tell Ashley the good news.

"Ricky, that was slick," stated Ken.

"Yeah, that was," chuckled Gary.

"Well, I have always been in favor of God having His own way in a service.

Why burden Caleb with undue pressure or stress in speaking to the masses here? I instantly felt he was the one to speak today. Do you guys agree?"

"Yes indeed, no checks in my spirit," replies Gary.

"I'm in full agreement," adds Ken.

Just before the revival is to begin Thomas Stanton Jr. approaches the side of the stage where his two good friends are preparing to play their instruments. He shouts in a low tone, "Hey, Andy and Steve, can you please come here a second? "

"What's up, Bro.?" shouts Andy.

"Hey, would you guys please do me a huge favor and grab your Grandpa and Bro. Gary because I need to tell them something important."

"Yeah, I guess we can," says Andy. "This revival is about to start any second, but we'll see what we can do." Andy and Steve go over to their grandpa and Uncle Gary on stage. Steve tells them that Thomas Stanton Jr. would like to tell them something, if they have a minute."

"Well, boys, we have just a few minutes," says Ricky.

"Yeah, just a few, guys," declares Gary with a smile. "But I think your grandfather and I can squeeze him in."

"Thanks! We appreciate it."

The two excited ministers are wondering what Thomas wants. They walk over to edge of the stage where Thomas is standing. "Hey, Thomas, what do you want to tell us that is so urgent?" inquires Ricky.

"Well, uh, uh, I just wanted to tell you, Bro. Ricky, I apologize for what I said about you two months back. I was dead wrong about you and Bro. Gary. I just want to tell both of you that you are men of God and that I love you and that I fully believe in your mission now."

"Well, Thomas, I appreciate all that you have said and I've seen you grow in the Lord over these last eight weeks."

"Thomas, thanks for the kind words," grins Gary. "We trust God that He is not just the author of your faith but also the finisher. And He is just beginning with you."

"Thanks, Bro. Ricky and Bro. Gary. I know the revival is just about ready to begin so I'll let both of you go." As he runs away smiling and looking for his parents, he yells, "Thanks!"

At precisely 1:00 PM, Caleb announces to the huge crowd, according to Sheriff Barnes, an estimated 7000 people are in the audience today. Barnes and his deputies have also found out from talking with the people that they came from across the country and around the globe. Almost all are Christians, but some are not. A few individuals were driving through the area en route to other places when something came over them and they were drawn to travel down unfamiliar roads to get an unknown destination that just happened to be where a revival was going to take place. Like steel is invisibly attracted to a magnet, they were not only pulled but also supernaturally guided to Woodcross. Caleb shares these things of interest to the people before him. Caleb has his dad pray for the success of the revival and that Lucifer will be bound and all that had come to the revival, or will hear it on CD or seeing it live on the internet or on video will be deeply touched.

At this time little do the Christians at the Double V Ranch know that God will do more than just tie the hands of the enemy but that he will destroy those who are coming to do them physical harm. After assessing the potential spiritual impact of the Golden Valley Revival, the leadership of the Adamic Society decided that they had to spin the story of what actually happened. Rumors were circulated on the internet and tabloid magazines that Perkins being raised from the dead was nothing more than a rumor, or an elaborate video hoax that was computer generated. Gary's, Ricky's, and Ken Hagman's integrity were repeatedly questioned. The story of former end time theological archenemies now becoming friends was played up from every angle in the liberal news. Talk of Ricky's and Gary's faithfulness to their wives was also brought into play with ridiculous allegations. When the Adamic Society first caught wind of another big and grandeur revival planned called Woodcross taking place in Golden Valley, they knew they had to eliminate the threat of the leadership of Fortress and the

Disciplemaker churches. They had their people who were 'biblical scholars' and were well versed in historical movements of false and true Christian revivals. The likes of the latter the Adamic Society dreaded like the plague. The Golden Valley Revival has been a rallying call to the declining fundamental churches and put wind in the sails of the true Bible based spirit-filled churches that were spiritually sputtering in the nation and around the globe. But the new awareness of remnant churches that are completely sold out to their Christian God unnerves those in the highest positions of the Society the most. Remnant churches are rock solid biblically based churches. They are churches that are not based on some wacked out silly doctrines of men or continual false prophecies of a so called prophet or prophets of God. The remnant Christians are bold, hungry, and desperate to see God's Spirit moving supernaturally in the hearts of men on the face of the earth at this time. The remnant church at Fortress is leading the worldwide charge with the continual ripple effects caused by the last revival in Golden Valley. Down through the centuries true revivals of God had been counter-productive to the goals and objectives of the Adamic Society. The Christians at the Woodcross revival are a vermin that have to be eliminated.

Colonel Krasnev was the logical choice of the Society to head up an assassination team to eliminate the Fortress leadership, the radical Christian masses who would attend Woodcross and the threat of the revival spreading.

Krasnev handpicked 44 former Spetnaz soldiers. These battle hardened special forces soldiers had served under his command in previous hotspots around the globe with the New International Union Security Forces. He did make a few exceptions but for the most part he personally knew each man and their area of specialty and qualifications. Each soldier chosen by him had been chosen for a specific job and was trained and schooled in that task for nine days prior to leaving their Boulder base in civilian clothing and vehicles loaded with their weapons, ammo, and gas masks in their unmarked vans and SUVs.

Also needed for this mission were five unrelated company marked semi-trucks. Two of these trucks carried a total of four specialized small camouflage 4x4 pickup style dune buggy vehicles and thousands of body bags. One truck carried two forklifts to help stack dead bodies inside the trailers of a large convoy of semi-trucks coming in later under the cover of night. Once the masses were all killed and Dominion Law imposed on Clark County, the operation could carry on throughout the night unhindered. Also, once any locals who didn't attend the revival heard of a number of packs of pitwolves that converged on the revival they would fear for their lives and barricade themselves inside their homes. Two of the five semi-trucks are carrying 30 of the largest giant pitwolves in each vehicle. Krasnev is in the semi-truck leading the convey with his driver transporting half of the pitwolves that had been brought up from Mexico. Their cages had never opened on the day of the big meteorite strikes in Colorado due to electrical glitches. The Adamic Society had saved them for such a time as this. Krasnev's unit was going to stage a false massive attack of pitwolves descending on the revival attacking, killing and eating their victims after they had all been gassed and killed. They were going to discredit the Fortress' leaderships claims of their property being divinely protected. Krasnev's military convoy was going under the radar. All soldiers wore civilian clothing on the day of the mission. When they got to Fortress they would put on their camouflaged charcoal lined military clothing, gas masks at the appropriate time, assault vests, check their sniper and automatic rifles to execute Christians that would survive being gassed with a highly concentrated poisonous nerve gas..

"Colonel Krasnev, this is Geneva. How is your reception on the satellite phone?"

"It is loud and clear."

"Good! Is the plan going according to schedule?"

"Yes, everything is a go."

"Excellent! What is your ETA at the revival?"

"We will be arriving at our destination at approximately 11:00 AM Mountain Standard Time, according to the plan."

"Excellent! You'll have time to get everything in place! Colonel, we already have the high frequency ultrasonic speakers already stationed in the vicinity to continually drive off any giant pitwolves within a three-mile radius of the revival. Your men will be free to engage the enemy without fear of attack from the beasts for the duration of your time there."

"Thank you, Geneva."

"Remember, your team's job is just to eliminate anyone who tries to escape from the ranch from the effects of the nerve gas. The helicopter will eliminate the vast majority of the human Christian garbage with the release of the projectile gas canisters shot out from overhead and by spraying the masses below. Set up a perimeter around the ranch and have your men and snipers to eliminate those that try to escape the grounds of the ranch. When the last Christian dies, and the nerve gas has dispersed have everyone safely in position in the reinforced trailer and then deactivate the remote high-frequency ultrasonic speakers. Then your team is to release the giant pitwolves from their sound proof trailers near the dead victims. After two days of the super predators not being fed and only given water, they will be ready to feast on human flesh and quench their thirst with human blood. Your camera man knows what pictures and videos to take from within his van. When he is through taking footage, activate the ultrasonic speakers from within the your semi-truck. The super predators immediately will flee into the forest and then terrorize the locals of Clark County."

"Colonel, if the plan is properly executed, it will bring an end to all this religious revival fanaticism. Once the last Christian dog is killed, set up Dominion Law and seal off all roads to the Double V Ranch until you are relieved. Major Ivan Brechennko will take command once he arrives and you have briefed him."

"Tonight, under the cloud of darkness, Brechennko will roll in with 80 semi-trucks and 300 Security Forces personnel, who will stack the dead, bloody carcasses of thousands of Christians, or should I say what's left of them, into body bags. Krasnev, your team will return to Boulder immediately for further details. Brechennko's men will clean up the mess at the so-called revival and take the dead bodies to an undisclosed rock quarry and dispose of them. Do you understand?"

"Yes, Geneva!"

"The helicopter that will be used today is equipped to jam all the smart phone transmissions from the ranch except yours. It will drop the nerve gas at precisely at 1:40 PM. Our news people will take the real footage that your camera man shoots, photo shop the footage, and spin the story to make it look like the masses have been overtaken and killed by hundreds of pitwolves converging on the revival. The anti-Christian public will gossip with fear in their voices about this incident for months to come. If you run into any problems, call us. Is everything clear, Colonel?"

"Yes, Geneva!"

"Over and out, Colonel."

"Sergeant, this mission is like taking candy from a baby. If I pull this mission off without a hitch, I might be adding new general stripes to my shoulders very soon."

"Sir, there should be no problems with this mission. It will be like shooting fish in a barrel."

"Yes, I also like that American analogy, Boris."

"Thank you, Sir. It's been an honor to serve under your command."

Krasnev's convoy travels down a two-lane road with a narrow shoulder on each side. It's been basically a lonely stretch of highway that winds through a valley with steep mountains on both sides. The driver spots something just up head of them that seems odd.

"Colonel, look up there high on that ridge on the right at a two o'clock position. What is that shining? Are those some kind of shiny rocks glistening in the sunlight?"

"No, Boris! They kind of look like giants dressed in white spread out across this mountainside, but I think my eyes are seeing things."

Boris drives a few seconds more, blinking his eyes, and says, "Colonel, I can clearly see now they are angels dressed in white robes with raised swords reflecting the sun. They are swinging them to the ground. Oh no! Oh no! It feels like an earthquake! I'm pulling over! The truck is swerving!"

"No, soldier! Floor the accelerator!"

"But, Colonel!"

"That's an order!"

"Sergeant, are you blind? The road is beginning to split right down the middle! Oh $#@& Colonel, the split is widening! We are going down into an abyss!"

"Hold on, Boris! HELP! HELP!"

The Colonel's semi-truck is momentarily airborne, then takes a nose dive inside a long chasm created from the earthquake with the other trucks and vehicles going down right behind him. The Colonel's truck crashes on a rocky ledge 40 feet below the road's surface. His satellite phone that had been on the dashboard falls off through the broken windshield and bounces off the rocks far below. The truck is barely hanging on, and creaking sounds can be heard as it hangs in the balance. Boris, the driver, is dead. The rest of the convoy have all fallen deeper into the mile long rift and plunged to their deaths. Krasnev is dazed and has suffered massive internal injuries and is seconds away from being cast into hell when he suddenly smells a stench in the air and feels heavy breathing down the back of his neck, followed by a blood-chilling, terrifying growling sound. He is going into shock, but still has enough wits about him that he quickly realizes his truck is mangled from the jagged rocks on a ledge it is resting upon and that a giant pitwolf has broken out of its cage, staring him down from behind for his last supper. He somehow fights the pain he is experiencing and musters all the strength he has to try to reach for his sidearm to shoot the beast when he realizes his right arm is pinned between his caved-in passenger door and his seat. It's impossible for him to unsnap his pistol, let alone pull it out and use it. The last sound Colonel Krasnev hears on this side of eternity is the crunching sound of the three inch fangs of the massive pitwolf behind him piercing and crushing his skull. Within seconds, another minor earthquake occurs at the hands of the angels' swords again striking the mountain above. It supernaturally brings the giant rift in the road back together within inches, entombing both the dead men and beasts below.

After Caleb makes the announcements Ricky Crawford prepares to give the opening prayer for the 7000 hardcore, born again Christians waiting in full anticipation of a tremendous move of God at Woodcross. He had been looking forward to sharing a message he had worked hard on, but he was both excited and proud that his son Caleb has apparently been chosen by God for the task. As Ricky approaches the microphone, there is a solemn and respectful attitude among the masses. Many had seen Ricky call life back into the mayor of Golden Valley on Videoalbum. Others had heard the account from their friends. This man of God has their attention as he cries out to God to move upon the hearts of everyone present at Woodcross. He calls out to both the young and old alike to become true disciples of Christ and not just settle for being Christians who say a one-time prayer and never grow or advance in their walk. He pleads for God to instill upon the believers' hearts to lay down their lives and to pick up the cross and follow Christ daily. Ricky acknowledges to God that he knows the time remaining for this present world is short. By the time he finishes his anointed time of prayer, many believers have already confessed their secret sins to God desiring victory in their walk with Him. Ricky finishes his time of prayer by shouting, "JESUS, JESUS, JESUS, JESUS, JESUS..." to the crowd that is made up mostly of teenagers to young adults up to age 30. But senior citizens and middle-aged couples with young children can be seen scattered throughout the crowd. The audience erupts into a frenzy, repeatedly shouting the name of Jesus while Ricky cheerleads them with his arms motioning to fan the flame of revival. Ricky knows there is a special anointing in the air. So far, it's like the Golden Valley Revival, but even stronger. After a few minutes, the intensity of the cheers dies down and Ricky motions for silence. When the crowd's voices die down, he announces that the crowd is in for a treat because his son Caleb Crawford is going to share from his heart after the band *Butterfly* finishes with worship. Sounds of whistling, cheering, and hand clapping are heard with the announcement. Ricky goes on to say that his son is a retired Navy SEAL Major who faithfully served his country and is now serving God full time as an assistant pastor at Fortress. He adds that he knows his son has a message that will both inspire and challenge them. But he announces that before Caleb shares, the group *Butterfly* is going to minister to the crowd's hearts through their anointed music. Thunderous applause erupts from the masses of Christians who have been captivated by the group since the last revival, as seen and heard on Videoalbum the short time it aired.

When Ricky hands Starlight the microphone, the audience goes wild. She smiles and says, "The spirit of revival is here! Can you spell and say revival?" as she extends her mike to the audience.

The hyped-up crowd yells to the top of their lungs, "R-E-V-I-V-A-L, REVIVAL!"

Starlight says, "I think that is why you guys came here today from the ends of this country and from halfway around the world. *Butterfly* and the leadership here feel you won't be disappointed. That being said, I want to dedicate this first song to the memory of the late great Rich Mullins and his Ragtime Muffin Band. She starts singing his hit song, *My Deliverer is Coming*. Only some of the crowd had ever heard the song before, but the crowd soon loves it and breaks into a cheer with the band's musical performance, Starlight's amazing voice, and the backup harmonizing vocals of River, Brenda Lee, and Emily. After *Butterfly* finished the song, something supernatural happens. All the applause is replaced with instant silence on the part of the crowd. It is like they can instinctively feel something big is about to take place. The band, on the other hand, keeps praising God with nods from Brenda Lee and Forrest. The band starts singing their new version of the old hymn *Revive us Again*..

What happens next is that an invisible wave from the back of the crowd starts moving forward to the stage. One by one, individuals yield themselves to the presence and power of the Holy Spirit. Some people in the crowd drop like rocks to the ground, others gently drop to their knees. God's glory has invaded the grounds of the Double V Ranch in a big way. *Butterfly* continues and an even greater anointing falls on them as they play their instruments and sing. All the Fortress leadership, along with everybody in the audience experiences this spiritual phenomenon.

The distinguished Baptist prophecy teacher Dr. Ken Hagman, with an earned PhD in theology, is on his hands and knees with his wife Lydia right next to him and is barely able to whisper to Ricky that he is having a hard time breathing. He struggles to say, "Ricky, the glory of the Lord has fallen." Hagman has a stream of tears falling on the stage. "I've never experienced the Holy Spirit to this degree. His presence is so thick you can almost cut it with a knife."

Ricky manages to say, "I know, Ken. The presence of God is even greater now than it was at the Golden Valley Revival, and that was awesome."

Lydia Hagman, always prim and proper and dressed stylishly with every hair in place, has make up running down her face as she weeps bitterly before the Lord about her unconfessed sins. She is almost beside herself, but manages to say, "Bro. Ricky, I just threw up something blackish in color and it evaporated before my eyes. What was it?"

Ricky struggles to respond, but blurts out to her, "It was probably a demon the Lord cast out of you."

"Oh, my God, Bro. Ricky! Are you joking?"

"No, I'm not!"

During this time, Brenda Lee is looking around wondering what to do while the other backup vocalists are repeatedly singing the chorus with an incredible anointing and unhindered in their breathing. She scoots over and bends down quickly to ask her Dad who is prostrate on the stage from the presence of God what *Butterfly* should do.

He responds in a calm, but strained, quiet voice because the Holy Spirit is all over him, "Keep singing, keep singing. Don't stop for anything." He is gasping for his breath and says, "God is cleansing His people of their sins. He is bringing revival His way, not our preconceived ways. Sing all the songs the Lord gives you."

"Yes, sir, Daddy!" responds Brenda Lee. All the band members have their eyes on her, following her lead. They shift their eyes back and forth and raise their eyebrows to each other in awe of what is going on, unsure of what will happen next and too afraid to stop playing and singing.

Mary Anne, Melody, Sarah, and Frances hold each other's hands like frightened school girls. They are on their knees huddled together praying intensely and interceding for grace and mercy for all those in attendance. Soon they succumb to the power of God's Spirit permeating the grounds of Fortress. They fall onto their backs still holding hands, gasping for air, and whispering prayers from the depths of their spirits. Caleb, along with the band *Butterfly*, is exempted from the heaviness of the revival spirit on the masses. John Blackhawk found Amy Choate earlier and they are side by side on their knees and elbows unable to get up. A purging of sin is going forth from their hearts and minds as they repent of deeds done in darkness, both past and present. Fear of the Lord has gripped Amy's spirit and soul and she knows there is no more compromise and straddling the fence with the Lord as in days past. John and Amy, like those around them, are finding it difficult to breathe in an atmosphere super charged with the presence and power of God.

The Christians in the crowd had come to the Woodcross Revival for various reasons. Some came to hear the anointed music of *Butterfly*. Starlight's pretty face and extraordinary voice had become an internet sensation. Others came out of boredom to check out all the excitement surrounding Woodcross and the Golden Valley Revival. Many Christians had to see firsthand the giant 100 foot wooden cross or to validate that the property of Fortress was truly supernaturally protected. Others wanted to meet and touch Mayor Perkins and talk to him about being raised from the dead. A number of Christians came to see for themselves that Dr. Ken Hagman was linking arms with the two most famous post-tribulationists in America. Ever since the Golden Valley Revival, Ricky's and Gary's books on prophecy have been flying off the bookshelves at the Disciplemaker Churches, Christian bookstore chains, and internet book retailers nationwide. Their ministry has been sending out tons of CDs and videos on their teachings. They had turned down all radio and TV requests since the last revival so they could devout their time, attention, prayer and ministry to Woodcross. Some Christians had come to Woodcross to witness a real miracle first hand. But the majority came to experience a personal revival in their walk with the Lord and then spread the fire of it around the world. Almost everyone had questions to ask Gary and Ricky about the revivals and end times because they believed these two men had the answers.

Regardless of their reasons for being there, heart surgery was the order of the day for the Great Physician's family members. A time of supernatural spiritual cleansing had come to the people at Woodcross.

In an atmosphere of awe and wonder *Butterfly* finishes up their time of worship with a jazzed up rock version of the old hymn, *I Have Decided to Follow Jesus*, as if on key everyone is now able to stand up with raised arms in worship. A smile graces everyone's face, with many having tears streaming down as they sing the song. Peace and serenity fill each Christian's thoughts, the sinful poison of the world having been bled from their hearts, souls, and minds. The blood of Jesus has washed the sins of believers present at Woodcross whiter than snow. The faith of each Christian man, woman, teenager, and child is being renewed. But the small number at Woodcross who are not saved are under great conviction from the Spirit of God and a healthy and holy fear of the Lord has gripped them tightly. A look of intense anguish is on their faces.

An hour before the revival began, the Holy Spirit had taken Caleb Crawford to a spiritual woodshed and dealt harshly with him about issues of sin in his life. Those sins are now under the blood of Christ and he has been emancipated from them. He feels clean and free in Christ. He was the only non-band member who was able to worship freely during the time of worship. Caleb was aware of everything taking place around him, but he was so caught up into his own deep, personal worship of God that no other things or people mattered at the time.

When Butterfly concludes their singing Caleb walks over to the microphone. All he can say is, "Wow!" and scratches his head for a couple of seconds. "I don't know about you guys, but I feel the Lord has been doing a deep spiritual work in all our hearts today. He did earlier with me in a unique way, and I know He has with you guys. God's spirit fell on the people at the Golden Valley Revival and it was amazing. But He has already fallen here in a new and wonderful way. I believe that God is taking His end time church through a process from glory to glory before He sends His Son Jesus. You and I are experiencing that process this very day."

"God has really renewed my love for Him today at Woodcross to a greater level than I have ever known. The Spirit of God has come down on us like a thick, warm, heavy blanket in a world that has grown ever increasingly cold toward Him. I don't know how else to describe it, but it has felt so wonderful. Everywhere I looked earlier during worship people had a hard time breathing normally. People were on their knees, flat on the ground, and some were in a fetal position because of the presence of God. Folks, God is doing a deep, deep work here today. You will never ever forget this day. I know I won't. The Holy Spirit was all over me in a very unusual way and I don't know why I was able to stand during the worship time and breathe normally. All I can say is if this is not true revival, I don't know what is. If you agree with me, please raise your hand." Almost every hand is raised.

Caleb, led by the Holy Spirit, senses a change in the direction of the service. Being obedient to the Spirit's leading, he calls the lost people in the midst of the masses to come forward if they want to surrender to Jesus to be their personal Lord and Savior. He cries out, "Please come forward now and accept Him before men. Don't hesitate! Come now! Behold, now is the day of salvation." Within a minute and a half, about 150 individuals come forward. All are under strong conviction from the Lord. Most are crying, many are wailing, and some are even trembling from the fear of the Lord. Caleb leads them in the sinners' prayer and they repeat it out loud.

He tells them, "If you just now sincerely prayed the sinners' prayer, then you are a true born again child of God. Your are saved from the pit of hell and bound for heaven. Please go back to where you were standing and ask the person you came with to either commit to discipling you or to help you find someone who is willing and able to do that. Everyone is praising God and shouting hallelujah for lost souls saved. Pure joy is written over all the faces of new believers in Christ and the former looks of intense anguish that many had before have vanished as they all head back to their families and friends.

Some teenagers, led by Wyatt Banks and his girlfriend Bobbie Jo Morgan who are on fire for the Lord, chant for several minutes, "Revival has come! Revival has come!" over and over again.

When everyone settles down, Caleb then says, "I think it may be safe to say we are all now on the same team. Amen?"

The crowd shouts, "Amen!"

"What I want to tell you now is that it was an honor and privilege to serve my country as a Navy SEAL. Some claim we are the world's best elite fighting force. But I declare to you that that is not true. I am looking at America's and the world's most elite fighting force. It's Christian soldiers right in front of me. And you know the gates of hell shall not prevail against God's true church." The crowd just explodes and goes wild praising God for a couple of minutes. As the sound of the crowd dwindles, Caleb continues, "Just you showing up here at Woodcross says you're really serious about the Lord. Now that you have experienced God showing up and touching you, you'll never be the same. We all went through some intense impartations today to be equipped for the Lord's army. A lot of what you need to succeed in your individual mission for the Lord's will for your life just got downloaded into your spirit. But I don't believe you are fully equipped yet and ready to be deployed on your mission. I think there is more to come today. What that is, I don't know exactly."

"But now I'm going to tell you a little secret that most of you don't know. Only some of the people here at Fortress know about it. This morning the Archangel Gabriel stopped me dead in my tracks while I was running on this very property. Now some may doubt what I'm about to tell you, but I have no reason to lie or misrepresent the truth. You are wondering what he told me? Well, he told me that God has heard the prayers of the saints at Fortress, in Golden Valley, and across the globe. The purpose of this Woodcross Revival is to help those who have been chosen in this last generation on earth to purge sin from their lives and for them to be endued with power from on high and to stand firm in the Lord. They must go through a baptism of fire to strengthen them for the hard times ahead. What that entails was not revealed to me. Gabriel told me, 'Your enemies will experience the strong arm of the Lord. Woe unto them who oppose the One and Only true living God and His anointed ones.' Then he said he must go in order to carry out the sovereign will of God. Then he disappeared and I didn't see him anymore."

No sooner does Caleb finish speaking these words, than extreme adventure seeker David Solomon who was only recently saved two weeks before yells out loudly, "Look!" and points up to a helicopter he spots at least two miles from the ranch. One by one, everyone's eyes quickly turn and move toward the sky. Sheriff Barnes pulls up a pair of binoculars and sees what appears to be a slightly altered KABZ news helicopter from Boulder. Ever since the Golden Valley Revival, no secular news program has given the ministry of Fortress the time of day to question them or for the leaders to tell the truth about what happened the night of the Golden Valley revival.

As the helicopter approaches the crowd from a distance, the pilot is contacted from Geneva about the status of Krasnev's convoy. The pilot is Major Braum of the N. I. U. Security Forces (Air Force) in civilian clothing flying a replica of the Boulder news team helicopter. He immediately pushes the electronic kill button that will knock out all the smart phones for a radius of eight miles from his location. Instantly everyone's phones at the revival are no longer functional. But the ministry's sound system works just fine.

"Hello, Major Braum, this is Geneva. We need a confirmation on Colonel Krasnev's team. Have you caught a visual of them and are they in place?"

"Negative, Geneva. No visible signs of his team. I have not picked up any radio transmissions either."

"Major, our satellite phone is not able to pick up any transmission from him and we have not received any recent update concerning his status."

"Geneva, apparently neither form of communication available to him is functioning."

"Major, what was the status of the highway Krasnev's team followed north of your present location along the designated route? Were there any signs of an accident or foul play?"

"We have had some minor technical difficulties on our end. But we do have two unusual confirmed reports of small earthquakes happening in the same region as Golden Valley."

"Were there any signs of the convoy having any accidents or mechanical problems?"

"Geneva, nothing out of the ordinary except an unusually long crack about a kilometer and a half long down the middle of one stretch of the highway. But other than that, no visual problems or accidents. Do you want me to abort the mission?"

"No, Major Braum. Proceed as planned, we must snuff out this Christian revival and all the religious fanatics involved at all cost. The nerve gas is highly concentrated that you will drop and spray on the masses and it should quickly take out all humans with the vicinity of the revival.

Hopefully, Colonel Krasnev got rerouted for some reason and can reestablish contact with us as soon as possible. Do you have a visual of the revival area?"

"Yes, Geneva."

"Are your orders clear?"

"Affirmative!"

"May Lucifer be with you!"

Once he is a mile away from center stage, Major Braum's eyes are opened into another dimension. It is a spiritual one. He sees giant, nine and ten feet tall angels standing shoulder to shoulder with large shining silver swords in their hands and bright golden breast plates on their huge chests. They are stationed around the perimeter fence line of the ranch. His first thought is that he is hallucinating. Braum shakes his head only to now see more angels high in the air right over the revival's stage. These angels are fierce looking and have their swords pointed right at him. Fear begins to seize the highly decorated combat veteran officer and his body trembles as he contacts Geneva to abort what seems to be a suicide mission.

In a nervous voice, Major Braum announces, "Geneva I need to abort the mission."

"What is it, Major?"

"I'm encountering thousands of giant war-like angelic beings in the air with large swords both around the property and in the air over the revival. I'm asking for permission to abort the mission. I do not believe my mission can be accomplished facing these hostile spiritual beings."

Immediately, Marla Wittenhaur yanks the microphone from the hand of the low level officer holding it. Marla and the Security Forces' top brass are far below the N.I.U. Security Forces' Headquarters in one of the Adamic Society's Secret Command Centers. The beautiful and evil Marla speaks into the microphone, "Major Braum, under no circumstances are you to abort this mission. You may not see them, but Lucifer has summoned an army of demons to do his bidding. They will enable you to complete the mission. If you do not fulfill your mission as previously ordered, you will never live long enough to see all your family members, who will be executed this very day. Is this understood?"

"Yes, ^%$&*#@$&, Geneva!

Caleb, who is very familiar with military and civilian helicopters, notices six suspicious looking canisters attached to the bottom of the news helicopter about 500 feet above ground level. The crowd is distracted and excited by the helicopter, as it is about 200 yards away. He believes the helicopter pilot is sweeping around to position the helicopter over the center of the crowd and hopefully gather as many together as possible close to the stage. Sensing imminent danger, along with a strong inner peace in his spirit, Caleb yells with his most commanding voice into the microphone that everyone needs to be still and see the salvation of their Lord. All eyes of the audience are upon the helicopter directly above them. Over half of the crowd is waving at the pilot in the fake KABZ helicopter. But some are wondering why Caleb said what he said. Some are puzzled about why their phones are not working and they can't take pictures and videos.

The Spirit of God rises up within Caleb and reveals that Lucifer has come to kill, steal, and destroy today at Woodcross. He shouts out to the masses, "The enemy of our souls has come and he is above us, but do not be afraid because no weapon formed against us shall prosper. I speak to Lucifer the god of this world and I rebuke you in the name of my Lord Jesus Christ, the Name which is above all other names. Be gone, you slithering serpent, because we are all under the blood of Christ here and God's holy angels will protect us!"

Braum knows he is on a suicide mission and hates to hear the Christian prayer from Caleb below. He pushes a button that fires the canisters in six different directions from the helicopter. The nerve gas is projected into a 360 degree direction away from the helicopter. By divine angelic intervention, the canisters never get close to the ground. All those assembled at the revival are given eyes to pierce into a rare spiritual dimension that few mortals have ever seen. Momentarily, all of them are given permission to see numerous giant warrior angels flying rapidly around in a circle creating a vortex. Green-colored gas is being released from the canisters as they are falling and then quickly caught up in the vortex 200 feet above the crowd. Also nerve gas spraying from the nozzles on the helicopter quickly starts encircling the aircraft. But no Christians have experienced the effects of the deadly gas. Four angels fan the nerve gas inside the helicopter with their wings. Braum's high-tech camera and communication systems at the top of his windshield are crushed by the swift, powerful swords of two fierce warrior angels.

Geneva's eyes are now gone as the event is unfolding. For the Christians below at Woodcross the portal into the spiritual dimension has been resealed. Now all that is taking place in the spiritual realm above and around the Christian masses is not revealed. They do not see a host of grotesque demonic forces trying their best to fight against Michael and the rest of his angelic army. Immediately, Major Braum starts choking on the gas, because there is a defective filter in his new gas mask. In a gasping struggle for life, Braum is barely able to say, "Mayday! Mayday! Geneva!" not knowing all his communication systems have also been destroyed.

Instantly, out of nowhere, the sky turns almost pitch black and a small funnel of a tornado forms over a one mile away. Braum, who is dying, is reaching for a spare gas mask to put on. His helicopter is stuck in a stationary position and spinning around in a circular fashion and he can't move it with his control. All the nerve gas is now inside the helicopter. Within a few seconds, all of Braum's gurgling for air and foaming at the mouth with a grotesque and contorted look on his face comes to an end. With visual and communication systems both down, the high-ranking Adamic members have a sinking feeling that their mission has become a complete disaster. In what seems like just a moment, the twister is rapidly gaining in size exponentially and is about a three quarters of a mile away from everyone. It forms a short but wide path of destruction outside the property boundary of the Double V Ranch. But once it reaches the fence line of the property no damage occurs after that time. It is approaching rapidly towards the outer edge of those at the revival. At this time, none of the angels are visible to the masses, but everyone knows they are still involved in an epic battle.

In the path of the tornado are 7000 born again Christians. Above them a helicopter is still in a fixed revolving position at 500 feet with a dead pilot aboard and enough poisonous nerve gas to wipe out a small city of 20,000.

The vortex of the tornado, is coming straight at them, but without the devastating winds or sucking up everything in its path like normal tornados. Six massive bolts of lightning are now visible and are continually striking inside the opening of the twister, as loud sounds of thunder clash at the top, which is at least a half mile wide. Some of the very young Christians not well versed in Bible prophecy are crying out, "God, is this the end of the world or it's the end of the world as we know it?" Almost all of the Christians want to run away, but it is as if their feet are stuck in mud up to their knees. Friends and family members hold hands tightly or embrace each other as they frantically murmur prayers of divine intervention by Almighty God. Amy, crying, turns to Blackhawk and tells him if they are going to die she wants to die in his arms. He tries to comfort her and tell her everything will be alright as he fervently prays. She clings to him and wraps her arms tightly around him with her head on his chest and her eyes closed with the belief that her allotted time on this earth has come to an end. Some of the children's teeth chatter for fear of the frightful sights that are playing out before them. The elders are trying to reassure everybody within the range of their voices that God will deliver them from the hand of the enemy.

When the rogue twister is less than four hundred yards away from the nearest person, the EF5 tornado instantly sucks the helicopter toward itself. Everyone sees it spin three cycles around the outside of the tornado's vortex. It then is hurled with great force far away from the vortex. The automatic pilot system kicks in, as it flies south away from the ranch, undoubtedly with angelic help, to an unknown destination with the deadly nerve gas aboard.

At this very moment, vision capability to the event unfolding in Clark County has been restored. The Adamic Society has their own satellite repositioned and beaming down at this very moment. Within seconds, another live visual feed from a small drone with a Live Pro wide-angled camera attached to it is circling the revival area from outside the fence perimeter of the ranch. Wolfgang Martin, Marla Wittenhaur, and the head of the N.I.U. Security Forces Five Star General Luther Hamburg had all been furious when the breakdown of communications occurred with Major Braum. General Hamburg has been in charge of the operation to neutralize and eliminate the revival threat in Colorado. Things have not gone according to his plan. But now, Major Braum and his helicopter's status and Krasnev and his team's whereabouts have all taken a back seat.

Tension and anticipation are mounting as the Adamic members are deep within the secret chambers of the Society's high-tech command center 150 feet below the N.I.U. Headquarters in Geneva, Switzerland. They are witnessing an unplanned EF5 tornado over a half a mile wide with six lightning bolts striking inside of the vortex in Golden Valley. It appears to be taking center stage literally. It has caught the members completely off guard and they are totally fixated on what is going to happen next.

Marla is so thrilled she screams, "Look! Mighty Lucifer has summoned the forces of the wind and fire from lightning bolts to do his bidding. Praise be to Lucifer!"

Others follow making declarations of, "Praise to Lucifer!"

The EF5 quickly continues in its path to the revival and it now supernaturally passes over the masses of Christians and the stage oddly without disturbing them, the 100 foot wooden cross, or even a blade of grass on the ground. In the invisible realm, hidden from all the eyes of those on earth, a major spiritual battle has erupted high and directly above their heads. It's the Army of God versus the Army of Lucifer fighting for the souls of mankind. Tremendous amounts of high-voltage electrical energy is being produced from the bolts of lightning repeatedly striking inside the vortex of the massive twister as it spins around rapidly at very high rpm. This natural phenomenon is producing the kind of electrical power that would meet all the electrical needs of New York City for a month if it could be harnessed.

President Cohen is now watching the event unfold. He has just been briefed and brought up to speed by his Chief of Staff and longtime personal confidant Tom Williamson about what has happened in Golden Valley. They are both now watching the event on the President's wide plasma screen inside his office. He had just finished signing a new Executive Order into law to further dismantle American Christians freedom to worship. The Oval Office and Command Center of the Adamic Society in Geneva are linked together on speaker phones as the events at Woodcross unfold. Isaac Cohen announces to Marla that he is ready for this

Woodcross Revival to be over and for this Christian radical fanaticism to stop. Cohen's sick and sadistic side can't wait for the carnage to begin.

Although he did not personally care for Dr. Von Gunten, his second cousin, he was still family. A vendetta against the God of the Bible would have to be paid in blood for the death of his family member. The horrible death of his dear mother's favorite cousin would be avenged today. Each of the five Adamic members know Lucifer has personally conjured up the EF5 tornado and that he and his army of demons will supernaturally dispose of the 7000 Christian fanatics assembled at Woodcross. Lord Lucifer had slaughtered millions through the centuries and he will take care of these small number of anti-progressive people in Colorado.

At first, one by one, the Christians underneath the monstrous high-voltage-charged tornado shooting out long sparks of electricity begin to fall to their deaths from being electrocuted by it. Then hundreds of Christians, and finally thousands, until no one is left standing. It all happens within a matter of several minutes. The law of death has claimed its latest victims. It appears Lucifer has gotten the upper hand on God this day. The glorious effects of the Golden Valley Revival and the hopes of Woodcross Revival were short lived. Three minutes have passed by since the last of the Christians have died at the hands of Lucifer and the deadly electrically charged EF5. There are no videos or pictures on the side of good to tell the true story of what has actually occurred here. Cohen and the Adamic Society will spin this story in another away that best suits their interests. Almost immediately, the huge tornado quickly dissipates after being stationary over the crowd of people at revival for only a matter of minutes.

Marla says, "Our Lord Lucifer has triumphed by bringing this deadly tornado and these six lightning bolts into being by his powerful hand to electrocute all these vile Christian dogs. Lucifer rules over all."

"All power and glory belong to him," shouts Wolfgang. With every Christian dead at the revival, the five wicked Adamic members hearts fill up with pride within themselves and begin to mock the Christian's God and celebrate their victory.

Each one also gives continuous accolades to Lucifer and to each other as they celebrate and toast each other with Champaign. But no sooner had they all taken their first sips than two brilliant rays of the Shekinah Glory of God beam down from Heaven. God Almighty Himself has thrown Glory down from His throne to Golden Valley. A bright almost blinding beam of golden light surrounds the dead body of Bro. Ricky Crawford, as does another one that surrounds Bro. Gary Kirkman's limp, cold corpse. The spirit of death flees from their bodies in the presence of the golden light sent from God the Father above.

In the midst of their evil party-like atmosphere, Marla is the first to notice the divine illuminating beams of light coming down from Heaven. Totally stunned, she drops her crystal glass, still almost full, on the concrete floor below. The sound of broken crystal startles everyone in the center in the midst of their celebration atmosphere and they are unaware of what just occurred.

Almost always in command of any given situation, Marla mumbles "Oh, my dear sweet Lucifer."

Slowly Ricky and Gary begin to move their bodies as if from a deep sleep. But, within 30 seconds, they both rise to their feet in full use of their faculties and bodies and shout to the top of their lungs in holy righteous anger and harmony by the Spirit of God, "Jesus Christ is Lord!!! In His name we command life to come back into our brothers' and sisters' dead bodies who lie before us. They are part of the Remnant Church that still has work to accomplish for God Almighty. We are the Army of the Living God. Lucifer, you cannot stop this revival from spreading to the ends of the earth in Jesus' name!"

After this declaration, all the Fortress leaders' and *Butterfly* band members' bodies begin to stir, followed by the leadership of the Network of Disciplemaker churches, and then all of the others in the crowd. Soon, within several minutes, an Army of God emerges - men, women, and children standing in the power and radiate glory of God and called for an end time purpose of spreading the Gospel around the globe.

Complete shock and disbelief are written on the faces of Wolfgang, Marla, General Hamburg, Tom Williamson, and President Isaac Cohen. Cohen is so furious and disgusted by what he sees that he clears his desk off with his right arm, throwing everything across the room in his Oval Office. He yells in a fit of uncontrolled rage, "Geneva, we have a serious problem on our hands!"

The Christians at Woodcross Revival are slowly realizing that they have indeed gone through a literal baptism of fire and have been protected by the divine hand of God. It begins to dawn on many that they were killed by the high voltage of electricity that the tornado was discharging and have been brought back to life. A crowd of 7000 radical Christians brought back from the dead lift up continuous shouts of praise and loud prayers of thanks to God.

In the midst of bewilderment and amazement, Gary Kirkman and his wife Mary Anne turn to their long-time friends, Ricky and Melody Crawford. Gary says, "Rick, I know in my heart that the huge tornado with the six lightning bolts that produced incalculable deadly watts of electricity was from Lucifer."

Ricky responds, "Yeah, that tornado was definitely from Lucifer, no doubt about it. But by God's grace and His mighty angels, nothing was disturbed on the ground. God kept that deadly gas from reaching us and kept that bird in the air and then cast it away from us. The pilot was dead when all that deadly gas was put into the helicopter. but we were all electrocuted."

Caleb runs over with Ashley and his two sons and says, "Are you guys alright?"

"Yes, we are, Son, by God's grace," declares Melody.

"Thank God!" shouts Caleb.

"Dad and Uncle Gary, we all died here today at the revival, didn't we?" asks Ashley.

"Yes, Ashley, we were all dead" replies Gary. "But the Lord was merciful and brought Ricky and me back from the other side. Then He used us to call life back into the bodies of our brothers and sisters in Christ. You know what this means, Ricky?"

By the Spirit of God and with full confidence, Ricky responds, "Yeah, we are standing on the brink of the unfolding events written in the book of

Revelation. The Spirit of God has moved here today like in the days of the Old Testament. He has used the people of Fortress located in Clark County, the most conservative, but the poorest, least progressive and smallest county in Colorado to help birth a great world-wide revival. God has done an incredible work and miracle here in the lives of the people assembled at Woodcross so that they can stand in the face of adversity and persecution in the days ahead. We were all dead and now we are all alive. None of us will ever be the same from this day forward to the glory of God. Lucifer's army is mad because they lost this battle today. Gary, from this time on, it's all-out war. God, help us or we won't survive! Surely the Tribulation must be beginning very, very soon!"

The End

Final Remarks

If you have enjoyed reading this book by R. E. Crofton please pass your copy along to a friend or tell others that it can be purchased on Amazon.com. The first chapter of this book can be read by all at author's website *fortressbookseries.com*. You must type it on the address bar at the very top of your smart phone or computer. If you would like to email a question about the book or for R. E. please send it to *fortressbook@yahoo.com*. A Fortress Book Series may be in the works depending on the reception of this book. Some material has already been written in advance. If you would like to be on a list to be contacted (for this purpose alone) if a book series becomes a reality, please send an email to the address above.

The story of <u>Fortress</u>: Divinely Protected is fictional. But supernatural churches like Fortress will come into existence during the Tribulation period. Revelation 12 makes it plain that the implied protected offspring (churches/Rev. 12:17) of the woman in the wilderness will be supernaturally protected from Lucifer by Almighty God. Do not confuse the fact that just because a church is in a remote area that it qualifies as a church in the wilderness according to Rev. 12. These churches in the wilderness will be pure, holy and will hold fast to the faith. I believe they will be the essence of what I call a true Remnant Church. Also, don't make the assumption that all members will permanently be part of a church in the wilderness for the duration of the Tribulation period. God may have other plans for them.

Another thing is don't make the wrong assumption that just because a Christian or Christians are not in a church in the wilderness that God will not do supernatural things in their life or lives. At the end of time all the children of God will triumph over Lucifer if they embrace the following;

"And they overcame him by the blood of the Lamb, and by the word of their testimony: and they loved not their lives unto death." Revelation 12:11

Maranatha,

Bro. R. E.

Made in the USA
Columbia, SC
18 June 2018